JOHNNY CASH
THE LIFE OF AN AMERICAN ICON

JOHNNY CASH
THE LIFE OF AN AMERICAN ICON

Stephen Miller

OMNIBUS PRESS
London/New York/Paris/Sydney/Copenhagen/Madrid/Tokyo

Cover designed by Michael Bell Design
Book designed by Lisa Pettibone
Line drawings by David Mackintosh
Picture research by Sarah Bacon

ISBN: 0.7119.9626.1
Order No: OP 49203

Exclusive Distributors:
Music Sales Limited,
8/9 Frith Street,
London W1D 3JB, UK.

Music Sales Corporation,
257 Park Avenue South,
New York, NY 10010, USA.

Macmillan Distribution Services,
53 Park West Drive,
Derrimut, Vic 3030,
Australia.

To the Music Trade only:
Music Sales Limited,
8/9 Frith Street,
London W1D 3JB, UK.

Typeset by Galleon Typesetting, Ipswich.
Printed in Great Britain by Creative Print & Design, Wales.

A catalogue record for this book is available from the British
Library.

www.omnibuspress.com

CONTENTS

DEDICATION

To my beloved wife and children for whom I try to walk the line.

PREFACE

Johnny Cash died aged 71 on September 12, 2003, just as this book was about to be printed. He passed away in a hospital in Nashville where he had been admitted for complications associated with diabetes which led to respiratory failure.

No one who saw the photographs of Johnny in a wheelchair attending the funeral of his beloved wife June in May of 2003 can have been unmoved by the sight of this immensely strong and brave man brought down by this unexpected tragedy. It was a hammer blow from which he never really recovered, but he nevertheless continued recording right up to the end.

The tributes were fulsome and well earned. "His music will go on forever, just like Elvis," said Jan Flederus of his European fan club, a sentiment echoed across the globe. Only weeks before his death Johnny added yet another accolade to his massive list of achievements by winning an MTV video award for 'Hurt', an extraordinarily apt tribute to an extraordinary career.

Johnny Cash truly was an American Icon.

INTRODUCTION

"Talking of Shawn Camp, here he is now."

I looked out of the window and saw a large, jet black pick-up truck pulling up in a sun-dried parking area protected from the ninety degree heat by a group of tall leafy trees. Out jumped Shawn, displaying cherubic good looks and designer jeans.

I was at The Cowboy Arms Hotel and Recording Spa in Nashville to interview Jack Clement, one of country music's original entrepreneurs and a long-time friend (and producer) of Johnny Cash. The interview over, I was asking about some of Jack's current projects when Shawn Camp's name cropped up. Jack introduced us. "You're writing a book on Johnny Cash!" Shawn exclaimed. "I've just been listening to 'I Walk The Line' in my truck. Man I *love* Johnny Cash. He's the greatest."

Some time later, one of my daughters phoned me from Australia. She had been travelling around that vast continent and had found work in the only bar in a tiny farming town miles from nowhere. "You won't believe it," she said, "but one of the most popular songs on the juke box is by Johnny Cash, something about a guy with a woman's name . . ." Such endorsements gave me an intriguing insight into the appeal and inspirational quality of someone whose first record came out in 1955, more than ten years before Shawn Camp was born. Not many artists from any musical genre manage to attain and sustain this kind of instant recognition and approval over a long period of time.

It was in the early Sixties that I first became passionate about popular music. However the name Johnny Cash didn't make much of an impression with me (and many others) on this side of the Atlantic until the end of the decade. By that time, he was well on the way to living legend status in America, and in 1969, he was even outselling The Beatles. Years of long, gruelling tours had helped to establish a substantial overseas following in Britain, Europe, Canada and Australia. Yet it was in his homeland that he was elevated to a figure of true significance.

When I started to research this book I only had a general outline of the life and career of Johnny Cash – a poor rural upbringing, a traumatic death in the family, immediate success with Sun Records in his early twenties, and stardom in the Sixties experienced through a haze of drugs and booze. That stardom almost became deification when reckless and negligent excess nearly brought about a premature end. Yet when a premature demise appeared likely, Cash somehow maintained his hold on life and continued to make great records. His marriage to June Carter helped to mend his ways.

However while his concerts continued to attract the faithful, commercial success in terms of hit singles and albums decreased. Cash was showered with awards and accolades; he was associating with American Presidents without making it clear where his political sympathies lay. Through it all he used his position to support the underdog; his name being associated with prisoners, Native Americans, the oppressed and the ordinary. No longer just a singer and songwriter, Cash became an American icon. The thinking man's John Wayne. Despite the comparative lack of enthusiasm for country music in most urban areas, if you asked the average person to name one country singer, it's likely they would respond with "Johnny Cash".

Something I knew little about was the role of religion in Cash's life. In the early Seventies I studied philosophy at university and one topic guaranteed to hold my attention was the ageless debate about belief in God. Voltaire said that if God didn't exist we'd have to invent him. After giving it much thought I was quite clear in my own mind that I could not take such a spiritual leap of faith. That was over 25 years ago and despite much reading, discussion and thought on the subject, my view has never changed. Johnny Cash made that leap. I wanted to know why he did it, what affect it had on him and whether I might find my own message in his experience.

As I talked to more and more people, a recurring theme emerged. No matter how badly Cash behaved – drug psychosis, missed shows, crashed cars, wrecked rooms, and worse – it didn't seem to diminish people's high regard for the man. Specific words kept cropping up again and again – integrity and, above all, honesty. Equally, when I asked what specifically made Johnny Cash special, "It's just his presence," "There's no one like him," and "He's totally original" were typically fulsome responses, illustrating that greatness is easy to recognise but harder to define. In taking on the challenge of writing a Johnny Cash biography I have attempted to define the unique circumstances which combined to produce a troubled man of spirit.

Stephen Miller
Edinburgh, June 2003

PART I

Hey! Porter

"If you listen to me you'll be glad you did."

1

THE PATERNAL ANCESTRY of Johnny Cash can be traced back to a pictur-esque rural part of Scotland some 30 miles north of Edinburgh, around the peaceful village of Strathmiglo in the ancient kingdom of Fife. Evidence of the historical presence of the family name is dotted about on maps of the area – Cash Mill, Cash Loch, Cash Feus (a feu being a type of Scottish landholding), Easter Cash, Wester Cash, the last two being old farms laid out around reassur-ingly traditional houses. The lady of Wester Cash, Sandra Black, runs a thriving bed and breakfast business from her property and though she has no way of knowing if it might be the site of the ancestral Cash home, she is not slow to realise the commercial possibilities of the connection and has gone to the trouble of having available in the residents' lounge copies of a document, evi-dently prepared with the involvement of Johnny Cash himself, detailing his family origins in Fife.

A short distance along the road at Easter Cash the welcome for an unexpected caller was friendly though measured and the lady of the house looked at the whole Cash thing rather differently. Of more advanced years than Sandra Black, long-time owner Mrs Shanks (first name not offered) agreed that people called Cash had lived in her part of the world for many years. However to suggest that her house, or her neighbour's, might be built on the site of the ancestral home of that famous singer Johnny Cash (yes, she did confess to quite liking some of his songs, the old ones anyway) was pure speculation; this general area perhaps but beyond that, who could say?

What is certain is that the name Cash, which is of Gaelic origin, is a very old name in the part of Fife which is home to Sandra Black and Mrs Shanks. It prob-ably refers to an area of land which was given to Duncan, Earl of Fife about 1160 by King Malcolm IV so it was originally royal demesne – land owned directly by the king and managed for the needs of the royal court – and goes back at least a thousand years. Historians are agreed that the original spelling was different from that of the present day but they are not agreed upon what it was. One local historian favours "casche", from the Gaelic word "caise" meaning steepness or place of steepness. This would make sense as it refers to the fact that the lands lie on the first rising terrain encountered for almost 12 kilometres when crossing the Howe of Fife from the east.

Another possible derivation is from the related words "casch" or "caschel", different historical forms both meaning "castle". Clearly the ideas of a steep place and a castle are not mutually exclusive and it is not hard to imagine that, as with all language, the particular form and meaning gradually evolved over many years. The area is a romantically appealing one in which to be able to trace family roots, especially for someone born and raised in a very different place and culture, thousands of miles away.

◆ ◆ ◆ ◆ ◆

There is great natural beauty to be found in the lands of Cash with ubiquitous vistas of fertile farmland and great swathes of golden bronze barley wafting around seductively in the breeze. To the south are the Lomond Hills, distant yet imposing, which between field and sky provide a rugged jagged border, purple with heather in the lower reaches. To the north is Pitmedden Forest whose Scots Pine and Norway Spruce are so densely packed in some places that only patchy shafts of light penetrate through to the ground below and you could walk over the springy carpet of dead pine needles in the rain and hardly get wet; beyond, the shimmering Firth of Tay.

To the east lies the medieval town of Falkland. With its cobbled streets and picturesque old houses, the impression is that modern life has not intruded much. The town boasts the internationally famous Royal Palace which was built between 1501 and 1541, an outstanding example of Renaissance architecture which was the country residence and hunting lodge of eight Stuart monarchs including Mary Queen of Scots. One of their majesties' favourite pastimes was to ride out from the palace to hunt wild boar in Pitmedden Forest and it is recorded that 12 shillings was paid "to Casche" for providing King James V with drink while he was out hunting on April 17, 1540.

To the west is the town of Kinross. Though much enlarged by modern housing estates catering for a necessarily mobile white-collar workforce, the town centre remains a place of some antiquity; a case of bustling market town by day, dormitory by night. Kinross also benefits from its idyllic location next to Loch Leven on whose western margin is a small island containing Loch Leven Castle. It has been derelict for many years but in the course of its colourful history it was visited by Robert the Bruce and also served as a prison for Mary Queen of Scots who was executed in 1587 for her alleged complicity in a plot to overthrow the Queen of England.

William Cash was born around 1653, probably in or near Strathmiglo, and his line can be traced directly to Johnny Cash. His uncle, also William, was a master mariner in the days of wooden sailing ships, long before the advent of powerful and reliable engines, radar and other navigational aids. He sailed the transatlantic routes in his brigantine *Good Intent* for many years, delivering cargoes of raw materials as well as Pilgrims in search of a better life in the New World. He settled in Salem, Massachusetts in about 1667 and a few years later brought over his nephew, the progenitor of the line which nine generations later would produce one of the great American icons of the twentieth century. Records show that William was "seated" in Washington Parish, Westmoreland, County Virginia (later the birthplace of George Washington) in 1677. He died in 1708.

When Johnny Cash made a detailed study of his ancestry some 20 years ago he was struck by the wording of some of the older family wills dating back to the early eighteenth century. Although these documents were principally concerned with the disposal of property and money after the testator's death, they started with the words, "In the name of God Amen!" and often included as a first bequest, "I give my soul to God which gave it . . ." It was also common for testator's to say prior to the specific legacies: "In sure and certain hopes of Resurrection and that I shall see my Saviour at the last day."

As a committed Christian for most of his life it is hardly surprising that such words should have struck a powerfully resonant chord. What he no doubt found equally striking, though a great deal less palatable, were the many references to slaves in these older documents. Two examples suffice to give a flavour of a way of life long since displaced but which nonetheless casts long shadows to the present day. From the will of Robert Howard Cash who died around 1770 are these directions: "Item. I give to my daughter, MARY LIVELY, a negro wench named Sarah." And later, from the same will: "Item. I give to my daughter MARY ANN, a negro boy named Ralph and also a bed and furniture and a cow and a calf."

William Cash's descendants remained in Virginia for two or three generations, in the counties of Amherst and Bedford. Virginia took a leading part in the American Revolution and at least some of William's descendants were soldiers who fought for the American cause. Thereafter the family line moved south to Georgia, the "Peach State", and joined other early settlers there. Like Virginia it was one of the original 13 states of the fledgling United States of America. Moses Cash, Johnny's great-great-grandfather, fought for the Confederacy in the Civil War. He survived but his Georgia plantation was razed to the ground by Union troops under General Sherman as part of his demolition of Atlanta, so Moses Cash moved his family west to Arkansas in an ox-drawn covered wagon.

One of Moses Cash's grandchildren, William Henry Cash, as well as being a cotton farmer, was a travelling Baptist preacher, a "circuit rider", who covered considerable distances to minister to his far-flung congregations. The roads could be dangerous and carrying a gun was considered a necessity even for a man of God. Though he didn't seek financial reward for his efforts, William's farm was invariably full of animals given to him as payment in kind. His wife Rebecca was also a Baptist preacher and it has been suggested that some of her ancestors may have been Native Americans, possibly Cherokees.

Though there is no hard evidence, many early articles and books on Johnny Cash routinely asserted his Native American ancestry, on the strength of flimsy evidence, something which Johnny himself either didn't contradict or positively endorsed for a time. In 1912, at the age of 52, William Henry died of Parkinson's disease, he and his wife Rebecca having had 12 children, four of whom died in infancy. By the time of William Henry's death all but one of his grown-up children had left home, the only one remaining being 15-year-old Ray Cash.

Ray, who had left school aged 14, stayed on to help run the family farm until his mother's death in 1916 at which point he enlisted in the Second Arkansas Infantry. After some involvement in resisting Mexican border incursions orchestrated by Pancho Villa, Ray was transferred to Camp Beauregard in Louisiana where he learned how to operate 155 mm mule-drawn guns whose purpose was to provide artillery cover for the infantry. The guns were so large and heavy that an eight-man team was needed to operate them and Ray, the number one man, had the job of pulling the lanyard, a kind of handle made out of rope. In 1918, at the tail end of the First World War, he was sent to France on what was then the largest ship in the world, the *Leviathan*, which the United States had captured from Germany.

In April 1919, Ray Cash was ordered to ride shotgun for a train full of beef from St Lazare to Paris under strict orders not to let anybody near the consignment. The train was due to leave St Lazare at five o'clock but Ray missed it and had to get on the next train to Paris where he received a severe dressing down from an American major. He was lucky though because, despite his dereliction of duty, the train had been traced and the beef duly delivered to its intended destination. No doubt Ray managed to avoid telling the major how it was that he had missed the train. He had met a "little gal" in St Lazare with whom he was participating in an engrossing cultural exchange, so engrossing that he just couldn't tear himself away. As he admitted later, "I was learning her English and she was learning me French."

Ray was discharged from the army soon after returning from France and despite the case of the missing beef, he was proud to be able to tell people that he received an honourable discharge and that the army rated his character as excellent. It has been said that love can build a bridge but for Ray it was a case of a bridge building a love when, soon after the end of the war, he and his brother were hired to work on a construction spanning the Saline River near the town of Kingsland, Arkansas. Ray boarded with the Rivers family for about four weeks and there he met Carrie Rivers who often served his food, something which she would continue to do for many years to come.

Carrie's father, John L Rivers, was from a family of farmers and both he and his wife Ruth were God-fearing churchgoers. John grew cotton and other crops though he also kept animals to meet the family food needs. In addition, he was a music teacher as, reputedly, his father was too. The Rivers' house was often the venue for informal musical gatherings with family and guests taking turns at singing and playing a selection of instruments – guitar, fiddle, organ and bass viol. No doubt wanting to make a good impression in the right places, Ray Cash enthusiastically joined in with the sessions on his increasingly frequent visits.

Ray and Carrie were married on August 18, 1920. Ray went to work on his brother's farm near Kingsland, at that time a small trading town in County Cleveland, with a population of around 200. The cash crop was cotton but the inhabitants were also self-sufficient in many of the essentials of life. Though the work was physically demanding, the rewards meant that the people were able to make ends meet even though years of cotton farming had taken the best out of the land so that successfully growing anything was a considerable challenge. The Cash family started to increase and by the end of the Twenties, they had two children, Roy and Louise, who would soon be followed by a baby brother, Jack. However, there were a number of dark clouds on the horizon.

◆ ◆ ◆ ◆ ◆

In the wake of the First World War, farmers had been encouraged to increase production in order to supply the seemingly insatiable demands of Europe whose agricultural production was in tatters. This had led to a mini-boom, with farmers taking out more loans and acquiring more land. Once European agriculture got back on its feet, demand from that quarter rapidly diminished and farmers in America found themselves producing more than was needed.

Cotton farming had taken a great deal of goodness out of the soil but farmers had little option but to keep on working the land. The result was that, after a few years, the land produced cotton of inferior quality, "strict low middlin'" as opposed to "fair to middlin'." The bottom line was less income, which naturally added immensely to the difficulties of sharecropping which even at the best of times was a borderline way of life. Things went from bad to worse with the economic earthquake which struck America, and soon much of the world, in the wake of the Wall Street Crash of October 29, 1929.

Before the Depression cotton would bring in about $125 per bale but by 1931–1932 that figure had tumbled to $25 for 500 pounds of cotton, a level which was unsustainable. Increasing numbers of farmers simply couldn't maintain loan repayments and, as the whole agricultural infrastructure started to unravel, most were badly hit.

With drought bringing an extra burden, whole families left Kingsland in search of work in the bigger towns and cities. Large numbers took to riding freight trains illegally, looking for the harvest, or any work. For some, though not the Cash family, far-off California was the promised land, despite myriad risks and uncertainties associated with travelling such huge distances with little or no back-up. The Cash family lived beside a large siding on the Cotton Belt railroad and would often see desperate people sitting on boxcar roofs waiting to be hauled away to another town in the hope of finding work. Although things were very difficult for the Cash clan, they would sometimes share what little they had with those who were even more unfortunate. In order to support his family, Ray Cash tracked down work wherever he could – working as a labourer on building sites, cutting down trees, washing dishes, and cleaning cisterns – even when it meant going long distances for meagre rewards. Sometimes he was paid in food or other essential supplies and when there was no work he shot possum, squirrels and rabbits in order to help feed the family. He became a rural jack-of-all-trades, prompting one subsequent description of him as "a farmer, hobo and odd-job labourer".

While most of the work kept him close to his family, on one occasion Ray received an offer he felt he couldn't refuse: 35 cents an hour to be part of a team dismantling a chemical plant in Charleston, Mississippi, about 150 miles to the east. The money was sorely needed so Ray reluctantly accepted but there were ugly scenes when some local unemployed men, desperate for work, offered to do the job for 15 cents an hour. Ray managed to keep his job but had a tense time from the local men who issued dire warnings about what they would do to the "intruders" if they came across them in town. Ray hid in his lodgings when not working, having cleared just over $60, a significant contribution to the family budget.

When the work ended, Ray sent the money together with his clothes on ahead to Carrie, something which, in those uncertain times, caused her more than a little concern considering that he was travelling on freight trains by "riding the blinds" (standing on the small platforms between two carriages) or, even more riskily, "riding the rods" (hanging on to the rods under a moving boxcar). During the journey back from Charleston, Ray crawled out from under a boxcar at night, only to be caught by a far from sympathetic railroad detective (or "bull"). Memories of the scene with the major in Paris might have flashed across his mind but this was an altogether more menacing situation. It was humiliating for Ray to have to beg, plead and grovel to be allowed to jump on a train to join his family. After some extremely harsh words and, according to Johnny Cash in his 1997 autobiography, a beating, both of which he had to take to avoid the risk of being prosecuted, Ray did manage to get on a train and made his way home, to his family's great relief.

◆ ◆ ◆ ◆ ◆

The Depression was a testing time for people of strong religious faith and the Cash family moved from house to house, even living for a time in a shack without any windows. The demands on their limited resources were about to be tested further still. On February 26, 1932 Carrie was heavily pregnant and close to term with her fourth child. In the morning Ray had headed off to the fields to plant potatoes but he was soon called back because Carrie had gone into labour and, shortly afterwards, JR Cash made the first of countless grand entrances. JR was a sickly baby and Carrie has said that he was anaemic in appearance at times, resembling a "foreign-country baby that's starving to death". When she was still breast-feeding him she took her concerns to the local doctor who determined that for some reason the mother's milk was insufficient for the infant. The doctor told her to give the baby cow's milk instead – a simple measure which quickly produced results. It has been said that Ray and Carrie simply called their son "JR" because they could not agree on what names to give him and this may be true but the use of initials rather than proper first names was by no means unheard of in the south at this time.

If there is truth in the proposition that babies growing in the womb absorb aspects of the world their mothers inhabit, then, given the upheavals and desperation of the times, the right epithet for JR Cash and his entry into the world would surely be "troubled". He had inherited a mix of qualities to stand him in good stead in later life though some were double-edged. Mixed up in the genes from his forebears were a willingness to work hard, a spirit of pioneering adventure, persistence in the face of adversity and its related (though less appealing) quality, stubbornness, risk taking, mischievousness and an affinity to the natural world. Music was in there too as was the genetic code for a voice of rare quality, so baby JR Cash clearly had a lot to work with.

In providing for JR and his siblings Ray and Carrie were still much at the mercy of events. Their existence remained hand to mouth and in addition to growing crops, Ray still had to take whatever work he could get to bring in sufficient money. Louise Cash Garrett recalls that her father was essentially a farmer, "so that when he took on other work to make money he was never quite so good at that. There were times when he worked for whatever people would pay, no matter how little." One job Ray found particularly distasteful was slaughtering 40 of the weaker cattle in his brother's herd. This happened in 1934 and was the result of a government initiative aimed at upping the price of cattle by reducing their number.

A good shot, Ray took a break at one point in order to throw up but he got through it because he had to in order to earn the pay of $2. Ray's brother reportedly told him that his "nigras" would claim the corpses but in fact his hogs feasted on them first. This was a particularly low point for Ray Cash who, along with countless others, longed constantly for better news. By the end of 1934 there were over 75,000 people in receipt of state benefit in Arkansas and half of them were farmers.

Trains and railways played a significant part in JR's life from an early age.

One of his earliest memories was seeing his father jumping out of a fast moving boxcar and rolling down the embankment into a ditch before clambering up on to the road which ran near their house as he returned from another far-flung job. As he said later, "My feeling for trains comes from lying awake in the hope of hearing the whistle that would bring my father back from the latest train-hopping search for work." One particular train he remembered, which he referred to as a "crack" train, was "Old 90" which would tear past the house at half past five in the morning "sounding like all creation fast and loose".

When he was older one of his uncles, a retired engineer, took JR for a run on the Cotton Belt line and as Johnny recalled later with barely concealed excitement, "He let me ride in the cab of the engine and it was the most awesome, powerful thing, a steam engine, and he let me pull the cord and blow the whistle when we came to a little town and I was thinking . . . I've got power, I'm running this train."

◆ ◆ ◆ ◆ ◆

Franklin Delano Roosevelt had been elected 32nd President of the United States in 1933 and though he came from a family of wealth and privilege, the like of which poor sharecroppers could not even dream about, he clearly understood that his overriding challenge lay in actively bringing relief to the Depression-induced sufferings of ordinary people. Things could not be left to free-market forces righting themselves over time – first he had to instil a sense of hope. Roosevelt was good with words, an effective communicator in modern parlance, and in his inaugural address he told people that they had nothing to fear but fear itself.

He also delivered deeds, and quickly. Within the first hundred days he enacted major laws designed to bring about industrial and agricultural recovery and though people understood that change couldn't happen overnight, there was a sense of the tide turning, that things were changing for the better. Roosevelt skilfully reinforced his message of hope with famous fireside chats in which he endeavoured to explain the steps he was taking to improve the economic situation and ameliorate the lot of millions of American citizens. In those days not everyone had a radio but those who did invited their neighbours in to listen and gradually the message of better times ahead under the New Deal spread.

Doubtless, the President had never heard of Ray Cash (though later Presidents would) but Ray would soon have reason to appreciate the efforts that Roosevelt was making on his behalf. One of the government's brainchilds was FERA (the Federal Emergency Relief Administration) whose basic idea was to provide targeted and constructive financial help to people, particularly those in the rural sector, by helping them get back on their feet and start making a contribution to the economy. This last factor was crucial because though it might have been popular in the short term simply to give handouts, Roosevelt realised the importance of getting as many as possible of the 30 million or so unemployed back into the workforce.

Towards the end of 1934, Ray Cash was listening to the radio when he heard about one particular "resettlement scheme" which appeared to provide the kind of news he had been hoping for. The government planned to buy large areas of land in America's farm belt which would then be split up into small parcels and given to selected individuals to work. One such scheme was to be in Arkansas. The idea greatly appealed because although Ray was able to scrape a living as a sharecropper he did not own his land and had little prospect of ever fulfilling this personal ambition. However it was not all plain sailing since the Arkansas scheme covered approximately 15,000 acres – room for only 500 families, a small fraction of those on relief.

Government officials would only select applicants they deemed to be of good character and likely to make a success of their opportunity. One unappealing feature was that the area designated for settlement consisted of low quality land, located in the middle of Mississippi County bordering the Mississippi River, with no nearby towns. It had been almost entirely overlooked by generations of previous settlers and while oak and cypress trees had attracted some logging activity in the past, the ground now showed the effects of near total neglect, being an impenetrable tangle of undergrowth and trees. Not only that but the swampy conditions were home to lethal inhabitants like wildcats, rattlesnakes and water moccasins.

Under the scheme each family would be provided with a house, 20 acres of land, a barn, a cow and a mule. They would have to clear the land first before farming it. There would be no down payment on the house and those selected would be "licensees" with full legal ownership being achieved only after the first three years. In addition groceries would be covered for a year though the cost would have to be recouped from the proceeds of the first crops harvested and sold. The government would create a basic infrastructure at the centre of the new community comprising churches, a school, a co-operative general store, a café and so on, from which 16 gravel roads would extend out, like the spokes of a wheel, to the 500 farmsteads. A basic drainage system and railway line would be installed, creating a connecting link to the outside world. The work involved in putting this infrastructure into place gave employment (at $5 a day, seriously good money at the time) to thousands of unemployed men but they had to work fast, with a team of 10 required to put up a five-roomed house in 16 hours.

A farmer without sons could not apply because whatever income the land generated, it would only ever be sufficient to support the family living on it, not hired hands as well. There was one other thing: the scheme was not open to blacks. The Roosevelt administration was progressive but only up to a point, even though 40 per cent of the population of Mississippi County was black. The authorities reckoned that white homesteaders simply would not accept black neighbours and that to insist on this would lead to insuperable race relation problems, dooming the whole project to politically unacceptable failure before it began.

The administrator of the Arkansas scheme was WR Dyess and it was after him that the "colony", initially described rather soullessly as "Colonisation Project Number One", came to be called Dyess. (Dyess never saw the scheme through to final completion because he was killed in a plane crash in January 1936.) Applicants had to attend the courthouse in the nearby county town of Rison and Ray, along with many others, duly presented himself there in his work clothes, full of optimism.

Having waited patiently for a considerable time, Ray was eventually interviewed by a government official. On one side was a be-suited official armed with a six-page form and numerous detailed questions. His motive: to assess whether the applicant merited the privilege of being given his own property at government expense. On the other, an ill-at-ease farmer in his working clothes, doing his best to give an honest account of himself. His motive: to gain a place he could call his own and be independent, no longer having to scratch a meagre living from someone else's land.

Ray Cash was surprised at the number of questions he had to deal with, about his family, his work history, his education and his military record. He also had to provide the names of people who could attest to his character. More interviews followed, more bureaucracy, more waiting; it seemed endless but in Ray's case, unlike those of many others, it was all worth it when he became one of only five Cleveland County men to be selected. Things were looking up, but though gaining a place was a cause for celebration, Dyess would also bring with it challenges to test the strongest of wills.

GIVEN THE UNCERTAINTIES and insecurities he and his family would be leaving behind, in all probability, Ray Cash overlooked the possible disadvantages in the move to Dyess. Part of his pleasure in being chosen was doubtless attributable to his having come through a rigorous checking procedure with flying colours. The family's sense of anticipation as the days ticked by must have been immense, though all Ray had really been given was a dream in the form of a share of a piece of economic engineering that represented potential deliverance, one that would need an enormous amount of strenuous effort to turn it to advantage. Adding to the family's excitement was the fact that they were put on 24 hours' notice of their departure time.

The waiting was extremely wearing but the day finally arrived and on March 23, 1935, the Cash family set out in a hired truck from Kingsland to Dyess. Reports of just how long the journey took vary considerably, from under one day to the best part of two, the reality probably being somewhere in between, though nobody was keeping an exact record. What no doubt started as an adventure for Ray and Carrie and their young brood soon became a gruelling ordeal as the children became bored, cold, tired and hungry, impatiently asking how much longer to go.

Carrie, Louise and new arrival Reba, travelled in the front alongside the driver while Ray, Roy, Jack and JR made do in the back, crammed in amongst the few family possessions and valuables worth taking. A rough tarpaulin provided little protection against the winter weather – cold rain fell, ice hung from the trees and the roads were covered in mud and riddled with potholes. The truck bounced along tossing the Cashes about, up and down and side to side, with relief coming only during brief pit stops and an overnight stay near a town called Marion.

Two of Johnny Cash's earliest musical memories date back to the journey to Dyess. In an attempt to comfort her brood, Carrie sang 'What Would You Give In Exchange For Your Soul'. At that particular moment the children could have been forgiven for answering, "A hot bath and a comfortable bed." It was during this journey that Johnny remembered singing for the first time, "seconding" with his mother leading on the appropriate 'I Am Bound For The Promised Land'. This was indicative of the powerful part the Christian religion played in JR's life from an early age.

The family eventually reached a rainswept Dyess in the early afternoon. Their house (number 266, Road 3) was just over two miles north of the centre of the colony. The yard was waterlogged and Ray had to leave the truck some distance from the house before he carried the young ones through the thick black Arkansas mud (or gumbo as they called it). Carrie Cash remembered how it stuck unforgivingly to her shoes, like wading through treacle. While hardly the most welcoming of sights, Ray Cash was not about to let any sense of anticlimax detract from his pride in having completed the move.

It was not possible to unload the truck that day but Ray was determined to inspect his land. Kitted out in thick rubber boots he headed off. Despite the seemingly impenetrable vines, unkempt trees and even an unscheduled dip in a well-disguised tree stump hole, he was not downhearted. Ray returned to the house and proudly announced that they were fortunate to have some "fine land". Although it was no mansion, the Cashes had a newly constructed house which they could now call home. The family slept under blankets on the floor in the glow of a fire prepared by Carrie with wood foraged from the surrounding land. Daylight allowed them to take full stock of their surroundings and unload furniture and other essentials from the truck. The house was white with green trim, and consisted of two large bedrooms, living room, dining room, kitchen, back and front porches, an outside privy, and barn with a chicken house and smokehouse added later. In the absence of a refrigerator (electricity would not reach the houses in Dyess for another 10 years), a smokehouse was a vital means of preserving the hog carcasses which Ray would kill in the winter. The smell of burning hickory for smoking the meat was one which would remain in Johnny Cash's memory throughout his life. Lighting came courtesy of kerosene lamps.

Being the equal of any man and undaunted by the prospect of hard work Ray Cash felt that his pride and sense of purpose had been restored. However, the financial strings on the FERA scheme were considerable, as Ray found out when he went to the administration office in the centre of Dyess soon after his arrival. The family's living expenses for the first year had been calculated in minute detail by the authorities and totalled $253.59, a figure which included an annual clothing allowance of $6.55 for young JR. This was paid in "doodlum", a form of voucher exchangeable for goods which was recoupable off earnings from the land, as was the cost of hiring the truck which brought them to Dyess.

The colony was not a charitable institution though repayment terms were not oppressive, with homesteaders being obliged to make such repayments as they could manage. The house and land would not legally belong to Ray until the ground had been converted into a viable commercial proposition and an amount had been paid to the administration reflecting the value of the house plus other necessary outlays. Until then Ray remained a licensee. The administration gave folks a chance through the incentive to succeed.

Ray was also issued with a scrawny beast of a mule. Not wanting to make a fuss but equally not wanting to be lumbered, he resorted to down-home diplomacy. Ray struck up an amicable conversation with the mule provider, manoeuvring the talk round to family origins. Before long they found that they had some common background. Cannily playing his hand, Ray made a comment to the effect that his mule was not the most impressive beast he had ever seen. Casting a knowing eye over the wretched animal, his new friend agreed and allowed Ray to pick a new mule which he named Joe.

The most pressing task ahead was to clear the land, rendering it fit for cultivation, a task made all the more difficult by continuing bad weather. Ray and Roy set about it with gusto, attacking the higher ground first before working their way down to the lower areas (much of it underwater). It was gruelling work especially for Roy who was only 14 but he didn't question what was expected of him. With a plough, heavy-duty saws and axes the pair got to work cutting down trees, clearing roots and breaking the surface of the land to ready it for seed planting, all the time keeping a wary eye out for the dangerous snakes which were their constant companions. Often they had to burn out tree stumps and sometimes it was necessary to use dynamite to blast out the more obstinate ones. Their work hours were governed by nature, starting at sunrise and only returning to the house as darkness fell.

With the arrival of spring and the easing of weather conditions, the land began to dry out making Ray and Roy's work slightly easier and, since it had not previously been cultivated, the soil was rich, considerably richer than the soil around Kingsland which had been denuded of its beneficial nutrients. By the time they had cleared a reasonable area of land it was late in the planting season. However, Ray was anxious to get to the stage of supporting himself and repaying the government money so he planted roughly three acres of land, mainly with cotton which would generate income but also with crops to feed the family such as beans, potatoes and strawberries. Corn was also grown for the animals including a recently acquired milk cow and hens. The soil yielded two acres of cotton which produced three bales, allowing Ray to reduce his debt to the authorities by $150. In less than a year, the Cashes were already moving towards self-sufficiency.

Whilst Ray concentrated on knocking the land into shape Carrie had her own set of challenges back at the house. The water in Dyess, while safe for drinking, was a nightmare for cooking. When boiled it turned black and if soap was added for washing it failed to dissolve properly, creating a kind of gooey mess not unlike the gumbo outside. With a typical combination of ingenuity and resolve Ray installed water barrels which were used to catch rainwater. One was filled with pump water and then treated with lime to produce water suitable for cooking and washing. Carrie also became adept at getting the best out of a government-issued pressure cooker which she used to cook foodstuffs, most of which were stored for use during the winter. It was understood that nothing could be wasted.

For four-year-old JR, or Shoo-Doo as his father called him, this was a lonely time. He had just moved to a strange, forbidding new world and the rest of the family were either toiling to make ends meet or at school so he found himself on his own for long periods of time. The high points of JR's day were when his mother sang him a song or his father bounced him and his little sister Reba on his knee and told stories, many from his experiences during the First World War.

Over the years many articles about Johnny Cash have stated that he came from an extremely poor background and that there were times when he nearly starved. Such assertions were always upsetting for Ray and Carrie Cash because though they rarely had money for luxuries, they always made sure that their children were fed and clothed as a matter of pride. Roy said in later years, "We were never hungry," and though conceding that the diet was repetitive, with beans featuring on the menu on virtually a daily basis, he went on, "but it was healthy, there was plenty for everyone and no one ever went without." Not content with his arduous land toiling, Ray also helped to complete the last houses in the Dyess community whose population grew rapidly. By the start of 1936 there were 139 families and by the end of the year the figure had grown to nearly 500, though the scheme did not work for everybody. A number of settlers found the land altogether too hostile and headed back to the hills they had come from, their hopes dashed.

Those who stayed helped the colony to prosper on a foundation of mutual support. As well as helping out with problems that arose – clearing particularly resistant areas of land, stuffing mattresses with ginned cotton, whatever needed to be done – there was also a co-operative economic structure developing in Dyess. The cotton produced was aggregated and sold "higher up the line" for better prices than lone farmers would have been able to achieve. Each home-steader also had a stake in the general store and shared in its profits. It was a kind of socialism or to use Johnny Cash's preferred description, "com-munalism", a concept which apparently met with his family's approval, though not everybody agreed. The landowners saw the Dyess experiment as a potential threat to their way of life and one which only a Democrat administration could have dreamt up.

Anything which smacked of socialism was anathema and they appeared little concerned that often the sharecroppers were unable to meet their rental commitments. For many, living with an ever-increasing burden of debt had become a way of life, of which there was little prospect of escape. It was ironic that the Depression helped a chosen few, like the Cashes, to make the break.

◆ ◆ ◆ ◆ ◆

Partly in recognition of the progress made and partly to generate favourable publicity for the scheme and keep the momentum going, First Lady Eleanor Roosevelt, plus an entourage of assorted dignitaries, swept into Dyess in June 1936. Amidst much pressing of flesh (and a fondly remembered hug for Louise Cash Garrett), speeches were made to boost morale at a time when the economic situation was particularly dire. The colony was told by Colonel Westbrook, deputy to Presidential Assistant Harry Hopkins and the man handling responsibility for the resettlement programmes, that "there is more real security here . . . than in the finest mansions in the most fashionable and arrogant residential sections of Memphis." It's unlikely that Ray Cash and the other workers saw it that way as they toiled for 14 hours a day, but they had reason to be optimistic as Dyess started to bloom.

Within a short time there was a garage, a printing house, a blacksmith, a furniture factory and a twenty-bed hospital. A rising birth rate, improving crop yields and other such local occurrences were reported in a fledgling newspaper, the *Colony Herald*. Doodlum was replaced as the unit of exchange by dollars and cents, and there was scope for goods and services beyond the bare necessities. A beauty salon opened up in the back of the barber's shop where ladies could avail themselves of a shampoo and finger wave for 40 cents.

For thousands of years the Mississippi River had meandered back and forth across the flood plains and, though it regularly overflowed its banks, Native American tribes simply accepted the whims of this life-giving artery and adapted to it. The arrival of European settlers in the eighteenth century resulted in various control measures being introduced. These principally consisted of the systematic construction of levees at those points deemed most vulnerable to flooding but, as with the Maginot Line some 13 years later, the defence measures proved wholly inadequate in the face of overwhelming and irresistible force. The Great Mississippi River Flood of 1927 broke through levees in more than a hundred places and flooded more than 26,000 square miles of land, forcing more than 600,000 people from their homes. In some places the river was 80 miles wide, up to 500 people died and countless animals drowned or starved.

In 1928, Congress passed the Flood Control Act under which the US Army Corps was given responsibility for controlling the Mississippi. In addition to levees, a series of spillways were created which were essentially doorways in the levees at various points which, when the river was dangerously high, would be opened to allow some of the water to flood along designated routes into nearby lakes and on to the Gulf of Mexico.

The Mississippi lay about 15 miles to the east of Dyess. Early in 1937, it started raining and didn't stop, raining heavily for the better part of a month. Water levels rose steadily and the steps leading up to the Cash house became partly submerged. Normal working life came to a standstill but of even greater concern was the fact that the level of the Mississippi had risen by nearly 40 feet in places (15 feet above flood level). The extra ingredient of strong winds made fears that the levees would break all the more real. One of Ray Cash's friends, Frank Huff, went to the centre of the colony where he measured the depth of the water, which he found to be three feet high, and rising. Back at house number 266 it was deeper still, reaching five feet and rising. If the levee broke, Dyess would be washed off the face of the earth.

With no let-up in the weather the colony's officials took the decision to abandon Dyess like a sinking ship. Ray and Roy decided to hold out in the hope that the situation improved. Carrie and the other children, Louise, Jack, JR and Reba, were taken from the house in a makeshift boat and put on waiting buses with the help of a piggyback ride from their dad. The farewells were heartfelt and tense, being the first significant separation for the family since Ray's far-flung forays to find work.

Taking only a few essential items with them the Cashes were driven by bus to the town of Wilson, a journey of about 12 miles marked out with poles to ensure the bus didn't drive off the road. The surrounding lands were underwater with bridges destroyed and crops ruined. On reaching Wilson, Carrie took one look at the government tents and queues for soup and decided to go on by train to Pine Bluff near Kingsland where some of her family still lived. JR, then nearly five, was largely oblivious to the tension surrounding the departure from Dyess and was hugely excited by the Lone Star journey on the Cotton Belt route.

JR proudly sported his best outfit, a Tom Sawyer suit bought from the Dyess co-operative store for $1.25, almost a quarter of his yearly clothes allowance. He let off steam by running up and down the aisle of the train, but his exuberant behaviour though understandable in the circumstances was in marked contrast to the apprehensive demeanour of many of the other passengers. The journey was painfully slow with the engine only making two or three miles an hour at times because the track was under water and the driver was concerned in case the train hit a hidden log across the track. The surrounding fields were flooded and it was often not possible to make out where the creeks had been. Carrie was relieved to reach Kingsland where her father was waiting to greet the tired and bedraggled group.

Ray stayed on at the house for another week; his and Roy's time being taken up with making preparations for the wave of flood water he assumed would come when the levees burst. After a week, with the rain still falling and the water still rising, they had no option but to leave Dyess and join Carrie in Kingsland. Ray jammed open the doors so as to reduce the impact of the water and also to ensure that as the waters receded, they would not be retained inside the house. He also made arrangements for the animals to be turned loose with food supplies left in the hope that they would still be alive when the family were able to return. By the time he and Roy left, armed law officers were patrolling the colony in boats to deter any would-be looters.

It was a tribute to the measures put in place by the Flood Control Act that for the most part the levees held, especially so since the flows of water in 1937 were bigger and stronger than those of a decade earlier.

Despite this, the Cashes and hundreds of other families were faced with the demoralising prospect of starting all over again. The wind eased, the rain abated and the waters receded. The family returned to Dyess about a month after they had left, to be met by a sobering sight. The place was a mess, caked in black Mississippi mud, with tide marks on the walls of the house, and the land completely waterlogged. Packs of wild dogs roamed at will and poisonous snakes, the conditions to their liking, had taken up residence in the barn.

The children initially appeared despondent. However, Carrie was quick to admonish them to get down to some serious tidying and cleaning, assuring that things would be back to normal in no time. The Cashes did return to some positive news. The Poland China sow, a recent addition to Ray's animal menagerie, had given birth to five piglets and the hens had been on a laying frenzy throughout the house. Not only that but the mud deposited on their land was exceptionally rich and helped to produce a bumper cotton crop the following year.

Life gradually returned to normal. Ray and Roy returned to the fields and did battle with nature whilst Carrie returned to her housekeeping role once the house was sufficiently clean again. The Cashes were lucky. Some people's houses had been rendered uninhabitable or had been partially demolished by the floodwater which meant that they effectively lost everything. The colony administration was involved in numerous expenses associated with the flood including evacuation costs, medical bills, and many other sundry costs, the net result being that the administration found itself nearly $50,000 in debt.

◆ ◆ ◆ ◆ ◆

Life went on in Dyess. Over the next year the cotton crop was good and the number of families in the colony increased to well over 600. For young JR it would be a time of formative experiences. His tasks included feeding and watering the animals, chopping wood to burn in the stove and picking the garden vegetables. He also took water to Roy and Louise as they toiled in the fields. JR soon learned about hard work from his father, as he said in his 1975 autobiography, "I don't believe a man ever lived who worked harder and was more dedicated to providing for his family than my father." Louise described him as the "Family motivator". Although JR formed a burning ambition to get away from Dyess and the backbreaking work that was demanded of its inhabitants, he nonetheless came to have a great admiration for people who were prepared to work hard to support themselves and their families.

And then there was religion. Carrie took the children to the Road Fifteen Church of God, but if the aim was to increase the size of the congregation the preacher had a strange way of going about it. For JR, his experiences there were often alarming and frightening. His voice rising, apparent breathlessness causing him to deliver shorter, stabbing sentences between gasps, the preacher worked himself up into a state of apoplexy as he delivered the message of God's love, and for JR the effect was confusing. Members of the congregation would raise their hands in the air, yell, pray, writhe around on the floor and burst into tears, and now and then the preacher would triumphantly give thanks to God as another one "Got the Holy Ghost".

Young JR thought people only acted like this when they were upset about something and the scenes in the church troubled him. On one occasion, as he was walking back from a service which featured dire warnings about Satan and damnation, he observed a skyline lit up by bright red, yellow and orange flames. It was in fact a distant forest fire but the little boy with the big imagination genuinely thought this must be the hell he had been hearing about in church and it made him tremble with fear as he hurriedly scampered homewards.

Yet he was struck by the fact that his mother looked rapturously happy after such occasions, leading him to wonder what it was all about. Carrie Cash had been brought up a Methodist but in Dyess she regularly took the children to the Baptist church. For such a small place, Dyess had seen a lot of churches spring up in a short space of time – there being, in addition to the Methodists and the Baptists, the Church of God, the Church of Christ and the Pentecostal Church. Carrie took the children to different churches depending on what services or revivals were happening and this may have helped to broaden her children's views to the extent that they came to appreciate the general message of the bible as opposed to believing that one particular religious doctrine had a monopoly on the truth. However, all churches served up conservative evangelical Christian religious philosophy, and non-believers were not welcome. In politics it is said that if you disagree with Marx you are a class enemy but in the religious world of the American South, if you disagreed with the Baptist credo then you were a Satanist.

The churches were believers' churches, there being no room for liberal doubts, and critical appraisal of the bible was tolerated only to the extent that it proved the veracity of the text. Despite this apparent intolerance, it could be argued that churches which propounded certainty in their teachings were a vital social prop in such difficult times. There was, however, one thing about the Church of God that made JR feel that visits were not all bad – they had no objection to folk using musical instruments to accompany the singers, and JR loved the music which began to stir something deep inside him. Perhaps fear of the preacher made him take refuge in the music in the way that a child will bury his head in his mother's breast to hide from some horror too frightening to face. Or perhaps some mystical conception between music and religion was forged. Either way, Christian religion and, of course, music would be constants in Johnny's life thereafter.

Although the Cashes, like everybody else they knew, had no option but to live by the "If you take care of the cents the dollars will take care of themselves" maxim, Ray and Carrie allowed themselves one luxury, a battery operated radio which Carrie selected from the Sears Roebuck catalogue. Sears Roebuck was a retail lifeline for countless Americans, particularly those in rural areas, because while the local shops catered for the essentials, Sears Roebuck offered affordable luxuries on hire purchase.*

JR began listening to the radio every chance he got and the sounds which reached his ears – sounds which were more sophisticated than those he heard at home or in church – ignited a passion which would become the guiding force in his life. On Sundays, he would look for the songs he was used to hearing in church while, at other times, he would surf the airwaves checking out the already considerable list of stations broadcasting to the pre-television masses, WWVA out of Wheeling, West Virginia, WSM (home of *The Grand Ole Opry,* the most popular country music show and the spiritual heart of country music in years to come) from Nashville, Tennessee, and XERL, Del Rio Texas.

This last station actually broadcast from over the border in Mexico which meant that it was able to achieve a much higher output than was permitted in the US. As one early fan put it, "You could hang a tin cup on any barbed wire in Texas and hear The Carter Family." The Cash family went to bed early, Ray being first at 8:05 after the evening news, but JR was allowed to stay up a little bit longer to listen to music on the radio. He would often try to push his luck by turning the volume as low as possible in the hope that he wouldn't be found out. Often his father would shout down to blow out the candle and go to bed but JR was always loath to turn the radio off. The music he was hearing was rapidly becoming the most important thing in his life, more than a mere pleasantry to pass the time as it was for most people. For JR, music was a form of escape from the harsh unrelenting drudgery of day-to-day life.

Dyess was a politically engineered answer to a particular set of economic problems, which could never prosper in the long term. Times were changing and people were gradually becoming aware of, and in some cases actually acquiring, a few of the luxuries modern America had to offer. Against this

---

* Sears Roebuck had been performing this valuable service since the end of the nineteenth century and it is a sign of changing times that their massive depository in Memphis, vacated in the early Eighties, remains derelict to the present day.

background, the prospect of a lifetime of physical demands and miserly returns from a small farm were hardly enticing and it was inevitable that the next generation would find that a far better quality of life lay elsewhere. As the Thirties drew to an end the population of Dyess declined to around 400 families.

Still, for Ray and Carrie Cash, industrious and thrifty as they were, the security provided by their way of life was still acceptable. Their needs were modest and could be met in Dyess and, what's more, the farm now legally belonged to them. Three years after they moved in, the property was valued at just over $2,000 (including a reduction to reflect the enhancement Ray had achieved through his hard work) and this was converted to a mortgage which Ray undertook to repay at approximately $110 per month.

After the insecurities of the past, this was an immense source of pride and since Ray and Carrie had made some very good friends they saw no reason to leave a place which felt like home. With the Mississippi flood a distant memory and a growing family to help run the farm, life seemed to be on the up again for the Cash family, and for a while that's how it was. But Dyess would also be the setting for intense heartache of a far more personal nature.

APART FROM THE HYMNS JR heard at church, Carrie regularly sang popular songs to the children at home. On occasion, Ray accompanied Carrie while she led the children in hymn singing. Johnny Cash also remembers, with great affection, musical evenings spent at the home of his maternal grandparents, John and Ruth Rivers, who liked nothing better than to invite family and friends to celebrate a birthday or similar special occasions. After a generous dinner, the table would be cleared and people took it in turns to sing traditional songs and old hymns as well as traditional Carter Family songs with young JR hungrily drinking it all in.

His affection for his maternal grandfather may have been enhanced retrospectively since, as his mother liked to tell him, it was from John L Rivers that he inherited his distinctive singing voice. JR also came to admire his grandfather's capacity for hard work, being greatly impressed that when he relocated his family from Georgia to Arkansas, he constructed the family house with his own hands. John even thought to create a special area under the house which was ideal for children to play in and a cool place to escape the summer heat. Family life was important to JR right from the start.

While living in an enclosed space was not always to his liking and may have led to tensions and friction on occasion, it did help to engender in him (and the other children) an ability to get on with a variety of people of all ages and to adapt to new surroundings and situations.

The radio introduced JR to his musical heroes. Lulubelle and Scotty, Lonnie Glosson, harmonica maestro Wayne Raney, Red Foley and The Carter Family, one of whose members was a young girl called June Carter who performed songs such as 'The Old Texas Trail'. JR knew them all, what shows and what stations they were on, and every song they played. He was also able to tune into stations broadcasting shows such as *Barndance*, from far off Cincinnati, Ohio, and heard music from a broad range of artists such as Bing Crosby and The Andrews Sisters.

His mother recalls JR paying rapt attention to stories on the radio which seemed to fire his imagination. When bringing water to his sister as she worked in the fields, Louise Cash Garrett helped JR to sing by delivering a line once or twice and then getting him to repeat it. In this way, Louise provided an early introduction to songs like 'Amazing Grace' and 'Will The Circle Be Unbroken?' JR's burgeoning musical passion was still a mere hobby, fitted around other more pressing needs. As the boy got older, he was expected to do his share of working the land and picking the cotton insofar as his school timetable allowed. Sometimes he went to the fields after school to do a few extra chores but the romantic image sometimes created in film and song was far from reality. The work was repetitive, boring and physically demanding.

A wagon was parked at one end of the rows of cotton (the Cashes grew the Delta Pine variety) and the pickers worked their way along the rows of plants towards it, plucking the cotton by hand before flicking it into heavy and cumbersome canvas sacks, six feet long for children and nine feet long for older children and adults. Once the cotton was pushed down into the sacks it was possible to get 30 pounds into the smaller ones and up to 40 pounds in the larger. On a good day a picker going hard at it for 10 hours or so might fill 10 sacks but the cotton bolls were mercilessly prickly and a moment's lack of concentration meant a painful puncture wound. Much of the time, pickers' hands were red sore with such injuries. Being the stoical type, Ray didn't complain, being pleased and relieved when both the quantity and quality of the cotton – "strict high middlin'" – generated sufficient income to support his family. When the cotton bales were delivered, graders would pull out a sample, tease it for a while and then give a verdict on its quality with strict low middlin' getting around 28 cents a pound, strict high middlin' selling for 35 cents a pound with fair to middlin' falling somewhere in between.

Apart from the physical demands, cotton picking could be demoralising in other ways. From spring onwards, the cotton was plagued by fast-growing weeds, one of the most pernicious being cow-itch vine – a robust, irrepressible type of creeper which wrapped itself around the cotton. As the weather got warmer, these weeds seemed to grow faster than they could be contained which made doing battle a never-ending, wearisome and demoralising slog. Even when the sultry August weather led to a brief lull in the cotton industry there were other jobs to do such as digging potatoes, mending fences and chopping wood. The awkward seasonal challenges that nature threw up included the sudden arrival of massive flies, which hassled the cow and goat herds and congregated en masse on windows. Worse still, unstoppable army worms could strip crops like a school of piranha fish. Nowadays crops are sprayed with the right pesticides but such remedies were not available to poor sharecroppers such as Ray Cash in Thirties America.

◆ ◆ ◆ ◆ ◆

Yet the Cash family were much better off than some. JR observed migrant farm labourers approaching his father to ask if there was any work they could do, perceiving him to be a man of some substance. Observing such scenes, JR came to realise that his father had moved up the ladder through his own efforts and thus acquired the kind of self-esteem that comes from owning property and having an independent means of support. Ray Cash was by no means rich but the people who asked him for work had little beyond the clothes they stood up in. It was reported that when a baby of such a family died, the infant was simply buried in a ditch at the side of the road.

School wasn't an especially appealing place for JR. He did reasonably well academically, being quick on the uptake, which was all the more frustrating for his teachers who shared with JR's parents their thoughts on how well he would do if he just applied himself more. Over the years JR's grades were in the C to B range on average, with the odd A– thrown in. English and History interested him most and he was an avid reader with a particular penchant for such heavy-weight authors as James Fenimore Cooper and Sir Walter Scott.

JR's youngest brother Tommy (born in 1940 – the last of seven children following the birth of another girl, Joanne) remembers him as a lanky, studious boy, the quietest member of the family and "not too interested in boisterous games with his little brother." Then again big brothers quite often don't have much in common with their younger siblings, especially as JR was very close to his brother Jack two years his senior.

Ray and Carrie were keen for their children to complete their schooling but despite JR's undoubted potential there was never any talk of him going on to any kind of further education. School in rural Arkansas did have one major compensating factor, music. There were a variety of opportunities to sing at school plays, social events and musical competitions, which JR increasingly grasped as he got older. He liked many of the popular country songs which he heard on the radio but such material was not deemed suitable for school settings where he invariably performed gospel songs and novelty numbers such as 'Trees'. Ray Cash recalled that JR won $5 in a school talent contest when he was about 10 or 11. "I believe the name of the song was 'Lucky Old Sun'," he said. JR first sang in public at a local Dyess church when he was about 12. His mother accompanied him on 'They Tell Me'.

After school or working in the field, JR might go with friends or family to cool off by the river. One favourite spot was known as the "blue hole", a particularly deep section of the Tyronza River that was perfect for diving and where full-immersion baptisms took place. Fishing was also popular. A pole, a line and a hook plus a little local knowledge and youthful dexterity could land a catfish, a carp or a bass for dinner. Sometimes, at the weekend, JR would head off with Jack or some friends, wandering around indulging in whatever impulsive pursuits appealed to them. As long as they were back in reasonable time for supper, their parents didn't worry.

There were of course times when he and his friends got into trouble but a number of people who knew the young JR all make the point that there was no "meanness" about him. If he was challenged, he would come clean even if it meant a "whippin'". Carrie Cash confirmed this when interviewed in 1981 though Johnny himself painted a different, more idealised picture in the course of an interview with the *Daily Telegraph* in 1996. "My parents never whipped me, which they do in the south you know . . . we didn't know we were poor and we loved each other."

In his 1997 autobiography, Johnny bemoaned the loss of simple pleasures for growing children and wondered if they could still exist in the modern world. "I think that even if such places do exist, our televisions have blinded us to them." Rockabilly singer Narvel Felts, who grew up in the nearby town of Keiser at about the same time, takes a similar view. He looks back fondly, though realistically, at a way of life that has vanished – ploughs pulled by mules, kerosene lamps for light but above all the lack of television. "The kids had to make their own entertainment and that's what's missing now."

JR had a dog he called Jake Terry and like most youngsters he was very attached to his pet. One day when JR was at school, the dog somehow got into the hen house and killed some of the family's valuable chickens. It was his misfortune that Ray caught him in the act, saw red and dragged the canine into the woods and summarily shot it. When JR came home from school, he went looking for his dog and found the gory corpse. When challenged, his father told the truth. They got over it but, not for the last time, JR had to learn to live with a new kind of pain. For his part, Ray regretted what he had done, despite the compelling logic of protecting his interests. Despite being a good family man, and a hard working one at that, it was said of Ray, by one of his neighbours, that he was "kinda highly strung". It certainly must have been a powerful emotional surge that would lead a man to kill his son's much-loved pet rather than take the more obvious step of making sure the hen house was properly secure in future.

◆ ◆ ◆ ◆ ◆

Jack Cash was a different sort of boy from JR. By 14 he was an excellent physical specimen, well toned and muscular (partly thanks to Charles Atlas), unlike JR who was skinny and slight. Though they could both swim and climb trees, Jack's abilities were more honed. In the evenings, when JR avidly listened to music on the radio whilst carving patterns on the dining room table, Jack lost himself in Bible readings. Louise Cash Garrett moved away from the family home when she was 19 and clearly recalls Jack coming to visit her. His visits were not always welcome. "He was a Christian young man. He used to come by my house and talk about Jesus and at that time I found it all too much. I just wasn't interested in hearing about that kind of stuff and he could be quite persistent. I was really more interested in making a living then."

Jack was clean living whereas, even by the age of 12, JR had discovered the delights of smoking. Even though he knew it was bad, it attracted him nonetheless. Ray Cash used to roll his own cigarettes with Prince Albert tobacco, and sometimes he would put temptation in JR's way by leaving a half-smoked cigarette in the ashtray, which his son would then furtively smuggle into the toilet to finish. Around the age of 12 he even tried sniffing glue, smoking grapevine and sniffing gasoline, though he soon gave up on the last of these because one time he "got too much" and found himself "running and screaming". The fact that his father had allowed him to drink strong coffee from a saucer as a treat from about the age of two might have possibly contributed to Johnny's developing taste for artificial stimulants. Apparently Ray reckoned it would make his sons tough – a privilege not offered to his daughters.

Despite their differences, there was a particularly strong bond between Jack and JR. As Johnny Cash put it in his first autobiography, *Man In Black* (1975): "I suppose no two boys in a family were ever closer to one another or loved each other more than me and my brother Jack." JR really looked up to his brother, so it was all the more shocking when Jack, already a stalwart of the church by age 14, used a swear word when caught up in the overwhelming excitement of killing a cottonmouth moccasin (a poisonous snake) during one of their rambles. "Die, damn you!" he cried. It was a sign of the high regard in which JR held his brother that he was so taken aback by what would now be regarded as a minor transgression.

It also illustrates another aspect of JR's country upbringing, an unsentimental attitude to animals other than pets. Animals were seen as commodities to use or threats which had to be guarded against. Hunting and killing snakes was regarded as a pastime, as were hunting frogs and hooking out spawning fish from holes in the riverbank. Their father had to slaughter cattle in an attempt to maintain the commercial value of the herd, which needed protecting from bobcats and wildcats. The pelt of a wildcat Ray had slain was long enough for a young JR and two of his siblings to sit side by side on when laid out flat.

From an early age Carrie Cash, a "practical Christian", held Bible readings for the children when she would discuss the meaning of particular passages, often ones about people worse off than them. However, it was more likely a result of Jack's influence that, shortly after his twelfth birthday, JR attended a two-week series of revival meetings at the First Baptist Church. One night, with Jack in the front row, eyes closed and singing hard, JR made his move. As he recalls it, there was no sudden or dramatic revelation, no words spoken to him by the Almighty, no bands of angels with a heavenly choir accompaniment. It was more a feeling of inevitability brought about by his parents' example of living by the tenets of their religious faith, the religious music he heard on the radio and, not least, the striking example of Jack, already destined to be a preacher. These things helped to form in JR a conviction that to give himself to Jesus was the right thing to do and, more importantly, not accepting Jesus would be tantamount to rejecting him. Put that way, acceptance was the only option, albeit not one devoid of pragmatism.

It must have been a nerve-racking moment when JR got up, walked past his brother in some trepidation and put his hand into the preacher's. As he said later he was "making a public show of repentance and acceptance of Jesus as Lord and Saviour." In the wake of his momentous decision JR became aware of two things; firstly, a sense of relief tinged with joy that he had now taken a step which, given the religious norms in his closed community, there was clear pressure to take. He had joined the club. Johnny Cash has talked of "reaching the age of moral and spiritual accountability" and of "the direction choosing time" of his life – advanced concepts for one only 12, although it's hard not to detect a rationalising gloss applied with the benefit of hindsight.

JR became aware of an even greater feeling of closeness to Jack. They had always enjoyed a special bond but now JR felt that he was his brother's equal, that having gone through this important rite of passage he had somehow acquired a degree of maturity and knowledge on a par with Jack's. Johnny Cash has said that they now had something more in common, that he and Jack could "walk like this forever – children of God." This was written in his 1975 autobiography when a middle-aged Cash was reflecting on his life, referred to as a "spiritual odyssey". Perhaps his remark about Jack should be set against this background.

◆ ◆ ◆ ◆ ◆

Many accounts of the death of Jack Cash have been written – hardly surprising in view of the special relationship he had with JR. All tell the same basic story with some containing more detail than others. So it was all the more surprising that out of the blue, in the mid-Nineties, Johnny Cash elected to tell a different story.

It was Saturday, May 12, 1944. The weather was warm and pleasant that morning and JR wanted Jack to go fishing with him but Jack had other plans. He had agreed to go to the high school agriculture workshop to help with various jobs including cutting oak logs into fence posts. As always, family money was tight and characteristically, Jack saw it as his duty to help out as working at the school would increase the family finances by $3. It seems Jack acted strangely in the house and was edgy and fidgety in a way that JR had not seen before. JR's main aim was to get him to forget the workshop but though he appeared undecided, Jack refused to go with his brother who has since suggested that Jack had some kind of premonition.

Jack fooled around doing Bugs Bunny impersonations, "What's up, doc?" apparently not wanting to leave. Yet he wouldn't go fishing with JR who sensed that he was in something of a quandary. Jack went to his room to read his Bible before deciding it was time to go to the workshop for which, uncharacteristically, he was already late. They walked the first mile together, all the time JR trying to persuade his brother to go fishing.

He may well have felt uneasy about letting Jack go in view of a dream he had had two weeks previously. "I dreamed an angel came to me to tell me my brother Jack would die, but that I must understand that it was God's plan and someday I would see that it was." When the boys came to a junction, Jack headed off determinedly to the school and JR made for the fishing hole. His last memory of Jack was him fooling around doing more imitations of cartoon characters. As he said later, "It wasn't like him and it didn't feel right."

JR's fishing expedition was unsuccessful and, lacking the hoped-for companionship of his brother, he packed it in early and made his way back to the house. It was when he reached the junction where he had parted from Jack not long before that the day turned into a living nightmare. He became aware of the preacher's car pulling up and his father gesticulating wildly from the passenger's seat for his wide-eyed son to throw his fishing line in the ditch and get in quickly. As they drove along, Ray blurted out a few vital details. There had been an accident at the workshop and Jack was injured very badly. When they reached the house, Ray took JR into the smokehouse and opened up a bag which he had noticed his father clutching onto in the car. He pulled out the shirt and trousers Jack had been wearing when the accident occurred; they were torn and saturated with blood. JR had the unnerving experience of seeing, for the first time ever, his father crying as he told his son that he feared the worst. JR was shocked and confused and overwhelmed.

Jack had been working, unsupervised, at a bench with a spinning circular saw blade at its centre when somehow he was yanked onto the saw. A cause was not given but one strong possibility was that a knot in the piece of wood Jack was pulling towards him caused the saw to jerk Jack towards it. Nowadays there would be a guard making such an accident impossible. The damage was done in a split second as the blade slashed violently into Jack's torso. The force was such that his leather belt, the one JR saw in the smokehouse, was sliced clean through but, more gravely, the saw sliced into Jack's abdomen causing massive injuries. Louise Cash Garrett explains that the injuries were made worse by Jack's attempts to get help. "He crawled to the door and got sawdust and dirt in his wounds and this of course led to an infection."

An ambulance was called and Jack was rushed to the colony hospital literally trying to hold his insides in. He was operated on but in reality it was simply a case of stitching up the wounds. Those close to him at the time said Jack knew he was going to die but though he was right, he somehow managed to hold on for over a week even showing signs of recovery at times, talking lucidly to his family and other visitors.

Roy Cash, who by this time was married and working in a munitions plant in Texas, came back expecting to say a final farewell to his brother but, in view of the apparent improvement, had returned to Texas. The doctor counselled against optimism because the internal injuries were too severe. The only aid he could realistically offer was to ease Jack's pain with morphine so that much of the time he was comatose. Days passed and still he lingered as prayers were said at local churches with the whole community rallying round. On one occasion JR visited his brother who was conscious and deep in conversation with his mother. He didn't seem to notice JR who was puzzled and a little offended at his brother's morphine-induced stupor.

Carrie was concerned that the doctor had not dressed Jack's fingers which had also been injured in the accident and ended up attending to the task herself. Eventually, the doctor advised Ray that Jack had blood poisoning and that he couldn't hold on much longer. Ray and Carrie and the older children with the exception of Roy, settled in at the hospital while Reba, Tommy and Joanne were taken to stay with a nearby neighbour. JR was the youngest child to be allowed to witness the death of his beloved brother and now faced the prospect of being the oldest son on the farm.

♦ ♦ ♦ ♦ ♦

Johnny Cash's recollection of the passing of his much-loved brother is charged with mystical overtones. In the course of his dying, Jack left JR with a spiritual experience that gave him what he took to be a vision of a world beyond this one. It was an experience which made an indelible impression on a young, deeply disturbed mind and almost certainly helped to reinforce JR's burgeoning awareness of faith so soon after his church initiation.

In both his 1975 and 1997 autobiographies, Johnny Cash describes his brother's death in detail, providing specific quotes of Jack's last words. The quotes differ but what they evoke is a dying boy, drifting between life and death and, before the moment of physical death, having what might now be called an out-of-body experience. On the morning of his death, Jack woke to find his family around him in various stages of emotional distress. He apparently asked his mother, "Did you see the river?" He is said to have spoken of going down a river, with fire on one side and heaven on the other and went on, "I was crying, God, I'm supposed to go to heaven. Don't you remember? Don't take me to the fire. All of a sudden I turned, and now, mama, can you hear the angels singing?" He started crying. He said the angels were "so beautiful". He spoke of the "beautiful place I'm going . . . what a beautiful city". Just before he died he said, "Oh mama, I wish you could hear the angels singing."

It's a powerful and moving picture but did it actually happen? Louise Cash Garrett, who was present, does not recall hearing the words attributed to Jack though she does recall her mother, "the spiritual leader of the family", later mentioning similar words. Jack was full of morphine, prone to hallucination and close to death. His body was giving out so who knows what chemical combinations were running through his brain as this happened. Hospice nurses confirm that those at the end of their lives often do have strange visions. Was he simply rambling about the house in Dyess and the local church choir? JR had recently taken an important decision to go forward in church and commit himself to Jesus Christ and was in the powerful presence of distraught believers. Was it a case of putting a particular interpretation on events years later to fit in with beliefs which became so much more to the fore many years later?

Of Jack, Johnny Cash later wrote: "There was such substance to him . . . or even moral weight, such *gravitas*." In later years when faced with difficult decisions, he often asked himself the question, "What would Jack do?" One beneficial consequence of Jack's death was that Ray Cash stopped drinking. The family dreaded the times he would come home drunk. Johnny recalls lying awake late at night silently praying his father would stop shouting aggressively at his mother; such incidents, not uncommon, were a source of considerable tension and fear within the family.

There is an intriguing footnote to Jack's accident. Although there were no eye-witness accounts, it has always been reported and assumed that what happened was an accident. However, in 1994, Johnny Cash contradicted this in an interview with Nick Tosches. Although clearly uncomfortable at talking about it in detail, Cash said that there had been another person, a neighbour, at the workshop, who disappeared after the incident. He was now hinting that Jack had been deliberately killed and as he said in the interview, "It was an accident only in the family's mind." But if so, why keep quiet about it for half a century? Why not give more information, why be enigmatic? Were the police involved? Apparently not. Above all, when he had the opportunity to set the record straight in his 1997 autobiography, why was Jack's death once more described as an accident?

Whatever question there may be over Jack's death there is no doubt that he and JR were intensely close, to the extent that other members of the family had found it hard to get close to JR. Jack's death highlighted behavioural traits that were already evident. Carrie Cash recalled that JR, though a happy, well-adjusted child, had always been subdued. After the tragedy, he became much quieter, appearing to withdraw emotionally. His younger brother Tommy recalls that JR "grew up quieter than most teenagers would have". In the wake of Jack's death JR started taking much more of an interest in writing songs and poems. Carrie Cash said that the happy laughing boy became a sombre boy. After investing so much time and energy in his friendship with Jack, there was a vacuum in his life which was at least partly filled with his own dark, brooding thoughts. Yet he still had to get through the rest of his childhood and more formative experiences along the way.

4

POST TRAUMATIC STRESS SYNDROME was unheard of in Dyess in 1944. JR had to deal with the terrible loss of Jack (and before that the brutal demise of his dog) as best he could, with the freely given support and sympathy of the family and community. He may not have expressed it at the time but it was his mother's plight which affected him most. With no space for any natural kind of grieving process, she was soon back at work, looking after the house, working in the fields, chopping down weeds and vines when all the time her heart was pining for the son she had just buried. Sometimes she would stop work and hang her head, waiting for the strength to carry on.

JR matured considerably in a short space of time. He came face to face with the kind of realisations about life that only mature adults should have to deal with. He learned that no matter what happens to a boy and his family, no matter how great the tragedy that befalls them, life has to go on. In a way the task was made easier in that the land had to be worked and the animals fed. JR discovered that no matter how massive the impact of his brother's death on his own life, for his friends, undiplomatic and tactless as youngsters can be, it merely became a boring subject that they soon tired of. Perhaps this was why Jack soon entered JR's most private domain, his dreams. In his 1997 autobiography, Johnny Cash claimed that from 1944 onwards Jack often featured in his dreams, having most recently appeared with grey hair and a grey beard, like one of the older representations of God – a preacher of repute with a clear understanding of his younger brother's inner thoughts.

Each year poor families would appear in Dyess looking for work. One such family, evidently with a different set of mores from the Cash household, set up camp about half a mile down the road from number 266. According to the story there were three brothers called Big'un, Littl'un and Cotch and a younger sister by the name of Annabelle, who took a fancy to JR. After introducing herself to the uncertain youth she tried to persuade him to accompany her into the undergrowth. Three or four years his senior but evidently light years ahead in terms of experience, she was too much for JR who ran off in terror despite his natural curiosity.

Later he became smitten with a girl called Virginia, though the outcome was no more successful. JR had been aware of Virginia for about two years and had suffered the angst of watching her date a boy from Osceola, a town not far from Dyess. That romance had ended, but still JR felt too shy to make a move, though he wrote some love letters which he didn't have the courage to send. One day he drove the family's car (their first) into town, but the old Ford was a sorry sight not least because the windows had fallen out, their place taken by haphazardly placed bits of cardboard. The town centre was a circular area with shops and other buildings around the perimeter. JR pulled up at the Dyess café, ready to make his move. Unfortunately the brakes weren't working properly and in the process of sliding the car to a halt, JR made contact with the front of the café's porch and the jolt caused the old Ford's "windows" to fall out.

As it happened, Virginia, who was outside the café, saw the whole thing and when JR got out of the car she had an enigmatic smile on her face. Taking this to be a show of friendliness, JR suggested a date but at this Victoria's demeanour changed, making it clear that until he got a car with windows he was wasting his time. JR got back in the car and drove off, rain blowing into his face. Upset and humiliated, his emotions raged around in his head. He cried, laughed and sang, all the while bumping along the rough gravel roads of Dyess with little thought for his own safety.

◆ ◆ ◆ ◆ ◆

While at this stage JR did not yet think seriously about pursuing a career in music, songs and writing nonetheless came to be ever-present features in his life, something Louise Cash Garrett clearly recalls. "JR was a storyteller, wrote poems and sang songs he had written from quite an early age." He regularly sang at school assemblies, performing songs such as 'Drink To Me Only With Thine Eyes' and 'The Whiffenpoof Song'*which had been made popular in 1936 by Rudy Vallee, though it was perhaps an unlikely choice for a poor boy living on a sharecropper's farm in the Mississippi delta.

Although JR was nervous, not least because the songs were invariably un-accompanied, the urge to sing in front of an audience was well established and vigorous. At this stage, in his early to mid-teens, his tenor voice was strong but of average pitch, markedly different from the trademark Johnny Cash bass bari-tone of subsequent years.

JR was greatly encouraged in his singing by oldest brother Roy who had

* The Whiffenpoofs were a renowned singing group formed in 1909 as an offshoot of the Yale Glee Club, whose members came from privileged families. The name came from a character in the 1908 Victor Herbert operetta *Little Nemo*.

formed his own band, The Dixie (sometimes Delta) Rhythm Ramblers. They often practised in the house, something JR loved to watch, being particularly impressed that his mother was able to play most of their instruments, including guitar, banjo and violin. The Rhythm Ramblers played popular country songs of the day and performed at small venues in Arkansas to which JR was taken on occasion as an enthusiastic and excited observer. JR was even more impressed when his brother's band got to appear on a radio show on local station KCLN, broadcasting out of the county town of Blytheville. Along with Carrie Cash, Roy was one of the first people to encourage JR to stick with his singing because he could tell that his little brother had real promise.

Though no recordings of The Dixie Rhythm Ramblers exist, it is said that Roy Cash had a strong voice and might well have had a bright future in the music business. However, along with the other members of his band he went off to fight in the Second World War and tragically three members of the band were killed in action, two of them at Pearl Harbor. After that Roy's heart went out of the idea of a musical career and he found work in the motor industry.

After Jack's death JR became closer to his sister Reba. Often when they were out working in the fields they would trade songs, though it was a rather one-sided exchange. Like most people, Reba found that when it came to her turn she could hardly remember any songs and often ended up singing the same one, usually 'You Are My Sunshine', over and over again. On the other hand JR, who inherited his father's exceptionally good memory, had already discovered a remarkable talent for remembering songs, even ones he had only heard once or twice on the radio.

He usually sang gospel songs, particularly those by Jimmie Davis, Sister Rosetta Tharpe and The Chuck Wagon Gang, whose angelic female tenor he particularly admired. JR's love of singing was furthered by working on the fields where a voice provided a means for people, exhausted from the relentless toil, to raise their spirits. Gospel songs were called on towards the end of the day when morale was often at its lowest. JR gained more musical inspiration from a friend and neighbour, Pete Barnhill, who was a useful guitar player even though his right arm and leg had been affected by polio. Pete was sometimes ridiculed by the locals as he hobbled to and from school and JR felt a strong sympathy for him as an underdog, struggling against the odds.

JR's mother had bought him a modest guitar some years before from Sears Roebuck but JR didn't show any interest in learning to play. However, he loved the way Pete played, forming the chords with his good left hand and knocking out a solid rhythm with his crippled right, leading and playing rhythm with his thumb. JR longed to be able to play like that. Maybe it would provide a way for him to somehow get on the radio – like Roy. JR spent hours after school at Pete's house, singing along on songs by Jimmie Rodgers, Hank Snow and Ernest Tubb, but though he tried to learn some chords, he found the awkward shapes too difficult.

JR was capable of displaying a lack of consideration which enraged his parents on occasion. Tommy Cash recalls one particular occasion when, as a special treat, he had been allowed to go to the "owl show" (the late film at the cinema) in Dyess. "JR had agreed to collect me in the family car, a black '42 Oldsmobile and that's why my parents let me go. It was quite a thrill for me. When the film finished I came out but there was no sign of JR. I hung around as everybody else headed off and eventually I was on my own and realised I was going to have to walk over two miles back to the house in the pitch dark. I could hardly see a thing. My parents were very angry with JR and told him so in no uncertain terms. After that I was never frightened of the dark though."

JR continued to listen to the radio whenever he got the chance. One of his favourite programmes was *High Noon Roundup*, broadcast on station WMPS from Memphis. It was a variety programme, featuring country and comedy, presented by Smilin' Eddie Hill. During the summer, carrying water to the pickers, JR invariably listened in during his lunch break. Lunch finished at one but JR often tried to sneak in extra time when Hill teamed up with Charlie and Ira Louvin, The Louvin Brothers. As The Lonesome Valley Trio, they sang gospel songs and read out dedications. JR couldn't contain his excitement when it was announced that, in a few weeks, the whole show would be broadcast from Dyess High School. JR got to the school hours before the show was due to begin, hanging around impatiently until the stars arrived. This was of course the radio age and JR had only seen black and white photographs of The Louvin Brothers.

He looked on enraptured as the limousine arrived and the equipment was unloaded and taken into the hall. He was fascinated by the organisation that went into putting on a performance; taking in details about the sound system, the guitars, even the souvenir programmes that would be sold in the foyer. He noted with approval Ira Louvin cradling his mandolin like a child and his heart missed a beat when Charlie Louvin approached him. A million thoughts went through his head as he tried to come up with something impressive to say. Actually Charlie wanted to know where the toilets were but that was good enough for JR. The radio star was eating soda crackers and, still tongue-tied, all JR could think to ask was whether they were good for his throat when he had a show to do.

For JR, the show was magical. Instead of listening to it on the radio and imagining, it was all brought to life in front of his very eyes. The performers easily lived up to the boy's expectations, reinforcing a growing desire to be involved in this kind of life. JR hung around long after the audience had drifted away and waited outside until the limousine departed. He was rewarded with a wave from Charlie. It was a precious moment, one which added another dimension to his excitement about all things musical. As he walked home in the dark, singing the songs he had just heard, he might well have been thinking, "I'm going to be like you." If so, it was a case of history repeating itself since The Louvin Brothers themselves had been similarly inspired by the sight of Roy Acuff driving by in a fancy limousine some years before.

◆ ◆ ◆ ◆ ◆

JR's interest in music did not have the unqualified support of both of his parents. Carrie came from a musical family and wanted to encourage JR in any way she could. Ray, however, had little time for the records JR listened to on the radio, dismissing them as "fake", unlike singing hymns in the house or at church which was the real thing. For Ray, the introduction of recording studios, disc jockeys and amplification devalued music, rendering it worthless. Ray sensed that his son was being inexorably drawn towards a life in music and wanted to divert him away from that path, one of his main complaints being that music would prevent JR from making a decent living. In contrast Carrie put herself out to support her son, taking in some washing duties to earn some extra money to pay for JR's singing lessons with an attractive tutor called LaVanda Mae Fielder.

In what may have been the first real indication that there was something unique about JR's vocals, Miss Fielder soon discontinued the lessons because she recognised a natural voice when she heard one, realising that it should not be interfered with or tamed. This was the beginning and end of any kind of formal musical training for JR Cash. Up until around the age of 16 JR's tenor, which had started to develop with the breaking of his voice around the age of 14, was not particularly deep, which was a puzzle to Carrie Cash. She felt that JR had inherited an aptitude for music and singing from her late father John L Rivers, but wondered why he had not received his deep rich voice. One day after JR had been out cutting wood for the winter fuel supply with his father (a dreaded job), he returned home singing 'Everybody's Going To Have Religion And Glory' at the bottom of his voice. The deep booming tone was so different from JR's voice up until that point and yet so familiar to Carrie Cash that she was moved to tears. Carrie urged JR to keep on singing and he was thrilled with the deep resonant tones he was now able to produce with ease. "God has his hand on you," Carrie is reported to have said, opining that Johnny would sing on the radio and perform for audiences far and wide. There was a sense that somehow this was a turning point, that a train of events had been set in motion, though where exactly it was headed nobody could yet say.

Another important point was reached in 1950 when JR graduated from high school. Once more it was an excuse for him to sing and for the occasion he chose one of his personal favourites, 'Drink To Me Only With Thine Eyes'. Completing his education had become the main reason for JR staying in Dyess; the land had become less productive in recent times and was barely able to support the family. Seeing the writing on the wall, Ray Cash decided to lease out his property and go to work at the Procter and Gamble oleomargarine plant in the nearby town of Evadale. Roy had already left home and JR soon decided to follow suit. For a young man of any ambition, Dyess was a town without a future.

JR took odd land jobs around Dyess but the rewards were meagre. He spent a miserable, though lucrative, few weeks in Pontiac, about 24 miles northwest of Detroit, working on the car assembly line at the Fisher Body Company. The trip was significant in one respect since it was here that JR had one of his earliest experiences with alcohol. His landlady gave him some wine to counteract the effects of a heavy cold but he hated it. Although coming home with well over $100, JR had found the work to be boring and demoralising, hardly surprising for someone so used to the outdoors. Nor did he like being derisively referred to as a "hillbilly" or "hick" by the other employees. Despite this experience he next went to work at the factory where his father was employed but if anything this was worse than the car plant – being employed as a general dogsbody, sweeping floors and clearing out foul-smelling residues from vats.

JR decided to follow the example of many poor young southerners and his own father, who had served in the Armed Forces, by enlisting in the Air Force. (He was not, as some have said, conscripted.) The idea of a stable job, which offered the prospect of training in new skills and a regular pay cheque, appealed to JR a great deal, though it was a potentially dangerous time to enlist. In June 1950, communist North Korea had invaded South Korea and when a United Nations resolution demanding the withdrawal of the North's troops to the thirty-eighth parallel was ignored, America found itself involved in war.

The question therefore arose as to where JR would be sent, though he wasn't nearly as troubled about this question as his anxious mother. He needed to do something, to get away from the dead-end existence he associated with Dyess. JR enlisted at Blytheville and soon found himself doing basic training at Lackland Air Force Base in Texas where one bonus was the marching music which he liked. In view of the huge demands placed on the Air Force infrastructure by the Korean crisis, the period of training had been reduced, and after a mere seven weeks, JR was presented with a number of training choices from which he selected radio operator. Intensive training followed, first at Mississippi's Keesler Air Force Base and thereafter with the recently created USAF Security Service at Brooks Air Force Base near San Antonio. Competition for jobs as radio intercept operators was intense but JR was one of those selected and his self-confidence received a timely boost as a result. With initials considered unacceptable, the Air Force referred to him as John R Cash.

On Friday nights, John would hit the town in San Antonio. On one fateful Friday he went roller-skating at St Mary's rink. His exuberance got the better of him and he collided with another skater who tumbled to the ice. "I'm sorry, I hope you're not hurt," he blurted out as he helped up the girl he had bowled over, and was immediately struck by her alluringly Mediterranean appearance. She was different from any girl he had known in Dyess and a spark of electricity passed between them right away. The girl was 17-year-old Vivian Liberto, a resident of San Antonio whose family were originally from Italy. They started dating but soon afterwards word came that John was to receive his first posting abroad. He was presented with a choice of locations, Germany or Adak Island in the freezing Aleutian archipelago off Alaska. By the time he sailed for Germany, he and Vivian were a couple though they had known each other for little more than two weeks.

John had to take a train from Memphis to McGuire Air Force Base from where he would fly out to Germany. Arriving in Memphis with his parents and Tommy in the family's silver grey '46 Pontiac, John stopped off to say goodbye to Roy and to eat when disaster struck as Tommy Cash recalls. "Unfortunately he left the keys in the ignition and when we came out from the restaurant the car had been stolen. Our mother was crying and our father was trying to comfort her. John had a train to catch so he simply had to put his bag on his back and run, and that was him away for over three years. It was a terrible parting."

It can only be imagined what Roy made of his brother going to Germany so soon after the end of hostilities in 1945, particularly bearing in mind the close friends he had lost. If he was familiar with German history then the name of John's destination, Landsberg, where the Second Mobile Radio Squadron was based, would no doubt have resonated with special significance. It was in the military prison at Landsberg that Adolf Hitler served a short jail sentence for his part in the abortive "Beer Hall" putsch of 1923/4 and where he wrote much of his autobiography, *Mein Kampf*. Though the charge against him was treason and a conviction would normally have carried the death penalty, the authorities were acutely aware of Hitler's growing popularity and chose instead to impose a five-year sentence of which he actually served less than one year. The prison was later used as a concentration camp.

Landsberg marked the start of a totally new phase in John's life. He was still relatively inexperienced in the ways of the world, having grown up in an isolated village in a climate of comparative poverty, in a family where money was always a worry, where luxuries were few and where battling with nature was an everyday survival issue. Now he had secure accommodation, a reasonable level of income ($85 per month) with plenty to spend it on, and no parents or religious strictures to cramp his style. Although the work in Landsberg was long and gruelling, John's time in Germany offered him the chance to learn and experience a veritable cornucopia of what the world had to offer.

Given the deprivations and restrictions of his upbringing it was hardly surprising that John threw himself into the task with excessive zeal. His initial instinct was to spend much of his spare time reading and writing home. In those early days, he didn't socialise much and felt intensely lonely at times. He often went to the base church, something his mother would have been proud of, but it didn't last. Initially wary of his companions who went on three day passes and got drunk the whole time, he eventually joined them, making up for lost time. He soon discovered the delights of German beer, then cognac though he would later disingenuously claim in his 1975 autobiography that he never really cared for the taste of alcohol.

Skirt chasing and fighting soon followed. A good night out would often involve a punch-up which for John seemed to be a way of letting off steam, so much so that he would actually go out of his way to look for someone to pick a fight with on occasion. It was hardly surprising that he and his friends regularly came to the attention of the polizei. John also witnessed what he later described as a race riot, black and white American soldiers who were supposed to be fighting on the same side. US military units had only recently been integrated and the tensions frequently surfaced. Despite not seeing any black people for most of his childhood, unlike some of his fellow airmen, John did not have a problem about sharing barracks with them.

His involvement with the opposite sex did not always run smoothly. One girl is reputed to have caused permanent impairment to his hearing after rummaging about in his ear with a pencil. How she came to be engaged in this particular activity is not clear. It wasn't all about the wild side of life. John also made some friends with whom he went walking and trout fishing. A favourite spot was Oberammergau, set amid beautiful mountain scenery, where the world-famous passion play is held every 10 years. On occasion they would cook their catch in the middle of the town square. John later suggested that the strong religious associations in Oberammergau somehow restrained the worst excesses of his behaviour and that his conscience reminded him that he was no longer going to church or making contact with his family, as he should. During his three years with the Air Force, John was not allowed one visit home and his phone calls were severely limited.

John honed his skills as a radio intercept operator to a high degree and was soon transcribing nearly 40 words a minute. With shifts consisting of eight hours of solid concentration, invariably he was exhausted by the end. There was one consolation though as the receivers could pick up radio station WSM all the way from America, so he could sometimes listen in to *The Grand Ole Opry* on a Saturday night. John was the first operator to pick up news of the death of Joseph Stalin in 1953. Although the Soviet operators could send Morse code to each other at the astonishingly high speed of 35 words per minute, John was up to the task of hearing and transcribing it. On occasion, the stress of it all got too much and some of his darker frustrations came to the surface. Once, when working an apparently normal shift, he threw a typewriter out of a window and then collapsed in tears after which he was given the rest of the shift off.

Presumably the Air Force knew when to turn a blind eye as John's outburst failed to diminish their opinion of his abilities. He may have been a silent type, at work and in his dealings with his superiors, but Sergeant Cash clearly knew his job inside out. As one of the top operatives in Landsberg, he was sent on special missions to bases in nearby countries. He also used some of his leave time to visit other European cities, taking in the *Folies-Bergères* in Paris, flamenco guitar playing in Barcelona and the gondolas in Venice, where he and friend Ted Freeman borrowed some café musicians' instruments to put on an impromptu performance of country songs by the likes of Hank Snow and Ernest Tubb.

John was pleased to discover a number of colleagues at the barracks shared his love of music. Informal music sessions soon started and a friend called Orvile Rigdon taught John a few chords. A group was formed which was christened The Landsberg Barbarians, possibly a comment on the laddish nature of the socialising which went on after rehearsals. They played well-known country songs by artists such as The Carter Family, Jimmie Rodgers, Roy Acuff and Hank Snow, a particularly strong influence of whom John later said, "He was my hero . . . he was breaking out of the mould with songs like 'Rumba Boogie' and 'The Golden Rocket', songs with a beat, with a tempo, exciting energetic songs and that's what I enjoyed."

The Carter Family also had a particular appeal for John because of their strong preference for religious material and as country music writer and historian Bill C Malone said, "Most of the Carter's religious songs originating in the fundamentalist tradition stressed the importance of holiness and emphasised the sadness and wickedness of this life and related the joys of the heavenly home beyond the grave." For all his new-found freedoms, John loved this music which resonated with much of his childhood experience, providing a spiritual connection to home. Jimmie Rodgers was also important because he had succeeded in synthesising pop, country, folk, blues and jazz, which prepared the ground for countless other artists.

♦ ♦ ♦ ♦ ♦

On occasion the Barbarians would take their instruments into town and play in some local tavern. John bought his first guitar for about 20 Deutschmarks (at that time about $5) and eagerly started honing his skills on the basic chords. He also continued to write poetry including 'Hey! Porter', an autobiographical piece about a homesick young man restless to get back to the welcoming familiarity of the southern states, which got published in the forces magazine *Stars & Stripes*. Even at this stage John showed interest in the idea of making and recording music, albeit in a primitive way, when he bought a reel-to-reel tape recorder with which to record the Landsberg Barbarians.

An experience in Landsberg also contributed a prominent feature to the physical appearance of one of the most famous faces in American popular music. John was troubled by a persistent cyst just below the right side of his mouth and he consulted a German doctor who decided that it should be surgically removed. John went along with this but unfortunately when it came time to carry out the procedure, the doctor was under the influence of alcohol and made a botched job of the operation. John was left with what would become one of the most commented upon minor facial disfigurements of all time, some reports suggesting that it was inflicted in the course of a fight.

And of course there was Vivian. John's family would no doubt have envied the number of letters she received but although John and Vivian hardly knew each other, the passion of their long distance love grew and grew. They did manage to speak on the phone (though John made himself unpopular by forgetting the time difference, waking her in the middle of the night). Marriage was proposed, and an engagement ring dispatched by post to Texas, but was this the best way to go about making a lifetime commitment? Although he had proved to be a first-class radio operator he didn't necessarily have the skills that would get him a good job back home. He liked singing but even though his ambitions lay in this direction, he couldn't really see music as a serious career. As his time in Germany drew to a close and home beckoned, there were more questions than answers swirling about in his head.

5

DESPITE THEIR SELF-EVIDENT mutual attraction, John and Vivian had been together for only three weeks, during most of which John was completing his training at Brooks Air Force Base. For more than three years they had communicated voluminously by letter with the occasional phone call thrown in. It was an extreme case of absence making the heart grow fonder, which had culminated in a proposal of marriage by phone approximately 18 months into John's time in Germany.

If wiser counsel had prevailed then perhaps they would have spent time getting to know each other again, finding out if they had anything in common, giving themselves time to see if they were right for each other. John would also have been able to investigate what direction he wanted to go in career-wise. Following his honourable discharge, Staff Sergeant Cash flew back to Camp Kilmer, New Jersey where members of his family as well as Vivian were on hand to greet him the next day. On a hot and humid day, amidst flamboyant Italian style celebrations, John and Vivian were married on August 7, 1954 at St Ann's Catholic Church, San Antonio, by Vivian's uncle, Father Vincent Liberto.

Vivian's strict Roman Catholic Italian background was very different from that of her new husband. Her father Tom, an insurance man whose hobby was amateur magic, was a keen opera fan. The Libertos didn't know anything about "hillbilly" music and Vivian had no particular interest in popular music, though intriguingly she did have a relative, "Wild Man" Ray Liberto, who had been a raucous honky-tonk piano player in his younger days. Unlike the Cash family, the Libertos were reasonably affluent. Tommy Cash has stated that when John got married to Vivian he was not aware of any tensions over their differing religious beliefs, and though there was some surprise that he should be marrying someone from such an opposite background, it was accepted.

However some of the older family members took a different view. Louise Cash Garrett recalled some concerns, as she said, "People didn't see that the Roman Catholics had the right ideas when it came to religion." It seems likely that there were devout believers on both sides who had misgivings about the union. John agreed that any children of the marriage would be brought up as Catholics and after he and Vivian were married, he actually underwent a course in Catholicism, which lasted six months. John had great respect for Vivian's father Tom, "One of the finest Christians I've ever known," as he put it in his 1975 autobiography. The experience helped develop in him a broad tolerance of different faiths, a trait not universal amongst southern Baptists. Aware of the disapproval some of his family evinced, the general subject of religion was one he sought to avoid.

◆ ◆ ◆ ◆ ◆

John had come back from Germany a changed man thanks to his army experience which had dragged on, especially towards the end. As he said later, "I spent 20 years in the Air Force from 1950 to 1954"; on another occasion, "I thought I'd thrown away my personal life." Family members noticed two things in particular about John, firstly, that he had filled out a lot and secondly, that he was edgier and quieter than before, as if some kind of barrier had been thrown up. Tommy Cash recalls, "This kid that I'd known had come back this big man. He had this persona about him that was different from anyone I'd been around."

He briefly returned to Dyess and stayed in the new Cash family home in the centre of the colony, the farm having been sold while he had been away. However Dyess had even less to offer him than when he was last there. The land was exhausted and unproductive and offered no future for a restless, worldly young man. For more than three years, subject to doing his job and abiding by Air Force regulations, he had been his own man, making his own decisions, indulging himself as he chose. He had discovered that alcohol could uplift his mood and obliterate his personal worries. However at the age of 22 he knew instinctively that this was not the sort of behaviour he wanted to pursue around his family.

In later interviews Johnny said that when he came out of the Air Force, "There was a rebel in me. I felt like I was caged, in prison." He also displayed a deeper insight when surmising that the restless feelings which beset him were, "Truly American. Maybe it's in all of us. After all most of us were losers and outsiders when we had to leave England [sic] and find a new country." Because so much of the music he had listened to over the years was broadcast from there, John was in no doubt that Memphis was the place to be. The newlyweds rented a four-room apartment in a modest residential area of the city. John put a down payment on a green '54 Plymouth.

Although he had built up some savings during his stint in Germany, he knew they wouldn't last long. Getting a decent job wasn't easy with the previous experience of agricultural handyman, and radio intercept operator unlikely to be of any immediate assistance. Given his forces background he considered a job in law enforcement. By a stroke of luck, the police officer who persuaded John that it might not be for him suggested he contact George Bates at the Home Equipment Company, who offered John a job selling electrical appliances. It wasn't so much that John was a lousy door-to-door salesman; his ability to relate to and get on with a wide variety of people pretty well qualified him for the job. It was more that his heart simply wasn't in it.

John drove around the poorer areas of Memphis, such as Orange Mound, making calls, going through the motions, breaking the golden rule of salesmanship by considering the best interests of the potential purchaser. He was a naturally open and honest person and his conscience got the better of him when realising that many people either didn't need the particular fridge, electric mixer or vacuum cleaner he was selling or couldn't afford it.

The net result was that he sold very little, making around $100 on a good week assuming all the credit applications were approved, and often many were not. He spent a lot of time sitting in his car, tuning into his favourite radio programmes such as Dewey Phillips' *Red Hot And Blue* show. Dewey was an anarchic disc jockey who played a broad variety of music that reflected his eclectic taste in blues, pop, gospel and country. He would think nothing of talking over songs and expressing wacky opinions about particular records, much as disc jockey Wolfman Jack later did.

John also came across a poor black musician called Gus Cannon,* sitting on his back porch playing a five-string banjo. John would listen to him play and sing and sometimes joined in. Like Elvis Presley, another young singer looking for direction around this time, John connected with the looser, more freed-up atmosphere of the black neighbourhoods. For a time, John pursued an interest in the idea of radio work and through an Air Force contact, he approached a station in Corinth, Mississippi, but his lack of experience worked against him. He then enrolled in the Keegan School of Broadcasting with a view to learning how to be an announcer or disc jockey, with the assistance of the GI Bill of Rights, to which he was entitled as an Air Force Veteran.

Under the Bill of Rights he had his tuition fees paid and received an allowance of just over $100 per month but it wasn't enough to live on, particularly since the couple found that they were expecting their first child. Juggling work and studying with the attendant travelling placed too many strains on home life and, despite the fact that he liked the course, John packed in his studies after five months in order to concentrate on selling appliances. His technique didn't improve and he and Vivian couldn't survive on what he was making. His boss, George Bates, had obviously taken a shine to him, and despite his young employee's obvious lack of success, he regularly took on the role of guardian

* Gus Cannon wrote 'Walk Right In' – a subsequent US number one hit for The Rooftop Singers in January 1963.

angel by lending him money. At one stage the debit balance got as high as $1,200.

Another guardian angel was a lady called Pat Isom who called into the Home Appliance Store when John was there. Perhaps it was the fact that he told her the $65 icebox she was interested in was worth less than half that amount which endeared him to her. The two got into conversation and John mentioned that he and his wife were looking for a new apartment. The fact was he and Vivian needed to reduce their outgoings, though no doubt he neglected to tell his prospective landlady that small detail. It so happened that Pat and her husband were in the process of dividing their house and she asked if John and Vivian would be interested in one half? It turned out that the rent, $55 per month, was $10 cheaper than they were paying at the time so they took the apartment on Tutwiler Avenue, not far from the Home Appliance Store. The arrangement worked well and later Pat Isom would say that the only thing that caused any problem was John playing his guitar for hours on end, sometimes late into the night. Even the fact that he was usually late with the rent apparently did not concern her because she knew that he would always pay eventually.

For all the tedium of everyday life, trying to make ends meet driving round town selling appliances, John got caught up in the urban buzz of Memphis. Traditionally the city's connection with the Deep Southern states of Mississippi and Arkansas was very strong and John was exposed to the music of the Mississippi Delta – blues, jazz and an embryonic rhythm and blues, all available in the music joints along legendary Beale Street. When money allowed, he went to the Home of the Blues record shop, also on Beale Street, where he bought albums by the black gospel singer Sister Rosetta Tharpe and seminal bluesman Robert Johnson. Legend has it that the man in charge, Ruben Cherry, used to keep a rattlesnake behind the counter to discourage potential shoplifters though unlike the amphibians John encountered in Dyess this one was made of rubber.*

One of John's all-time favourite albums was (and still is) *Blues In The Mississippi Night* which featured songs and spoken reminiscences by such greats as Memphis Slim and Big Bill Broonzy. It was recorded by the eminent folklorist, the late Alan Lomax and the sounds John heard created a heady mix when factored in to the country, folk and gospel he had grown up with. This might just have been the final piece of the jigsaw. The process had been building gradually, but music now represented the directional force in John Cash's life – something which could not be satisfied by giving endless solo performances to his neighbour through the wall.

Once more John's brother Roy did his bit to help on the music front. John had written to Roy from Germany saying that he intended to become a

---

* When the snake went missing it was rumoured that it had been stolen by a former customer, one Elvis Presley.

recording artist on his return home and the pair often talked about John's musical ideas, listened to songs and Roy gave feedback which John valued and respected. Roy and his wife Wandene also moved to Memphis and Roy introduced John to two mechanics – Luther Perkins (nickname Ellum) and Marshall Grant – who worked at the garage on Union Street where Roy was service manager.

Luther and Marshall both played guitar to a modest standard but, for them, music was a hobby to be fitted round the more serious business of servicing engines and installing car radios (one of Luther's specialities). They did play the occasional informal gig with another mechanic friend, Red Kernodle, as, according to some reports, The Tennessee Three. Marshall came from a large family of sharecroppers who lived in a tiny hamlet in the Smoky Mountains of North Carolina called Flatts. He moved to Memphis and trained as a watchmaker but gave it up because of eye-strain, switching to mechanics in 1946.

His first impressions of John Cash were telling. Roy had arranged for them to meet at the garage and Marshall observed John as being tall, dark and edgy, with something about him that just grabbed his attention. Luther Perkins, the son of a Baptist minister, came from Mississippi and in the words of singer George Hamilton IV, who knew him in the early days, "Luther was a good ole country boy, real folksy and approachable, who loved to trade stories, but he didn't have so much of a business side to him the way Marshall did."

John, Luther and Marshall had all listened to the same kinds of radio stations as they grew up and all had similar religious backgrounds. The trio quickly built up a firm friendship though John instinctively felt closer to Luther than Marshall. Right away they got into regular get-togethers, playing music late into the night at each other's houses and soon friends and neighbours came to listen, liking what they heard. Early on, John realised that in order to get a better sound, like the music on the radio, they would have to change from the format of three acoustic guitars. It made sense for him to stick with rhythm since he did just about all of the singing and wanted to be able to concentrate on that, so he suggested that Marshall switch to bass and Luther to electric guitar. Buying new equipment was out of the question at this stage but they managed to persuade friends to lend them some instruments.

Luther eventually bought a Silvertone amplifier from Sears Roebuck. Marshall had no idea how to play bass so he got Luther to play particular notes on the guitar, tuned the bass to the notes and then marked them on the neck of the bass with pieces of sticky tape. Apart from John's handful of singing lessons not one of the trio had any formal musical training but this undisciplined approach undoubtedly contributed to their raw sound. Talking about Luther, Johnny later said, "From the very first time I rehearsed with him it felt right. I loved that beat, I loved that rhythm. I guess it was like a train rhythm or a pile driver. He wasn't such a great musician but he was a great guitar stylist."

Playing shows in a public setting was the next logical step and an opportunity arose when a neighbour asked them to perform at a church service. The trio decided on a uniform appearance, but the only shirts they had which were alike were black. At this stage, black wasn't any kind of trademark and John would be just as likely to wear a red or blue jacket as a black one. The evening gave John a chance to set out his stall by singing gospel songs, taking the opportunity to do one he had written himself, 'Belshazzar'. It was a serious piece, demonstrating a concern for religious themes, in marked contrast to much of the candy pop music and romantic ballads coming out of the radio at the time. Despite the palpable presence of religion in many people's upbringings, it's hard to imagine many other aspiring young recording artists writing lyrics like:

> Well the Bible tells us about a man,
> Who ruled Babylon and all its land,
> Around the city he built a wall,
> And declared that Babylon would never fall.
>
> He had concubines and wives,
> He called his Babylon "Paradise",
> On his throne he drank and ate,
> But for Belshazzar it was getting late.
>
> For he was weighed in the balance and found wanting,
> His kingdom was divided, couldn't stand,
> He was weighed in the balance and found wanting,
> His houses were built upon sand.

John, Marshall and Luther put on another show in a drive-in restaurant in Summer Avenue to raise money for a friend of Marshall's who had been injured in a motor-boat accident. It was another important step in that people actually handed over some of their hard-earned cash to hear them play.

John's long-suffering boss George Bates continued to employ and support him even though his weekly returns sometimes dipped as low as $20. Bates knew John wanted to make it in the music business and he helped to give his fledgling career a leg up by arranging for the Home Equipment Company to sponsor John's appearance on a radio show at a cost of $15 for 15 minutes. Between songs, in the manner of *The Grand Ole Opry*, the company received plugs which were dutifully delivered by John himself. Marshall was desperately nervous though the others felt reasonably confident. They did eight shows but if they had been thinking the appearances would lead to overnight success they were to be sorely disappointed. The telephone didn't ring.

◆ ◆ ◆ ◆ ◆

John found some inspiration from another young sharecropper's son, who was causing a bit of a stir in Memphis, called Elvis Presley. His first single 'That's All Right (Mama)' b/w 'Blue Moon Of Kentucky' was doing well in the local charts and he was performing all over town. John caught his show a couple of times, first when he was singing from a flatbed truck to provide publicity for the opening of a drugstore. He and Vivian spoke to Elvis afterwards and were delighted to receive an invitation to Presley's next show at a club called the Eagle's Nest. The venue was a bad choice since it was an adult club and teenagers weren't welcome. The result was that fewer than 20 people actually caught the show.

Elvis' appearances made an enormous impression on John even though he just kept on playing his two hit songs over and over again like a faulty jukebox. He was especially struck by the charisma of the man and his dazzling rhythm guitar playing. He loved the way Elvis sounded then with Scotty Moore and Bill Black, what he later described as "Seminal Elvis", but even better when it was just the man and his guitar. Regardless of the actual music he was playing, Elvis clearly had an influence on John's forward planning and the instrumental line-up he chose for The Tennessee Three mirrored that of Elvis and his backing musicians.

Marshall and Luther were not typically aspiring pop stars. They were both married and settled in good jobs which they were reluctant to give up. For John it was a different story entirely. The monotony and futility of doing a job he was no good at drove him further in the direction of music, despite the imminent birth of a baby and Vivian's reported desire to leave Memphis and return home to San Antonio. Through all these pressures, John's thoughts stayed with music and in particular the idea of trying to record some songs. His desire made him bold. He had heard that the man to speak to in Memphis was Sam Phillips, for whom Elvis recorded, and he resolved to do just that.

◆ ◆ ◆ ◆ ◆

Samuel Cornelius Phillips is assured of legendary status in the annals of popular music because, as writer Jeff Gordinier put it, "Sam Phillips poured hillbilly twang into a vial of African-American blues and Pow! Invented what is now known as rock'n'roll." From Alabama, Sam Phillips was born on January 5, 1923, working as a radio announcer after dropping out of high school in 1941. Keeping his options open, he studied podiatry and embalming but was soon successful enough as a disc jockey to concentrate on that full time.

With money he had saved he opened a recording studio, "The Memphis Recording Service", at 706 Union Avenue, Memphis in October 1949 – his business card boldly proclaiming: "We record anything – anytime – anywhere." Phillips initially recorded black rhythm and blues artists, including BB King, and then leased the songs to independent labels. One of the songs he recorded, 'Rocket 88' by Jackie Brenston (with the young Ike Turner on piano), has often been claimed as the first ever rock'n'roll record. In 1952, in partnership with his brother Judd, Phillips decided to start his own label. Amongst the early Sun artists were Junior Parker, Rufus Thomas, and The Prisonnaires, who really were prison inmates, a fact that caused no end of logistical problems when it came to cutting a record.

Major commercial success eluded Phillips until 1954 when a 19-year-old employee of the Crown Electric Company called by to record a couple of songs for his mother. The studio was administered by a woman called Marion Keisker who was more than a little impressed by the customer's rendition of 'My Happiness'. Of her own volition, Marion taped some of Elvis' singing, saying later that she remembered Phillips saying what he really wanted to find was a white man who had the negro feel to his singing. Phillips denies making such a claim but there can be little doubt that he saw the massive commercial potential of finding a kind of music which would appeal to the exploding teenage market which, with the strictures of the war years now receding, possessed a growing economic clout.

Phillips wisely perceived that Elvis oozed talent and charisma and was ready as one writer put it, "to knock the doors down". Things moved quickly and the first single – 'That's All Right (Mama)', a joyfully liberated up-tempo version of the Arthur Crudup blues number backed with a souped-up rockabilly version of the Bill Monroe bluegrass classic, 'Blue Moon Of Kentucky' – released in 1954 started Presley's phenomenal rise. Phillips was suddenly a busy man with Elvis in big demand. He already felt confident enough to claim that there was no other studio of any consequence in the south. Therefore it's hardly surprising that John Cash had problems making contact with Phillips and initially spoke to him by phone saying that he wanted to record some gospel songs.

Phillips was sympathetic but dismissive. He loved gospel music and appreciated the uninhibited testifying and inspiring sermons served up by the charismatic Reverend Brewster at the church at East Trigg. At a time when the small number of blacks attending Hank Williams' funeral were segregated from the rest of the congregation, Reverend Brewster was passionately proclaiming, "that a better day was coming in which all men would walk as brothers". However, he knew from past experience that a small label like Sun wouldn't sell sufficient numbers of a religious record to justify the outlays involved.

John tried to see Phillips in person but he was invariably away from the studio on business or tied up in a meeting. Eventually John went to the studio early in the morning and waited for the studio boss to arrive. When he showed, John said, "Mr Phillips, sir, if you listen to me, you'll be glad you did." Phillips was either impressed with his self-confidence or too worn down to resist and invited John in to the studio and for much of the day, listened to him singing a variety of songs by Hank Snow, Jimmie Rodgers and The Carter Family, as well as some of his own including 'Belshazzar'.

It was a sign of Phillips' acumen that he got John to hone his own songs. Though sometimes accused of being more interested in drinking coffee and eating at the diner next door, Phillips had the ability to spot talent and the necessary vision to match artists to songs. He realised early that most people who succeeded in the music business did so on the back of original material or at least unfamiliar material which could come to be identified with the artist. He saw definite possibilities in 'Hey! Porter', the lyrics for which John had written in Landsberg.

Phillips told John to return the next day with his musician friends so that they could make a recording. Although Johnny Cash is widely referred to as a Country or Country and Western singer he was drawn to Sun, a predominantly non-country label which produced innovative rhythm and blues and pop, with the aim of singing religious music. As writer Greil Marcus said of Sun, "It was a space for freedom, a place to take chances. Its music was as authentically new as any music can be."

John, Marshall and Luther duly turned up the next day with their Heath Robinson equipment (Marshall's bass was held together with tape) and John apologised profusely to Phillips about not having a professional band. They also had with them Red Kernodle on steel guitar and though Red's abilities were basic to say the least, writer Colin Escott reckons that on a technical level, he was no worse on his chosen instrument than Luther Perkins was on his. However, he couldn't play for nerves and after messing around on a few songs he realised that a career in music wasn't for him, took his leave, and rushed off into the footnotes of history. One can only speculate how things would have turned out if Red had been up to the task and the early Cash material had been sweetened with pedal steel.

Speaking in 1980 Cash himself said he thought the trio's raw unadorned sound was the key to their success, very different from the mainstream country, "A steel guitar would've taken us more towards Nashville." Phillips assured John that the fact the sound was basic was not a problem because he already realised it had a distinctive quality which he felt had great possibilities, particularly Johnny's voice and Luther's guitar. Phillips also appreciated that what John and the group brought was a complete sound which for all its technical faults, should not be radically altered and did not need much in the way of additional voices or instruments. He wanted the music to retain its spontaneous feel, but Marshall Grant has said that in view of their limited technical ability and nerves in the studio, it was necessary to have things rehearsed in advance to quite a considerable degree.

The first song they recorded was 'Wide Open Road' which John had composed in Germany. On hearing the playback, he reckoned it sounded awful. Phillips really liked the sound of 'Hey! Porter' and casually mentioned that he would be prepared to release it. John couldn't believe his ears. Phillips wanted another strong original number for the flip side, a love song, a real "weeper" as he put it. The trouble was John didn't have another song ready, but he didn't admit this to Phillips. What he produced was a weeper but not in the conventional sense. 'Cry! Cry! Cry!' was a contemptuous put-down of a woman whose wayward lifestyle was bound to end in tears and the sentiments and the way they were so brutally expressed, made the song highly unusual in the context of the bland love songs prevalent in the hit parade.

Opinions vary as to the precise origins of the song but it seems most likely the inspiration came from John hearing disc jockey Eddie Hill admonishing his listeners to stay tuned because he had some great songs including "sad songs that'll make you cry, cry, cry". After a false start when the boys arrived at the studio to find that Phillips wasn't there, they recorded it some weeks later along with some other songs. John kept on rearranging the song and Luther kept on messing up his leads (despite their simplicity) so it took 35 takes to perfect. The net result was the first single by Johnny Cash and The Tennessee Two. Many reports say that "John" became "Johnny" at the behest of Sam Phillips who reckoned "John" would be too staid for the younger market. It has also been suggested that when Vivian Liberto first met her future husband, he introduced himself as "Johnny". Apparently, Johnny wanted the name of the group to be The Tennessee Three, arguably a strange choice since none of the band hailed from Tennessee. However, the others insisted that Johnny Cash and The Tennessee Two was more appropriate given Johnny's leading role and it was agreed that earnings would be split 40-30-30.

For Johnny this was the chance to express himself in the way that he had been desperate to do for so long and in a sense he had been building up to this moment for much of his life. For Luther and Marshall on the other hand while it was all a bit of excitement, it did not occur to them that it might result in them having to give up their well-paid day jobs. (Luther was not the only one in his family with musical aspirations. His brother Thomas Wayne was a singer who had a hit with 'Tragedy' in the late Fifties and who signed for Sun in the Sixties.)

In musical terms what happened in that small Memphis studio was truly cataclysmic – something which only happens when a number of chance events conspire together at the same time. A star, and a sound with which he would be forever associated, had been born and it had all been done on a shoestring in a studio not much bigger than the living room of an average house. The raw, driving fricative sound recorded that day, which has been so widely admired and imitated ever since, was simply a case of three modest musicians playing and singing to the best of their limited abilities. Luther's contribution was vital though largely unwitting; he really was not a good guitarist in a technical sense and found it hard to get the simplest of lead breaks right first time. However by simply playing a note and then immediately dampening the strings with his right hand and doing a snappy up and down action on the strings before hitting the next note he gave the world the boom-chicka-boom sound, one of rock'n'roll's most compulsive rhythms. However all this alone would not have added up to all that much, a few local hits maybe. The X factor was Johnny Cash, mysterious, flawed, driven. Whatever the others might have made of it all Johnny knew he had now started down a road that would go on forever.

PART II

Ride This Train

"Sometimes I didn't know if it was New York or New Year."

6

IN 1955, two momentous events occurred in Johnny's life within the space of a month. On May 24 his first child, Rosanne, was born and on June 21, after what seemed like an interminable delay during which Johnny wondered if it was really ever going to happen, his first record was released, 'Hey! Porter' b/w 'Cry! Cry! Cry!'. When receiving a contract from Sam Phillips, Johnny felt elated despite not having any money. In fact that same day, he walked out of Sun with 15 cents in his pocket which he gave to a bum on the street whom he reckoned needed it more, jumped in his car and ran out of petrol just before he reached his house.

Johnny was keen to do whatever he could to promote the record. Before its official release, Sam had given him an advance 78, which he proudly took along to a local disc jockey, Bob Neal, who played one side but then accidentally dropped the record which broke. Johnny thought he had lost his chance not realising that Phillips would have plenty more copies back at the studio. He may have been naive in that respect but he was sufficiently switched on to express his concern to Phillips that the single be released on Sun rather than Flip, a label used for lesser, experimental records with fewer commercial prospects.

Once the record was released, Johnny drove to nearby towns (nearly crashing his car the first time he heard his own record being played on the radio), trying to set up appearances in theatres, school halls or outdoor arenas. The strictures of his upbringing meant that he initially avoided premises selling alcohol, even though many of these featured live music, but commercial imperatives soon overcame this particular restriction. At the same time Johnny was still trying to sell electrical appliances though he was now more motivated than ever to get into the music business.

The response to the record was better than he could have hoped for, though radio stations initially picked up on 'Cry! Cry! Cry!' rather than 'Hey! Porter', which had originally been intended as the A-side. One local disc jockey known as Sleepy-eyed John played both sides and then predicted, "It won't be the last time you hear them." He wasn't the only one who liked it. The record, with its combination of Johnny's authoritative bass baritone and a restless rhythmic urgency from the instrumental backing, immediately struck a chord with the public and was soon at the top of the Memphis country charts and number 14 in the national country charts with sales exceeding 100,000. Bookings became easier to obtain and more lucrative, though the three of them might still be splitting as little as $50 per show with ticket prices of about 50 cents, which, after expenses, meant they were making very little for themselves.

However low profitability wasn't the only problem. Johnny recalls trying to persuade the owner of one theatre in Joiner, Arkansas to let them perform but being told to his fury that "goddamn hillbillies" weren't wanted there. When he did play, Johnny performed both sides of his single and added other favourites such as Hank Snow's 'I'm Moving On', Lead Belly's 'Rock Island Line' and a recent pop hit, 'Memories Are Made Of This' by Dean Martin. In a short time, Johnny Cash and The Tennessee Two played many small, sometimes unsavoury, venues with bar room audiences in particular not yet convinced that they were seeing anything special. It was the price of an education and Johnny began to discover how to engage, work and win over new audiences. By this time he had also managed to secure a regular fifteen-minute slot on radio station KWEM.

Johnny was keen to capitalise on his initial success by getting another record out as soon as possible. However, Sam Phillips was busy with Elvis Presley and things didn't happen as quickly as his eager protégé would have liked. The songs chosen were 'So Doggone Lonesome' and 'Folsom Prison Blues', a song inspired by *Inside The Walls Of Folsom Prison*, a film Johnny had seen in Landsberg. Apart from a distinctive sound, the subject matter of his songs was proving to be anything but typical of the day's chart music. 'Folsom Prison Blues' had as its main theme the thoughts of a man serving life for murder, being best known for two famous, some might say notorious, lines, arguably the most famous Cash lyrics of all, "But I shot a man in Reno, just to watch him die." When asked about the lines Johnny has said that he tried to think of the worst possible reason a man could have for killing someone and that's what he came up with.

Leaving aside the jurisdictional question of why the subject should be serving his sentence in far-off California, 'Folsom Prison Blues' was remarkable for a number of reasons. In the hours they spent on the arrangement of the song, Johnny and Luther came up with a lead simple enough for the latter to master even though it had him spending more time than usual away from the bass string. Yet it was memorable and catchy enough in its economy to endure for nearly half a century. The lyrics served notice of the arrival of an artist who was able to capture succinct insights into the human mind and condition, more befitting somebody of advanced years.

Prison songs had long been an established part of country music but the sentiments and stories tended to be fairly predictable; men regretting their actions, longing for their sweethearts, perhaps languishing in prison for a crime they hadn't committed. In 'Folsom Prison Blues' the protagonist hates being in prison though he knows he deserves to be there. The pay-off comes in the last verse when the character proves to be unreformed:

> Well if they freed me from this prison, if that railroad train was mine.
> I bet I'd move it on a little farther down the line.

On another level the song is a general comment on the human condition, as Cash himself put it, "Most of us are living in one little kind of prison or another, and whether we know it or not the words of a song about someone who is actually in a prison speak for a lot of us who might appear not to be, but really are." The song would come back to haunt him in later years. Johnny had first recorded a version at one of his initial sessions at Sun at a time when he had to come up with new material fast. The trouble was that 'Folsom Prison Blues' was largely lifted from a song called 'Crescent City Blues' by Gordon Jenkins which came from a concept album called *Seven Dreams*. Jenkins did not sue in 1955 but he did later when a live version of the song, recorded at Folsom Prison, became a worldwide hit.*

The fact remains that while many people have heard of 'Folsom Prison Blues', 'Crescent City Blues' remains in relative obscurity, but this act of plagiarism in no way detracts from Johnny's undoubted gifts as an original songwriter. A lot of potential hassle could have been avoided if the appropriate permission had been obtained but when Johnny wrote his version of the song in Landsberg, he had no inkling that it would ever become a big hit so it probably never occurred to him that there would ever be an issue over the song. Perhaps he didn't understand the legal principles involved. Though the song is now one of Johnny's best known, he nearly didn't get to record it. One day, his eye was caught by a note on Phillips' desk, suggesting that 'Folsom Prison Blues' might be suitable for Tennessee Ernie Ford. Johnny made it plain that he wanted to record it himself.

On a creative level the relationship with Phillips suited Johnny well. Having laid down the law about not doing gospel songs he basically allowed Johnny his own head much of the time. Like Johnny, Phillips was a maverick, not quite fitting in with the music industry. He had recognised something special in Johnny and his authoritative, bass baritone voice and wasn't put off by the lack of professionalism on the instrumental front. Indeed he astutely recognised that the simplicity of the musical backing enhanced the distinctive power of Johnny's voice. There was no studio clock ticking so Johnny had plenty of time to express himself, encouraged by Phillips who often got caught up in the excitement of the creative process.

The scene was in complete contrast to the major studios who were working to

---

* Recent releases of the song are now credited to "Gordon Jenkins – Johnny Cash".

formulas that would produce guaranteed hits in as little studio time as possible. Indeed, it's barely conceivable that any major label during this time would have expressed interest in Johnny Cash. Above all Phillips recognised the importance of keeping it simple, stripped down and uncluttered with Johnny's voice well forward in the mix. The fact that Johnny went out of tune on occasion didn't seem to matter. Embellishments were few, though Sam did thicken out the sound with distinctive slapback echo which enhanced the sparseness of the early recordings. The two men worked together effectively and shared countless hours in each other's company, but for all that Johnny always called Sam "Mr Phillips", as did the office staff.

Not everything they tried was successful. There were a range of sounds in the Sun hothouse all vying for attention at that time: rock'n'roll, rockabilly, rhythm and blues and pop. Not surprisingly, Johnny tried them out – with fairly awful results, on occasion. One example, 'Leave That Junk Alone', had Johnny upping the pace, trying to add in vocal jerks and generally sounding self-conscious and totally in the wrong place. Listening to it now is like seeing a film clip of a famous actor in his first, wholly miscast part. He could be forgiven for attempting this kind of material given the success of Elvis Presley and Carl Perkins, whose song 'Blue Suede Shoes' would soon become a major hit worldwide.

Johnny had met Perkins – a sharecropper's son from Tiptonville, Tennessee on the other side of the Mississippi – and the two quickly became close friends. The idea for the title was given to him by Johnny recalling an Air Force friend (a black staff sergeant by the name of CV White) who, when getting dressed up to go out at the weekend, would admonish those near him not to step on his blue suede shoes, even though his shoes were not actually made of blue suede which, it appears, was just wishful thinking on his part. (Another version has it that Perkins got the idea after seeing some kids by a bandstand who were visibly proud of their new shoes. Remembering this, Perkins woke up in the middle of the night and wrote the song out on a potato sack.) Sam Phillips placed a great deal of importance on Johnny's contribution to the song. In his letter rebutting a claim for breach of copyright, he pointed out that 'Blue Suede Shoes' was the original creation of two of his artists, Carl Perkins and Johnny Cash.

◆ ◆ ◆ ◆ ◆

By the end of 1955 things were starting to move faster. 'Folsom Prison Blues' was released and showed up well on the local charts; reaching number five on the country charts. Johnny Cash and The Tennessee Two were playing a lot of dates, some of them further afield. In October 1955, they played in Cherry-spring, West Texas, on a bill which featured Elvis Presley, Wanda Jackson and Porter Wagoner. Johnny also appeared in a showcase for new talent at the Overton Park Shell in Memphis, organised by DJ Bob Neal (the previous year,

Elvis Presley had been the rising new star). Later in the month, the trio played at the Fair Park Auditorium, Lubbock, Texas, the opening act for the show being the duo, Buddy (Holly) and Bob.

In December, they supported George Jones, who was touring his first hit 'Why Baby Why?' at a show in Texarkana. Another legendary Memphis show featured Carl Perkins headlining, followed by Elvis Presley and then Johnny Cash and The Tennessee Trio. It was a show which gave Johnny a crash course in developing an audience rapport. As he was about to start his set, problems with an amplifier meant that a nervous Johnny had to stand in front of the audience, feeling increasingly ill at ease and, like them, wishing that the problem could be quickly resolved. After a few minutes, with the audience restless, he broke the ice with, "Has anybody got a deck of cards?" and soon after the amplifier problem was resolved.

Johnny received his first royalty cheque from Marion Keisker at Sun, for, according to his recollection, $6.42 (other reports mention even lower figures) and had just paid $15 to join the American Federation of Musicians. By April 1956 the money was still not great, and for one session he was paid $82.50 which was noted as an advance on royalties. However, in the wake of the success of his first two singles, Johnny's next cheque was for over $5,000, which meant that he could at last put the horrors of being a salesman behind him, though it would be some time before Marshall and Luther gave up their day jobs.

A piece of good fortune came their way when being asked to appear on the radio show *The Louisiana Hayride,* an appearance which would lead to a regular slot and a great deal of publicity though not much money because like *The Grand Ole Opry,* the *Hayride* paid union scales, $12 per person per show which barely covered petrol costs. *The Louisiana Hayride* was the only radio show which came anywhere near *The Grand Ole Opry* in popularity and was broadcast from Shreveport which meant a 700-mile round trip every Saturday. They must have made an odd sight in Luther's 1941 Pontiac with Marshall's double bass strapped onto the roof, pulling an aluminium teardrop trailer painted with multi-coloured spots. For Johnny it was worth it for the moving experience of finding himself standing on the same stage that childhood heroes like Wayne Raney, as well as the recently deceased Hank Williams, had stood.

The demands on Johnny's time and attention were increasing and strains at home started to show although, at this stage, Johnny made the effort to be at home as much as he could. Vivian, pregnant again, was wary of the music scene which she feared was not compatible with her idea of a conventional marriage. While she of course wanted him to do well in order to attain a more secure financial situation, Vivian really had no interest in music and wanted, above all, to have a reasonably normal home life. She didn't like being left on her own so Pat Isom arranged for a door to be installed between their two houses so that

Vivian could pop in anytime she wanted some company. Vivian was seen in public with Johnny on occasion, but was becoming apprehensive about the future. On a more prosaic note she was very particular about who she left baby Rosanne with, so any outing meant arranging for some trusted family member to be on hand.

There was a definite momentum building which Sun Records were keen to maintain with another single. One night Johnny was backstage killing time with Carl Perkins before a show in Gladewater, Texas, and was messing about with some unusual sounds he had first heard in Landsberg. When coming off a night shift, Johnny had played a tape he'd made of the Barbarians but it didn't sound right. The sound was eerie and otherworldly and seemed to include the word 'father'. It turned out he had put the tape spool on the wrong way and what he heard was a recording of the Landsberg Barbarians reversed, the sound of which stayed with him. It was the distinctive chord progressions of the tape in reverse which struck Carl as unusual, prompting him to suggest that Johnny should write a song around it. Later, conversation turned to what guys on the road get up to and this soon led to the subject of men cheating on their wives and girl-friends. Johnny, still very much loyal to Vivian said, "Not me buddy, I walk the line." There was a brief eureka moment and Johnny wrote what would become one of his biggest ever hits in about 15 minutes; as he said later, "The lyrics came as fast as I could write."*

Sam Phillips immediately recognised the originality of the song when Johnny played it to him. It was recorded in April and released, with 'Get Rhythm' on the other side, in May. The production was a classic case of less is more, with the normal order of strong chords followed by less solid ones needing resolution being reversed. Listening to the record now, it's striking just how little instrumentation adorns the song, reinforcing its stark impact and compulsive sound. The addition of backing vocals or steel guitar would have taken away from the effect but there were still some neat touches. Before each verse, Johnny hums for about three bars creating a distinctive lead-in to the verse, though at least one writer has subsequently claimed that Johnny said he merely did this to help him stay in tune. According to another report the idea came to him from a doctor in Dyess who constantly hummed as he worked. In addition Johnny threaded a piece of folded up wax paper through the strings of his acoustic guitar and this added a percussive, snare-like effect to the rhythmic sound of his Martin guitar, something also featured on earlier Cash records. Phillips has claimed it was he

* According to an article in the magazine *Country Music International* in 1994, the song was inspired in part by stories of railroad workers far away from home trying to stay out of work camp brothels and according to this view, the "line" was the railway line next to which brothels rapidly sprung up. The challenge for the railway workers was to keep on walking the line and not succumb to temptation.

who advised Johnny to do this, being a technique he'd used with rhythm and blues artists previously, though according to some, this was Johnny's own idea.[*]

The sound thus created echoed the "crack"' rhythm of Hank Williams, with the electric guitar keeping time on the deadened bass strings which emphasised the beat. Such extra ingredients were evidence of a Cash/Sun knack for coming up with unusual and distinctive touches which added interest and individuality. In addition, there are changes of key for the start of each verse and although this has always been a widely used technique it is one that Johnny Cash in particular would use to great effect repeatedly. It's as if the song receives a sudden charge and the effect is attention-grabbing, akin to a car's sudden acceleration after changing down a gear. The restless, agitated rhythm owed more than a little to Johnny's time in Germany as he later explained. "That rhythm of Morse code had a lot to do with the rhythm I felt in my music. I realised that it's got a rhythm that just begs to have a drum added to it, or a guitar. After I got out of the Air Force, I could still hear it and when I started writing songs again, I had that rhythm in my head." Another feature, particularly of the earlier songs, is the lack of a conventional chorus. Already the deep Cash voice was well established, though his singing did still sound a little strained, as if he were trying just a bit too hard, though this may have been due to the tempo. Johnny is usually referred to as a baritone or a bass baritone but in 'I Walk The Line' he actually hits a low C with ease, giving him good claim to be described more accurately as a bass.

Once a song was chosen Phillips would usually let Johnny record it his own way. However, sometimes he did override his wishes when he was sure he knew best and 'I Walk The Line' was a case in point. Johnny felt it was too fast and when he first heard it on the radio he phoned Phillips and pleaded with him to withdraw the record in favour of a slower version. As it climbed the charts Johnny's objections soon evaporated, although in a 1973 *Rolling Stone* interview, he maintained that it "still sounds bad". The song as a whole was, like so many Impressionist paintings, greater than the sum of its fairly basic parts.

◆ ◆ ◆ ◆ ◆

Johnny Cash has said that Marshall and Luther placed limits on the kind of songs he could take on because of their limited abilities. Against this, he also said that Luther's guitar sound was "a key factor to making my early records successful". As Ernest Tubb put it, "A guy in a bar listening to it could say, 'Well I could do that.'" There is some truth in both opinions but the fact is, particularly when it comes to the Sun output, Perkins hit upon a guitar style which helped to define the Johnny Cash sound. When asked about it later he would smile and

[*] This simple technique is now demonstrated every day as part of an informative guided tour of Sun Studios in Memphis.

say of guitarists far more able than himself, "Man, they're still looking – I found it." The way he picked out lines which were somewhere between leads, bass lines and percussion was the perfect backdrop to the Cash voice. It sounded great but it didn't steal any thunder.

It's clear beyond question that Luther was no virtuoso and that he knew it. He removed the metal plate from his guitar in order to mute the strings because he wanted to cover up his limited playing but by doing so he simply contributed further to Cash's distinctive sound. It would have been easy to have replaced him with a far more technically able guitarist, but it seems that Luther's contribution to the sound was recognised as an integral part of the group's success. The sound they created was recognised when The Tennessee Two won *Jamboree* magazine's award for instrumental group of the year in 1957.

If three guys with no musical training could get together and be successful then why couldn't others follow? In proving the thesis that you don't have to be technically brilliant to make music, Johnny Cash and The Tennessee Two could be seen to be providing an example for such musical styles as skiffle, rockabilly, punk, garage and even rap, though that particular style perhaps owes more to Johnny's outsider image.

That Johnny Cash was free of compromise from an early start is a testament to Sam Phillips who had the vision to give reasonably free rein to his artists and was not hidebound by rigid demarcations between different kinds of music, believing that music should be "universal". His astuteness lay in allowing his artists to try out different things in the studio until he heard the one that was different or right for that particular singer. The contrast between Johnny Cash's early songs and those of Elvis Presley and, later, Jerry Lee Lewis could not be starker. Many are classics but those of Presley and Lewis were patently targeted from the neck down. In the case of Johnny Cash the head was also stimulated with a message delivered with intensity and earnestness. Having said that Johnny possessed a manly physical appeal combined with great personal charisma, sexually attractive in anyone's language. Along with Elvis and Jerry Lee, he was a star with real pizzazz; new and invigorating whom teenagers could call their own and of whom their parents would disapprove.

◆ ◆ ◆ ◆ ◆

'I Walk The Line' was an immediate hit and stayed in the country charts for a staggering 10 months, though it just missed out on the number one spot. More significantly the record crossed over into the pop charts and made it to number 19 – a breakthrough in terms of the demographic range of his audience. It gave Johnny his first gold record and won a BMI (Broadcast Music Inc) award. His country background allied to his populist instincts meant that he was able to make an important contribution to the process of breaking down the barriers between country and popular music. The impact of 'I Walk The Line' deflected attention from 'Get Rhythm' on the flip – an outstanding piece of jerky rock'n'-roll. It was originally intended for Elvis but Johnny decided against telling his friend about it, perhaps fearing it would have given Elvis a hit at his own expense.

Being signed to a new booking agency, Stars Incorporated (run by Bob Neal), Johnny's meteoric rise led to the group being booked for shows further afield. In May, Johnny and Vivian had their second daughter, Kathy, but for Johnny there was less and less time for a home life as the tour dates continued to flow in, playing shows in Canada during August. Soon the prices the group commanded began to rise steadily and in the course of 1956, Johnny Cash and The Tennessee Two found themselves on bills with such stars of the day as Webb Pierce, to whom only a short time ago they had been listening on the radio, and many more starting out on what would become successful careers such as Jim Reeves, Roy Orbison, Jean Shepard and Faron Young. At *The Louisiana Hayride* they were billed as "Special Guests" and Sam Phillips pulled out all the stops on publicity posters for 'I Walk The Line' describing Johnny as "One of the truly great talent finds."

Johnny's sudden rise to fame had an affect on other members of his family too. At the time, his sister Louise was working as a secretary at the Christian School in Memphis and recalls one incident in particular which demonstrated that his notoriety was not yet universal. "A book saleswoman came in selling some stuff one day and the principal of the school introduced me as a famous person, 'Because she's the sister of Johnny Cash.' The saleswoman said, 'Who's he?' I was not at all happy about this and asked the principal not to introduce me like that again." Roy Cash made jokes about it and if somebody said to him, "Are you really Johnny Cash's brother?" he would reply, "Yeah, but don't blame me, I didn't have anything to do with it." Tommy Cash says that he would be having a conversation and people would refer to him as "Johnny".

June Carter ran like a thread throughout Johnny's life from early on. She made her first appearance in Dyess when, as a young girl, she had appeared on border radio stations as a member of Mother Maybelle and The Carter Sisters. June sometimes toured with Elvis Presley who was a big Johnny Cash fan. Elvis played Johnny's early hits repeatedly on the jukebox and encouraged June, who was married to country singer Carl Smith at the time, to listen to them, hence her first introduction. June had married Carl Smith in 1952, the pair having struck up a relationship following a session where he had recorded some gospel songs with the backing of Mother Maybelle and her daughters. There was also a more practical reason for Elvis playing Johnny's songs; he tuned his guitar to them. Johnny and June would soon get to meet in person.

Although it was only a year since his first record had been released, the response to 'I Walk The Line' in particular had been such that he was invited to join the cast of *The Grand Ole Opry* and for Horace Logan, programme director of *The Louisiana Hayride*, this was depressing but unsurprising news. He regularly complained that his show was just an audition for *The Grand Ole Opry* as one star after another moved on to the *Opry* after a short time; Hank Williams and Elvis Presley to name but two. One of the artists Johnny admired most, Ernest Tubb, "The Texas Troubadour", was very supportive of efforts to get Johnny onto the *Opry*. The pair had toured together and, as Johnny later put it, Tubb had coached and taught him some invaluable lessons. "Make those people know you believe in what you're singing. When you're singing 'Folsom Prison Blues' . . . make them feel the misery of the lyric . . . when you're singing 'I Walk The Line' give them a twinkle in the eye once in a while and let them know it's light-hearted."

Tubb recognised the importance of attracting a younger crowd to the *Opry* and realised that Johnny was just the sort of hot new singer to help achieve this. He also told Johnny to stick with his own style and to be himself even though he knew there would be those more conservative elements at the *Opry*, alarmed at Johnny's rockabilly and rock'n'roll overtones, who would try to persuade him to be more country. The two men were similar in that they both had deep voices, which was quite uncommon for chart singers at that time. As Colin Escott said, they "both worked the low vocal range with minimal instrumental support." Johnny was delighted that Tubb, a man he respected and was influenced by, recorded some of his material including an early Cash composition, 'So Doggone Lonesome'.

Johnny's first appearance at *The Grand Ole Opry* came in July. He played two short spots on the hallowed stage of the Ryman Auditorium, one of which was sponsored by Coca-Cola, to an audience numbering 3,800. That night June Carter was also performing at the *Opry* and for his début appearance, Johnny was introduced by her husband Carl Smith as "The brightest rising star in the country music of America." Johnny and June met backstage, a moment recorded in a photograph in which he seems to be half on his knees, looking towards the camera with a sheepish, guilty sort of look, as if he had been caught red-handed, which in a sense he had, because during this first meeting he reportedly told June he would marry her one day. She seemed amused and not offended by this exchange which was unusual to say the least given that they were both married to other people.

Johnny's début was met with much excitement in the local press with the *Nashville Banner* headline reading, "Johnny Cash Achieves Life's Ambition. Wins *Opry* Hearts." The sub-heading said much about where Johnny's main competition lay, " 'Probably better than Elvis Presley who had same manager' national country music expert predicts." This comment reflected a Cash–Presley rivalry stirred up by the press at this time with one report in *The Tennessean* referring to the "Johnny Cash vs Elvis Presley 'Battle of the Charts' raging in *Billboard* magazine." The article about Johnny's début at *The Grand Ole Opry* went on to say, "Johnny Cash has sincerity, he has bombast, he has tone that carries to the rafters. The top row hears him. He's a true country singer and Presley isn't and never has been." *Opry* favourite Minnie Pearl could not contain her excitement. "Look at that handsome Johnny. He's scared to death. Wish I could get stage fright again . . . If I was 30 years younger and 30 years lighter he'd be courtin' tonight."

Not all artists gave him such a warm welcome. Apart from the suspicion that he was connected to that dreadful rock'n'roll music and wasn't really country at all, some artists lost their slots on his début night because the crowd demanded so many encores. Johnny was moved by the occasion and said afterwards, "I'm grateful, happy and humble. It's the ambition of every hillbilly singer to reach the *Opry* in his lifetime. The crowd was mighty kind, the nicest kind of folks." Showing early diplomatic skills he went on to say, "The fact that some of the songs have definite rhythm beat does not make them rock'n'roll songs."

Despite the help of a number of big names, getting onto the *Opry* had not been all plain sailing. The booking manager at the time was Jim Denny, who kept Johnny waiting two hours and then brusquely asked him why he thought he should get on. Johnny respectfully pointed out that his records were popular and that there would probably be quite a few people who would like to see him perform at the Ryman. The problem which the more conservative elements in the country music establishment had to struggle with was the balance between maintaining traditions and bowing to commercial realities.

In the late Fifties, ticket sales for the *Opry* fell dramatically as pop music took off in a big way, and it turned out that Jim Denny was moonlighting for a publishing company dealing in pop, which led to his summary dismissal. A further irony is that Johnny Cash, the man some in the country music establishment mistrusted as being too closely associated with this newfangled rockabilly and rock'n'roll, turned out to be one of the most stalwart champions of the traditions of country music and its older stars, who would be largely ignored in the rush to support the new breed of country singers.

Appearances at the *Opry* helped to firm up Johnny's sartorial style as he reacted against the "rhinestones, flashy things and spangles" that so many of the artists wore, which he felt detracted from the music. Johnny preferred the simplicity of black, which he had worn regularly but by no means exclusively up until then. Though it was a great honour for Johnny to be part of the *Opry*, the strictures placed on artists proved unacceptable to him. Artists had to agree to play 26 Saturdays each year at minimal rates of pay and for the major artists this was commercial suicide when they could be on the road making far more money and reaching a wider audience. Thanks to Bob Neal that is exactly what Johnny did though his touring was largely restricted to the country circuit.

◆ ◆ ◆ ◆ ◆

Soon after the release of a third single, 'Train Of Love' b/w 'There You Go', another success though not on the scale of its predecessor, Johnny got caught up in a legendary gathering at Sun which has taken on a life of its own. On December 4, 1956, there was a recording session for Carl Perkins at Sun with a still unknown Jerry Lee Lewis on piano. Carl's brothers Jay and Clayton were there as well and on drums was WS Holland universally known as "Fluke". By this time Elvis had left Sun for RCA under the guidance of Colonel Tom Parker. Elvis was cruising Memphis in his Cadillac with then-girlfriend Marilyn Evans when he saw that something was on at Sun and decided to drop in. An informal jam session started up, and Sam Phillips, wise to the commercial possibilities of such a gathering, called up a reporter from the Memphis newspaper the *Press-Scimitar* and told him to get along quickly. He also phoned Johnny who was now the biggest star at Sun and he and Vivian called by shortly afterwards.

In no time at all, Elvis was at the piano with Carl, Jerry Lee and Johnny grouped around him. According to *Press-Scimitar* reporter Bob Johnson, "An old-fashioned barrel-house session with barber shop harmonies resulted." Later in his report, Johnson said, "That quartet could sell a million." Some reports, including one in a very detailed account in Peter Guralnick's book, *Last Train To Memphis – The Rise Of Elvis Presley,* suggest that Johnny only stayed for a short time and then left, possibly to do some Christmas shopping, though Johnny himself doesn't accept this for a minute. He reckons he was there pretty much for the duration and that he took part in a lot of the songs, more than the eight to 10 he is sometimes credited with. He recalls the gathering singing hymns and folksy gospel type things like 'The Old Rugged Cross', 'Will The Circle Be Unbroken?' and 'Blue Moon Of Kentucky' on which he sang high tenor. Certainly the famous photograph of the session, the one that has Elvis at the piano looking up into Carl Perkins' face with what appears to be religious devotion (and which usually cuts off Marilyn Evans who was sitting on top of the piano), gives the impression of all four participants being heavily involved in the sing-a-long, though of course the cameraman may have just told them to "move a little closer boys", for the photograph.

Johnny did say that the microphone was at the far end of the studio, so it's perhaps not surprising he can't be heard clearly though he had the most powerful voice of the four. Based on the session recordings, there is little in the way of aural evidence that Johnny sang. It was a chaotic scene with musicians coming and going, but once the principals started, Sam Phillips signalled to a recently hired engineer, Jack Clement, to roll the tapes. Johnny said that the tapes would never be officially released because they were "too bad" but, needless to say, this didn't stop bootlegs appearing. The trouble is that there are very few complete songs, mainly false starts and chat but nonetheless the session does make fascinating listening as the boys excitedly talk about and play Chuck Berry's 'Brown

Eyed Handsome Man' (Perkins had just come off a tour with Berry) and Elvis babbles on about someone, a "coloured guy", in a group called Billy Ward and His Dominoes, who tried so hard and came up with a better version of 'Don't Be Cruel' than him. It may be that the true details of the "Million Dollar Quartet" session will never be known and perhaps it's better left that way.

◆ ◆ ◆ ◆ ◆

By December, with 'I Walk The Line' still riding high in the charts, 'Train Of Love' selling favourably and plenty of demand for the live services of Johnny Cash and The Tennessee Two, 1956 had been a memorable year. Cash was the year's third biggest selling country artist, bettered only by Marty Robbins and Ray Price. In *Cash Box*'s poll of the year 'I Walk The Line' was voted third best single of the year, behind 'Don't Be Cruel' and ahead of 'Blue Suede Shoes'. Johnny was also voted the most promising Country and Western singer of 1956. Johnny's financial position was transformed and in the course of the year he had been able to repay his accumulated debt to George Bates. Marshall and Luther still couldn't quite believe that music was now their main job and as a compromise they asked for and got a six month leave of absence from the garage. Needless to say they never went back. However their mechanical skills were invaluable because on the road tours covering thousands of miles, Johnny's green Plymouth would invariably need a major service.

The pressure on Johnny to keep coming up with the goods was immense and came not least from Sam Phillips who was only too aware of the maxim that you should "Get it while you're hot because you're a long time cold." Sam had invested a lot of money in promoting Johnny and it had paid off. Apart from tours and one-night stands, there were numerous personal appearances on radio stations, and Johnny was also given a guest spot, for 10 shows to Elvis' five, on the Jackie Gleason television show. Unlike Marshall, Johnny is on record as saying that he does not look back on this time with affection. Although he was doing what he wanted to do, the burden of continuing success rested heavily on his shoulders and while he was making money he was spending very little free time with his growing family or his friends.

In April 1957 another single was released, 'Next In Line' b/w 'Don't Make Me Go', a sensitive ballad, but it did not do so well in the charts, possibly because for all of Johnny's appeal, the burgeoning teenage market was looking for something lighter. It may be that Phillips heard warning bells which encouraged him to devote more time to his other artists. Whatever the reason, he decided to pass much of the responsibility for producing Johnny's recordings to a man who had joined Sun only a short time previously, someone who would become a lifelong friend and musical collaborator, a member of the Cash inner circle. That man was the engineer who had set the tapes rolling during the Million Dollar Quartet session, Jack Clement.

7

A NATIVE OF MEMPHIS, Jack Clement came out of the Marines in 1952 having completed a four-year stint and, as with Johnny, music was in his soul. Like Sam Phillips he loved the atmosphere at the Reverend Brewster's church at East Trigg in Memphis. "It was black gospel kind of stuff. There was a beat that got into my head, a backbeat. White people had a tendency to put it on the upbeat, black people put it on the backbeat." Clement could play a number of instruments proficiently, including steel guitar, ukulele, dobro and bass. He also sang, wrote songs, played in various bands and did some comedy work as part of a bluegrass duo called Buzz and Jack before working as a ballroom dancing instructor for a time, waltzes and tangos being his specialty. Clement was bowled over by Elvis' rendition of 'Blue Moon Of Kentucky' saying, "It was just what I'd been wanting to hear, it was real and I loved the simplicity of it."

To keep his options open he had also studied journalism and formed a record company whose main asset was an old Magnacorder recording machine which he acquired from Memphis disc jockey Sleepy Eyed John who also had a band that Clement emceed for. He recorded a song by Billy Lee Riley, a capable though unremarkable singer. He needed to have the record mastered and as he puts it, "Sam Phillips was the only one in Memphis who could do it reliably." Phillips actually gave Clement an audition which he passed but he claims now that Phillips reckoned he was a little too good for Sun, though soon afterwards he was taken on as a trainee engineer at a starting salary of $60 a week. Clement was of course aware of Johnny Cash, and respected the fact that Phillips had given him the kind of chance he would never have got from any of the major country labels in Nashville.

However he didn't like 'I Walk The Line' when he heard it at first, "Too crude," he says, but adding, "I love it now, of course." Once settled in at Sun, Clement was handed the job of trying to maintain Johnny's success rate, being acutely aware that the last record had not done nearly as well as the previous two. He was also aware that Johnny was "Sam's pride and joy".

There was a creative tension between Johnny Cash and Jack Clement from the start. On a personal level Jack took to Johnny immediately, appreciating his sense of humour and his straight dealing, and for his part Johnny has said of Jack, "He, more than anyone, knew my limitations but also my potential." They did not see eye to eye on everything though. Like Phillips, Johnny always tended to prefer a stripped down uncluttered sound, for him the unadorned song was (and is) paramount, the rest being a secondary issue.

For Clement, embellishments were of more importance and over the years some commentators have been critical of Jack Clement, accusing him of seriously impairing the essential Johnny Cash sound with intrusive and unnecessary backing vocals and orchestrations, or as one put it, "Trying to force Johnny Cash's country purity into a crass pop formula." It is something of a conundrum that despite his obvious affection for Clement, Johnny, without referring directly to him by name, has often voiced criticisms of the production techniques employed on his music at various stages of his career. On the other hand Johnny has always been an innovator, keen to try out new ideas from a diverse range of people, and on this the two were most certainly on the same wavelength.

On Johnny's next single, 'Home Of The Blues', Clement managed to introduce some piano and gentle backing vocals and the song fared better than its predecessor. Vocally Johnny was going from strength to strength with his trademark bass baritone settling into what sounded like its natural pitch, the effect somehow enhanced by the impression that he was suffering from a cold or a hangover. On the flip side was a ballad, 'Give My Love To Rose', a song with a basic country feel, not perhaps the sort of thing to impress Clement, who, while not disliking it, thought it was insufficiently commercial. Jack gave a lot of thought to Johnny's next single but there were other developments before then.

◆ ◆ ◆ ◆ ◆

In September, Sun released the first Johnny Cash LP, *With His Hot And Blue Guitar*. It contained 12 songs including four of his hits plus the old traditional 'Wreck Of The Old 97' as well as the gospel song, 'I Was There When It Happened', already a firm fixture in their live shows, which unusually featured Marshall and Luther on backing vocals. The tours and live appearances continued relentlessly, with the band honing their show by travelling further and further to reach new audiences. They appeared on the live west coast show *Town Hall Party* and, in the latter part of 1957, toured Florida with George Jones and Jerry Lee Lewis, now a rapidly rising star on the strength of 'Whole Lotta Shakin' Goin' On'. Johnny now had a considerable repertoire made up of his hits, some gospel songs and a few traditional folksy numbers and for a trio of such limited abilities, they put on quite a show. Johnny of course was the centre of attention, looking intently into the audience as he sang, jerking his head back equine fashion as if to provide momentum for delivery of the next line. When he wasn't singing he moved slowly and unpredictably around the stage, sometimes pointing his guitar at the audience in a way described as "phallic-like" by some and armed robbery by others.

In between songs Johnny would chat to the audience and though often appearing nervous, and talking quite fast to overcome it, it was clear that he knew how to handle a crowd. Right from the start there was a genuine quality to his engagement with his audience. As George Hamilton IV puts it, "There was no Hollywood smile." While Johnny was the essential fulcrum, Luther and Marshall made totally different yet important contributions to the spectacle. Luther stood expressionless as he picked out his elementary leads, hardly allowing any expression to animate his facial features, and spent most of the time on stage stock-still, swallowing hard. Luther was the butt of Johnny's jokes but though he sometimes appeared to be the subject of ridicule long-time Johnny Cash fan and authority Ian Calford says, "There was a real rapport between the two men and Johnny relied on Luther a lot. The straight man funny man bit was all part of that." Johnny would pretend to take the audience into his confidence. "Luther? Don't worry about him, he's been dead for two years."

For all that his onstage persona might have helped Johnny, Luther quaked that he would do on stage what he did regularly in the studio, namely mess up his parts, particularly the solos. Appearances on Tex Ritter's television show *Ranch Party* around this time caught him looking like he wished he could be anywhere else in the world but where he was at that moment. Playing his short and simple solos he looked round nervously at Johnny as if expecting some rebuff.

Marshall on the other hand was a non-stop bundle of energy. He appeared to use his double bass as a piece of exercise equipment, jumping around like a chimpanzee on speed, smiling from ear to ear. He had a great fondness for exercising his jaws on stage and for a joke Johnny sometimes introduced him, "And on my left, on chewing gum, we have Mr Marshall Grant." Johnny manfully concentrated on the job in hand, throwing in the odd smile along the way, but singer Narvel Felts remembers that Johnny always came over as more nervous than Elvis on television. Compared to so many popular musicians in later years, Johnny Cash and The Tennessee Two performed with very little frills. They nonetheless provided, with a combination of straightforward songs, raw enthusiasm, wit and imagination, shows which invariably left their audiences wanting more.

These were heady times indeed and Johnny received invitations to appear at important events in the country music calendar. In June 1957, he appeared with two of his great heroes, Hank Snow and Ernest Tubb, at the Meridian country music festival to mark the twentieth anniversary of the death of Jimmie Rodgers and to pay tribute to the many people who had died over the years working on the railroad. Prominent political figures such as Adlai Stevenson were in attendance as was the widow of the legendary engine driver, Casey Jones, and Jimmie Davis, the former Governor of Louisiana who had co-written 'You Are My Sunshine'. The crowd numbered some 20,000. Johnny later spoke of his admiration for Jimmie Rodgers. "Jimmie is terribly important to country music. Not only did he revise and keep alive some old songs . . . but he wrote from a gut level, the life of the working men, the common men, the down and outers, the hobos, the men on the move, the men who built our country."

After the *Town Hall Party* appearance in August Johnny met Don Law, a record producer for Columbia Records, one of several meetings the two men had. Law, a dashing Englishman who emigrated to America in the Twenties, was a highly experienced player in the music business and the fact that he was given the important job of luring Cash away from Sun to Columbia Records gives an indication of his business acumen. In his time, Law had signed such legendary figures as Bob Wills and Robert Johnson to the American Recording Corporation. He obviously spoke Johnny's language because they soon came to an understanding and Johnny signed an option to move to Columbia in approximately one year, after his Sun contract expired. Ray Price said of Don Law, with whom he worked for many years, "He was the kind of producer who let an artist be an artist." No doubt a man like that would have appealed greatly to Johnny, whose musical horizons, even at this early stage, stretched beyond churning out three minute hits aimed at the country and pop charts.

Quite apart from anything else Law made it clear to Johnny that he would be able to record the religious songs which he had not been able to do at Sun. This was important to him, so much so that from early on in his career Cash vowed that at least 10% of the material he recorded would be sacred songs. He shared concerns with singer Sonny James, a committed Christian himself, that it wasn't right that he was only doing secular songs. Thinking about a future with a major label must have been barely credible for Johnny Cash who, a mere two years before, had been a failure at selling electrical appliances around Memphis.

◆ ◆ ◆ ◆ ◆

For some time Johnny had been experiencing the kind of health problems singers dread, namely throat ailments. His doctor felt that his tonsils should come out but there were concerns about the possible effect of surgery on his singing voice because once out of childhood, the more serious the procedure it is. Sometime in October Johnny did have his tonsils removed and after the successful operation, Johnny had a period of rest and recuperation in Hollywood with manager Bob Neal. While there, they took the opportunity to visit some of the major movie studios and had discussions with producers of Western films and TV shows about the kind of openings there might be for Johnny.

Up until this point Johnny had, quite remarkably, written every song chosen for his singles. However, Jack Clement had a song of his own that he was confident had what it took to emulate the success of 'I Walk The Line'. It was called 'Ballad Of A Teenage Queen' - a bouncy, teen-orientated soap opera type story about a girl who gets the chance to make it in the movies but eventually gives it all up in order to live happily ever after with the boy next door. Sam Phillips was said to hate the song and it certainly wasn't typical Sun output. Over the years many others have criticised the busy, overladen Clement style of studio production as some kind of aberration, with writer Colin Escott describing it's ending as "So sugary it could put a diabetic into a coma."

The basic track was overdubbed with prominent Fifties pop style vocal backing courtesy of The Gene Lowery Singers which vies with Johnny for the right to be heard. It was certainly a radical departure from anything he had released up to then and while Johnny was on good form vocally he sounded more clean-cut than on previous outings, lacking any dark menace and accordingly less special. Jack Clement simply says that Johnny recorded the song because when he played it to him he loved it and wanted to record it. This is not so surprising when considering that, throughout his career, Johnny Cash has shown a remarkable propensity to listen to other people's ideas, to try out new things and to take risks. 'Ballad Of A Teenage Queen' may simply have been an early example of this. However, some of Clement's crasser lyrics – such as "She was queen of the senior prom, she could cook just like her mom" – ended up on the studio floor.

The song was obviously aimed at the teen market and on that basis the vocal additions were just right for those who liked and expected that sort of sound. Unfortunately, with the passage of time, though Johnny's voice remains impressive, the backing vocals sound dated, making the song a reasonably pleasant period piece. It seemed Clement had worked his magic when 'Ballad Of A Teenage Queen' went to number one in the country chart (a position it held for eight weeks), and number 16 in the pop chart; a remarkable feat considering Clement had produced a record that sounded as sophisticated as material being turned out by the big studios with Sun's limited facilities. Most assumed that Johnny had written the song himself, since he had composed all of his other hits but he graciously went out of his way to tell interviewers that it was the work of Jack Clement.

In retrospect many would rate the flip 'Big River', as the stronger side. A hard driving, bluesy number (on which Clement played lead guitar and bass drum simultaneously), it had started out as a slow number and was destined to become one of the high points of Johnny's concerts. With 'Ballad Of A Teenage Queen' being promoted on posters as a "pop hit" (with "pop" underlined), the clear disparity in styles between the two songs led reviewers to refer to the single as a "dual-market contender". 'Big River' grew from an article Johnny saw about himself with the headline, "Johnny Cash Has The Big River Blues in His Voice."

Though probably apocryphal, some reports say he had the song written inside his head before he finished reading the article.

The release of 'Ballad Of A Teenage Queen' occurred close to the time when Johnny Cash and The Tennessee Two undertook a two-week tour of Canada. As part of the promotion for the tour and single, a contest was held in each city to select their own teenage queen. On the afternoon of each show, Johnny flew into town, did some personal appearances and then turned up at a record shop where he selected the teenage queen by pulling names out of a box, one for the winner and one for the runner-up. In order to get your name in the box you had to prove that you had purchased a copy of the record. The strategy was stunningly successful and whereas Sam had estimated they might sell an absolute maximum of 15,000 copies of the record in Canada, it ended up shifting nearer 100,000.*

◆ ◆ ◆ ◆ ◆

Back in America, the musical revolution which began with Elvis in 1954 continued unabated. Classic songs from the Sun artists, as well as many other overtly teen-targeted stars, were being released as if there was no tomorrow. When he was six years old, Rodney Crowell was taken to see Johnny Cash, Jerry Lee Lewis and Carl Perkins at the old Magnolia Garden bandstand in Channelview, Texas. There had been torrential rain throughout the early part of the show but just before Johnny took the stage, the rain stopped and the sky cleared. Catching the mood of the moment Johnny stormed into 'Five Feet High And Rising', a song inspired by his family's experiences during the Mississippi flood of 1937. For Rodney the experience was uplifting and inspirational and he recreated the atmosphere in his autobiographical song, 'Telephone Road'.

> Magnolia Garden bandstand on the very front row,
> Johnny Cash, Carl Perkins and the Killer putting on a show,
> Six years old and just barely off my daddy's knee,
> When those rockabilly rebels sent the devil running right through me.

Narvel Felts, by his own admission quite a shy youth, described his own awe at the music even more graphically. "I sometimes wonder, if I'd never heard all that music would I still be hauling bags of cotton and would I still be a virgin." Musician Charlie Musselwhite, who grew up in Memphis, said, "Johnny Cash sang songs from the earth especially when he recorded for Sun. He seemed like he was one of us and was singing about us, about the life we knew. In that sense he served the role of a bluesman." Nashville singer/songwriter Bob Cheevers, who occasionally exchanged a wave with Elvis Presley in Memphis in his

---

* There was one choice footnote to the competition held in Saskatoon. The winner unexpectedly died and so the runner-up got to be teenage queen. Her name? Joni Mitchell.

younger days said, "When that music came on the radio and me and my friends heard it we took a left turn and never came back, especially a few of us who went into a career in music."

However, it was not universally popular. Inevitably there were tensions from the older generation who really didn't understand the music and saw it as immoral and wanton. They were not the only ones who felt threatened. Artists who had enjoyed previous success saw themselves losing ground to all the new-comers, especially Elvis Presley. Mitch Miller said, "It's not music, it's a disease," while Frank Sinatra said, "Rock'n'roll is lewd, in fact plain dirty. It's phoney and false, and sung, written and played for the most part by cretinous goons." Billy Graham expressed doubts about letting his children go to see Elvis though ironi-cally some of his sensual jerky movements on stage could be seen as similar to the ecstatic dance of people giving their praise to Jesus at altar calls in many southern churches every Sunday. Hank Snow received a salutary lesson about the new order of things when he found himself top of the bill on a show in which he followed Elvis Presley. The reception for Elvis had been so ecstatic that Snow was reluctant to follow him.

The constant touring and recording meant that the normal home life which Vivian craved was impossible. Everything seemed to be happening so quickly and towards the end of 1957 she discovered that she was pregnant with their third child. Of course Johnny was making a lot of money, enabling them to buy their own house in the more upmarket Sandy Cove area of Memphis, and also making it possible for Johnny to buy fishing gear, guns and cameras. However, it was all so chaotic that Vivian might well have preferred it if her husband had gone back to selling reconditioned vacuum cleaners. As Louise Cash Garrett put it, "I got on well with Vivian but she was really a home maker."

At first, when success beckoned and Johnny talked about going on the road, she thought he meant a few towns in Arkansas, possibly Texas. In truth she never liked it when he went away; not least because she was a young mother of two with a baby on the way and wanted her husband by her side. She was supportive up to a point but increasingly her interests were ignored as the demands placed on Johnny increased dramatically. Vivian was in no doubt that her duty lay with her children but while Johnny loved his daughters, nothing could deflect the upward curve of his career. Everybody has choices in life and Johnny could have given it all up and chosen to spend more time with his family but few in his unique situa-tion would have made that choice. Even if Johnny had given up at this point, the chances are that he would have regretted it and come to resent those who had thwarted his ambitions. Success made a failure of their marriage.

◆ ◆ ◆ ◆ ◆

Johnny and the boys soon discovered that much of the touring process was routine, repetitive and boring. In the early days, they adapted to life on the road in their own way. Tiring of snack food in the car they acquired a small stove and created fry-ups for themselves at the side of the road, usually laying into steaks, bacon or chops with their bare hands, a reflection of their rural upbringings where the niceties of table etiquette were not of great importance. Sometimes they sneaked the stove into hotel rooms in defiance of the rules, and later came up with some more off-the-wall entertainments to break the monotony. They carried shotguns with them and if they spotted a suitable target, such as an unsuspecting bird, they would stop the car and jump out with all guns blazing. More dramatically, Marshall used the long journeys as an outlet for his fascination with explosives.

Sometimes it was just a case of letting off some home-made firecrackers at the side of the road but soon the intrepid bassist graduated to full-scale bombs consisting of sticks of dynamite tightly wrapped up with string which, when detonated, blew crater-like holes in the ground. Another favourite was a small cannon, which was fired in hotel corridors and sometimes at concerts to indicate that Johnny Cash and The Tennessee Two were about to take the stage. Despite all these shenanigans Johnny still found time to write new material; in the back of the car, in motel rooms or backstage, so that when he came back from a tour he would have numerous scraps of paper with lyrics and ideas scrawled over them.

As 1958 wore on and the time for Johnny's departure for Columbia approached, rumours of his plans abounded and Sam Phillips soon got wind of what was happening. He confronted Johnny and asked him straight out if the rumours were true. Uncharacteristically Johnny lied and Phillips subsequently said that he could tell Johnny was lying though he didn't say so at the time, feeling hurt and let down. Sun had been able to nurture and encourage Johnny's talents in a way the bigger companies could (or would) not have achieved. Ever pragmatic, Phillips resolved to get as much new material out of Johnny as possible and ordered him into the studio to lay down tracks. Johnny baulked at this but it was Jack Clement who persuaded him to co-operate because his job was on the line over it, pointing out that Phillips was due more sessions in terms of their contract. Johnny reluctantly agreed but held back much of his better material for Columbia.

Phillips was left with the distinct impression that the material he recorded at this time, though reasonable, was below what Johnny was capable of. This presented a further opportunity for Clement to put forward another of his own songs, 'Guess Things Happen That Way'. Once more, the production owed much to Jack's vision of what the younger teen market wanted with sweetening backing vocals and some robust "Ba dum ba dums" juxtaposed with Johnny's reflective and maudlin delivery. Clement was acutely aware of the success of artists such as Ferlin Husky and Marty Robbins with material of this ilk. The choice of song was inspired and the message was simple and direct, something everybody could relate to. As with many classic country songs, the lyrics, particularly the chorus hookline, have the quality of a proverb or an aphorism. The original inspiration for the song in terms of the rhythm and the feel came from Dean Martin's hit 'Memories Are Made Of This.'*

It was another smash hit, soon making number one on the country charts and showing up in the pop charts as well. Johnny's last recording session at Sun took place on July 17, 1958 when two tracks were laid down, 'Down The Street To 301' and 'I Forgot To Remember To Forget'. It's doubtful if there was one sole reason for Johnny's decision to leave Sun, yet he didn't linger long over making his move despite the debt he owed to Sam Phillips. Although the magnitude of Sun in the mid-Fifties increases as it recedes further into history, it was nonetheless clear at the time that Phillips' set-up was something out of the ordinary. On the most basic level, Phillips decided whether particular artists were taken on and he had given Johnny Cash the break he sorely needed.

However, leaving loyalty aside, Johnny had paid back a lot of the debt owed to Sun and Phillips by helping to fill his coffers on the back of a string of solid hits. Johnny wanted to do religious material but in all his time at Sun he was only able to record two such songs, one of which was his early composition, 'Belshazzar', and this clearly was a source of frustration. Despite the money he was generating for Phillips, Johnny felt he was being insufficiently rewarded. For recording and songwriting he received 3% of 90% of retail, when the going rate at the majors was 5%. The songwriting figures were the same so the difference between the remuneration at Sun and what Johnny could expect to receive at one of the majors was significant. He was effectively still on a basic rate which he should clearly have gone beyond in view of the sales he was generating.†

It may well be that it had simply dawned on Johnny that he had outgrown Sun. Columbia, in the person of Don Law, doubtless offered Johnny the money he wanted and also creative freedom to record religious music. There was also the kudos of being on the same label as some of the biggest recording artists of the day. Sam Phillips has also suggested that there was a lot of jealousy among his artists, who were in the main inexperienced country boys in unfamiliar situations. Personal fortunes went up or down regularly in the music business and if they felt that Phillips was paying more attention to one artist over another they tended to feel insecure and resented it. Phillips' unwritten rule was that the more established artists on Sun's roster should realise

* Clement later unsuccessfully tried to get Dean Martin to record a version of 'Guess Things Happen That Way'.
† Phillips has since said that he did not realise Johnny intended to leave Sun and that if he had been given the chance to match Columbia's offer, he would have paid him what he asked for.

and accept the fact that he could not give them his undivided attention when he had new talent to nurture.

By the time Johnny was established, albeit with some records doing better than others, Jerry Lee Lewis exploded onto the scene with 'Whole Lotta Shakin' Goin' On' which outsold Johnny's latest offering. One day Johnny called into the studio wanting to have lunch with Phillips to discuss various things but Phillips was too busy with Jerry Lee. Johnny took offence at this and also resented the fact that Carl Perkins was given a shiny new Cadillac when 'Blue Suede Shoes' hit big when Johnny had not received such a reward for any of his major hits. Jack Clement has said that Johnny doesn't like to argue and is just as likely to store up resentment and walk away from any kind of confrontation. Clement also confirms the point that Phillips himself pretty much conceded that he could only really concentrate on one artist at a time.

If Johnny felt put out by this he wasn't the only one. The late Rufus Thomas claimed that he and Phillips had been "Tighter than the nuts on the Brooklyn Bridge," but that when Elvis, Johnny, Carl and Jerry Lee came along and started selling records, Phillips quickly lost interest in Rufus and the other less-successful Sun artists at the time. Rufus turned it into a question of race but Phillips has always denied this, though it certainly is striking that up until Elvis Presley the Sun roster was predominantly black and that immediately after it became virtually all white. However, if Sam was in any way prejudiced, why would he have gone to the trouble of starting a label specialising in black blues artists? Perhaps it was simply a purely pragmatic commercial decision based on the comparative success of the respective groupings. If so, it didn't work out in the long run because Elvis' contract was sold to RCA, Johnny left for Columbia, Jerry Lee's personal life caused his career to hit the buffers in the most dramatic and public way and Carl Perkins was taken out of action when he was seriously injured in a car crash on his way to a rehearsal for Perry Como's television show. It was only after they left Sun that Roy Orbison and Charlie Rich enjoyed their biggest hits.

In the wake of the departures and the British invasion of the Sixties Sun didn't produce another star of any significance. Speaking in 1982, Johnny said of his defection from Sun, "Sam couldn't see me wanting to go to another record company, but I could. I felt like at Sun I would be limited in what I could do, where with a major record company I could do all that and reach more people with my music. I think I was right too." To this day there are those who feel that artistically Johnny Cash has never bettered his two tumultuous years with Sun in Memphis, and that the batch of singles he recorded there have stood the test of time in a way that comparatively few others of the era have. Many say the same of Elvis Presley. Certainly it was at Sun that the Johnny Cash *sound* was created, a sound which was to remain his trademark formula.

The essential Johnny Cash sound was in place when the group first auditioned for Phillips. As *Record Collector* magazine put it, "When Johnny Cash arrived at Sun he had a style already formed and neither the hot blast of rockabilly nor the attempted sophistication of the later Sun recordings did more than mask the style." Jack Clement says he was surprised that Johnny left Sun and reckons Phillips had the money to promote him properly and that sooner or later he would have let him do religious music. Sam's brother Judd, speaking in 1972, took a rather different view, believing that Sam's problem was essentially that he didn't really believe in his major artists, "He never really believed that Elvis Presley, Jerry Lee Lewis and Johnny Cash would be the giants they are today. He thought it was just a passing situation and as a consequence we let all these artists slip away from us." A nostalgia industry has grown up around Sun with some feeling that there was so much inherent magic surrounding the studio that it came through on every release. That certainly isn't true. However, for a few short years some of the most exciting rock'n'roll ever produced came out of Sun Records in Memphis.

◆ ◆ ◆ ◆ ◆

Sam and Johnny did not part on good terms – due to Sam feeling that his old friend Bob Neal, Johnny's manager, had taken Johnny to Columbia behind his back. Time being a great healer, in 1984, when Phillips was honoured at a special dinner in his home state of Alabama, Johnny and Jack Clement drove down from Nashville to take part in the celebrations. There were reminiscences, hugs and some tears. As Johnny said in his 1997 autobiography, if it hadn't been for Sam Phillips he might still be working in a cotton field.

When Johnny left Sun, it was part of the deal that Carl Perkins also went to Columbia (though, in Perkins' case, the arrangement turned out to be unsuccessful). Bob Neal closed down his Stars, Inc. organisation and managed the two from his house. Neal wasn't the only one looking after the business side of Johnny's life. Stu Carnall, a native of California, was a young tour promoter who had heard 'Hey! Porter' on a jukebox in Phoenix towards the end of 1956 and realised right away that he was hearing something out of the ordinary. He tracked Bob Neal down with a proposition that he set up a tour of central California.

Carnall got to know the band as he drove them from show to show. The contrast was striking. Carnall was well-educated, cultured, with a taste for snazzy clothes, and his new clients were unsure how to deal with him because the musicians and managers they had dealt with up to then had been from their part of the world, in many cases from similar backgrounds. The trio might have been testing his reactions or merely acting naturally but Carnall was put out by their habit of dropping fruit peel in his immaculate new convertible and eating with their hands at restaurants but he put aside his personal mortification and attempted to maintain decorum.

Despite these differences they hit it off and 'Stew' went on to become heavily involved in the management of Johnny Cash and The Tennessee Two (or "His" Tennessee Two as they were sometimes billed), alongside Bob Neal. Johnny was earning $750 per Californian show, which was big money, though already he was waking up to the business side; principally the fact that Luther and Marshall, the petrol, the hotel costs and so on were paid out of his fee. Johnny Cash has always hated this aspect of the business, preferring to perform, entertain, and to get a reasonable return for what he does, or as Jerry Lee Lewis put it rather more bluntly, "Just gimme the money and show me where the piano is."

Carnall became more and more involved in organising shows and eventually did a deal with Neal whereby he bought half of his contract and the two co-managed Johnny for a time. By 1959, Stew and Bob had ended their business partnership and, for a brief time, Carnall was exclusively responsible for managing Johnny's affairs. That same year, Johnny made his first foray across the Atlantic to England, where he appeared on Marty Wilde's television show *Boy Meets Girl*, performing 'Five Feet High And Rising' and 'I Got Stripes'. Union rules in Britain prevented Johnny from using The Tennessee Two and one member of his hired British backing group was teenager Joe Brown, then an unknown guitarist, later a successful artist in his own right, who quickly had to master Luther Perkins-style guitar. Brown was given an album of Cash material to listen to a short time before the recording.

"I'll never forget it as long as I live," Brown recalled. "I did the wrong style of picking . . . it was similar to the Chet Atkins style. The truth was I got a bit fed up with the Luther Perkins stuff during 'Five Feet High And Rising' and played a lick or two in the middle of it. Johnny walked over to me and said, 'There'll be no picking thar.' He actually stopped the recording of the show which was unheard of, causing all sorts of technical problems. I got the sack as a result but when Johnny heard about it he put in a good word for me and I got my job back. It was really kind of him. I was just a nobody at the time."

Despite the inauspiciousness of this encounter Joe got to back Johnny on other occasions in England and when Johnny returned to America he sent Joe a gift – a considerate gesture but one which created a problem for the then impoverished Brown. "I got a note from Customs and Excise that there was a parcel for me . . . I got there to discover that it contained these beautiful cowboy boots worth $200. I was absolutely devastated when I found out that I couldn't afford to pay the duty on them. The guy took pity on me. He said, 'Let's have a look at them on you son.' I put them on and walked about and he said, 'Tell you what, one second-hand pair of boots, four quid.' I had just enough money on me and took them home. I've still got them."

◆ ◆ ◆ ◆ ◆

Johnny was hardly ever back in Memphis, and when he was there was always work to do in the studio. Consequently, he saw very little of Vivian and the girls. The Carnall connection meant that Johnny started doing more shows and generally spending more time in California. He was on a roll, attracting large crowds wherever he played and selling huge quantities of records. However, that restless creative energy was already looking for a new outlet and Johnny was increasingly drawn to the idea of acting. It was by no means unheard of for singing stars to make it in the cinema, Bing Crosby and Frank Sinatra being recent examples. If you had the looks or the name then acting was an optional extra, so long as you could make a good attempt at appearing reasonably comfortable in front of the camera (something Elvis Presley was to have some difficulty with). One possible scenario would be for Johnny to work on films with Vivian and the girls living nearby, thus enabling him to be close to his family for long spells, but with the prospect of keeping his touring and recording going between shooting engagements. Without too much debate he decided that it would be a good move to relocate to California.

JOHNNY CASH was introduced to the illicit world of drugs at an early age. When he was 11 years old in Dyess, he broke a rib during a wrestling match with a pal without realising he had done any damage, only to wake up in agony during the night. His father took him to the hospital in a mule-drawn wagon, still screaming, but when the doctor gave him a shot of morphine, the boy was amazed that the pain disappeared. That first shot of morphine didn't create Johnny Cash's drug dependency, though on a subconscious level it may have triggered some inner connection. Later, in Germany, Johnny, along with many others, had acquired a taste for alcohol but there is little evidence that it became a major problem. Indeed he claimed that once he got back to America and settled down with Vivian, he didn't drink much at all.

The real problems started when the uncompromising demands of touring – driving through the night from one town to the next – meant that Johnny was losing sleep yet needed to be on top form for each show. He claims he was first offered amphetamines in 1957 during a tour with Faron Young and Ferlin Husky, though other reports suggest that the first opportunity arose when he was driving Ernest Tubb's tour bus. Johnny was impressed and relieved that he had found what on the face of it was a simple way of staying alert and which helped him with his pre-show nerves and onstage confidence. As with the morphine for his broken rib, Johnny simply saw it as a case of taking medicine to cure an ill. In fact, it was uncommon for a performer in his situation *not* to take speed. The pills had different names, Benzedrine, Dexedrine and Dexamyl ("bennies", "dexies") being amongst the better known, but they were all amphetamine-based and, in those days, cost less than $10 for 100.

As well as enabling him to stay awake and bolstering his stage performance, Johnny discovered speed made him less shy around people, though many noticed that he was shifty and awkward when it came to one-to-one talk away from a larger group. In this there were similarities with the late Hank Williams, whose first wife Audrey said, "When he walked on the stage it was the only time

Hank was ever really sure of himself." Johnny found that in a psychological sense, pills gave him the confidence to effect changes to his personality and character, something which in itself many would see as indicative of an addictive personality though he put it more simply, "I liked them, they made me feel good."

Initially it was simply a question of going to a pharmacy and buying the pills over the counter. The next step was contacting hotel doctors, explaining that he was on tour and might not be able to get to a pharmacist. In this way, he managed to obtain substantial supplies in one town after another. All the time the demands of punishing schedules, with venues hundreds of miles apart, were pushing Johnny harder and harder so the need for the pills was gnawing away at him all the time. Soon friends and fellow musicians noticed the effects – twitchiness, irritability and an inability to sit down for more than a few moments without wanting to get up and move around. He looked nervous and tense – the very symptoms he thought the pills were eradicating.

◆ ◆ ◆ ◆ ◆

On the music front, the switch to Columbia signalled the early release of a batch of new material. Having signed a full contract in August 1958, a single, 'All Over Again' b/w 'What Do I Care?' was released in September. At the same time, Sam Phillips competed by releasing some of the leftover Sun material, including an EP of Hank Williams' songs with subsequently added overdubs. November saw the release of Johnny's first Columbia album, *The Fabulous Johnny Cash*, which contained a varied mixture of songs. Despite his undoubted affection for Jack Clement, Johnny stated that he didn't like the way much of his later Sun material was produced, complaining there were too many backing vocals and other techniques to fill out the sound. On that basis, his first Columbia album came as something of a surprise since much of the same approach was adopted on songs such as 'Run Softly Blue River', and 'The Troubadour', the main difference being that the overall production was smoother and the backing singers were of a higher calibre.

With Luther's inimitable boom-chicka-boom picking placed to the fore, it was as if Columbia were trying to bring two styles together without diminishing either, being keenly aware that both had reaped considerable financial rewards. The album was also notable for the début appearance of two Cash classics, 'I Still Miss Someone', a straight from the heart tale of lost love co-written by Johnny and his cousin Roy Cash, Jr, and 'Don't Take Your Guns To Town', a story-ballad with a Western theme which went on to be a number one hit on the country charts. It's likely that Columbia were particularly keen to capitalise on this song in the wake of the success two years previously of 'Tom Dooley' by The Kingston Trio, a murder mountain ballad which helped to create a resurgence of popularity for the genre. As was common in the late Fifties US record market,

The Original Man In Black. (*Michael Ochs/Redferns*)

The Cash family home in Dyess, Arkansas. Though times were hard, in later years, Johnny's brother Roy Cash proudly claimed, "We were never hungry". (*The Cash Family Collection*)

The influential Carter Family, circa the early Thirties. L-R: Maybelle (in later years known as Mother Maybelle Carter, mother of June Carter), AP, and then-wife Sara. According to one early listener: "You could hang a tin cup on any barbed wire in Texas and hear The Carter Family." (*Glenn A. Baker/Redferns*)

Johnny (right) as a youngster with his elder brother Jack and sister Reba. Johnny never got over Jack's death from a freak accident, aged 14. (*The Cash Family Collection*)

John R. Cash as an airman in Oberammergau, Germany, 1952. Although broadening his outlook, the experience became a drag, as Johnny later commented, "I spent twenty years in the Air Force from 1950 to 1954." (*The Cash Family Collection*)

Johnny with first wife, Vivian Liberto, and the first of many awards. The couple's whirlwind two week courtship resulted in marriage in 1954 soon after Johnny's discharge from the Air Force. (*Courtesy of Nashville Public Library*)

Johnny with fellow Sun Records recording artist, Elvis Presley. With the success of 'I Walk The Line',
the local Tennessee press tried to stir up a Cash – Presley "Battle of the Charts" rivalry. (*Pictorial Press*)

The legendary Million Dollar Quartet session at Sun Studios, Memphis, December 4, 1956 (L-R: Jerry Lee Lewis, Carl Perkins, Elvis Presley and JC). Some reports suggest that Johnny only stayed for a short time, though Cash refutes this. (*Pictorial Press*)

The young June Carter, 1956. She first heard Johnny's records when mutual friend Elvis Presley played them to her. (*Courtesy of Nashville Public Library*)

"He was as straight and moral and clean-living as any guy I'd ever worked with" said neighbour Horace Logan. "But as it happened with so many others before him, the pressures and demands of sudden fame were destined to take a heavy toll." (*Redferns*)

With mentor Ernest Tubb at the *Grand Ole Opry*. Tubb coached Cash by saying "Make those people know you believe in what you're singing. When you're singing 'Folsom Prison Blues'… make them feel the misery of the lyric… when you're singing 'I Walk The Line' give them a twinkle in the eye once in a while…" (*Courtesy of Grand Ole Opry*)

Johnny ended 1956 as the year's third biggest selling country artist, 'I Walk The Line' was voted *Cash Box*'s third best single of the year, behind 'Don't Be Cruel' and ahead of 'Blue Suede Shoes', and Johnny was also voted most promising "Country and Western" singer. (*Redferns*)

Johnny arrives at London Airport on September 17, 1959, for his starring role in the TV pop show, *Boy Meets Girl*. (*Corbis*)

Now all in black, circa the early Sixties, Johnny strikes a pose alongside the original Tennessee Two, Marshall Grant (left) and Luther Perkins (right). (*David Gahr*)

Johnny after being arrested on October 4, 1965 at El Paso International Airport, Texas, for attempted drug smuggling. (*Michael Ochs/Redferns*)

Cash Pleads Guilty in Drug Case

Johnny Cash, 33-year-old writer and singer of many of the decade's most popular folk and hillbilly songs, pleaded guilty yesterday to the charge of possessing illegal drugs at an arraignment in El Paso, Tex.

Sentencing of the tall, dark-haired Arkansas native—whose many recordings of his own songs include the country-and-western standard "I Walk The Line," the folk ballad, "Don't Take Your Guns To Town," and the 1964 hit "Understand Your Man"—was deferred indefinitely by U.S. Dist. Judge D. W. Suttle.

Asst. U.S. Atty. Harry L. Hudspeth said the maximum penalty on the charge to which the singer pleaded guilty—possession of depressants and stimulant drugs for which he had no prescription—is a $1,000 fine, a year in prison, or both. The offense is a misdemeanor.

CASH, FREE under a continuing $1,500 bond, was accompanied at the arraignment by his wife, Vivian, a native of San Antonio. Attorney Woodrow W. Bean of El Paso said Cash had no public statement.

The singer was arrested by federal customs agents Oct. 4 at El Paso's International Airport. He was charged with possessing 368 tablets of Dexedrine, a stimulant, and 475 tablets of Equa-

(Turn to Page 2, Column 4)

—AP Wirephoto

EL PASO, Texas — Johnny Cash, recording star, at left, leaves the federal courthouse with his wife Vivian, and attorney Woodrow W. Bean after pleading guilty to possession of drugs.

The *Tennessean* newspaper clipping (dated 29/12/1965) reporting on the Cash drug case that led *Thunderbolt* magazine (with the possible support of the Ku Klux Klan) to wage a hate campaign against Cash and his "negress" wife. (*Courtesy of Nashville Public Library*)

"I don't like being referred to as a country singer, call me the way you see me," Johnny said in 1966.
"I've sold more records in pop than in country, so don't categorise me or stereotype me."
(*Michael Ochs Archives/Redferns*)

the album was released in the form of three EPs. *The Fabulous Johnny Cash* was solidly successful with initial sales in the region of 400,000, accompanied by a respectable pop chart appearance, becoming *Billboard*'s Country and Western album of the year.

In 1959, Johnny had the pleasure of introducing a newcomer to *The Grand Ole Opry* stage, 13-year-old Dolly Parton. Though she was understandably nervous, her performance was received with rapturous delight, and it was fitting that Johnny should have introduced her since he was an inspirational figure to her. Writing in her autobiography, Dolly described an occasion when she and her uncle waited to meet Johnny after a show at the Ryman. It was getting late and she was sleepy and about ready to go home when, as she explained, "A man stepped out of the stage door and walked over to us and there was no other time. There was only this moment. There was only me and Johnny Cash. I have never seen a man with such a presence, tall, lanky and sexy with that trademark voice that cut through me like butter. Now I knew what star quality was. He had it. It was a combination of personal charisma and intense sex appeal . . . I was blown away. I was just a young girl from the Smokies but I would gladly have given it up for Mr Cash right there in the parking lot . . . apparently what I said to him was 'Oh, Mr Cash I've just got to sing at *The Grand Ole Opry*.' He looked at me as if he realised I was serious."

Enjoying his liberation from Sun, Johnny was keen to lay down as much religious material as possible, spending many hours in the studio. The album *Hymns By Johnny Cash*, featured standards such as 'Swing Low Sweet Chariot' and 'The Old Account' and, in accordance with then common practice, Johnny claimed credit for arranging and adapting the songs. There were also a number of Cash originals such as 'It Was Jesus' and 'Lead Me Father' and a composition by Johnny and his father Ray, 'I Call Him'. A few months later Columbia released another album, *Songs Of Our Soil*. The liner notes referred listeners who liked the album to Johnny's earlier release, *The Fabulous Johnny Cash*, but not *Hymns By Johnny Cash*, a possible indication of the record company's view of its limited commercial appeal.

Columbia clearly wanted to capitalise on their new asset with a more mainstream album following so closely on the heels of the religious album. The sleeve photograph featured a clean-cut Johnny playing his guitar, looking contemplatively upwards. His name has been painted on to the neck of the guitar; perhaps by the sleeve designer as an afterthought in a conscious effort to provide an accoutrement to emphasise his star quality. In terms of production both albums were in similar vein to Johnny's Columbia début. There were backing singers aplenty, smooth and sugary "oohs and ahhs" with some deep bass lines every bit as low as Johnny's own thrown in to add a gospel feel. Luther added his onomatopoeic "boom-chicka-boom" contribution.

Vocally Johnny was on top form sounding relaxed and confident, with a rich and pleasing timbre. Unlike some of the early Sun material, the music was imbued with an easy listening quality which was quite deliberate on Johnny's part who invariably tried to give the listener an easy tune and memorable melody. From the point of view of the average record buyer, *Songs Of Our Soil* was the more attractive proposition. The album may have been easy on the ears musically but lyrically it was anything but bland, containing the veritable Cash classic, 'Five Feet High And Rising', inspired by his family's experiences during the Mississippi flood of 1937. Religion was again predominant on 'The Great Speckled Bird' – credited to "J Cash" on the album sleeve which must have come as a surprise to the many people who believed the song was written by the Reverend Guy Smith in 1937 when "J Cash" was five years old. It was a virtuoso performance of this song which had earned a young Roy Acuff a rapturous reception at *The Grand Ole Opry*, leading to him being offered a permanent place there after five years of unsuccessful attempts.

There were folksy ballads and also a song alluding to the sufferings of Native Americans, 'The Old Apache Squaw', an early indication of Johnny's interest and concern for this particular group of people. The traditional 'I Want To Go Home' (later adapted by The Beach Boys as 'Sloop John B') was also included, though the jaunty beat, emphasised incongruously by tom-toms, was somehow at odds with the sad yearnings of the song's hero. 'The Caretaker' was an early example of a type of song which came to be very much associated with Johnny Cash, being a simple story about a cemetery caretaker who watches relatives gather to bury their departed and from a distance he imagines their squabbles and in-fighting over the family inheritance. The caretaker lives in a small house in the cemetery and at night he sleeps soundly like those beneath the ground, but he has no family and wonders about his own death and who will take care of his simple wishes for his own burial arrangements. In a few verses Cash paints a vivid and poignant character portrait, much in the way of the great painters such as Vincent Van Gogh.

The solemn, reflective tones of his voice, with a maturity beyond his 27 years, merely added *gravitas* to the song. While Columbia retained much of the sweetened production techniques favoured by Don Law, Johnny ensured that lyrically the songs were free of the banality of much pop and country music including his own 'Ballad Of A Teenage Queen'. Sam Phillips was equally determined to maximise his original investment by releasing singles and also a hits album, *Greatest Johnny Cash*, featuring contractual commitment material.* Inevitably, the songs were of mixed quality with catchy but inconsequential numbers such as 'Goodbye Little Darlin'' and 'It's Just About Time' sufficient to secure respectable if unspectacular chart placings. The album included Johnny's own

---

* Phillips would continue to do this for years and on occasion would enjoy more commercial success than the Columbia releases he was competing with.

Luther Perkins tribute, 'Luther Played The Boogie' which neatly summed up his guitarist's appeal with the line, "Now didn't Luther play the boogie strange?"

◆ ◆ ◆ ◆ ◆

Early in 1959, as his recording career with Columbia was in overdrive, Johnny moved his family into television personality Johnny Carson's old house in Casitas Springs, an exclusive area of Encino in the San Fernando Valley, for a reputed $175,000. On the site, they built their own house, a ranch-style affair called Las Casitas where, as a reminder of his roots, Johnny planted some cotton. However, fuelled by those little pills, he soon abandoned his home and family for his musical career. Given the emphasis placed on the value of family life in his Christian philosophy, how could these two things be reconciled? In simple terms they could not be.

As a young man Johnny Cash had realised that he had a rare talent, or as his mother put it, that God had His hand on him. This gift took the form of writing and performing songs that connected with people from all sorts of backgrounds, but especially those from the blue-collar, or working-class, sections of society. For all the hedonistic excesses a musical career on the road held, Johnny still felt that religion was a vitally important part of his life. However, fate dictated that before success could occur he should literally crash into Vivian at a San Antonio roller-skating rink and that the two of them should get married without any conventional courtship. Being from opposing religious backgrounds, it may well be that the arrival of three children in quick succession was a reflection of Vivian's strict Catholic upbringing. Having got himself locked into responsibility, Johnny's musical ambitions were suddenly being realised.

If events had happened differently, Johnny would have been free to devote himself to his career without any sense of guilt which the pills helped to alleviate. This is not to say that Johnny Cash didn't love his family but, as a performer, he could never have been content solely in a domestic situation. It was an immensely difficult dilemma for a principled man to have to confront but when it came down to it there really was no choice; music was always going to win out. For Vivian the performing circus which Johnny found himself dragged into was alien and threatening. In the early days she had accompanied him to shows because she was keen to show support for her new husband's career, but she was horrified at the sight of Elvis Presley being mobbed by rampant teenage girls and would have been even more horrified at the notes they regularly hurled onto the stage. Was this going to happen to her husband as well?

On one occasion she accompanied Johnny to the DJ Convention in Nashville. For Vivian it was a miserable time especially when, late one night, there was a call to their hotel bedroom from June Carter saying she was with Don Gibson, and would Johnny care to join them to trade a few songs? He enthusiastically agreed, triggering a mammoth row with Vivian who simply wanted to spend as much time with her husband as possible. In the end he did go to visit June and Don, thereafter hopping about from room to room, talking excitedly and making music into the wee small hours. It was another example of how when it came to a choice between Vivian and the music, between the normality of conventional married life and the craziness of the entertainment world, the latter invariably won. And of course those pills helped to make the decision easier.

1959 saw Johnny's popularity spread further as he undertook his first appearances in Australia and re-recorded two of his songs for the German market: 'Wo Ist Zu Hause Mama ('Five Feet High And Rising') and 'Viel Zu Spat' ('I Got Stripes'), a song whose melody was based on the blues standard, 'On A Monday'. Johnny had already shown an interest in acting, and in June he got the chance to play a psychotic killer in a low budget film provisionally titled *Five Minutes To Live*. Despite the presence of some bankable names including Pamela Mason (wife of James Mason) and Merle Travis, the film ran out of money and was only rescued when Johnny injected $20,000 from his own resources into the project. The film didn't fare well with Johnny looking gauche and ill at ease in front of the cameras with only the obvious assets of his striking appearance and distinctive voice making his performance in any way memorable. He later remarked, "I had no idea what I was doing."

A similarly undistinguished title song was consigned to oblivion when the film was changed to *Door To Door Maniac* late in the proceedings. Johnny's fame meant that producers were keen to use him in cameo roles, the mere presence of a big-selling singing star helping immensely in the promotion of films and television. Johnny gave them what they wanted but there was nothing to suggest he was to be an actor of quality. Johnny was meeting new people and making friends in the course of his hectic schedule. One man he particularly took to was Johnny Horton. Seven years his senior, Horton was a sharecropper's son from California who was married to Hank Williams' widow Billie Jean and had rocketed to stardom in 1959 with 'When It's Springtime In Alaska (It's Forty Degrees Below)' and more especially 'The Battle Of New Orleans' which topped the country charts for 10 weeks and the pop charts for six. The song was banned in Britain because of its reference to the "Bloody British" and skiffle king Lonnie Donegan had a hit with it only after he had made appropriate changes to the lyrics.

The two Johnnys were great fishing buddies. Horton was a real expert; able to cast a line to exactly where the fish were feeding. He set up his own fishing tackle company which Cash helped to underwrite. In contrast to Cash, Horton was not a drinker and did not take drugs but the two of them had a strong religious faith in common as well as a taste for practical jokes. When one of the musicians on tour was constantly complaining about how heavy his suitcase was, the pair surreptitiously added small weights to the case each day in order to really give the man something to complain about.

Horton was interested in spiritualism and psychic phenomena and tried to get his friends involved too. His manager, Tillman Franks, recalled an incident when Horton hypnotised Cash and took him back to when he was six years old, to a classroom at school. Apparently Horton was able to get Cash to remember precisely things like the colour of his teacher's dress, and to sing some of the very first songs he ever knew. However when he tried to get Cash to go into the future he reportedly became very upset, pleading not to be sent into that dark and scary place.

Horton had premonitions that he would die young and he was proved right when a drunk driver rammed his car head-on at high speed in November 1960 as their two vehicles were crossing a narrow bridge in opposite directions.

Johnny Cash later said, "Three months before his death I had a dream about him. I woke up one night and told my wife I dreamed I was walking to Johnny Horton's funeral." Horton's death was all the more upsetting for Cash because his friend had been trying to get hold of him shortly before the crash, but had been unable to do so because, according to Billie Jean, Cash was stoned at the time. One of the remarkable coincidences surrounding Horton's death was that his last ever gig was at the Skyline Club in Austin, Texas, the last venue Hank Williams played before his untimely death in 1953. By this stage Johnny Cash didn't need an excuse to take pills but on hearing of his friend's death he increased his intake. On a more positive note, he later wrote an instrumental number as a tribute to Horton's three children, the title being a play on their names, 'Jeri And Nina's Melody'.

Vivian has said that after Horton's death, Johnny's nervousness seemed to increase and that he was particularly restless at night. It was difficult for her to know how to handle these situations because, before meeting him, she had led a fairly sheltered existence, explaining later, "I tried to discuss the pills with Johnny many times but he always convinced me, at the beginning, that there was nothing to worry about." Johnny could certainly afford to indulge his pill habit because according to his friend, the writer and broadcaster Hugh Cherry, Johnny was already earning around $200,000 a year by this time.

Despite the burgeoning drug madness and its unpleasant side effects, Johnny still managed to be creative. In September 1960, Columbia released the album *Ride This Train*, which Johnny has maintained is one of the works of which he is most proud and which sold well right up into the Seventies. It was an unusual album for a singer aiming at success in the country and pop charts since it was not particularly commercial, but its quirkiness contributed to Johnny's growing reputation for creating music from serious and historically evocative subjects. *Ride This Train* was a concept album, painting a picture of a vanished world, the rural America of the eighteenth and nineteenth centuries. There is a remarkable sequence at the start of the album where Johnny reels off a list of American towns followed by a list of Native American tribes delivered in the quickfire style of a tobacco auctioneer. As so often in art, less is more and such a straightforward idea, enhanced by the Cash voice, comes over as evocative, colourful and compulsive. Clearly Johnny's real life experiences of the country and trains, as well as his passionate interest in Americana, fired his imagination.

Ride This Train is made up of different character sketches; a train driver, a lumberjack, a doctor, a plantation owner, an outlaw (John Wesley Hardin). As with 'The Caretaker' powerful images are conjured with a few words. Like all good storytellers Johnny made the characters real, and the stories had the power to entertain, inform and move the listener. For example, Doc Brown looked after the people in his town, never charging more than he thought people could afford and sometimes charging nothing at all. He died alone, his final act being to write off all outstanding fees due to him, but there wasn't enough money to pay for his own funeral and the local undertaker provided a metal casket that he hadn't been able to sell.

The individuals came from all over America and their stories are linked by the device of train journeys, evoked by the haunting sounds of a steam engine. As the engine roars and the whistle blows Johnny delivers earnest linking narratives between the songs. Johnny used to lie awake at night listening to those railroad sounds and was there when steam trains were still roaring across America. The steam train was a powerful symbol of freedom and progress and though young JR would not have viewed it on this level, it subliminally made a profound impression on him.

Musically some changes were made to fit in with the mood of the album. The sound was stripped down and folksy, though some sympathetic piano and dobro backing was applied at points where their presence added to the overall effect. Gone were the sugary backing singers and the trademark Luther guitar licks, nothing was to compromise Johnny's vocal presence. Writers of real stature contributed songs: Merle Travis ('Loading Coal'), Tex Ritter ('Boss Jack'), Red Foley ('Old Doc Brown') and folklorist Alan Lomax, who co-wrote 'Going To Memphis' – a song about men on a chain gang wishing they were free but, as in 'Folsom Prison Blues', without any thought of rehabilitation: *"Like a bitter weed, I'm a bad seed."*

The song's driving groove is set over a beat created by the sound of hammers hitting rocks and nails and the background rhythmic grunting from other members of the gang complete the effect. The brutal realities of life are spelt out graphically:

> *If you complained about anything,*
> *They'd just be liable to give you a chance to get away,*
> *They'd take the chains off your legs*
> *And beg you to run so they could shoot you.*

The sleeve shows Johnny dressed in cowboy gear; unshaven and looking at the camera with a slight air of menace, whilst toying with his gun. Was he getting ready to fire or about to put it back in its holster? The landscape is rocky and arid against a blue sky and, in the background, a goods train heads off into the distance. In the early Seventies, Johnny said he had the idea of a "country opera" in mind when he came up with *Ride This Train*, claiming it as the first concept album with gospel overtones though both Merle Travis' *Down Home* and Gordon Jenkins' *Seven Dreams* were earlier albums which could be said to fall into this category. Regardless, the album is an early Cash classic which easily justified Columbia's slogan, "Nobody but nobody more original than Johnny Cash", lending weight to *Life* magazine's later observation that "He is at his best when singing of a bygone era."

With its weighty worthiness mixed with simple accessible songs, the album stood in stark contrast to the crazy drug-fuelled roller coaster ride that Johnny had now embarked upon. It was a ride which was also driven by a restless desire to try new things musically, as if he was somehow making up for lost time. It was a ride which would also produce some of his greatest work and help to make Johnny Cash an indelible part of popular American culture.

9

AT THE END OF 1960, hard on the heels of *Ride This Train*, Johnny Cash took the unusual step of releasing a tribute type collection, *Now, There Was a Song!* The album contained songs by a variety of older as well as more recent country stars such as Marty Robbins, Ernest Tubb, Bob Wills, Ferlin Husky, Hank Snow, Ray Price, Hank Thompson and George Jones. There were potential commercial risks in giving widespread exposure to songs associated with artists some of whom were Cash's commercial competitors, but despite the mixed reception he had received from some quarters of traditional country music, Johnny genuinely admired and respected the people he saw as outstanding talents, alongside the older artists he had listened to when growing up in Dyess. Johnny shared the same bills with a lot of these artists as they criss-crossed America on manic touring schedules or television and radio appearances.

The album was a further sign of Columbia's willingness to indulge their new star since such an album had less commercial potential than more conventional country or pop music. It was in the course of 1960 that Johnny added drummer WS Holland so The Tennessee Two now became The Tennessee Three. Like Johnny, Holland was not musically trained and had been given initials for a name, something which would cause him endless hassles at passport controls over the years when touring abroad. WS was invariably known as "Fluke", a nickname derived from a word he invented, "flukus", meaning "thingamajig". WS had been Carl Perkins' drummer, played on 'Blue Suede Shoes' and had also been around for the Million Dollar Quartet session so he slotted in well to the Cash set-up with which he was already familiar. Marshall and Luther were long settled into marriage and had only recently been persuaded that there was a career in music. They were not unattractive men but, like Bill Haley before them, they didn't have sex appeal and neither did Fluke. Also married, he was quite stockily built and handsome though the effect was spoilt by a disconcerting squint. This was in contrast to Johnny who was blessed with conspicuously good looks and an imposing presence. He looked serious and edgy most of the time so his winning smile, when it came, was all the more affecting. There was no attempt to disguise the fact that he was married with children and so, in theory at least, unavailable.

Touring continued to take up a substantial amount of Johnny's time because he was, as Bob Neal liked to say, "Hotter than a two dollar pistol." When he was in California, Johnny invited 35-year-old Rose Maddox to be part of his touring show. The two of them had appeared together before at such venues as *The Grand Ole Opry* and *Town Hall Party* and since her career was in the doldrums at the time she accepted the offer with alacrity. Rose recalled arriving at hotels when Marshall and Luther would put on a special reception for dapper manager Stew Carnall, who affected a walking stick and often wore a Derby hat. The boys would arrange to roll out a red carpet at the front of the hotel and announce Stew as the "Baron of Bellflower". When he was asked to sign the register the hotel receptionist would be told that he never signed anything because it was beneath his dignity.

Although she was more than five years his senior and an established artist, Rose, like many people first meeting Johnny, felt intimidated. When the unwelcome attentions of a booking agent involved in the tour were thrust upon her, Rose still felt uncomfortable about approaching him for help. Eventually Johnny got to hear about her problem through Gordon Terry, one of the other musicians on the tour. Johnny was volatile and unpredictable thanks to his pill consumption, and something about the situation made him snap. He cornered the agent, towering over him with barely concealed rage and told him, "If you don't leave Rose alone, you're gonna be a dead man!"

It worked but Rose still wasn't in the clear, because she still had Johnny to deal with. First there was his wicked sense of humour, as she found when he arranged for her to help him get rid of some unwanted female fans in his room. She recalled that he told her to join him in the bedroom next door where the two of them began an impromptu argument, shouting at the tops of their voices. After a while Johnny roared, "That's it. I'm going to kill you, bitch," and fired a gun, after which the unwanted fans legged it in a state of alarm. On another occasion during the tour Rose was suffering from food poisoning and wasn't able to appear on stage, so Johnny solemnly told the fans that she was very ill, suffering from a serious infection and that gangrene was setting in.

This black brand of humour, while no doubt amusing for Johnny and his cronies, was upsetting for people who couldn't see through it. Rose Maddox was not particularly streetwise and was initially oblivious to the fact that Johnny was taking large quantities of drugs. As far as she was concerned he was invariably polite, in a rural southern sort of way, and considerate, even though he was a little rowdy at times. Gradually, the chaotic nature of his life became clearer to her. At this time Johnny's marriage was in serious difficulty as his fourth daughter, Tara, was on the way. Vivian made a last-ditch effort to save the marriage, and to persuade Johnny to accept some of the responsibility for looking after their children. Sometimes he would head back to California with little or no notice, leaving the rest of the troupe to sort out the resultant mess but it was all to no avail. On the rare occasions he did return home the children barely knew their father, drug ravaged and incoherent as he often was, and were afraid of him.

Vivian said that she had to "feel her way" when he came back to the family home, "So as to see if he was in a mean mood or not." He had little to do with the girls, missing out on birthdays and end-of-term school celebrations. When he did make it back to the house he would barely re-establish contact before heading off into the country in a camper van with a friend of his called Curly Lewis. They'd be out all night or longer, with Johnny hoovering up large quantities of pills, walking about the countryside and living rough. Vivian had probably realised there was no hope for their marriage ever since Johnny's first big hits but her religious beliefs made her keep on trying to find a way to rescue the situation. The late Horace Logan, programme director at *The Louisiana Hayride* up until 1958, was a neighbour of the Cash family in California. He remembered Johnny's appearance as being particularly striking and quite a contrast to the way he remembered Johnny when he appeared on the *Hayride* in the Fifties. As Logan put it, "He was as straight and moral and clean-living as any guy I'd ever worked with. But as it happened with so many others before him, the pressures and demands of sudden fame were destined to take a heavy toll."

Now as a result of his dramatic rise to fame Johnny had lost weight, his eyes were sunken and surrounded by dark rings. As many others noticed, he was on edge and jumpy much of the time, being in such bad shape that the dread thought occurred to Horace that Johnny would go the same way as Hank Williams. If so, at the age of 27, he only had two years to go.

Even when he stayed with the troupe, Johnny's erratic behaviour had a major impact on their shows. Sometimes he would turn up shortly before a performance, causing the others, who had no idea if he would appear or not, to make frantic efforts to rearrange the programme without him, only to see him stroll in and head out onto the stage at the last minute. At other times he was too far gone to perform, and the show had to go on without him; the audience being told he was unwell. Johnny was letting his audience down; an unhappy indictment given that so many looked up to him as a man of integrity. This didn't register strongly enough to persuade Johnny to change his ways and it wasn't in his nature to apologise for his behaviour. The troupe started playing smaller venues because if Johnny failed to turn up, the amount of compensation promoters might seek wouldn't be so great.

Much as Stew Carnall liked and got on well with Johnny, it all became too much for him. His wife had recently given birth to their first child and he decided to quit, his place being taken by Saul Holiff, who would remain Johnny's manager until the early Seventies. A Canadian Jew of Ukranian origin, Holiff, like Cash, had worked his way up out of a poor background. He had served time in his family's fruit business and the Canadian Air Force, thereafter trying various business enterprises before getting into concert promotion throughout Canada. His managerial involvement with Cash began, at Johnny's suggestion, during a tour through Nova Scotia and Newfoundland, possibly because Johnny had been impressed by Holiff a couple of years earlier when he was promoting a show in Ontario. The two of them got into a lengthy wrangle over the interpretation of one small part of a contract, the amount at stake being $40. Perhaps Johnny felt that someone who was prepared to put up such a spirited fight over such a small amount of money should be on his side.

When shows were cancelled and dates rescheduled because of Johnny's condition, Rose Maddox lost money too but that wasn't her main concern. One night Johnny asked if he could come up to her room since he was once more besieged by fans in his own room. Rose agreed. "Sure, if you want, you can sleep in the other bed." He got into the spare bed but as Rose put it, "He was real restless over there." Eventually he got up and said, on the way out, "I'm going back down to my room, I can't stand being this close to you." Rose, being fairly naive, only figured out later what that meant and it played on her mind. As the tour neared its conclusion she confronted Johnny as to what exactly he wanted of her. When he told her what she had already worked out for herself, Rose declared, "John I am married, I have never cheated on my husband and I have no intention of cheating on him." Eventually the emotional pressure coupled with the constant hassle over rescheduled and missed shows forced her to quit the Cash show. She was relieved and for some of the troupe, the feelings were mutual. Johnny Western, a Cash regular when Rose was on the tour, described her as an awkward woman with a number of personal issues which made her hard to get on with.

◆ ◆ ◆ ◆ ◆

The on-the-road madness may have ended for Rose Maddox but the mayhem associated with Johnny Cash tours continued unabated for some time with very little of what went on straying beyond the inner circle. As with the future President John F Kennedy, there was an unwritten rule that personal indiscretions were matters which a close circle of colleagues and reporters knew about but didn't disclose to outsiders. For the most part Johnny Cash fans saw a charismatic performer who put on an electrifying show and they went home happy. Many were impressed by the religious piety expressed through numbers like 'Will The Circle Be Unbroken?' and 'I Was There When It Happened', having little idea of the extracurricular activities which went on behind the scenes.

Writing some years later in his autobiography *Living Proof*, Hank Williams, Jr gave a graphic account of life on the road during this time. Although younger than Cash, Hank got into touring at an early age and was criss-crossing America not long after him, sharing stages together from time to time. Most artists observed an unspoken code of silence but Hank had no such compunction: "A lot of artists say they've never met a groupie on the road. I know they're lying because there's always women, as many as you could want in as many different varieties as you could think of, some pretty, some downright ugly, all willing. At first when you're young, you wonder what makes them do it . . . after a while though you don't think about it much any more than you'd think about water coming out of a tap when you've turned it on. The road is its own world with its own moralities and its own laws. Nothing from the outside counts even a little bit. In the country song, there's always a distinction between a honky-tonk angel and the girl who waits at home. On the road that distinction is very real." On his many travels, English country singer Frank Yonco was mystified as to why, when people *did* show some awareness of what went on, they tended to assume it only happened in rock music circles.

Groups like The Who may have thought they were the first to vandalise hotels but, if so, they were wrong. Johnny Cash and his cronies could have written a thesis on the subject. However, in total contrast to Johnny Cash, The Who used destruction largely as a publicity gimmick. The contrast with the way Johnny went about it could not have been greater, though from a hotel manager's point of view such distinctions were academic. Nobody will ever know the exact details of every hotel incident that occurred from the late Fifties to the mid-Sixties, but the escapades could fill a book on their own. Some reported examples, doubtless exaggerated and embellished with the passage of time, serve to give a flavour.

Johnny was in the habit of booking adjoining rooms for himself and the band but one time in Georgia this wasn't possible so the boys got hold of a fire axe and smashed a hole in the wall between their rooms. Another trick was to saw the ends off table legs and then put them back together so that the tables collapsed when unsuspecting staff cleaned them the next day. Painting the walls and even the furniture and television sets in their rooms was another favourite (Johnny explained that he preferred colour television). Johnny was also known to dismantle the insides of television sets and then put the shell back together again, leaving cryptic notes for the poor man assigned the task of repairing the set. Marshall's penchant for making bombs was also utilised, such as the occasion in New Jersey, on tour with Marty Robbins, when he dropped a bomb down a lavatory bowl and then flushed it. The bomb exploded a little way down the piping, destroying the bowl, causing an explosion in the men's toilet below and spraying 20 or so shell-shocked customers.

This particular incident did result in the police being called though no charges were brought against the band, who all pleaded ignorance of what had happened. Surprisingly the long-suffering hotels rarely did call the police though this was often because Johnny agreed to pay for the damage caused as part of what might loosely be referred to as out-of-court settlements. It was the price of his fun and he was making so much money that he seemed to accept it philosophically. In Germany, Johnny was enraged by an anti-American remark made by another resident and vented his anger on an expensive painting on the wall of his room by hurling knives at it, incurring a supplementary charge of $1,000 in the process. On another occasion in Frankfurt, as they were leaving their hotel, Johnny appeared at an upper balcony, suitcase in hand. He decided he didn't want the trouble of taking it all the way downstairs so he threw it out into the street. Luther reckoned he would do the same but unfortunately his case wasn't of such good quality and, on impact, it violently burst open, sending his clothes and other possessions flying in all directions.

On one tour in the early Sixties, fiddler Gordon Terry performed a novelty song called 'Johnson's Old Grey Mule' which had him braying at the top of his voice. Late at night, back at a hotel in Minneapolis, Gordon shattered the peace by letting out his loudest bray in the courtyard, followed immediately by Marshall setting off his cap and ball gun, causing residents to rush to their windows expecting to see a donkey being put to death. The boys expanded upon this particular idea when they bought some hay and manure and dragged it into the hotel by a back entrance, spreading it about the corridor of one of the upper floors. In the middle of the night, Gordon Terry once more let out one of his piercing brays and Marshall once again responded with his gun. The manager and members of staff appeared to see what was going on but Cash and his band staggered out into the hall pretending they had been asleep and, like everybody else, were wondering what all the noise was about. At the Hyatt in Los Angeles, a favourite among musicians over many years, legend has it that Johnny made up a bed for himself in the lift, even moving in some furniture. Despite the obvious inconvenience he caused Johnny resisted attempts to move because, as he explained, it was so cosy in there.

On one tour Johnny got it into his head that he wanted to buy around 50 baby chicks to take back to California with him. It may have been a misguided attempt to do something decent for the daughters he was neglecting but, if so, his good intentions backfired. Johnny put the chicks in a drawer in his hotel room and positioned a lamp over the drawer to keep them warm, but when he was out the light fell into the drawer and most of the chicks suffocated. Being transported back to Los Angeles aboard a TWA flight inside the band's pockets, the survivors escaped in mid-air, eventually being retrieved by harassed air stewards. Johnny eventually got some of the chicks back to his house in California, but most of them were eaten by a dog that had been given to him by Stew Carnall.

The boys rarely heeded the advice of Fluke who, unlike the rest, neither drank nor took drugs. "The secret is: go when you gotta go, sleep when you can, eat when you can. If you don't get the right kind of food (Johnny ate prodigious quantities of junk food on the road) and the right kind of rest you can't do it. That's why they take pills." What seems to have been the principal motivating factor for the various pranks and acts of vandalism was the sheer joy of the practical joke that went off well. The fact that at times the jokes could be destructive didn't seem to trouble the boys and, after all, hotel managers who complained could usually be bought off without the matter going any further.

It was all very innocent in a schoolboyish manner but did not always go down well with some of their fellow musicians such as Jimmy Dean who complained that he kept getting turned away from hotels that the Cash troupe had trashed. Johnny usually avoided trouble with the police but not always. In 1961, he forfeited a $5 bond in the Nashville city court on a drunkenness charge. Johnny and songwriter Douglas Glenn Tubb, Ernest Tubb's nephew, had been arrested at 3.30 am following a session in one of Nashville's illegal after-hours drinking clubs, and held in custody for four hours before being released. Interestingly, on the police report form, Johnny gave his job as "actor".

There were probably a number of reasons why such mayhem on the road appealed to Johnny. In the first place, touring could be mind-numbingly boring. Distractions were necessary, but why so extreme? Part of the explanation is surely to be found in Johnny's childhood, deprived as it was of so many material luxuries and with the constant threat of penury hanging over the family. Success and wealth meant Johnny was like a child in a toyshop. In addition, as has been commented on by many people not least himself, Johnny had a mean streak. In Dyess, when still very young, he used to take pleasure in smashing bottles just to hear them break. When Johnny's parents asked him to teach his younger brother Tommy how to swim, Johnny simply took Tommy to the deepest part of the river and threw him in. In Landsberg he sometimes went out on a Friday night specifically looking to pick a fight and at times his sense of humour could be cruel.

As his friend Merle Travis later put it, "There ain't no twilight and there ain't no dusk to Johnny Cash – he's like a sunny day or he's completely dark." Tommy Cash also believes that there is a dark streak in there somewhere. "Yeah, he could be belligerent and antagonistic sometimes. It kinda crept up on him and then he'd be OK again. I think to a large extent though, it was a combination of all the pressures he was under and the drugs." Johnny had certainly learned how to let go in Germany but with the addition of success, fame and money, Johnny could give free rein to his unconventional sense of humour by being able to move into a different league beyond the reach of most people. Damon Runyon's assessment of Frank Sinatra some years previously has a particular resonance, "He's about as normal as any 23-year-old who's just made a million bucks."

Carl Perkins made a similar point about the way money and fame could change people in a *Rolling Stone* interview. "You can't take a poor fellow, take him out of a pair of overalls and dress him in a three-piece sharkskin suit, set him in a Fleetwood Cadillac, with a gold record fixin' to come and a royalty check that's bigger than what the bank has in that little town he was raised in, and expect that dude to stay like he was. Somewhere or another, it pushes something away." Little Richard summed it up with "he got what he wanted but he lost what he had."

♦ ♦ ♦ ♦ ♦

It's ironic that while all of this was going on in the early Sixties, Johnny was leading a dual existence by recording more religious material for Columbia. 'God Must Have My Fortune Laid Away', 'He'll Understand And Say Well Done', 'When He Reached Down His Hand For Me' and an eleven-minute narration, 'A Day In The Grand Canyon' were recorded for an album entitled *The Lure Of The Grand Canyon*. It was something of a miracle that anything was laid down in the studio at all since Johnny's erratic lifestyle meant that he missed more sessions than he turned up for, in stark contrast to the early Sun days when he was hungry to be in front of a microphone.

Even when he did make it to the studio, his larynx was so dried out from the effects of heavy smoking and lack of sleep that many sessions were in vain. Despite these impediments, significant recordings were pulled out of the hat not least 'The Big Battle', one of Johnny's early social commentaries on the needless killing of war. The message is that the *real* battle occurs after the war has ended, in the hearts and consciences of the people who have suffered loss. Producer Don Law showed considerable restraint and allowed Johnny a degree of leeway.

Towards the end of 1961, when talking about a new girl singer for Johnny's show, Saul Holiff mentioned June Carter, suggesting she do one show at the Big D Jamboree in Dallas. Johnny needed little persuasion.

Apart from his obvious interest in June, from his earliest days he had a respect verging on reverence for The Carter Family, the midwives of traditional country music whose influence was detectable in the work of countless artists who followed them. The original group consisted of AP Carter, his wife Sara and Maybelle Carter, June's mother, who was married to one of AP's brothers, Ezra, better known as Eck. AP and Sara had a love of music in common and after they married in 1915, they spent much of their spare time making music at their home in Maces Springs, Virginia.

Apart from singing Sara was proficient on banjo, guitar and autoharp. AP had worked as a travelling salesman and absorbed many old traditional songs on the road. He didn't think of himself as a musical archivist, more that he wanted new material to perform with his family and friends. However, in the process he built up a collection of songs, many of which would become the basis of modern country music, and he could perhaps be forgiven for claiming the songs he rescued as his own when The Carter Family embarked on their recording career in the late Twenties. AP was endlessly curious about the world, a lover of books and a seeker of knowledge, roaming restlessly about the valleys and mountains around his home "searching for something he couldn't quite find" as one writer put it.

Maybelle Addington was descended from Henry Addington, Tory British Prime Minister between 1801 and 1804. She too came from a musical background and it was inevitable that once she married Ezra she would become involved with AP Carter and Sara. Soon, The Carter Family was born. AP heard about an audition being held by the Victoria Talking Machine Company, organised by Ralph Peer at Bristol, Tennessee and was keen for the group to attend though he encountered some resistance from his brother as Maybelle was seven months pregnant at the time, and a journey of 25 miles along dirt roads in the stifling midsummer heat was not what the doctor ordered. Eventually the group did go and Ralph Peer immediately recognised that he had struck gold. Johnny Cash later said that the Bristol sessions were the single most important event in the history of country music. The Carter Family broke new ground because of their style of close harmony singing and their use of guitar and autoharp on which Maybelle was able to pluck out melodies.

Many of the songs AP collected had been performed without instrumental backing, though some did have very basic accompaniment. The Carter Family used their instruments to provide melodic as well as rhythmic backing and their close harmony singing, enhanced by the special blend that is said to be achieved by voices of members of the same family would soon be widely copied. Similarly, Mother Maybelle's guitar style, the "Carter scratch" or "lick", would prove to be highly influential. She picked out a melody on the bass string while keeping up the rhythm with chords on the treble strings – picking as well as strumming. Songs were arranged around three main chords and a 4/4 tempo which proved to be innovative and highly influential to countless artists up to the present day.

Despite his hedonistic self-indulgence, Johnny undoubtedly approved of the Carters' strong religious beliefs and the modest handbills for their shows unselfconsciously bore the legend, "The program is morally good." Some years before the Bristol sessions, AP and Sara had been offered the chance of recording square dances by Brunswick which AP turned down because he knew that his parents would disapprove on religious grounds. The combination of rural values, earnest religious overtones and musical tradition would have been hard for Johnny to resist and, from June's point of view, the arrangement was attractive too. Despite their present-day legendary status the fact is that by the dawn of the Sixties the Carters were largely forgotten. The original group had split a few years after AP and Sara divorced in 1939, their fortunes not helped by the fact that a cover feature in *Life* magazine was pulled at the last minute following the Japanese attack on Pearl Harbor in December 1941.

June did become part of the "continuation" Carter Family, also known as Mother Maybelle and The Carter Sisters (Maybelle's three daughters June, Helen and Anita) who were so small when they started out that they had to stand on boxes to be able to reach the microphones. The family appeared at *The Grand Ole Opry* and cut records, putting together a repertoire which attempted to balance old Carter Family material with newer songs but by the mid-Fifties, they were not in great demand, being superseded by the sounds of modern country, pop and rock'n'roll. By the late Fifties many of their records had been deleted, meaning that the royalty cheques dried up. Maybelle had to take what she could get and, ironically, the group found itself as part of a vaudeville-style tour billed as a rock'n'roll revue with the Duke of Paducah, a country comedian who invariably finished his shows with the line, "I'm goin' back to the wagon, boys, these shoes are killin' me."

Eventually she had to take work as a night nurse to the elderly for $12 per shift to help make ends meet.

June was by now into her thirties, with a failed marriage to singer Carl Smith behind her, and a young daughter, Carlene, to look after. Her second marriage to ex-football player and garage owner Edwin "Rip" Nix was in trouble and she had another daughter from that relationship, Rozanna Lea (known usually as Rosey) to consider as well.* June has never been forthcoming about the failure of her marriages but, like Johnny, there is little doubt that the competing demands of marriage and a musical career presented her with a dilemma brought about by her conservative religious beliefs and a puritan upbringing in the Clinch Mountains of southwest Virginia. As she put it in her 1979 auto-biography, *Among My Klediments*, "God's order to wives is an important part of a successful marriage, and I'm afraid I fell short of what a wife should be. I con-tinued to work with my mother and sisters . . . if a wife expects to keep her husband she must think first of God's order – be a helpmate and forsake mother and father."

June decided to try acting following an offer to study under leading director Elia Kazan. She flew between Nashville and New York and to earn extra money wrote commercials for Kelloggs Cornflakes, Pet Milk and other *Opry* sponsors, as well as continuing to put in appearances with her mother and sisters. June also got some television parts and made some useful contacts in New York such as Robert Duvall, in whose film *The Apostle* she later appeared (as his mother). Less memorably, she co-starred with Faron Young and Ferlin Husky in the film,

---

* Rip Nix would later work as a police officer and was in charge of the investigations into one of the numerous car crashes Johnny caused.

Country Music Holiday which, according to writer Bob Millard, is "Generally considered the worst country music movie ever made."

June came up against the seedier side of thespian life when the head of a famous studio arranged a late night audition for her. She was to play the part of a prostitute and he the client, but despite a residual degree of rural naivety, her suspicions were aroused when she realised there was nobody else in the building. She kicked him in the shin and showered him with a tirade of the worst language she could think of. It became obvious to June that music was still her first love and she was keen to find a way back into it to boost her career prospects. An offer to join the Johnny Cash show was too good to miss even if it was initially for one show only.

Whatever attracted Johnny to the idea of June being on his show it can't have been her singing. Even her own mother said that June had the weakest voice of her three daughters which is probably why she learned to play a selection of musical instruments and also honed various comedy routines which were regularly used as show warm-ups. (A typical joke: "I always wanted to wear my mommy's girdle but I didn't have the guts.") A solo singing career that could provide any kind of decent income was realistically out of the question so the opportunity to be part of the Johnny Cash show was welcome. June was a highly experienced performer and was very much at home on stage, more so in many ways than Johnny and with the various skills she possessed she would be an obvious asset to a varied troupe like the Johnny Cash show. After her début in December 1961 at the Big D Jamboree, it was Johnny who suggested that she become part of the show. The arrangement turned out to be rather longer lasting than either of them could possibly have expected at the time. Or was the attraction between the two already so strong that they instinctively knew they were right for each other, no matter what hardships had to be overcome?

10

JOHNNY MIGHT WELL CLAIM that June had been his first real love, well before he was married to Vivian. As an 18-year-old in the *Opry* audience, he had fallen for "Junebug" and her toothy smile. Undoubtedly, he reached the conclusion after he became successful in the late Fifties that the only relationship that could survive was with one who shared and understood his itinerant lifestyle. June fitted the bill perfectly, The Carter Family connection being a strong bond, and the two shared a similar rural upbringing. No doubt June could do what Johnny complained city women couldn't do in an interview with *Mademoiselle* magazine – namely light a match in the wind.

Because of their strong religious faith, it's hardly surprising that their relationship was hushed up at the start. They were each married to other people and, given their chaotic lifestyles and the less liberal attitudes of society in general, they might well have been fearful of doing anything that might conceivably jeopardise their rights to see their children. In Johnny's case, Vivian had plenty of grounds on that score already, while June's second husband Rip Nix, became suspicious about their relationship, and threatened to drag the Carter family name through every mudhole in the state of Tennessee.

English country singer Frank Yonco who appeared on bills with the Cash troupe on quite a few occasions in the Sixties says it was obvious they were an item when he worked with them in 1963. In their subsequent public pronouncements Johnny and June have been a great deal more circumspect, though in his 1997 autobiography Johnny indicated that there was something very special about June right from the start, "This thing between us has been happening since 1961." June herself later described the kind of traumas she went through as her feelings for Johnny grew, "It was not a convenient time for me to fall in love with him and it wasn't a convenient time for him to fall in love with me. One morning about four o' clock I was driving my car just about as fast as I could. I thought why am I out on the highway this time of night." She suddenly realised the truth. "I'm falling in love with someone I have no right to fall in love with. I was frightened of his way of life. I'd watched Hank Williams die . . ."

When June joined the tour, Johnny made sure that she rode in his car. "I liked Luther, Marshall and Fluke but not the way I liked June Carter. I made the implications of that point clear to the boys . . . I let them know from day one: 'Don't mess around with June Carter. I'm covering her' . . . she didn't mess around . . . if she played at all, she played for keeps." Johnny made sure that Saul Holiff booked her for all his tours from then on. In her own memoirs, June simply denies that anything other than a friendship, a professional relationship and some degree of mutual attraction occurred between them for years after they first started working together. Given their constant road tours and Johnny's heavy amphetamine use the opportunities to spend what might be referred to as quality time together would have been fairly limited.

Right from her first tour, June's close involvement with Johnny suggests something beyond a merely platonic relationship. On one occasion, shortly before he was due on stage, June told him that he couldn't possibly go on in a crumpled shirt. While Johnny resented being spoken to that way, he did submit to her wishes and gave up his shirt for ironing.

In no time, June was routinely looking after Johnny's clothes, taking care of such chores as washing, ironing and sewing, though none of this exempted her from the touring pranks. Soon after she joined the show, the entourage were staying at a roadside motel. Because it was a hot day, June had left her windows open. As if it was the most natural thing in the world, some of the boys climbed into her room with a large barrel crammed with confetti. After a short speech welcoming June on board they proceeded to empty out the entire contents of the barrel, leaving her standing knee deep in confetti.

♦ ♦ ♦ ♦ ♦

Johnny had moved to California largely because he wanted to make progress with a film career but it wasn't really happening. He obtained parts in the TV shows *The Rebel* and *The Deputy* and the film *Night Rider*. However, because he wasn't a natural actor, he was usually given cameo roles in Westerns where, no matter what name his character had, he was typecast as Johnny Cash. Producers wanted him because they knew that his presence would attract a bigger audience but it soon dawned on Johnny that his natural talent lay in music. Over the years, he continued to take minor film roles but for the most part it was a case of indulging a hobby which his celebrity status made possible.

There were logistical problems, too. Johnny's house in Ventura was about 75 miles from the Hollywood film studios, which involved five hours travelling on top of everything else. Add to this his drug consumption and the breakdown of his marriage and it was fairly obvious that the pull of being on the road was going to win over movie making. Nonetheless he continued to jeopardise his success with reckless behaviour. One of the most remarkable examples of this came in 1962 with a Carnegie Hall show in New York which should have been a pivotal moment in his career. Johnny had been on a three day, sponsored moose hunt with his friends Merle Travis and Gordon Terry, an outing which turned into a marathon pill-popping session.

By the time Johnny got to New York he was a wreck, his voice all but gone. While he managed to stumble through press and television appearances he was really in no fit state to sing. Johnny took the stage after performances from Merle Kilgore, Tompall and The Glaser Brothers and The Carter Family. For reasons best known to himself Johnny decided to include songs by Jimmie Rodgers throughout his set. He had long been a fan of Rodgers and in 1957, when still a junior star in the country firmament, he had been invited to appear at the annual country music festival in Meridian to mark the anniversary of Rodgers' death.*

While some of the audience might have heard of the Singing Brakeman they were baffled by Cash's decision, not only to sing his songs but also to dress like him. He arranged for the house lights to be dimmed, walked out onto the stage carrying Jimmie's railroad lantern and then started playing the Rodgers classic 'Waiting For A Train' in anticipation of a roar of appreciation and recognition that didn't arrive. The audience couldn't grasp what he was doing and started shouting out for his hits. Johnny might have been able to rescue the situation if he'd simply changed tack and given the people what they wanted but his attempts to do so were largely foiled by a voice that was shot to pieces. He apologised, the usual stuff about his voice being worn out from a heavy touring schedule, and whispered his way through some of his best-known songs. It was an astonishing example of hubris to assume that people who had paid top dollar to see Johnny Cash perform his most well-known songs would appreciate a hoarse tribute to an influential albeit obscure singer who had been dead for 30 years.

Don Law had been planning to record Johnny's segment but in the event the tapes never rolled. June tried to be sympathetic after the show but Johnny was beyond consoling though the cloud did have one silver lining. Johnny met a folk singer called Ed McCurdy backstage with whom he hung out for a while in New York. McCurdy introduced him to Peter LaFarge, a Hopi Indian who helped to open Johnny's eyes to the many issues affecting Native Americans.

◆ ◆ ◆ ◆ ◆

Meanwhile, Johnny was looking for a new female singer to feature in his show and had Patsy Cline in mind. With the popularity of such Fifties names as Ernest Tubb and Hank Snow having waned considerably, Patsy and Johnny were

---

* Cash acquired the screen rights to Carrie Rodgers' biography of her late husband, though no film was ever made.

arguably the two top attractions in country music at the time. She appreciated Johnny's outsider image and also welcomed the opportunity to spend time with her close friend June Carter. The two had met on an aeroplane some years before and became close. Patsy saw June as something of a confidante who she could turn to when things got too much, particularly when she had rows, sometimes leading to physical violence, with her husband Charlie Dick. Patsy had reciprocated with powerful support when June's first marriage to Carl Smith disintegrated. The pair played a number of shows together though, as June later explained, their roles were very different. "We sung together, I'd do the harmony part or whatever but I wasn't in any kind of competition with her as a singer because I wasn't what I consider a great singer . . . I would draw people from the fact that I was a comedienne."

When playing a show together at a race-track in Philadelphia, they saw a horse collapse and die, and were both upset by the experience. Patsy reached into her purse and took out a green speckled capsule which she said would calm June's nerves. When June naively asked what it was, Patsy assured her that it "wasn't much more than an aspirin." June stayed wired for three days but afterwards saw the funny side. June thought her friend had strayed from the straight and narrow by indulging in "All that runnin' and jumpin' and playin'" (Patsy's euphemism for one-night stands on the road), and could be encouraged back onto the righteous path with the aid of some Bible readings.

Ironically not long after she joined Johnny's show he tried to add her to his list of conquests but as with Rose Maddox he was rebuffed, only in Patsy's case, the language used was considerably less ladylike. Patsy confided in June her belief that she would die young and even wrote out some instructions she wished to be carried out after her death. In all too short a time, June had to visit Patsy's family to pass on this information.

Initially asked to appear in a show dubbed "Star Cavalcade", Patsy was a part of the Cash show on and off for over a year and was able to earn up to a considerable $750 per show. Some described her as pure dignity, others as "hillbilly with oomph", but either way audiences adored her. The Star Cavalcade also brought together some of Johnny's old friends including George Jones and Carl Perkins, who often looked back in wonder at these packages where members of the public could see such an impressive array of talent for a dollar. In a letter to a friend Patsy talked about life on the road with the Cash troupe, referring to them as a "swingin' bunch of nuts". Another star turn on the tour was Cline's young prodigy, Barbara Mandrell, of whom Patsy said in her letter, "My ole ears have never heard anything like that. She's 12, plays sax and sings, looks like a blonde doll and boy what a show-woman, she's great."

In July, Patsy co-headlined the First Giant Folk Western-Bluegrass Spectacular with Johnny at the Hollywood Bowl. Despite the presence of many country stars, the actual word "country" was conspicuous by its absence which probably reflected its fall in popularity at the time. Other featured acts were Flatt and Scruggs, Don Gibson (writer of such country classics as 'Sweet Dreams', 'I Can't Stop Loving You' and 'Oh Lonesome Me'), Leroy Van Dyke, Faron Young, The Carter Family and Hank Cochran. Advance sales for the show were disappointing in line with the general decline in country music sales and writer Hugh Cherry recalls that Johnny was in particularly bad shape. "There was a record company cocktail party before the show and Johnny looked really bad, I reckon he was down to about 150 pounds and his face was gaunt and sunken. He couldn't stand or sit still or carry on a conversation for more than about three minutes. His voice was terrible and when it came to the actual show his spot was cut short." At a later show in Stafford, Arizona, a five-year-old Tanya Tucker came backstage to sing for Cash.

A typical show during this time would start with Johnny Western singing Western-themed material followed by June with a combination of comedy and novelty songs. Then came Carl Perkins doing his rockabilly-country-rock'n'roll thang, Barbara Mandrell with steel guitar and saxophone, and then George Jones finishing off the first half of the show. It must have been galling for Perkins to be billed below a twelve-year-old, no matter how talented. Patsy would open the second half followed by the star of the show. One of the problems associated with such a large array of performers was that none of them carried their own band so everybody was backed by The Tennessee Three, which meant an awful lot of boom-chicka-boom for the audience!

Gordon Terry was given some extra money and told to hire some more pickers. One of those he hired was Roy Nichols who went on to become a mainstay of Merle Haggard's band, The Strangers. There was always room for flexibility on the musical front and sometimes Luther swapped his electric guitar for an acoustic and Marshall switched to doghouse bass. Some of the other artists brought along friends to introduce variety in an informal way. George Jones was already developing a fearsome reputation as a heavy drinker and there were doubts about his reliability. All in all, it was a different proposition from today's smoothly drilled concerts, not least for the simple fact of having so many stars on one bill.

During Johnny's set, June would join him for a few songs and some repartee, which often centred around their three year age difference. He would say with a devilish glint in his eye, "I've been listening to you on *The Grand Ole Opry* since I was a little kid." June would come right back with, "Well that's true folks, I'm a little older than him but by the time I gotta hold of him he had so many miles on him I could never catch up with him anyway."

Johnny's voice was often in a bad way and part of Patsy's job was to soft soap the audience by warning that he wasn't well, that he should really be in bed and that he was appearing against doctor's orders *but* he didn't want to let anybody down in best show-must-go-on tradition. When he did turn in a substandard performance the crowd would still give him a good reception and often, because of the pills, his determination and pure animal magnetism, the crowd would still be screaming for an encore even though his voice was barely audible.

Another crowd pleaser was Johnny's remarkably accurate Elvis imitation, something he had included in shows since the Sun days. This involved him combing forward his swept-back black hair and jerking his leg around. For many, this was the high point of the show. Sometimes, Johnny violently threw his guitar over his back, as Presley did, and on occasion when the strap broke, the guitar would go flying towards the back of the stage. It was Johnny's good fortune that Marshall, a world-class power-boat racer with lightning quick reactions, caught it one-handed while trying to play bass.

At the end of 1962, Johnny performed what he saw as his patriotic duty by offering to entertain US troops in Korea. So popular were his shows that the original 20 planned performances had to be increased to 30 in the space of a week, during which time he was seen by 26,000 servicemen and women.

◆ ◆ ◆ ◆ ◆

More recorded material continued to be released in 1962. Sam Phillips put out *All Aboard The Blue Train*, consisting of 12 tracks with railroad themes – a flimsy excuse to get more mileage out of songs like 'Folsom Prison Blues', 'Hey! Porter' and 'There You Go'. From Columbia came *Hymns From The Heart* and an album of more mainstream, non-religious material called *The Sound Of Johnny Cash* which, in a 1973 *Rolling Stone* interview, Cash said was one of his worst albums. Of the 12 songs only two were Cash originals, 'You Remembered Me' and 'Sing It Pretty, Sue', the latter being a retread of 'Ballad Of A Teenage Queen' minus a happy ending. The opening track, 'Lost On The Desert' was a ballad about a convict who returns after serving his sentence to reclaim the stash of money he had hidden in the desert only to be thwarted by the Devil and his own conscience. Cash expressed his dissatisfaction to *Rolling Stone*, "It was a perfectly good song which I re-wrote and there was no need in that."

The producers tried to retain Luther's presence alongside the Nashville Sound heavenly chorus backings; an uneasy compromise in which Luther came off second best with his limited riffs sounding lame and tired despite the addition of some modest sweetening to brighten up the sound. However Johnny was convinced that for all their limitations, Luther and Marshall made a vital contribution to his sound and insisted on using them in the studio when most major artists of his stature might have switched to top session men.

On the traditional 'In Them Old Cottonfields Back Home' Johnny appeared to take his voice to new depths, though he later said in the same interview that he had no business recording that song in the first place, dismissing it as "a kind of showbiz cotton patch song". The album lacked any standout tracks with the strongest numbers being covers such as the Jimmie Rodgers standard 'In The

Jailhouse Now' and the murder ballad 'Delia's Gone'. Columbia also released a number of singles including 'Tennessee Flat Top Box' and 'Bonanza', which added lyrics to the theme music from the popular Western television series. The album's liner notes contained an ironic reference to Johnny's personal life, "When he is not travelling, Johnny lives in Casitas Springs, California with his charming wife and their four young daughters."

◆ ◆ ◆ ◆ ◆

When he did make it home to California, life for Johnny was as manic as ever. As with many of the practical jokes on the road, a consistent feature was the desire to shock members of the public. Such an occasion occurred when Johnny and a couple of friends arranged for a crony to be sitting on a bench in busy Hollywood Boulevard. They roared up in Johnny's Cadillac, dressed gangster-style in dark suits, jumped out, grabbed their accomplice and bundled him into the car, driving off at high speed. What disappointed them was how people in the street seemed to take little notice.

On another occasion the boys reportedly tied up singer Warren Smith (who had recorded the Cash composition 'Rock And Roll Ruby' at Sun) and placed him in the rumble seat of an old 1932 Plymouth Roadster which Cash owned. Carrying an array of guns including a Colt .45 and Winchester rifle, they stopped outside a bank in the style of Bonnie and Clyde. Despite their fearsome appearance the only response they got was a request for directions to Hollywood and Vine from a member of the public.

Johnny would often stomp around the house at night, waking and frightening the children with his unpredictable behaviour. They knew he was their father but he did not behave as their friends' fathers did. The fact that he was rich and famous was of little interest to four young girls who wondered why their dad was never at home. On the occasions Johnny was staying at the house Vivian and the girls were used to hearing him head off into the night – alone or with friends. He would cruise the streets or drive off into the country – Death Valley being a favoured destination – wired and dangerous. Johnny was involved in numerous crashes, leaving a trail of wreckage in his wake.

Ray and Carrie had followed Johnny to California and were running a trailer park in nearby Ojai, which he had bought them as an investment. On one occasion Ray was persuaded to accompany Johnny and his friend Curly Lewis on a nocturnal mission. The trio headed into the Mojave Desert in Johnny's camper van. Ray assumed that when they came to a gate with a sign reading, "No Trespassing. US Naval Proving Grounds – USN Ordinance" Johnny would stop the vehicle. Instead, true to form, he drove right on through. After a few miles they found themselves along a dirt track which led to a road dotted with burnt out military vehicles and what appeared to be bomb craters. In the distance they could see flashing lights belonging to a military vehicle. For Ray Cash the whole experience was a nightmare with memories of his dressing down in Paris all those years ago flashing through his mind.

The Navy officer didn't approach because of the lurking danger of hundreds, possibly thousands, of unexploded bombs and land mines. As in countless incidents before and after, Johnny was utterly reckless with his own and, on this occasion, other people's safety because it was only by chance that they weren't blown to smithereens. Any sign of authority or control seemed to provide an irresistible urge in him to disobey. The outings and adventures continued but after that particular scrape Ray Cash and Curly didn't join in. On one occasion Johnny jumped out of a moving truck just before it went over a 600-foot cliff in California. On another night, crying like a baby, he drove off the road, turned out the headlights and careered over rough and rocky terrain, virtually destroying his jeep in the process. He was also involved in mishaps on the water, which resulted in the sinking of two boats.

Johnny had given up on the elaborate scams required to get pills out of pharmacists and doctors by making contact with pushers who could get him any quantity he wanted, *when* he wanted, with no questions asked. Being strung out, he often paid over the odds. As the Sixties wore on his consumption increased dramatically, sometimes getting through a hundred pills in two days often washed down with beer, vodka or wine. These were powerful drugs; one in particular, the "LA Turnaround", was said to be able to keep a truck driver awake on a round trip from New York to Los Angeles. Johnny's weight continued to fall and he started hearing voices with which he held conversations during his night-time forays.

Like other areas of his life at this time, Johnny's personal finances were a mess. On one occasion he bought some groceries but the shop wouldn't accept a cheque. Incandescent with rage at this perceived slight, he reportedly went back to the house and scooped up some of the piles of cash left lying around the house (his daughters sometimes played with the attractive bundles of notes). He returned to the shop with a bagful of dollar bills, which he handed over to the assistant telling him to take what he needed and to give back the rest. There was about $15,000 dollars in the bag. In another example of financial foolhardiness, Johnny had been persuaded to invest in a race-horse which he named Walk The Line. Unfortunately, it went lame having never won a race and anyway Johnny hardly had the time to actually go and see the nag run. He lost thousands of dollars on the venture.

Surprisingly, Johnny still found time for religion. There were times when he was clean, sometimes days or even weeks on end and at those times his conscience was able to speak to him. He took the opportunity to rededicate his life to God by becoming a member of the Avenue Community Church in Ventura where he met and became friendly with the pastor, Floyd Gressett. However this failed to curb his habit and he was often heavily under the influence of drugs when visiting his pastor. The pastor knew of Johnny's condition and Johnny knew that he knew but the topic was never mentioned. Gressett came to Johnny's rescue, giving him understanding and food in equal measures when the singer's strung out condition verged on serious malnutrition. It's hard to believe that the pastor would have gone to so much trouble for *all* of his congregation.

In his 1975 autobiography, Johnny reflected, "I know that the hand of God was never off me, no matter what condition I was in, for there is no other way to explain the many, many accidents I had." Such an assertion lacked credibility and logic. Did God not have his hand on Johnny Horton and all the others who didn't make it?

◆ ◆ ◆ ◆ ◆

The start of 1963 saw the release of a new album, *The Legend Of John Henry's Hammer*. While not exactly a concept album, the songs centred around themes of railroads, prisoners, chain gangs and hard times for the working man. Unusually the title track written by Johnny and June – an amalgam of a number of traditional ballads - was over eight minutes long. Half dialogue, half song, the man versus machine saga bemoaned the advent of soulless industrialisation as it rendered manual labour redundant.

Johnny provided the rhythm by banging two steel bars together. Such was the depth of his involvement in the task that his hands were bleeding by the end of the session. According to legend, John Henry was a steel driver, his job being to drive holes into mountain walls in which explosives were placed. In Johnny's version, John Henry laid railroad track, driving spikes into ties to hold the rails in place and is pitted against a steam hammer. Though he wins the contest, it costs him his life. Many enjoyed the pathos of the song and it became a regular Cash concert favourite for several years.

Another standout was the Harlan Howard song 'Busted', originally the story of a miner who has lost everything but, in Johnny's hands, he became a washed up, cotton-growing sharecropper. 'Casey Jones' had a certain schoolboy charm and indeed became a favourite on the British radio programme *Children's Favourites*. A Jimmie Rodgers song was inevitable and Johnny gave a strong reading of 'Waiting For A Train', chosen perhaps for its resonance with Johnny's father's experiences during the Depression. Like the other recordings from that era, the album suffered from incongruous, rich backing vocals which were often inappropriate for the material. This was particularly evident on the song 'Chain Gang', another Harlan Howard effort, featuring what sounded like a Sunday school choir singing gaily along with Johnny:

> *I dig that ditch, I chop that corn,*
> *I curse the day that I was born,*
> *I believe it's better for a man to hang,*
> *Than to work like a dog on a chain gang.*

His voice sounded particularly sharp-edged on *The Legend Of John Henry's Hammer* but the impact of the songs which Johnny delivered effectively were blunted by the bland and sugary backings.* It was like pouring treacle on a pepper steak. One song which escaped this treatment was 'Another Man Done Gone', a traditional song adapted and arranged by John Lomax, Alan Lomax and Johnny. It was arranged as an unaccompanied call and response spiritual with Anita Carter on outstanding form and was one of the album's high points. It's unfortunate that Johnny did not do more duets with Anita, though perhaps family politics dictated it was unwise for further collaborations.

The Legend Of John Henry's Hammer won many critical plaudits and a good opportunity to try out the material presented itself in the appropriate setting of San Quentin Prison as Johnny's first show of 1963. Johnny had first played there in 1958, and in the audience was a young Merle Haggard who later described the experience as the turning point in his life. He recollected being impressed that Johnny had received such a good reception from the inmates since he had the challenging job of following a group of strippers. Haggard also remembered that about 40 guitar playing inmates spent the next few weeks trying to master Luther's guitar style.

Despite the plaudits and the consistent record sales, the fact remained that Johnny Cash hadn't had a major hit single since 1959. That would be remedied in 1963, thanks to the magical combination of a dream, the help of an old friend and an inspired partnership.

* Perhaps a future re-release of Cash material from this time could restore the tracks with the obtrusive backing stripped away.

11

WRITTEN BY JUNE CARTER and Merle Kilgore, 'Ring Of Fire' was originally intended for June's sister Anita. Based on a poem, 'Love's Ring Of Fire', written by Bob Johnston, the original title was 'Love's Fiery Ring'. As soon as he heard it, Johnny Cash was keen to record it himself but agreed to hold off for six months to allow Anita's relaxed folk version (as 'Love's Burning Ring Of Fire') a clear run.

Johnny first met Merle Kilgore in the late Fifties and they soon became close friends. Merle was a multi-talented artist, a successful singer who also had the ability to write hit songs, such as 'More And More' for Webb Pierce and 'Johnny Reb' for Johnny Horton. Like Cash, Kilgore got hooked on pills, though in his case they made him talkative, sociable and magnanimous rather than edgy, restless and withdrawn.

The song's inspiration is surely that of June falling hook, line and sinker for Johnny (around 1962 when the song was written). The lyrics suggest that the relationship described was anything but platonic, though the woman who falls, or rather has already fallen, is portrayed as a helpless ingenue:

> *I fell in, to a burning ring of fire*
> *I went down, down, down*
> *And the flames grew higher*
> *And it burned burned burned*
> *The ring of fire.*
>
> *The taste of love is sweet*
> *When hearts like ours meet*
> *I fell for you like a child*
> *Ooh but the fire went wild.*

Johnny had the tune in his head for some time when one night he dreamt about it, though he has always been at pains to point out that there was nothing mystical in the experience. "I dreamed I walked on stage with The Tennessee Three. It was in a coliseum that was overflowing with more than 12,000 people. I stood at centre stage acknowledging the applause and then two trumpeters appeared on my right and kicked off 'Ring Of Fire'."

What stayed with him when he awoke was the idea that the song should be recorded with Mariachi horns to the fore. Country music recording studios did not talk that kind of language in Nashville in the early Sixties, but Johnny felt strongly that that was what the song needed, even though Don Law would not welcome the idea of a brass section. Johnny hadn't forgotten his old producer Jack Clement, and felt it necessary to contact him to help put the song together. Clement was placed in an awkward situation. "When Johnny Cash asks you to do something, you do it but he already had producers at Columbia who weren't going to be too happy about somebody else coming on to their territory," he correctly predicted.

However, Jack went to Nashville and came up with what proved to be a crucial contribution: the simple catchy horn riff which became the song's instantly recognisable trademark. As Clement put it, "I always liked crazy stuff like that and of course when you're Johnny Cash, people expect different stuff and people loved it right away."* It's just as well that the horns took such a prominent part because Cash was not on particularly strong vocal form, singing flat and off-key at times, yet his voice was compulsive and command-ing, winning through with what one writer described as his "emotional mono-tone". Of course he often recorded material where his voice was slightly off-key but for Johnny Cash, rough around the edges never proved to be a dis-advantage. Tommy Cash who was in the studio when the song was recorded talks of the "awesome" sound coming out of those big speakers at Columbia's Studio B. He thought it would be a big hit the first time he heard it. He was right.

The song took off quickly and soon made it to number one in the country charts where it stayed for seven weeks (during a six month run) and 17 in the pop charts, receiving a Columbia Gold Guitar Award. Columbia attempted to cash in on the single's success by putting together *Ring Of Fire – The Best Of Johnny Cash* which included recent releases such as 'I Still Miss Someone', and 'The Big Battle' as well as religious numbers like 'Were You There (When They Crucified My Lord)'. '40 Shades Of Green', a cloyingly sentimental song, may have only been recorded because at the time Johnny was under the mistaken belief that his family line went back to Ireland rather than Scotland. 'The Rebel-Johnny Yuma' was the theme music for a half hour television series

* On the session, Clement played an old guitar he bought in 1951, which now hangs in his studio in Nashville.

called *The Rebel* in which Cash made an appearance.*

The liner notes eschewed the usual blandness of the era and provided an unusually perceptive view of Johnny Cash's appeal. Referring first to the contribution of "The Tennessee Two" (actually The Tennessee Three by this time), Joe Goldberg said, "Their sparse accompaniment strips the outlines of a song to its bare minimum, creating an often bleak atmosphere that is instantly identifiable even before Johnny begins to sing. And when he does, the feeling is increased: his is a dark, lonely sound, often intentionally impersonal, as if to focus attention on the song itself." Johnny rounded off 1963 with another themed album, *The Christmas Spirit*, his first Christmas recording, which contained a mixture of religious and secular songs. By today's standards Cash's output was prolific but in the early Sixties albums could be turned out in next to no time – all the songs for *Now, There Was A Song!* were reportedly recorded in one three hour session.

◆ ◆ ◆ ◆ ◆

It was around this time that Johnny first crossed paths with Bob Dylan. He had been impressed with Dylan's early albums, in particular *The Freewheelin' Bob Dylan* which he played repeatedly, later praising him as "one of the best country singers I'd heard." Johnny invited Bob to stay at his house but they kept missing each other. According to one story, when Dylan made it out to California, he couldn't find Cash's house. Dylan was very much associated with urban folk music although he liked rock'n'roll and some country (being a fan of Hank Thompson). Despite his reputation as a country singer, Cash had credibility in the folk world. Legend has it that he once wandered into a Greenwich Village coffee bar unannounced, sang a few folk ballads and walked out again. This quite possibly apocryphal story spread round the folk contingent and helped to raise Cash in their estimation; he seemed like someone they could identify with.

It was in Greenwich Village that Johnny finally met up with Dylan backstage at a café where Native American musician Peter LaFarge was playing. LaFarge was the son of Pulitzer prize winning author Oliver LaFarge and with the aid of enigmatic and florid prose, he recalled Cash as "ungrateful to his legend, acrawl with nerves, charred by his own poetry leading a mighty wake, and singing down great storms of beauty." The relationship with LaFarge was one destined to produce artistic dividends.

In some respects Dylan and Cash had things in common. They both spoke up for the underdog in society through their music and, in this way, were part of a line that could be traced back through Woody Guthrie, Hank Williams

---

* He also took small parts in other popular Western TV programmes such as *Wagon Train* and *Shotgun Slade*. It was clear where the demand for his acting services was most likely to come from.

and Jimmie Rodgers. They were both anxious not to be stereotyped or irretrievably linked to a particular cause or movement, wanting to be free to associate themselves with issues that moved them, whatever they might be. Above all, they rejected being hailed as spokesmen or figureheads for those issues they pursued.

Additionally, they were not above weaving a few myths around their personal histories. Dylan, a college kid from a fairly well-to-do background, told stories about having been a teenage hobo who had run away from home, cruising around the country in railroad trucks picking up blues tunes from itinerant musicians. Cash was said to be part Cherokee and no stranger to prisons. It was only later that he made it clear that he had no Indian blood and that he had never served a sentence but these stories helped consolidate the picture of the outsider.

If there were similarities there were also contrasts. Johnny's concern for the underdog was based, at least to some extent, on real life experience, and some who came to be his most loyal fans identified with this through their own hardships. The average prisoner at San Quentin Prison would have had little time for a middle-class, well-educated folkie preaching about the struggles of the working man. As critic Robert Shelton said of Dylan in the liner notes to his first album, "He is consciously trying to recapture the rude beauty of a Southern field hand musing in melody on his porch. All the 'husk and bark' are left on his notes and a searing intensity pervades his songs." In the case of Johnny Cash, it was already there.

Cash's songs such as 'Don't Take Your Guns To Town' or 'I Still Miss Someone' were direct narrative stories translated into a readily accessible form. Dylan's lyrics were austere, accusatory and heavily political, with a song like 'With God On Our Side' being a vitriolic indictment of mainstream religion. For some Cash fans Dylan represented everything they despised, a middle-class intellectual whose questionable support was enmeshed in liberal views they found abhorrent. Similarly, for the more cerebral Dylan fan, Cash was some kind of redneck figure. Even if his heart was in the right place, the folkie found his blue-collar homespun philosophy, with its strong religious content, deeply unhip. Supporters on each side found their respective hero's mutual admiration rather mystifying.

George Hamilton IV heard details of one of the earliest meetings, possibly the first, between Cash and Dylan, from June Carter. Dylan had been a fan of Johnny's music since the Sun days, 'I Walk The Line' being a particular favourite. When Dylan heard that Johnny was in New York, he sent a note to say that he would like to meet and it was arranged that he would visit Johnny at his hotel. There was a knock at the door, Johnny let him in, saying, "Hi, how are you?" but Dylan didn't reply. He circled Johnny for some time, "like he was a monument", maintaining his silence, leading Johnny to wonder what kind of weirdo he had allowed into his life. After a few moments he stopped, stared at Johnny and said, "I don't dig you man, I breathe you." For George Hamilton IV, Dylan's view of Cash was "some kind of credit . . . I get the impression that Bob Dylan doesn't waste five seconds on people unless they interest him."

In 1964, Johnny met Dylan backstage after his triumphant appearance at the Newport Folk Festival. He had performed a thoughtfully balanced selection of his own best known songs as well as the Dylan classic, 'Don't Think Twice, It's Alright' and the controversial Peter LaFarge song about the life and death of a Pima Indian, 'The Ballad Of Ira Hayes', which had been brought to him not long before the concert. The Carter Family were starting to enjoy a degree of recognition and Johnny helped by including 'Keep On The Sunny Side' in his set – a song of great personal relevance dealing as it did with a fundamentalist view of the two sides of life. *New York Times* critic Robert Shelton was glowing in his praise for Cash's set. "Johnny Cash, the Nashville star, closed the gap between commercial country and folk music with a masterly set of storytelling songs." Afterwards Johnny was in a state of speed-induced excitement as one observer recalled: "He was really wired; he looked like a puppet whose strings were all tangled up, half cut and half held together and he was just jiggling around." It may well have been Johnny who helped to rescue Dylan's major label contract. There were voices at Columbia who had doubted the wisdom of taking Dylan on in the first place and in some quarters he was referred to as "Hammond's Folly", a reference to John Hammond, the Columbia A&R man who had originally signed Dylan in 1961.

♦ ♦ ♦ ♦ ♦

It was an employee at Columbia Records, Gene Ferguson, who had first alerted Johnny to 'The Ballad Of Ira Hayes', who was immediately drawn to it, particularly when Peter LaFarge helped him to see the character as representative of a people who had suffered oppression over many years. The song was released in June 1964 and unwittingly or otherwise, Johnny provoked the ire of many sections of the country music establishment. These factions had their doubts about Cash in speaking up so passionately for Native Americans and, by implication, criticising the American establishment. Many disc jockeys refused to play the record, it still managed to make it to number three in the country charts, making no impression in the pop charts, though this can partly be attributed to the British Invasion which was in full swing. From today's vantage point, it's difficult to conceive just why the song could arouse such negative feeling until considering that John Wayne was at the height of his all-American popularity, cowboy and Indian films were ubiquitous and there was no doubt in middle American minds who the good guys were. The stories about the historical treatment of Native Americans were just that, so Johnny was opening a potential can of worms by recording the song.

'The Ballad Of Ira Hayes' brought together two important and emotional aspects of American history; namely the latter stages of the Second World War and the issue of Native Americans and their treatment by successive American governments. Ira Hayes was a Pima Indian who enlisted in the Marine Corps at a time when he had hardly travelled outside his reservation. His chief told him that he should be an honourable warrior and be a source of pride to his family and once in the Marines he proved to be a dedicated and steady soldier. His qualities were much needed towards the end of the war as the Americans and Japanese fought a fierce battle for an island that was of strategic importance to both armies. Iwo Jima was only seven and a half miles long yet the battle to gain control of it and in particular its highest point at the top of Mount Suribachi was fought out with such intensity on both sides that by the time the Americans prevailed they had suffered around 30,000 casualties, including nearly 7,000 dead, while virtually all of the 22,000 Japanese defenders perished.

The raising of the flag atop Mount Suribachi has become one of the most famous and enduring images of America's involvement in the Second World War, and made national heroes of the men involved, one of whom was Ira Hayes. On his return to America, Ira was feted by President Eisenhower and everywhere he went people slapped him on the back and shoved a drink into his hand. Returning to normal life proved to be impossible for Ira. When he returned to his reservation and tried to resume everyday life, he was never left alone. Tourists would track him down and ask to have their picture taken next to this heroic figure. Ira was invited to attend military ceremonies such as the dedication of the two Iwo Jima monuments in Washington in 1954 and to support campaigns to raise money through war bonds.

Through it all Ira became increasingly morose about the friends he lost in the campaign (the great majority of his platoon were killed) and took to hiding his grief in alcohol. He drowned in a shallow ditch after a drinking binge in 1955 aged 32 at the same time as a 23-year-old Johnny Cash was enjoying his first success with 'Cry! Cry! Cry!'. 'The Ballad Of Ira Hayes' was a tragic story, as was that of its writer Peter LaFarge who died at the age of 34 in 1965 from causes which have been the subject of debate. The official cause of death was a stroke, though there were rumours of suicide. Johnny's version of the song is emotionally powerful not least in the way he spits out some of the words, with a rare venom unheard on his contemporary studio recordings. The presence of those wretched backing vocals diminishes the overall effect, particularly on a song with such a strong message, and it's difficult to understand how commercial considerations could have got the better of artistic judgement.

Johnny has referred to 'The Ballad Of Ira Hayes' as "the only good song to come out of a war." A true patriot despite the criticisms of successive American administrations referred to in the song, he was infuriated by the response of the music establishment. In what he later described as "One of my wilder moments," he put his head above the parapet and placed a rambling and at times obtuse full-page advertisement in *Billboard*, which nonetheless gave some telling insights into Cash's own view of his outsider status, both in terms of his music and politics:

"DJs, station managers, owners, etc., where are your guts? I'm not afraid to sing the hard bitter lines that the son of Oliver LaFarge wrote . . . Classify me, categorise me – STIFLE me, but it won't work . . . I am fighting no particular cause. If I did it would soon make me a sluggard. For as time changes, I change. You're right! Teenage girls and Beatle-record buyers don't want to hear this sad story of Ira Hayes – but who cries more easily, and who always go to sad movies to cry??? Teenage girls. Some of you 'Top 40' DJs went all out for this at first. Thanks anyway. Maybe the program director or station manager will reconsider. This ad (go ahead and call it that) costs like hell. Would you, or those pulling the strings for you, go to the mike with a new approach? That is, listen again to the record?

"Regardless of the trade charts – the categorising, classifying and restrictions of airplay, this is not a country song, not as it is being sold. It is a fine reason though for the gutless to give it thumbs down. 'Ballad Of Ira Hayes' is strong medicine. So is Rochester – Harlem – Birmingham and Vietnam . . . I've blown my horn now; just this once, then no more. Since I've said these things now, I find myself not caring if the record is programmed or not. I won't ask you to cram it down their throats. But . . . I had to fight back when I realised that so many stations are afraid of 'Ira Hayes'. Just one question: WHY???"

♦ ♦ ♦ ♦ ♦

In response to his written tirade, there were angry comments about Johnny Cash being too sophisticated for the ordinary folk who buy country music. Some of the more traditional quarters called for Johnny to be deprived of his membership of the Country Music Association. One country music magazine editor suggested Cash should do the decent thing and resign on the grounds that, "You and your crowd are just too intelligent to associate with plain country folk . . ." None of this prevented Columbia from releasing a whole album of Native American orientated music, *Bitter Tears – Ballads Of The American Indian* in September 1964, which comprised eight songs of which five were written by Peter LaFarge, and two by Johnny.

The album enhanced the description of Cash as "The first angry man of Country and Western music." According to Johnny, the idea for the album was apparently inspired by a dream in which he was talking to Willie Nelson. After listening to 'The Ballad Of Ira Hayes', Willie suggested he should do a whole album of Indian songs. The marathon opening song, 'As Long As The Grass Shall Grow' indicts American Presidents from Washington to Kennedy for breaking treaties and thus depriving Native Americans of their lands, forcing them to watch helplessly as sacred burial grounds were flooded.

'White Girl' tells the story of an Indian who falls in love with a white girl but though she returns his love and introduces him to her world, she refuses to marry him and in the end he returns to his reservation bitter about having been merely a "White girl's pet", developing, like Ira Hayes, an irresistible thirst for whisky. 'Custer' is a critique of General Custer, a hero for many Americans, which Johnny delivers in bitingly sarcastic tones though some of the lyrics ("I will tell you buster, I ain't no fan of Custer") are banal. He also takes poetic licence in rhyming massacre with victory by pronouncing it "massacree".

Much of the musical accompaniment on the album is noticeably restrained with Johnny's vocals to the fore. On 'The Talking Leaves', the lugubrious female singers provide a dreamy backdrop as Johnny narrates, rather than sings, the story of a father explaining to his son the betrayal of Indians through the white man breaking treaties which just become "White leaves that blow away in the wind." The album sold about 100,000 copies in the months after its release; a reasonable commercial result in the circumstances, though Columbia were no doubt anxious for Johnny, as quid pro quo, to release a more commercial album in the near future. *Bitter Tears* was nominated for a Grammy in the Best Country & Western Album category (though in the event it lost out to a Roger Miller album). It was selected by the Library of Congress as, "truly representative of American Indians", and bolstered the growing view amongst commentators and critics that Johnny Cash was one of the most creative forces in country music. Once more it set him apart from most of the artists he had started out with; the notion of Elvis Presley or Jerry Lee Lewis having the clout and single-minded determination necessary to produce such a work would have been highly improbable.

By 1964, it was becoming increasingly rare for Johnny to spend time in California. When he wasn't on the road, he preferred to stay around Nashville, where of course June lived. Despite June's coyness on the subject, all the evidence points to their relationship being well established by this time, though her marriage and Vivian's adamant resolve that she would not give Johnny a divorce for religious reasons made things difficult to say the least. It would have been naturally unthinkable for Johnny to have visited June's home, where she lived with Rip Nix and her two daughters, so he spent increasing amounts of time at June's parents' house instead.

Maybelle and Eck Carter were fond of Johnny but they were fearful of his involvement with drugs, especially since, early on, he told Eck of his love for June. With mixed feelings Eck merely expressed the wish that the two of them would be able to "work it out", but the situation was worrying, not least because both Maybelle and June had spent time on the road with Hank Williams and had seen at close quarters the misery drug abuse caused.

In addition to washing Johnny's clothes and ironing his shirts, June found the pills he hid in dressing rooms and hotel rooms and flushed them down the toilet. This led to some furious exchanges but it was Johnny's devotion to June that prevented him from expelling her from his life. During the time when any kind of public acknowledgement of their relationship was not possible Johnny became more and more a part of the Carter family in Nashville. Maybelle and Eck understood that Johnny needed support and they made sure that there was always a room for him whenever he wanted it. They even remained tolerant when he turned up in the middle of the night and simply broke the front door down in his impatience to get in.

Friends of Maybelle and Eck recall the impact of Johnny's unexpected arrivals. Board games were popular in the Carter household and sometimes, just when they were lost in concentration, the door would burst open and as Minnie Snow, a great friend of Maybelle, put it, "A lot of those games would end suddenly when Johnny Cash arrived, sweating and pale, his eyes wide as flapjacks, knees trembling and arms jerking." Another friend, Dixie Deen, who had been brought up in England and who married singer-songwriter Tom T Hall, recalled that he would pace the floor, "higher than a kite" while Maybelle tried to talk him into going to bed. Pop (as Ezra was generally known) would try to calm everyone down by saying that the Lord had his hand on Johnny Cash and that "nothing gonna happen to him", though given the evidence of his state, this was surely said more in hope than expectation.

Talking about drugs some years later Johnny was not exaggerating when he said, "I'd been converted when young but I gave my body to the devil and I really went through hell." For Mother Maybelle the craziness of the situation was not entirely new since, in the Forties, she had provided sanctuary for Audrey Williams when Hank was going crazy and threatening to shoot her. The Carter house did become like a second home for Johnny. He went fishing with Maybelle and even curbed his tendency to swear. If he jabbed himself with a fish hook and an expletive slipped out, Johnny would feel deeply embarrassed even though the only reprimand he ever got was a disapprovingly prim, "Oh John."

As for Eck he introduced Johnny to myriad books from his large collection, many on the subject of religion. As the two spoke, they became closer and Johnny felt that he became reconnected to God through these conversations. For Maybelle and Eck the idea of a famous singer being interested in one of their daughters was not new. Elvis Presley had fallen for Anita some years before and his infatuation persisted despite some rebuffs. On one occasion, Elvis turned up late for a show and the Carters had to fill time. He eventually turned up and went out on stage, but when he broke a string and asked for a replacement guitar, Anita handed him the guitar, ran her finger down the side of his sweaty face, licked it, and pretended to gag.

On another occasion, after a show before which he had been feeling unwell, he headed for the Carters' car and fell into Anita's lap and pretended to faint. She started screaming that he was about to die and Colonel Tom Parker, who had wanted Elvis to go out and sign autographs, panicked because he was worried that there might really be a problem with "his boy". Maybelle signed Elvis in to hospital but next morning Presley turned up in perfect health, the whole thing having been a ruse aimed, unsuccessfully, at arousing Anita's sympathy. Johnny Cash had no need of such tricks in his pursuit of June.

Apart from June's involvement as part of Johnny's touring troupe, Mother Maybelle and her daughters featured on the album *Blood Sweat And Tears*, receiving a prominent credit, and Anita gave an outstanding performance in her duet with Johnny on 'Another Man Done Gone'. It's been suggested over the years that the involvement of the Carters was detrimental to Johnny's career and that as soon as June became part of the touring show, she manipulated things so that the rest of her family got to be involved in Johnny's reflected glory. Johnny specifically rejected this view in his 1997 autobiography. "From day one . . . it was a great feeling for me to have their support out there on the stage, a great honour and opportunity."

Although Mother Maybelle had given a well received performance at the 1962 Newport Folk Festival, it was only when Johnny asked her to join June as part of his troupe that Maybelle felt secure enough to give up her nursing job, something Johnny was proud to help bring about. An album of her own material was released by Columbia the following year, something which would not have occurred without Johnny's influence. For him, the presence of Maybelle, one of the original members of The Carter Family, as part of his troupe lent a new layer of historical depth to his concerts. For Maybelle it was a case of bringing her music to a larger audience and making it relevant once more. And, of course, financial security.

It was an arrangement that suited them both, though the idea of Maybelle performing alongside electric guitars and drums was a prospect which appalled some purists who reckoned AP Carter must have been turning in his grave. For Johnny Cash, the welcoming and forgiving embrace of the Carter family during his personal struggles was one of a number of factors that almost certainly helped to save his life which was in danger of spiralling completely out of control.

12

IN 1964, Johnny's younger brother Tommy got first-hand experience of how Johnny's business affairs were being affected by the singer's unpredictable behaviour. Johnny hired Tommy to open an office in Nashville's Music Row to run two of his publishing companies, JC Music and South Wind Music. As usual Johnny's wish was to keep things in the family and where possible he would do his best to ensure that job positions were filled by relations, friends or musicians who had supported him over the years. Tommy was heavily involved in the arrangements of decorating the office with gold carpets and garish orange and black wallpaper.

However, once the new Nashville office was up and running, Johnny would regularly let himself in at night and tear the place up; throwing filing cabinets onto the floor, smashing the coffee pot and generally leaving the office looking as if it had been ransacked by an amateur burglar on speed. Sometimes Tommy would come in at nine to find the door had been left wide open, so that anybody could have come in and stolen all the equipment and business files. He did his best to make Johnny see reason. "You hired me to run this office and it's all about your image and my image and we're proud of this office, so please don't come in here and do this again."

Johnny was invariably apologetic but, despite assurances to the contrary, similar incidents happened repeatedly. Patience exhausted, Tommy eventually decided to quit working for his brother. Did something about the neatness and order of the office rile him, as Tommy speculated? Nowadays, Johnny explains away his behaviour to the drugs. Initially his family hadn't appreciated the seriousness of his condition, being dazzled by JR's success, and thought, like Johnny himself, that he had control. Once he was famous they didn't see that much of him at all. However, on visits home it gradually dawned what kind of condition he was in. It got to the stage where the family couldn't see how he could live much longer but any entreaties to clean up his act fell on deaf ears, as Tommy puts it, "Until a person wants help they're not going to get it. They have to decide they want to change. All we could do was tell him we loved him and that's what we did."

◆ ◆ ◆ ◆ ◆

Meanwhile, Johnny further increased his musical road show towards a permanent troupe of performers under the general heading of 'The Johnny Cash Show', which was easier to manage than an endless line of package tours involving an ever changing variety of performers. Along with Mother Maybelle and her daughters were The Statler Brothers, a gospel-flavoured harmony quartet from Staunton, Virginia who were originally known as The Kingsmen.* The group only featured two real brothers, Don and Harold Reid (who delivered the group's distinctive bass vocal), the other members being Lew deWitt and Phil Balsley. They had a strong interest in religious music, an obvious attraction for Johnny Cash who they originally met in the late summer of 1963. Harold approached Johnny after a show in Roanoke and explained the kind of music they performed and succeeded in getting an agreement in principle that The Kingsmen might be able to appear as part of a future Johnny Cash show.

It actually took more than six months of uncertainty before the quartet made their first appearance with Johnny and in the meantime they had changed their name to The Statler Brothers, having apparently taken the name Statler from a brand of tissue paper. It was another case of Johnny Cash helping less well-known artists and, in the case of the Statlers, shifting them from local celebrity status to national prominence. They were well aware of the significance of the deal for their careers and as Don Reid put it, "When we got the news that Johnny finally wanted us, we were the four drunkest guys you ever seen in your life."

Johnny's appreciation of Bob Dylan's work was much in evidence around the mid-Sixties and in October 1964 Johnny released a pounding version of 'It Ain't Me Babe' as a duet with June. Columbia accompanied the release with a poster featuring close up photographs of Johnny and Bob Dylan (in Cash's case a rather unflattering profile) with the rather laboured slogan, "A new single from Bob Dylan on a new single sung by Johnny Cash." In their review *Billboard* commented that, "Cash duets with a mystery girl", indicating that despite her very obvious presence as part of the live shows, June's general profile was still low. The single reached its highest position, number four, in January 1965 and two months later was featured on the album *Orange Blossom Special* along with two other Dylan songs, 'Don't Think Twice, It's Alright' and 'Mama, You've Been On My Mind' (of which, Dylan said, "It's an old tune based on another old tune by Bill Monroe").

The album only featured two songs written by Cash, the acoustic 'You Wild

* No relation to the Pacific Northwest Sixties group who had a hit with 'Louie Louie'.

Colorado', and 'All Of God's Children Ain't Free', a song with a combined religious and political message which succeeded in arousing the opprobrium of those who had berated 'The Ballad Of Ira Hayes'. Cash's vocal performances were mixed. On the title track he sounded weaker than usual, possibly the result of his abusive lifestyle, and on others, particularly 'Mama, You've Been On My Mind', his pitching and timing are way off at times. 'Don't Think Twice, It's Alright' suffers in comparison to the Dylan original; Cash's limited and inflexible vocals were not really capable of doing justice to the song's nuances. In addition, Luther's same old riffs detract from the song just as the gentle picking on Dylan's version enhanced it. Cash sounds more assured on the murder ballad 'The Long Black Veil', the Harlan Howard prison song, 'The Wall', yet another outing for AP Carter's take on 'Wildwood Flower' and 'All Of God's Children Ain't Free'.

'It Ain't Me Babe' and 'When It's Springtime In Alaska (It's Forty Below)' were duets with June though Anita would have been a far better vocal foil for Cash. The song also featured Mexican brass à la 'Ring Of Fire' but it added little, serving merely to clutter the production. Johnny preceded a sentimental version of 'Danny Boy' with a nostalgic spoken narrative about his father Ray via his involvement in the First World War, his courting of Carrie and working the land. It may not be Cash's best album but it did contain a wide range of material covering the secular, the religious and the current. Some of the songs went on to become concert standards for years to come. The album reached number three in the country charts and just scraped into the pop Top 50. The single 'It Ain't Me Babe' gave Johnny his first British hit though it only just made it into the Top 30 during a run which lasted two months.

The lengthy liner notes were entirely devoted to information on Ervin Rouse who wrote the song 'Orange Blossom Special' (but who never actually travelled on the train which had inspired the name). Speaking in 1994, Johnny said that a lot of people who had previously recorded the song invariably claimed the arrangement because nobody knew who wrote it originally. It was Mother Maybelle who told him it was Ervin Rouse and that the last she'd heard he was in Florida. Johnny called a Florida DJ called Cracker Jim Brooker who said he knew Ervin and that he lived with the Seminoles out in the swamp, making swamp buggies for a living. Jim put out an announcement on air, "Hey Ervin, you call me and I'll give you Johnny Cash's number, he wants to talk to you."

An hour later Ervin called, got Cash's number and was asked if he would appear with Johnny at an upcoming show in Miami. According to Johnny, Ervin and his brother Gordon turned up for the show in the clothes they worked in. Johnny described Ervin as a sweet, humble man and his total lack of commercial acumen – he openly confessed that he had no way of proving he wrote the song – appealed to him. 'Orange Blossom Special' became a staple of Johnny's repertoire for years, though it did give him something of a commercial dilemma. A vital component of the song was the harmonica breaks, but the Cash troupe didn't have anyone who could play harmonica. Rather than hire a harmonica player, Johnny learned to play it himself, or at least sufficiently well to do that number and his use of two harmonicas which he threw into the audience after the song became one of the most eagerly anticipated sections of his shows.

◆ ◆ ◆ ◆ ◆

The gruelling tour schedule continued unabated and by the mid-Sixties, Johnny was performing around 300 shows a year. Most of the time, he concentrated his efforts on America (though the troupe also performed shows across the border in Canada) getting to know the vast continent like the back of his hand. As he put it in his 1997 autobiography, "I can wake up anywhere in the United States, glance out the bus window, and pinpoint my position to within five miles . . . I've been everywhere, man. Twice."

The only reason Johnny went back to California, where he felt he never belonged, was to see his daughters, but his frazzled condition meant that he was in no shape to spend any quality time with them. His eccentric behaviour included erecting a ten-foot aluminium cross on a hill behind the house which was lit up at Christmas and Easter, and a powerful amplifier on top of the house, blasting out Christmas carols at maximum volume during the season of goodwill. The locals were divided in their response; some thinking it quite a thrill to have such a colourful neighbour, others calling on police assistance to silence the racket. Did Johnny think he was above the law? Why did someone so concerned about the plight of others do things without showing the slightest regard for those around him? Was it the result of immaturity mixed up with money, fame and adulation? Did he think his daughters would appreciate being the centre of attention in this way? They certainly hated the taunts of "Cash trash" they received at school. Of course it would be up to Vivian to deal with these little traumas.

With all this in mind, it's surprising that Rosanne Cash ever became involved in the music business. In a recent interview with *Country Music People*, she said, "When I was a kid, looking at fame, I thought it was the most terrible thing that could happen to a person. It seemed to keep you away from home and make you crazy, and break up your relationships. Why would anybody want that?"

Not all of the scrapes Johnny got into were self-inflicted. According to one story, he was driving a tractor in the grounds of his property, clearing brush behind the house, when he opened up a rattlesnake's nest. Johnny has a morbid fear of snakes despite encountering so many in his childhood, and jumped out of the tractor which eventually came to a halt. However, a stray spark from the engine started a fire in the brush which was extremely dry. Johnny ran to the house but it was locked and Vivian didn't hear him knocking because she was listening to Elvis records at full volume. In a panic, Johnny broke a window to get in, severely cutting his arm in the process. When the fire engines arrived,

Johnny loaded the family into his car in order to take them to safety but, as he drove off, the car's bumper got caught in a fire hose jerking it out of the fire engine, causing Johnny to lose control of the car.

Ironically the incident which proved to be most costly came about as the result of an accident. Johnny had a camper van, with blacked out windows to allow sleep during daylight hours, which he used for many road trips into the countryside. On one occasion he had been driving around the Los Padres National Wildlife Refuge not far from Ventura and, aware of a squeaking sound coming from one of the wheels, he pulled off the road near Sespe Creek, where, apparently, oil from a cracked bearing dripped onto the wheel, now red hot, immediately setting fire to the grass. Within no time, a major blaze was underway which Johnny was powerless to control. The fire took over 400 fireman, eight aerial tankers and four helicopters two days to extinguish. The real tragedy was that the area was home to an endangered species of bird, the California condor, and only nine out of 53 previously recorded condors remained in their refuge. The camper van was destroyed and Johnny ended up sleeping rough before eventually hitching a ride home; having declined an earlier offer of a lift in the back of a truck loaded with occupied beehives.

This was just the start of his troubles as Cash, along with the vehicle's owners Don and Reba Hancock (Johnny's brother-in-law and sister), were sued by the US Government over the incident, not only for starting the fire but also failing to keep the vehicle in good repair and failing to alert the authorities about the fire. The lawsuit sought a total $125,000 as compensation for the ravaged hillside ($123,801 for the expenses involved in extinguishing the fire and $1,325 for re-seeding the burnt land).[*]

When news of the court case became public, the Indian Land Rights Association expressed a desire to help their champion and indicated the possibility of filing claims on the land, having taken the first step of electing Johnny as their president, in the hope of thwarting the proposed action. However, the case proceeded and Johnny later conceded that he was belligerent and unreasonable in dealing with the authorities, showing no remorse for the fire's impact on an endangered species. He generally gave sarcastic and wilfully unhelpful answers to questions which echoed the flippant responses he gave when being interviewed on television before the disastrous Carnegie Hall show.

"Did you start this fire?"

"No. My truck did and it's dead so you can't question it."

♦ ♦ ♦ ♦ ♦

Although Johnny claimed the fire was an unavoidable accident, he had been aware of the wheel problem for some time, though how he or anyone else could

[*] Around a million dollars in today's money.

be sure of the exact cause of the fire, given that the vehicle was quickly destroyed, is not clear. The fact that Johnny walked away and started fishing, feigning ignorance of the inferno raging nearby is not suggestive of a responsible reaction but of course people on drugs don't tend to act responsibly. George Hamilton IV, an understanding and forgiving man, brushes aside criticisms of Johnny over such incidents, explaining, "When he behaved badly and let people down, he really wasn't being himself."

The supreme irony of the incident is that someone with such a deep love of nature should cause serious harm to an endangered species and, even if it was a complete accident, expressed little or no regret. In his introduction to the 1967 annual of *The Legend* (The Johnny Cash Society magazine), Johnny played down the incident while taking the opportunity to restate his innocence. The case had clearly been dragging on and it appeared that some new stage in the process had reared its ugly head with Johnny referring contemptuously to, "This little renewed incident with the Federal Government." After informing his fans that he had to fly to Santa Barbara to give a deposition, he finished by saying, "I sure hope we win."

In the event the case dragged on for some years and was eventually settled out of court in 1969. According to his 1997 autobiography, Cash paid out the full amount sought, which most contemporary reports quoted as $82,000. The terms of payment consisted of $10,000 to be paid immediately with the balance payable by quarterly instalments of $3,600. In the end, after lengthy negotiations and a further court case, Johnny eventually recovered the money from his own insurance company, arguing successfully in court that the damage was covered under the homeowner's policy for his nearby residence.

◆ ◆ ◆ ◆ ◆

One of the more surprising and incongruous moments in Johnny's recording career occurred in 1965 when he recorded 'Thunderball' – one of a number of contenders for the title song of that year's James Bond film. Like 'Five Minutes To Live', recorded in an attempt to cash in on a film, the song was not one of Johnny's most distinguished efforts, sounding more like a theme to a low budget television Western than an international thriller. Unsurprisingly his offering wasn't chosen, the honour going instead to the more conventional Tom Jones.

That Johnny's version of the song was not chosen came as no surprise at all. For all his popularity in America, he was not able to cross international boundaries in the way that Elvis did. Presley's appeal was across the board but although Johnny Cash built up a large and loyal following in many parts of the world, much of his musical and cultural references were so firmly rooted in American folklore that there was an inevitable limit to his popularity.

In the summer of 1965, Johnny threw himself headlong into the controversy that erupted at the Newport Folk Festival when Bob Dylan had the audacity to "go electric" for his spot. Although the folk revival of the early Sixties was part of a freer expression of left-wing political views and the promulgation of liberal cultural values in the wake of the McCarthy era, the Newport ethos was musically conservative with an unwritten but widely observed rule book. Later, such constraints would attract contempt from commentators who talked of the artists at Newport "playing protest ditties" to like-minded liberal audiences and of "preaching to the converted".

One of the ultimate breaches of folk etiquette was the electric guitar. Even the great Muddy Waters was asked to cast aside the electric blues he had been delighting audiences with for years, and serve up a more "authentic" country blues style. Dylan wouldn't play ball and his performance caused great tension between the traditionalists and the modernists with invective hurled from both sides. Johnny Cash, whose 10-year track record of different musical styles made him difficult to categorise ("I play Johnny Cash music," he was fond of saying), was incensed by the attacks on his friend. In another of his wilder moments, Cash placed a piece of prose in *Broadside*, the magazine of the alternative folk music scene, in protest at what he perceived to be a reactionary attack on one of the great talents of the age.

His outpourings kicked off with an obscurity which Dylan himself might have appreciated. "I got hung but didn't choke, Bob Dylan slung his rope." As it went on however the message became clear, "Came a Poet Troubadour, singing fine familiar things. Sang a hundred thousand lyrics, Right as Rain, Sweet as Sleep, Words to thrill you . . . And to kill you. Don't bad-mouth him, till you hear him, Let him start by continuing, He's almost brand new, SHUT UP! . . . AND LET HIM SING!" When specifically asked in 1966 if he was a fan of Dylan's harder-edged work such as *Bringing It All Back Home*, *Highway 61 Revisited* and *Blonde on Blonde*, Johnny diplomatically stated they were all right but that he preferred Dylan's earlier albums.

A measure of the impact that Dylan's work made on Johnny's career in the Sixties had been shown by the release of his 1963 single, 'Understand Your Man'. Besides its folkie feel and Dylanesque phrasing, the song utilised almost exactly the same melody as Dylan's 'Don't Think Twice, It's Alright'. Perhaps wisely, Cash chose not to suggest the song when the two men recorded together later in the decade.

◆ ◆ ◆ ◆ ◆

Although Johnny was always welcome at Maybelle and Eck Carter's home, he felt that he should have his own base in Nashville and so he rented a small, first floor, one bedroom unit in Madison, off Gallatin Road on the outskirts of the city. Despite its modest proportions, he decided to invite a friend with whom to share this "crash pad". To the objective observer, the name of Waylon Jennings would not have been the most sensible choice since, as like Johnny, he had a well developed pill habit at the time. Ironically it was June Carter who had introduced the two of them some years previously, when Waylon was working as a disc jockey. Waylon and June's paths crossed a number of times after and, when they met in 1964, Waylon dryly observed (in *Waylon,* his 1996 autobiography) that "She had John in tow."

Interestingly, Waylon observed that during a subsequent meeting when the subject of sharing an apartment was first raised, Johnny told him he was "Experiencing some trouble at home trying to get June to marry him," though at that time the more immediate problem was trying to get Vivian to divorce him. Still somewhat in awe of Johnny, whose first hit 'Cry! Cry! Cry!' had been one of his favourite songs as a teenager, Waylon was unsure of the advisability of sharing an apartment, not because of his wild reputation – Waylon could match him punch for punch and pill for pill on that score – but rather because they still weren't close friends by this stage and the proposition was that there would be two king-size beds in the one bedroom in the apartment.

Mother Maybelle heard of the proposed idea and thought that the two of them would be "good for each other" which proves that age doesn't always bring with it wisdom. According to Waylon the two of them "were feeling uncommonly sorry for themselves," each being in the process of trying to get rid of a wife while trying to develop a relationship with another woman. In his autobiography, Waylon gave an evocative account of Johnny's domestic abilities when describing his attempts at cooking, "He'd be stirring biscuits and gravy, dressed in one of his thin black gabardine suits, and the flour would be rising in clouds of white dust all over him." Mother Maybelle and June cleaned up after them now and then and June would flush any pills she found down the toilet.

For such macho men, they were absolutely hopeless when it came to looking after themselves on a domestic level; a result of going on the road and becoming successful at an early age meant they could get other people to do all the tedious little chores like cleaning and cooking. On occasion, when locking themselves out of the apartment, they simply kicked in the door to gain entry. Even though they both took large amounts of speed, they were strangely reticent about discussing it even though each knew what the other was up to. They certainly never shared their supplies, though on one occasion when his own supply ran out, Johnny broke into Waylon's new Cadillac and ripped out the glove compartment in a desperate though fruitless attempt to locate a hidden stash. Waylon and Johnny were two peas in a pod but, in fact, due to the large amount of time devoted to touring and partying, they did not spend a great deal of time together at the apartment. As Waylon said, "We usually only slept there as a last resort." Despite or perhaps because of the shared experiences in the apartment, Waylon went on to become one of Johnny's closest friends.

13

ON THE MORNING of October 3, 1965, having wound down a tour with a show in Dallas the previous night, the various members of the troupe were due to fly off to multiple destinations, in Johnny's case to Los Angeles, for a little rest and recuperation. As they assembled in reception, they learned that Johnny had checked out of the hotel at 2 am without having gone to bed. After phoning some of his friends and contacting various airlines in a vain attempt to track Johnny down, there was nothing further they could do.

On the following Monday, June got a call in Nashville telling her that Johnny had been arrested at El Paso International Airport trying to smuggle a large quantity of drugs into the country as he was returning from Mexico and that he would shortly be appearing in court to answer charges arising from the incident. It seems the disc jockey who broke the news to her had worked out that she was to all intents and purposes his next of kin. Johnny was doubtless aware that Ciudad Juarez, just across the Rio Grande from El Paso, was an easy place to score. His habit ate away at him as he recalled in his 1975 autobiography, "I'd talk to the demons, and they'd talk back to me – and I could *hear* them. I mean they'd say, 'Go on John, take 20 more milligrams of Dexedrine, you'll be all right.'"

At El Paso, Johnny was found with 668 Dexedrine and 475 Equanil tablets and thousands of dollars in cash stuffed in his pockets and the inside of a guitar he had bought in Mexico. He was either totally confident about not getting caught or else he *wanted* to get caught, a not uncommon occurrence amongst addicts who, realising that things are out of control, take bigger risks in the subconscious hope that they get caught and referred to the appropriate authorities for help. Although Johnny stood out like a sore thumb, the actual reason he was targeted was because the police thought he might have been looking to buy more serious drugs like heroin and they were keen to get leads to help nail some major pushers they'd been after for some time. Johnny had the jolting experience of being held in jail overnight and, at his arraignment, the press reported that he had become agitated by the close attention of reporters in the court and tried to grab their cameras.

Vivian got to hear the story from her mother-in-law Carrie Cash, who June had phoned, and on December 28, she accompanied Johnny, Don Law and the Reverend Floyd Gressett to El Paso for Johnny's next court appearance in the hope that the presence of this worthy triumvirate might persuade the judge to show mercy. In his defence, Johnny explained that after performing two weeks of one-night stands, he'd been so utterly exhausted that he was past caring about his actions. A number of testimonials were handed to US District Judge DW Suttle, one of which was from the Department of Justice praising Cash for his work entertaining the troops. Before sentence was passed Johnny said, "I would like to ask for leniency from the court. I know that I have made a terrible mistake and I would like to go back to rebuilding the image I had before this happened."

Johnny was let off with a $1,000 fine and a suspended 30-day jail sentence; his response being a simple "Hallelujah". One of the most memorable aspects of the whole episode, and one which must have come as a shock to his more conservative fans, was a widely published photograph of a handcuffed Cash, walking between two police officers. In the shot, all three men are sporting swept-back hair, dark suits and sunglasses – resembling a Johnny Cash look-alike contest at first glance.

Johnny's misdemeanour had further, even more bizarre, consequences. A press photograph of Vivian taken as she was walking down the steps of the court building in El Paso made her look remarkably like a negro woman. The picture found its way into *Thunderbolt* – a magazine published by an organisation similar in its beliefs to the Ku Klux Klan and possibly a front for that organisation. In the magazine and handbills which included reproductions of the photograph, Vivian was described as a "negress" and Johnny was said to be the father of "mongrelised" children. Apparently, country singer Porter Wagoner first saw the handbills when he was playing a show in Ponchatoula and brought them to Johnny's attention.

Johnny was incandescent with rage and promptly announced his intention to sue for defamation adding that any money he received would be given to the national defence budget. Johnny made it clear beyond question that he had nothing against black people, citing what he then understood to be his own Indian Irish ancestry which made him "a real mongrel", but explained, "What I resent is the attempt at defamation of character and the attempt to make my children ashamed they were born."

In expressing his support Ernest Tubb stated, "Although I can only speak for myself, I think Nashville's country music people will rally around Johnny. I'm behind him 100% on this; this is a vicious thing involving Johnny and Vivian and their children and it makes me sick." Referring to the prospective court action he declared, "I hate that it even had to be dignified but he had to do something to protect his family." In the event, Cash never did take any action because of legal advice to the effect that an action against such organisations as the Klan or the publishers of *Thunderbolt* would be likely to fail, particularly as it was not clear exactly who had published the claims about Vivian.

Johnny believes that the photograph of Vivian which appeared in *Thunderbolt* had been tampered with to make her complexion appear darker, though virtually anybody looking at the original of the photograph who did not know otherwise would almost certainly think the woman in the picture was black. A possible reason for the picture being doctored was a desire on the Klan's part to get back at Cash for his support of one of their pet hates, American Indians. The Klan made a death threat against Johnny prior to an appearance in Greenville, South Carolina and one night in Nashville, a car pulled up outside the Columbia studios on Music Row where Johnny was recording with Don Law and a mystery man asked if Johnny Cash was in the building. Nothing came of it but Johnny spent a nervous night at Don Law's apartment clutching a shotgun Eck Carter had lent him. Mother Maybelle gave what comfort and understanding she could as Johnny raged about the slur on his "babies". Speaking years later about the ups and downs of his career, he reserved some of his most bitter vitriol for the Klan. "It's good to know who hates you, and it's good to be hated by the right people. The Klan is despicable, filthy, dirty, unkind. It's a shame sometimes that we have all these freedoms, 'cos freedom allows them to exist. I'd love to see them all thrown in prison."

Johnny ran into other problems in 1965. During an appearance at *The Grand Ole Opry*, he became irritated when he was unable to adjust a microphone stand and, losing his cool completely, attacked the footlights with the stand, smashing more than 40 of them in the process. Before he went on, he had been warned about his failure to adhere to the *Opry*'s rules about performing a set number of Saturdays each year and this may have shortened his fuse. According to some reports, his response to the admonition was that it didn't matter because it would be his last night at the *Opry* anyway. It was a terrible way to treat such a revered institution, not to mention the paying public. (Years later he tried to play it down joking that "Those lights were hurting my eyes," and on another occasion he claimed that he "was just having fun".)

When Johnny came off stage the manager Jim Denny told him he wouldn't be able to use him in the future and, while Denny's decision was completely understandable, it also fuelled Johnny's simmering resentment that his "rocking sound" had never really been accepted by many at the *Opry*, despite his respect and reverence for the artists. Johnny talked June into lending him her car and in a fury of rage and self-recrimination, he wrapped the car around a utility pole causing about $2,000 worth of damage, as well as breaking his nose and knocking out four of his teeth. Over the years, Johnny crashed many cars, breaking over 20 bones, as he later ruefully reflected, "It's the grace of God that one of those bones wasn't my neck." The police were involved in this particular incident though the reporting officer, one Charles Hay, despite writing "none" under details of driving licence, did not charge Johnny with any offence. The owner of the car was listed as Mrs June Carter Nicks [*sic*], she of course still being married to Rip Nix. Johnny was invariably fearful of telling her about such incidents but she always got the calls in the end.

Johnny was fortunate that a record executive, with whom he'd had a meeting earlier in the evening, found him, took him to hospital and put him up for the night. Despite his injuries, Johnny stayed awake for hours listening to records and taking pills, uppers plus painkillers from the hospital, washed down with beer. He eventually passed out, possibly with the assistance of the barbiturates which were a necessary antidote to the uppers, but when he showed no obvious signs of life, his host began to panic. The man phoned Luther Perkins who, having seen it all before, said, "Put him to bed. He'll sleep for 24 hours. If he wakes up he's alive. If he doesn't he's dead."

Johnny woke up but missed a show, adding to his well-established reputation for unreliability.

◆ ◆ ◆ ◆ ◆

Back on the recording front Johnny released a single, 'The Sons Of Katy Elder', the theme to a Western starring John Wayne. Johnny's intense fascination for the history of the American West culminated in the release of a twenty-track double album, *Johnny Cash Sings Ballads Of The True West*. The idea had been suggested in 1961 by Don Law, who saw Johnny as a natural for such a project. Johnny immersed himself in a series of publications such as *True West* and *Western Publication* as well as books by expert authors, including John Lomax and Carl Sandburg, which gave him much background material for the project. However, what he found most helpful was personally talking with people who had direct experience of the West and its folklore and music. Tex Ritter and Peter LaFarge provided invaluable support and encouragement; Ritter in particular helping him to narrow down a list of 300 songs.

He also received visits from folk singer "Ramblin'" Jack Elliott who, as Johnny put it in his sleeve notes, advised him "when he didn't know gee from haw". None of this expertise improved the quality of the cover photo which caught Johnny resembling nothing so much as a caricature baddie in a low budget Western. His moustache lends a notably seedy air and the weight loss from his drug intake was also apparent. A few titles – 'Bury Me Not On The Lone Prairie', 'The Ballad Of Boot Hill' and 'I Ride An Old Paint' – give a flavour of the album. Being Johnny Cash he did also find room for the occasional leftfield song such as 'Twenty Five Minutes To Go' by former *Playboy* cartoonist and idiosyncratic songwriter, Shel Silverstein, about a man standing on the gallows with the clock ticking, bemoaning his fate and the fact that "The whole town's waiting just to hear me yell."

'The Streets Of Laredo', according to Johnny's liner notes, was "A British tune, the original is supposed to be about a man who died of syphilis in a London hospital." He goes on to say that, "The second and third verses (author unknown) are from 'Cowboy Songs' by John Lomax." The provenance of many Western songs was often obscure and it was common for singers to describe them as "arranged by" themselves. It was in this way that AP Carter came to be credited with many folk songs performed by The Carter Family, though it's also true to say that it was he who had put a great deal of work originally into discovering them and coming up with authentic arrangements. On this album Johnny claimed the arrangement of six songs for himself. Old-time country music expert Brian Golbey points out that including songs which were many years old added an authentic slant to Johnny's output and, of course, also served to revive songs which were long forgotten.

The sleeve notes also provide a glossary of Western terms for the uninitiated from which it is learned that "High lonesome" means "Big drunk" and that a "Judas steer" is "A steer trained to lead the others to the slaughterhouse, then return to lead another bunch." Though it would not be a commercial success, the loose arrangement between Cash and Columbia was such that they would support such ventures so long as he kept on delivering commercial hits as well. Attempts were also made to cash in on his popularity abroad and in October 1965, Johnny recorded 'Wer Kennt Den Weg' – a German version of 'I Walk The Line'.

＊ ＊ ＊ ＊ ＊

In 1966, the Johnny Cash show acquired one other member who would solidify a classic line-up capable of putting on a show with nothing more than honest-to-goodness folk, country, gospel and rockabilly in a way that would satisfy audiences around the world for years. He had hit the jackpot early on but after the initial eruption caused by 'Blue Suede Shoes', Carl Perkins' career stalled and never fully recovered after the serious injuries he sustained in a car accident on the way to a Perry Como show rehearsal. His move to Columbia with Johnny was short-lived and unsuccessful. Though he had sold two million copies of 'Blue Suede Shoes', in many people's minds, the song came to be associated with Elvis. One of his brothers suffered injuries in the accident from which he later died and Carl found solace in alcohol.

He got some much-needed financial assistance when The Beatles recorded 'Everybody's Trying To Be My Baby', 'Honey Don't' and 'Matchbox'. Johnny had hit it off with Carl as soon as they met and June could have been forgiven for feeling deep apprehension at their friendship. The last thing she wanted was another poor country boy made good with unresolved problems and a chemical addiction problem. The two of them would sit at the back of the tour bus, getting wrecked on the substance of their choice, shedding tears over their dead brothers, leaving June feeling demoralised though undaunted. As with Mother Maybelle, there is the suggestion that Johnny was being charitable in rehabilitating Carl Perkins' fading career, though Jack Clement's view is that while there might have been an element of sympathy, the fact is that the two of them were friends and "Carl was a genuinely great picker." Lou Robin's similar view is that sympathy did not come into it and that Johnny took Carl on because of his admiration for his abilities.

In May 1966, the troupe (consisting, on this occasion, of Johnny and June, The Statler Brothers and The Tennessee Three) undertook a tour of Britain and Ireland which helped to establish a substantial and devoted fan base there. David and Pat Deadman, who ran The Official (UK) Johnny Cash Appreciation Society for a number of years, were at Heathrow to meet Johnny & Co when they arrived in London and the events of the day were chronicled in a report entitled, "A Dream Come True" which breathlessly began with precise details of flight numbers, take-off and landing times ("The time . . . 9.33 am . . . Johnny Cash, accompanied by his manager Saul Holiff . . . June Carter . . . and The Statler Brothers, stepped through the arrivals door, to commence Johnny's 1966 tour of the British Isles . . . Destined to be the biggest thing to happen to country music in England to date . . .")

What followed was a fan's eye account of their frustration as they waited for Johnny, catching tantalising glimpses of him as he made his way through customs and collected his luggage ("once down into customs, we lost sight of them . . .") and then eventually actually meeting their hero. They were impressed with the rest of the troupe too. "All wonderful people, and typical of the type of people connected with country music." Clearly the experience had been worth the wait, "This was a morning we would never forget . . . When a dream came true . . . When a voice and a name materialised into a wonderful person . . . THE GREAT . . . JOHNNY CASH." The next day, the Deadmans attended a press conference at the Pickwick Club in London, taking with them their "complete collection of Cash discs for Johnny to see." Before Johnny arrived they had an "interesting" chat with The Statler Brothers who informed them that they "owed their success to Johnny, and that he is a very wonderful person . . ." In order to maintain their privacy, it's understood that Johnny and June accepted an offer from promoter Mervyn Conn to stay at his apartment in London during the visit.

The tour consisted of nine appearances: six in England, and one each in Scotland, Ireland and Northern Ireland. The shows opened with an instrumental spot by The Tennessee Three which was followed by The Statler Brothers, dressed in brown suits, red ties and pink shirts, doing a set which included their major hit 'Flowers On The Wall' (a song recorded by Don Law during a session meant for Johnny but which he missed because his voice was too dried out by drugs), as well as songs from a forthcoming album. The Statlers were something of an all-round variety act, very much in keeping with the vaudeville feel of the show, and as well as songs they did imitations of a drunken Dean Martin, Eddie Fisher, The Maguire Sisters, Bing Crosby and The Ink Spots. It was perhaps presumptuous to assume that a British audience would be amused by imitations of such American household names, some of whom would have been little known in 1966. June Carter's segment featured some tunes such as 'Thirty Days', some comedy routines including one about English girls and mud holes and finally a medley of Carter Family songs.

Following an interval, The Tennessee Three took the stage and played an opening theme in anticipation of Johnny's imminent arrival, and then Don Reid introduced Johnny to rapturous applause. Dressed in a black suit, white shirt and black tie, he ran through many of his hits from the Sun era up to date before being joined for the last part of the show by June and the Statlers who used their vocal skills to imitate Mexican horns for 'Ring Of Fire'. Bearing in mind the inclusion of some religious songs such as 'Were You There When They Crucified My Lord?' and 'Amen', Johnny could reasonably claim that his show, like that of The Carter Family years before, was "morally good".

In Liverpool, he light-heartedly told the audience that he had meant to learn a Beatles song, "but hadn't had time." When somebody in the audience called for something by Jimmie Rodgers, Cash promptly tore into 'Waiting For A Train'. During The Tennessee Three's instrumental version of 'Cattle Call' at London's Hammersmith Odeon, Johnny did his level best to distract Luther by pulling faces and walking in front of him but as always Luther remained imperviously stony faced. Johnny's sister Reba felt compelled to later write that Luther's stage demeanour was merely an act and that he was in fact a warm and friendly person. In one interview, given at Hammersmith, Johnny was asked if he had any Cherokee blood to which he mischievously replied, "I believe I've still got some if the beer hasn't drained it all away." Tommy Cash has said that Johnny's views on his supposed Indian ancestry varied in accordance with his chemical intake. "The higher he got, the more likely he was to say he was a quarter Cherokee but when he was sober it would only be an eighth or less." It appears from later press interviews that the basis for Johnny claiming he had Indian blood at all was the part of America in which his maternal great-grandparents lived.

The tour was generally successful though not a sell-out and for the first performance at Manchester the auditorium was only half full and at Birmingham one reporter estimated that about 40% of the seats were empty as the show started. There was however sufficient demand for an extra London show to be squeezed in for which most tickets were sold. For an artist who had seen so little chart action in Britain the number of tickets sold was a tribute to Johnny Cash the man, and possibly to the fact that his music was being regularly featured on Radio Luxembourg.

On a day off, Johnny travelled to Wales to meet Bob Dylan who was playing a show in Cardiff. A version of 'I Still Miss Someone' with Bob on piano was recorded, which has yet to be released.* There was an organisational cock-up in Dublin when, having played their show there, the tour party found that the plane they had chartered to take them to Belfast was too small. Johnny made a fuss about insisting on them all travelling together and so at great expense a larger plane was chartered which was far too big for their purposes. Johnny and June were nervous flyers, and Johnny sometimes got so frightened that he could hardly breathe but it could be that drug-fuelled bravado led him to make a stand on the issue when they could easily have taken the train for a fraction of the cost. At the end of the tour the Deadmans presented Johnny with a combined cigarette lighter and case, engraved with his initials.

◆ ◆ ◆ ◆ ◆

Back in America, the effects of Johnny's drug habit were reaching a critical stage. While those around him were greatly concerned about his seemingly inevitable demise, the man himself showed all the recklessness of a person to whom life or death held no great attraction. In Toronto, Johnny turned up for a show virtually incoherent and it took the combined physical force and willpower of Harold Reid and Tex Ritter to force him onto the stage. As so often happened, he got through the show but later disappeared from the hotel. June raised the alert in the middle of the night and it fell to Marshall Grant on a cold autumnal night to try and track him down. Eventually Grant managed to locate him in a nightclub owned by Ronnie Hawkins and left a message, reminding Cash that the troupe were due to play a show in New York.

Johnny made it back to the hotel but when Marshall knocked on his door there was no reply so he broke in and found Johnny unconscious, slumped on the floor in amongst half-peeled potatoes. Marshall really did think he might be dead this time since he could detect neither pulse nor breath, so he laid him out on the floor and gave him artificial respiration. After a while there were some grunting noises and the thought went through Marshall's mind that they might make the matinee performance after all. Marshall and June bundled Johnny into the back of the tour bus and covered him with a blanket so that the border guards were entirely unaware of his presence. Having apparently been at death's door a few hours previously, Johnny made it to the theatre on time, though Marshall and June let him sleep through most of the first half before waking him up. Marshall watched with a mixture of admiration and exasperation as Johnny walked out to another hot and rowdy reception and growled the most

* Footage of their meeting was included in DA Pennebaker's unreleased Bob Dylan tour film, *Eat The Document*.

superfluous words in country music, "Hello, I'm Johnny Cash," though of course the audience would have felt cheated if he hadn't uttered them. It seems clear that without the support of those closest to him at this time, Johnny Cash's name would have been another statistic.

◆ ◆ ◆ ◆ ◆

By Johnny's recording standards, *Everybody Loves A Nut* was an anomaly. Although the producer credits go to Don Law and Frank Jones, it was Jack Clement who shouldered much of the responsibility for what transpired. Johnny's amphetamine-driven craziness contributed to the character of the resultant album, though the spontaneous and lateral thinking input of Clement no doubt helped as well. The cover is a cleverly constructed cartoon tableau featuring the cast of characters populating the songs. Johnny is in the role of the nut (whom everybody loves, naturally) with one foot resting on a 'Dirty Old Egg Sucking Dog' and the other in the mouth of a 'Boa Constrictor', right up to the knee. On 'A Cup Of Coffee', Johnny is a horribly convincing drunk driver while a risqué ditty, 'The Singing Star's Queen' describes what Johnny gets up to with Waylon Jennings' wife while the latter is away on tour.

Clement wrote four of the songs including the best known, 'The One On The Right Is On The Left', a successful single that made number two in the country chart, and which took a wry look at political divisions in a folk group. In many ways, the most engaging song on the album is 'Joe Bean'. Given the nature of the album and the title of the song, the listener is primed for comedy but lyrics about a miscarriage of justice and a boy about to be hanged on his twentieth birthday for a crime he didn't commit stir the liberal outrage so strongly associated with Johnny Cash. For a time it seemed he was going to end the album on a serious note but there is a black twist in the tale. Joe Bean was a killer by the age of 10 and the only reason his mother knows he didn't kill a man in Arkansas is because she knows he was robbing a train on the day of the murder. A request for a pardon is made but when word eventually comes through from the governor it is not only to tell him that there will be no stay of execution, but also to sing 'Happy Birthday' to him accompanied by a heavenly chorus of pleasant female voices, during which there is the graphic sound of the trap opening and Joe's neck breaking. Johnny Cash protested when prisoners were treated unfairly, but he didn't appear to have any qualms with the idea of capital punishment if the crime was sufficiently serious, a recurring theme in his songs. While feeling sympathy for a prisoner and his family going through the horrors of death row, the pay-off in his mind seems to be, "Did he have it coming?"

Everybody Loves A Nut demonstrated the quirkiness of Johnny Cash and the casual record buyer who, having quite liked 'Ring Of Fire' and 'I Walk The Line', might well have felt justified in asking for their money back. Then again, Cash never claimed to be just a country singer, as he made clear in a 1966

Melody Maker interview. "I don't like being referred to as a country singer, call me the way you see me. I've sold more records in pop than in country, so don't categorise me or stereotype me." Over the years, he has given many interviews where he referred to himself as a country singer, his attitude appearing to be fluid on the subject, depending upon the circumstances and context. *Everybody Loves A Nut* was a kind of *Beverly Hillbillies* version of *Rowan and Martin's Laugh In.* * The album was a million miles away from, and made no concessions whatsoever to, contemporary fads and fashions.

In 1966, there were the stirrings of psychedelia in The Beatles' *Revolver* and Jimi Hendrix and Cream released their first records. Johnny showed his individuality by sticking to the territory he knew best. It was as if The Beatles and the Stones had never happened and indeed in an interview at the time he referred to pop types as "A breed I know nothing about." Many of his conservative fans doubtless queried the moral good of many of these new artists but popular music flows from the same font: The Beatles had recorded songs by Carl Perkins, and Eric Clapton and Jimi Hendrix were expert exponents of the blues music which emanated from Johnny Cash's South. As for the wild pop star lifestyle, Johnny could have taught them all a thing or two.

In accordance with the Columbia deal, *Happiness Is You* (released in November) represented a return to mainstream Johnny Cash. If 'Ring Of Fire' was June's declaration of love for Johnny then the title track of this album was his reciprocal declaration, though the song was jointly written.

> *I tried to doubt you and live without you,*
> *Tried to deny that I love you like I do,*
> *But I realise now and I'll admit it,*
> *You'll always be a part of me, and happiness is you.*
> *No more chasing moonbeams or catching falling stars,*
> *I know now my pot of gold is anywhere you are,*
> *My heart won't miss you, my heart goes with you,*
> *Loneliness is emptiness, and happiness is you.*

Cash fans who never thought of their idol as a comedy turn were reassured by the return to an easy-listening country style though the pace of the album is either funereal (particularly 'Is This My Destiny?') or mid-tempo, that a lively rendition of 'Wabash Cannonball' as the finale comes as something of a relief. It was becoming aurally obvious that though The Tennessee Three contributed in the studio with Luther's distinctive, unchanging sound still part of the equation, more and more session instrumentalists (guitar, dobro, piano and organ) were making a contribution.

---

* The late Sixties zany comedy show which launched the career of Goldie Hawn amongst others.

Johnny benefited from improved studio technology and the greater use of multiple-miking meant an enhancement of his sound, though unlike other artists he did not overuse the advances in technology to add in sounds just because it was possible. Though the Luther Perkins sound was less dominant, he was still a crucial excitement-generating component of the Johnny Cash sound in a live context. Among the songs on the album was a re-recording of 'Guess Things Happen That Way' (overlaid with clean-cut vocal 'ba da ba da's of which Johnny made clear his dislike in later years), and the powerfully evocative 'She Came From The Mountains' – a lengthy, half-narrated tragic love story written by Peter LaFarge. One surprising inclusion was 'Happy To Be With You', written by Johnny, June and Merle Kilgore. A strange, overproduced song with jerky and intrusive vocal backings competing with swinging Sixties-style electric organs and guitars, it comes over as dated and out of place; sounding like an ill-advised attempt to keep up with contemporary trends.

Johnny's weight dropped as low as 150 pounds (he should have weighed over 200 pounds) and photographs from this time show a man literally wasting away. It was perhaps for this reason that CBS chose to dispense with a photograph on the cover, going instead for a plain, rather underwhelming charcoal drawing. The sleeve notes were surprisingly tacky; talking about the song, 'For Lovin' Me', the writer states, "Johnny gets back at all the girls who have loved and run and left him with shadows for companions. A brassy comment on life and love, it's a good bit of delightful listening." Elsewhere, Johnny's 1963 hit song is referred to as 'King Of Fire'. The album was considerably more successful than its predecessor and enjoyed a chart run of six months, peaking at number 10.

* * * * *

Although Johnny's marriage to Vivian had effectively been over for some time he nonetheless returned to California on occasion to see his girls and maintain the charade that they were still a family. However, after one particular tour ended in June 1966, he decided that enough was enough and that he would henceforth treat Nashville as his home when he wasn't touring. Soon afterwards Vivian decided to go against her religious principles and instituted divorce proceedings. All of this came at a delicate time in his daughters' lives, especially 12-year-old Rosanne, who, even by this early age, had a way with words. Some of the pain she felt at the unsettled state of her parents' marriage was revealed in early writings which were, with an irony obvious in retrospect, published in a magazine devoted to heaping praise on her errant father.

14

THE LEGEND, the official publication of the Johnny Cash Society, was initially run from California by Johnny's sister Reba. It consisted of letters from Johnny and Reba to the fans and reports from other fan clubs giving news on what had been happening in their part of the world. Also included were numerous photographs, newspaper articles, and adulatory features on Johnny and members of his family. References to drugs or missed shows are conspicuous by their absence.

In 1967 and 1968 there were photographs of Johnny's four daughters, Rosanne, Kathy, Cindy and Tara, together with their poems and letters. Rosanne's poem, 'Life' revealed a troubled view of the world:

> *As we walk on through life's surge,*
> *With our slow and faltering way,*
> *We pause and look back over the years,*
> *And have nothing much to say,*
> *For as we remember our past life,*
> *We see that faults are many,*
> *And we promise ourselves to do better,*
> *And see that faults aren't any.*

The following year Rosanne's letter contribution was written in a mature style – spelling mistakes and all:

> *"In September I began adjusting to a new school – Holy Cross – and a new grade – Eighth. I haven't really adjusted yet, tho. The nuns are very strict (to put it mildly) but next year I'll be going to St Bonaventure High, which is really supposed to be a tuff school. (If that's possible!)"*

Years later, talking about her father's visits to California, Rosanne lifted the veil a little on her childhood years, remembering her father as being "So wired you would almost break down in tears to be in the same room with him . . . He seemed so miserable." Like the sleeve notes on Cash's albums from the time, the quality of the magazine was basic at best and the "interviews" with Johnny invariably unrevealing.

Q. What would you say is your most embarrassing moment?
A. I don't know, or remember.
Q. What is your greatest dislike in the world today?
A. The war and world unrest.
Q. Would you tell your fans who some of your favourite artists are?
A. I have many favourites. No one in particular.
Q. Do you like German Folksongs?
A. Not especially, I don't know any.
Q. Do you like Lorretta [sic] Lynn?
A. Very much.

The Legend reported a visit to Dyess by a friend of the Cash family. The federal administration building, where Ray Cash had reported soon after his arrival in 1935, had been converted to flats on the ground floor and a meeting hall for the Masonic Lodge on the first. At the time of the visit in 1967, a government official was inspecting the building for possible use as a nuclear bomb shelter; the Cuban missile crisis being fresh in the memory and the Cold War still very real.

The friend also visited Dyess High School. The original building burnt down in 1963 and Johnny made a substantial contribution to the cost of rebuilding it. Next to the main school was the building containing the industrial arts workshops which escaped the fire, and the scene of the accident which claimed the life of Jack Cash – an event commemorated in a memorial plaque in one of the science rooms which read, "The equipment in this room was donated by Johnny Cash in loving memory of his brother Jack Cash who died in 1944."

Towards the end of 1966, on the same day that Ronald Reagan was elected governor of California, Johnny played a show at the state's high security Folsom Prison. He had played shows in prisons on a number of occasions in the past, usually with little or no fanfare, and had always got a great charge from the intense atmosphere the prisoners generated. In fact he was keen to record a live concert in a prison but, thus far, the otherwise indulgent CBS had resisted his wishes. The '66 show featured The Tennessee Three, The Statler Brothers and Mother Maybelle and The Carter Sisters, June, Helen and Anita. In the audience as guests of honour were Sara Carter Bayes, one of the original members of The Carter Family and her husband Coy. One Folsom "moss-back" was heard to say after the show, "I've been here 11 years and thought I had learned to hate everything connected with the prison, but I enjoyed this show. This is the first thing I've enjoyed in those 11 years." Warden Oliver said to Johnny, "You can come back to Folsom any time you want to, and stay as long as you like."

Johnny's peripatetic existence was becoming problematic. He had a number of places he could stay but each one was unsatisfactory for different reasons. Given the presence of June and the Carters, his recording commitments and other connections to the country music scene, Nashville was the natural choice for him to acquire a proper family home. Buying a house there would be a symbolic act of putting down roots, a significant change for the man who for almost the whole of the past decade had lived a wild, unpredictable and nomadic existence. Another factor was the need for Johnny's daughters to have a homely place to stay when they visited their father. With his earnings in 1967 reported to be around $600,000, there was certainly no financial impediment to the idea of a house purchase, and there were other reasons why it made sense. Johnny did not have a stable base but he was now 35, and his relationship with June needed to be taken a step further. Despite her strong love for Johnny and a single-minded determination to wean him off the pills (even taking some of his tranquillisers on one occasion to try and scare him. He was shocked but it didn't work), she made it clear that her patience was not infinite and that if he did not sort himself out then she might throw in the towel. It also did not strike June as acceptable that her young daughter Rosey sometimes got roped into search and destroy missions for his pill stash even if the youngster thought it was some kind of treasure hunt.

Given her own abstemious ways, June could perhaps have been forgiven for failing to understand why Johnny couldn't kick so easily. Writing later, Hank Williams, Jr gave an insight for the uninitiated into the overpoweringly seductive charms of drugs, as opposed to alcohol, for the road musician. "Fifteen minutes after taking a few pills the whole world took on a rosy glow and pretty soon I started to see what Daddy and Cash and (Merle) Kilgore saw in the stuff. With liquor you'd always have to face the inevitable morning after with your mouth feeling like used steel wool and your temples trying to figure out a way to get out of your head. With pills you can postpone that morning after for a hell of a long time, weeks in fact and also you could play the shows all night if you wanted to and you could spend the whole next day pretending to be the happy man and wife scene."

Despite these attractions Johnny conceded that drugs did not aid his writing, no matter how much he might try and convince himself otherwise. Looked at when he was straight, his scribblings invariably turned out to be "Wild impossible ridiculous ramblings you wouldn't believe." His pal, Waylon Jennings, was characteristically blunt on the subject. "As far as the drugs are concerned, there's no real excuse for it. There's really not. Except stupidity maybe." Surprisingly, despite his condition, Johnny was able to remember the words to numerous songs. Deep down, though he might not be ready to admit it to others, Johnny knew he was in serious trouble and that he would have to straighten himself out sooner rather than later. It wouldn't happen overnight but the decision to buy his own home marked a turning point in his life. Speaking 10 years later to

Rolling Stone, Johnny said he had a feeling that things were going to change and that he sensed that he had seven big years ahead if he could "just get myself out of this mess."

Being Johnny Cash, the process of acquiring a property was far from smooth and much of the eccentricity and farce involved is graphically detailed in Christopher Wren's 1973 Cash biography, *Winners Got Scars Too*. Johnny asked Braxton Dixon, a self-made house builder who had left school in his early teens, to show him any suitable plots he had for development. Unfortunately for Dixon (who was quite taken with it himself), he showed Johnny a large unfinished house in Hendersonville, about 20 miles north of Nashville. The structure, extending to roughly 10,000 square feet, was set into a hill overlooking Old Hickory Lake and was built of stone and timbers collected from old houses and barns in 14 neighbouring states, with large picture windows overlooking the lake and a roof partly covered in thick sods of grass. The house contained cantilevered circular rooms with balconies and ceilings featuring wooden spokes creating the effect of large wagon wheels. After a quick walk through the house Johnny told Braxton that he wanted to buy it and calling on his best powers of persuasion, Johnny secured a deal, at a reported price of around $200,000, over a Budweiser.

Although the house wasn't finished, and although it created potential insurance problems (if burnt down before completion there would be no cover), Johnny began staying at the house if he wasn't crashing out with Maybelle and Eck or staying at the apartment with Waylon Jennings. There were times when, after going on a bender in downtown Nashville, he would be found in an alley by the police or wind up at the house of a stranger, with no recollection of how he'd made it there. For the local press he had become something of a sad joke and some Nashville pundits and Cash watchers reckoned it was only a matter of time before Johnny joined Jimmie Rodgers and Hank Williams.

Johnny continued to stretch the tolerance of Maybelle and Eck to its absolute limit, arriving at all hours, breaking down doors and damaging furniture as he rampaged around the house, though he was invariably apologetic afterwards and, on occasion, made good his vandalism. When Braxton Dixon went to the house in Hendersonville he invariably found cigarette butts scattered about, and since the house was mainly a wood construction, this made the worries over insurance all the more real. Another of Johnny's tricks was to rip out the telephones when he didn't want to answer them, and some ended up in the lake. Despite Johnny's behaviour, Dixon and his wife allowed themselves to get caught up in the chaos, joining in the pill hunts, on occasion, providing a bed and food and showing forbearance when house payments weren't made on time.

On one occasion the Dixons called the police when Johnny failed to appear for supper after he had mentioned that he was planning to do some fishing on the lake. It turned out he'd capsized the boat and swum to shore, terrifying a few people in the process by knocking on their doors seeking help, before trudging miles back to the Dixon house. Perhaps it was being associated with a celebrity, or Johnny's vulnerability, but those who became involved with him seemed to be possessed of remarkable reserves of tolerance, far and above the call of duty. There was the occasion when Johnny went back to the new house late at night but was unable to get in (was he *ever* able to accept responsibility for holding on to a key?); the front door was a large wooden affair and Johnny, on a short fuse, got an axe from the garage and hacked his way in. Dixon had agreed the sale but had only received a small fraction of the price. Thanks to Johnny's habit of missing shows, his finances were not in good shape.* Dixon was evidently reassured by Johnny's persuasive words and after the incident with the axe, Dixon found a scrawled note from Johnny on the front door, "Braxton – I'm sorry, truly sorry. I love this place, I'm so proud of it. I'm still the man it was built for."

Even when Johnny was able to pull himself together enough to perform, he was unreliable; on top form for one show, sluggish and poor for the next. Eventually, Marshall Grant mooted the possibility of having Johnny compulsorily detained (as his friend Merle Travis had been), stressing that he was only thinking of Johnny's best interests. Saul Holiff was in agreement and, heartbreaking though it must have been, Johnny's parents indicated that they would be willing to sign the necessary papers. June however resisted, sensing that locking Johnny up to tame his demons would do more harm than good.

◆ ◆ ◆ ◆ ◆

In May 1967, the Cash family came together for a reunion, partly to mark the 23rd anniversary of the death of Jack. Johnny had been visiting his daughters in California and returned to Nashville along with his parents. According to Tommy Cash, who collected them from the airport, his brother was at his absolute worst at this time. Johnny had been put off the plane at Memphis because he was incoherent and acting strangely to the extent that passengers were alarmed. The American Airlines pilot felt he had no option but to land at the earliest opportunity.

When they finally arrived, several hours late, Tommy said to Johnny, "Is your show about over with for today?" "What do you mean by that?" Johnny said angrily. "You know perfectly well what I mean, look how you're embarrassing our parents," Tommy replied. With that, Johnny blurted, "Why you little punk," and hit Tommy. "He got me on the left jaw and knocked me flat on the ground. It was a sucker punch. I was startled. I was fit and he wasn't and I was

---

* The touring troupe covered for Cash as best they could, playing shows and then not getting paid because of his absence. At one stage, Marshall Grant complained that he was earning less than when he worked as a mechanic.

damn sure I was going to retaliate. My anger was probably out of control." However, Ray Cash intervened by standing between his warring sons, extending his arms. "You boys are not going to fight in front of your mother. If you're gonna fight, get out of the airport." The next day Johnny gave Tommy a precious coin from his collection as a peace offering, which was accepted with good grace.

Despite being on the receiving end, Tommy Cash is understanding about Johnny's behaviour. "Even with the little popularity I enjoyed myself, I didn't always find it easy to maintain my behaviour and to remain myself. You get into this monotonous routine but you still want to do it, you're getting booked and you're getting crowds and you have a payroll to meet. For my brother you multiply all of this by thousands."

Tommy explained that most of the Cash clan have "addictive personalities", afflicted by what Johnny refers to in his 1997 autobiography as "the family disease", making drink and drug abuse an easy escape. Johnny was extremely remorseful since he had never before stooped so low as to hit a member of his own family in front of his parents in a public place. Despite the trauma at the airport the family celebrations at Johnny's house went ahead, with Johnny carefully organising a number of events throughout the day. A photographer with a flash bulb had been hired to follow people around so that every detail of the reunion could be recorded for posterity. For the evening's entertainment, the family were to have been taken to the CBS studios on Music Row to witness a recording session, a case of mixing business and pleasure, but this was abandoned when news came through of the death of Luther Perkins' mother.

In the evening, in place of the proposed recording session, Reba reported that "Miss June Carter had come by and that little gal just couldn't be kept still . . . break out the guitars and autoharps she did. We had our very own country show that night with Cash, Carter and Cash." Reba also noted that despite the lateness of the hour, Johnny got it into his head that he had to have some roasted peanuts and popcorn and took Tommy off in the middle of the night to track some down ("peanuts" and "popcorn" being code for amphetamines). Tommy recalls other bizarre behaviour. "Johnny had a huge, dark brown, antique chest with really big drawers. He put a pillow and a blanket inside it and slept there so nobody could find him. I suppose it was another example of what drugs can do." Some of the photographs featured in *The Legend* reveal a palpable degree of tension on the faces of some of the family members, particularly Ray and Carrie Cash and their eldest child, Roy. Johnny himself, though smiling through it all, looks gaunt and unhealthy beside a fit and well-looking Tommy.

Roy Cash recalled being at the house in Hendersonville on another occasion when Johnny pulled up in a brand new Cadillac. To Roy's total amazement when he looked inside, the back seat was covered with rocks. Tommy Cash recalls receiving an urgent late night phone call from his brother. "He called me from the Andrew Jackson hotel in Nashville and said he was starving and could I do something about it. My then wife Barbara went to a lot of trouble to defrost some chicken, made biscuits and gravy and then we went over to the hotel. We were told he wasn't there. I decided to go up to the room to check that he definitely wasn't there or wasn't dead or something but he had definitely headed off. I mentioned it to him later and he had absolutely no recollection of it at all."

The warm words and cosy family photographs of the reunion (featured in *The Legend*) failed to disguise Johnny's ongoing problems. Having resisted the idea of Johnny being compulsorily detained, June realised that the kind of help he needed came within the scope of a psychiatrist's expertise. Her instinctive feeling was that Johnny had never adequately dealt with Jack's death and that his marriage to Vivian had failed to ease his aching hurt. June and Mother Maybelle were the prime movers in applying pressure on Johnny to go and see nearby Madison resident Nat Winston, a psychiatrist who was also State Commissioner for Mental Health. They hoped that Winston would be able to connect with Johnny, not least because he was something of an eccentric character himself. Away from his office Winston lived on a spread overrun with animals, wore blue dungarees and played banjo in the style of his close friend, Earl Scruggs. In his 1973 Johnny Cash biography, Christopher Wren referred to Winston as having become, "The unofficial 'shrink' to all those country music performers back in Nashville who didn't believe in psychiatrists."

Winston was wary of taking the case mainly because, suspecting Johnny was too far-gone, he didn't want to be the last doctor to treat him with all the high profile questioning that might attract. As well as this, since his government appointment, Winston no longer held a current practising certificate as a psychiatrist, laying himself open to financial disaster if things went awry. Despite such concerns, he got involved, trying in vain to have Johnny sign himself into private clinics. Like June, he too was opposed to the idea of compulsory detention.

The question of Jack's death as the origin of Johnny's psychological problems has been commented upon in many quarters. Nat Winston and Rosanne Cash are both quoted on the subject in Nicholas Dawidoff's book, *In The Country Of Country*. It's Winston's view that Johnny had "A severe amount of guilt" for having "gone off fishing while Jack Cash died for $3," while Rosanne was quoted, "His enigmatic, restless, constant seeking and self-destruction all goes back to that defining moment when he lost his brother. There's tremendous grief and guilt." On the other hand, Tommy Cash, who claims to have spoken to his brother many times on the subject, is adamant that Johnny does not feel guilt over Jack's death: "He didn't feel there was anything he could have done. Devastated – yes. Guilt – no."

During a visit to Johnny's house, Nicholas Dawidoff noticed a picture of Jack. Looking at it Johnny said, "That was not long before he died. I probably never did get over it. We were so close. It was like, you know, I've never been that close to anybody since." Apparently the subject came up during some treatment Johnny underwent in the early Eighties. The assumption was that he must have been suffering the burden of "unresolved grief" but further exploration of the subject drew a blank and as Johnny said, "I haven't grieved over him since I was a kid," but then again grief isn't the same as guilt. No doubt Johnny experienced a range of contradictory emotions in the years following Jack's death but his assertion to Nick Tosches that Jack's death was "murder" and that some mystery person had disappeared after the incident is certainly intriguing. Was this his enigmatic way of saying that he felt in some way responsible? Was it perhaps a way of expressing the inevitable but hopeless "if only", common to anybody close to such a sudden and avoidable tragedy?

◆ ◆ ◆ ◆ ◆

Johnny missed a lot of recording sessions at this time and even when he did turn up, "I'd come into the studio with a fog over my head, not really caring what condition I was in. Just go in on sheer guts and give it a try." However Johnny did still manage to lay down some new material and, in February 1967, the single 'Jackson', a bouncy up-tempo duet with June, was released. The song did well commercially, making number two in the country chart, becoming one of the best loved and most eagerly anticipated numbers in Johnny's repertoire. Some took it as a kind of affirmation of Johnny and June's love, helped perhaps by the songs opening words, "We got married in a fever." However it's actually about the end of passion giving it an ironic juxtaposition *vis à vis* the Cash-Carter ring of fire, as it had been featured in their live shows for about three years. Far more to the point was their version of John Sebastian's 'Darlin' Companion' which Johnny and June sang, staring into each other's eyes with a mutual magnetism impossible to disguise.

In March, *From Sea To Shining Sea* was released, which amounted to a highly personal, patriotic-feeling celebration of ordinary aspects of American life. As Johnny put it in the sleeve notes, "I sing mainly about things I have heard of, or things and places that I have seen. I have been in all 40 states . . ." The traditionally orientated songs cover topics which had become firmly associated with Johnny Cash such as 'Frozen Four-Hundred-Pound Fair-To-Middlin' Cotton Picker', 'Walls Of A Prison', 'Flint Arrowhead' and 'Cisco Clifton's Fillin' Station.' The latter painted an evocative and nostalgic picture of a dignified old timer struggling to preserve his business in the face of the relentless march of progress in the shape of a new interstate which will inevitably draw off many of his customers. As with other songs such as 'The Legend Of John Henry's Hammer', Cash bemoans the passing of a way of life while pointing to the inevitability of change. A number of the songs feature narrations and it was Carl Perkins who made the astute observation that many of Johnny's fans would be just as happy to hear Johnny talk as sing.

'The Masterpiece' is a song whose sugary religious sentiment was maximised by a heart-tugging harmonica accompaniment. Likewise, 'Call Daddy From The Mine' is overwhelmingly sentimental and, as Johnny explains, he had written both songs 10 years before but forgotten about them. When they resurfaced, he played them to June who suggested he record them. 'Shrimpin' Sailin'' is preceded by an extraordinary, incoherent outburst from Johnny of the kind which producers and record executives would normally have deleted. He seems to be complaining about "Cajun boys" doing something to or with "blackberry jim jams" and making marks on his table. Johnny wrote and arranged all of the songs though at least one melody, 'The Walls Of A Prison' was, as he acknowledges, originally a British tune called 'The Unfortunate Rake'.

Despite grooming and make-up as well as a serious moody pose, the sleeve photograph, taken on the balcony of Johnny's second storey bedroom overlooking Old Hickory Lake, could not disguise the fact that he looked old before his time. A photograph taken in the same place (and published in *The Legend* around the same time) found him looking even worse. He made an effort to smile but an unnatural facial thinness lent a spectral character to his appearance. The cast-iron eagle featured in the sleeve picture weighed about 250 pounds. A large hawk had nose-dived into it and broken its neck, so Johnny had it stuffed and displayed in his kitchen.

Johnny's condition was not helped by the fact that he continued to maintain a punishing schedule of concerts and tours throughout 1967, only taking any significant time off in July and December. The fans still loved him and turned out to see him in large numbers but despite this level of approval he still felt worried and nervous before he went on stage, as he put it, "I always had that fear that somebody's gonna throw eggs at me." Johnny did come in for some severe stick from one of his fans when he got into trouble with the police again in November. Ralph Jones and his wife were big Johnny Cash fans who owned every one of his records. So it was with a sense of disbelief, excitement and apprehension that Ralph learned that he was going to be dealing with Johnny in the course of his professional duties as the Walker County sheriff based in Lafayette, Georgia. Johnny had been picked up the day before, having been assessed by the arresting officer as drunk and incapable. It seems he had been indulging in one of his favourite pastimes, wandering around old Civil War battlefields looking for relics while sustained on handfuls of pills, when he had been spotted staggering about on a public highway.

As a measure of Cash's popularity, Sheriff Jones overlooked booking Johnny on a number of counts and the next morning he was genuinely upset as he gave Johnny back his possessions, including the pills he'd had on him. Johnny was mystified and said so. As Cash recorded in his 1975 autobiography, Sheriff Jones gave it to him straight, "It broke my heart when they brought you in here last night. I left the jail and went home to my wife and told her I had Johnny Cash locked up. I almost wanted to resign and just walk out because it was such a heartbreaking thing for me."

Realising he was going to be let off once more, Johnny told Sheriff Jones that he wouldn't regret it, but the good sheriff wasn't finished. "You know better than most people that God gave you free will to do with yourself whatever you want to do . . . now you can throw the pills away or you can take them and go ahead and kill yourself." Johnny was inspired to change and left the station ever more determined to kick his habit. Events were building up towards some kind of resolution but given the extent and duration of Johnny's habit, and with the degree to which his system physically depended on a daily intake of chemicals, giving up was not about to be achieved in one simple exercise.

◆ ◆ ◆ ◆ ◆

September saw the release of the last Cash album to be produced by Don Law, who resigned from Columbia earlier in the year. In keeping with his habit of breaking new ground with each release, *Carryin' On With Johnny Cash And June Carter* (also simply referred to as *Jackson*) was made up entirely of duets with June. The sleeve photo showed a blooming, effervescent June next to a sheepish, sick-looking Cash. Johnny had never looked worse for an official publicity shot.

The album featured the earlier hits, 'Jackson' and 'It Ain't Me Babe'* plus a selection of undistinguished songs serving no other purpose than to provide an informal vehicle for Johnny and June to let their hair down, while attempting to cash in on the success of 'Jackson'. The album's finale is an execrable version of Ray Charles' 'What'd I Say', the soulful nuances which made Brother Ray's version a classic being well beyond the limited Cash vocal range, never mind that of June. As with the light, jazzy numbers that he tried on Christmas albums, Johnny should have been advised to leave well alone. The mock put-down sleeve notes, written by Carl Perkins, included a paragraph which, knowingly or otherwise, got close to the bone. "June is affectionately known as 'Brindl', and poor little Brindl has had a tough time these last few years. She has fought a battle to tame a man with a wild streak – trying and succeeding most times in eliminating the streak."

The album made number five in the country charts during a four months' chart run – a tribute to the selling power of Johnny Cash since June is on particularly poor vocal form, at times woefully off key and rarely anything above ordinary. Not even her trademark laryngeal growls save the record. However June's vocal ability or lack of it was not the crucial part of the equation in her relationship with Johnny. June was not only a member of his beloved Carter Family; loving, attractive, sassy and confident on stage, but religious and conservative in

---

* Columbia sometimes released the same song three times within a year.

a way that resonated with Johnny's roots, someone who might stand up to him but who would always stand up *for* him.

It must have been hard for June, a professional performer aware of her limitations, to find herself on stages and studios backed by singers with far more ability. Apart from the undoubted pleasure and fulfilment she experienced as a performer, at the back of her mind was the knowledge that if she didn't get involved with Johnny professionally, then he would be adrift, and she felt she had to be there for him.

◆ ◆ ◆ ◆ ◆

Don Law's retirement led to Johnny being teamed up with Bob Dylan's Texan-born producer, Bob Johnston. Up until this point Johnny had not been able to persuade CBS to let him record a live album in a prison, because from their point of view, it wasn't a commercially viable idea to have robbers and rapists entertained in this way; what would religious organisations and conservative country music fans make of it all? Johnny had been keen to record an album in front of a prison audience for some time, especially since the Reverend Gressett had set up the appearance at Folsom. He knew that there was an open invitation to return to the prison so might Johnston be able to persuade the head honchos at Columbia to bankroll the idea?

On another important front, Vivian's divorce was progressing through court and, barring any hitches, Johnny would be a single man again, free to consider a future with June. However, more pressing than either of these matters was the question of Johnny's drug addiction. He had left Sheriff Jones full of good intentions but within a short time he was back pill popping as normal. What would it take to drop his vices and move on?

PART III

King Of The Hill

"Creative people have to be fed from the divine source."

ONE NIGHT, Braxton Dixon called by Johnny's house but though his black Cadillac was parked in the drive there was no reply when he rang the front door bell. Panic gripped him as he looked out towards the edge of the lake and saw Johnny's tractor on its side in the water. Fearing that Johnny was trapped underneath he was just about to dive in when he noticed a figure in a black leather coat clinging to a nearby tree. It was Johnny, sodden and frozen, too weak to move, shivering and a breath away from hypothermia. Braxton did what he could by dragging Johnny into the house but, stirring slightly, Johnny astonished Braxton by breaking away to frantically dig for the pills he had secreted in the garden. By chance June and Mother Maybelle called round and between them the three managed to get Johnny to bed though June was crying tears of anger, ready to give up.

It was around this time that Johnny, feeling he was "barely human", having let down himself and those closest to him, decided, as he said in his 1997 autobiography, to "Go into Nickajack Cave and let God take me from this earth and put me wherever He puts people like me." These words obscured the question of whether he intended to commit suicide, though he was clearer when, talking about the many amateur cave explorers who had lost their lives there, he said, "It was my hope and intention to join that company . . . I couldn't get along with anybody because nobody could get along with me. Paranoid, everything else . . . I was so down on myself, so disgusted with my health and what I had done to myself and my loved ones that I couldn't face life any more, I couldn't go on. It took the dark to bring out the light."

Johnny had been up for about five nights without eating when he went to visit a friend in Chattanooga near Nickajack Cave. Behind a massive entrance (now closed off), a series of caves stretched for many miles, where American soldiers slaughtered the Nickajack Indians. In happier times Johnny had visited the caves with friends searching for relics such as antique guns and minié balls (primitive bullets). He loved the historical associations of the caves, his imagination fired by thoughts of Civil War soldiers hiding out there, sometimes scratching their names in the walls. Hank Williams, Jr, who had accompanied Johnny on one of his cave trips, described the kind of recklessness that helped to define the Cash character in his autobiography, *Living Proof*. "He was a lot like I imagine daddy must have been. I was fascinated by his total disregard for his own safety and well-being . . . in the caves, if there was a sign that read 'Proceed No Further – Danger!' that was like waving a red rag in front of a bull, it darn near guaranteed that Cash would pick up his flashlight and get down on his belly if necessary and crawl back into that hole." Johnny obviously knew only too well what he was doing when he went into the caves, further and further along unknown routes, walking, crawling, driven on by a desire to terminate his pain once and for all. He crawled for hours until his torchlight battery died and he was utterly alone, in total darkness deep within the bowels of the earth.

In his 1997 autobiography, Cash explained how his emotions went from the abject loneliness of being "As far from God as I have ever been," to a major spiritual epiphany. "I thought I'd left Him but He hadn't left me." At least one (anonymous) person close to the situation pours scorn on Johnny's version of events but, with no witnesses, Johnny's is the only available testimony. He claims that having wandered directionless and forlorn into the caves, his energy sapping by the minute, he eventually lay down drained, unable to continue. Suddenly, he felt he had a new energy and though he couldn't see where he was going, he started to crawl through open passages, eventually feeling fresh air on his back which told him he was near the entrance. He eventually made it out of the caves and back to the house where he found June and his mother waiting for him. His mother had flown in from California, evidently sensing that things were seriously wrong with her errant son.

Johnny was finally ready to accept help and an *ad hoc* team under the direction of Nat Winston, who was taking a professional risk, was hurriedly assembled. Johnny's parents (who were now living in Nashville in a $50,000 house he had bought for them across the road from his own home), June, Mother Maybelle, Eck Carter, Luther, Marshall, Carl Perkins, WS Holland, and Braxton Dixon and his wife Anna were all involved to varying degrees, though June apparently baulked at staying overnight initially, not wishing to give such public expression to their relationship. Eck told her not to be concerned, seeing as she wouldn't be the only one there and it was all in a good cause.

Nat Winston saw two things as vital: firstly, that Johnny not be left alone at any time and, secondly, that in order to avoid a total collapse of his system, he be weaned off drugs gradually by reducing each dosage. His first edict proved to be well-founded since within a short time, the local pushers were at the front door trying to do business. June was particularly robust in seeing them off. In the days that followed, the team made Johnny comfortable, reducing his pill intake, finding and destroying the supplies he had secreted around the house, forcing him to eat to build up his weight which had fallen to around 140 pounds (it soon moved up towards 200 pounds, more appropriate for his 6' 1" stature), encouraging him to walk and run in the grounds to gird his strength but above all being close at hand during the terrifying nightmares which plagued him in the early stages of withdrawal.

Johnny gave a graphic description of the torment he went through when coming off drugs in his 1975 autobiography. He said he was "walking the floors and climbing the walls", but the most terrifying aspect were the nightmares, with unbearable stomach cramps, which haunted him night after night. In a state somewhere between sleeping and waking ("I couldn't close my eyes and I couldn't open them"), he imagined a glass ball expanding in his stomach and getting so big it lifted him up off his bed towards the ceiling and then when he went through the roof the glass ball would explode and "tiny, infinitesimal slivers of glass would go out into my bloodstream from my stomach. I could feel the pieces of glass being pumped through my heart into the veins of my arms, my legs, my feet, my neck, and my brain, and some of them would come out the pores of my skin."

Nat Winston visited every day to give Johnny advice, encouragement and support and to boost the morale of June and the rest of the team. Gradually Johnny came round, the cravings diminished and his general health picked up. If the human body has remarkable resilience, then in Johnny's case, it was stretched to the limit. For June, it was God who gave Johnny his life back. Johnny took a similar view stating that God had surrounded him with people who cared enough to devote their time and effort to helping him pull through. Johnny later wrote that while others had helped and he was eternally grateful to them, it was he alone who had actually succeeded in taking the vital step, who faced up to the harsh reality of a life without drugs. While every addict has to ultimately deal with his own demons, this is perhaps being a little uncharitable. The fact is that if his team of loved ones had not rallied round as they did, and left him to his own devices, it's extremely unlikely that Johnny Cash would have survived the Sixties.

◆ ◆ ◆ ◆ ◆

While Johnny recovered away from the spotlight, his fame ensured he was in constant demand. His first show, post-recovery, was a benefit concert in Hendersonville, to raise money for children's band uniforms in order for them to play Miami's Orange Bowl. Johnny was pleasantly surprised to find that despite initial nerves, having a clear head didn't prevent him from performing well. He was in good physical shape, telling a reporter at the time, "I feel real good. I weigh 213 pounds, more than I ever weighed in my life, and I'm full of vinegar." Soon afterwards, he was back on the road, urging Carl Perkins to follow his example by giving up his vices, not least because Perkins was in the habit of appearing drunk on stage.

On a sunny California day in January 1968, one of Johnny's long cherished ambitions came to fruition. Bob Johnston had realised the possibilities of recording a live album in front of a prison audience and was able to persuade reluctant executives at CBS that it was worth the risk. Once more the Reverend Gressett was involved in the arrangements for setting up the show with Folsom's recreation supervisor, Lloyd Kelley. The troupe plus Bob Johnston and his team of recording engineers moved, *en masse*, into a Sacramento hotel two days prior to the show and set about rehearsing in a large banqueting hall with different components of the troupe practising different songs at the same time. The unruly scene wasn't helped by the fact that a women's fashion show was being held in a nearby area of the hotel with attractive models in various states of undress wandering about all over the place. The evening before the concert the Republicans were holding a $500 per plate fundraiser during which Governor Ronald Reagan, attracted by the intriguing sounds coming out of the Fiesta Room, dropped in to wish everybody well.

The next day a convoy of limousines and trucks travelled the 25 miles to Folsom, California's second oldest prison. The guards allowed the vehicles in, two at a time, through the complex of gates protecting the prison entrance. Some prisoners who happened to be in the yard waved, but were forbidden to shout a greeting as the prison rules insisted on silence. The show was to be held in the prison dining area, a large high-ceilinged barn of a hall, capable of accommodating the 2,000 or so prisoners who would make up the audience. A large banner hung in front of the low stage proclaiming, "WELCOME JOHNNY CASH". The informal impression created by the numerous tables and chairs laid out around the hall was rather spoilt by the discovery that they were all screwed to the floor. The troupe, accompanied by the half a dozen prison guards deemed necessary to guarantee their safety, were led through to the kitchen which had been converted into a makeshift dressing room. Bob Johnston and the engineers got to work on setting up the recording equipment.

Just before the show, Johnny asked Johnston if there was anything in particular he wanted him to say before the first song to open the recording but Bob just shrugged and so in the absence of anything better to say Johnny immortalised the classic line, "Hello, I'm Johnny Cash," for posterity. The performance (lasting an hour and three quarters) that followed captured the raw, visceral essence of the Johnny Cash experience. Though his voice was ragged and off key at times, Johnny entertained and related to his audience in a way that the convicts could identify with. The wide variety of songs chosen for the occasion defied categorisation, something Johnny himself always saw as a pointless task as he reiterated in an interview. "People are always trying to classify me or define my type of music, but it doesn't work. I'm just me. I don't fit into any category and I try not to. I'm singing songs as honestly as I know how and I'm doing it the same way now as I did when I started recording." Writing about the concert in *Jazz and Pop* magazine, critic John F Szwed said, "Ventures such as this are object lessons to those who would divide the world of music into enemy camps."

What's more the album was achieved against the odds on a technical level, being recorded in a steel beamed, high ceilinged dining room with walls lacking any sound baffles, sophisticated acoustics or sound enhancing equipment. The actual recording equipment was 300 feet away behind a stone wall. Apart from reeling off such classics as 'Folsom Prison Blues' (naturally), 'The Long Black Veil', 'Orange Blossom Special' and 'Jackson' Johnny also featured some Jack Clement nuttiness with 'Flushed From The Bathroom Of Your Heart' (a much maligned comedy effort which is nonetheless full of slick lines such as "Up the elevator of your future I've been shafted," which went over well with the men) and 'Dirty Old Egg Sucking Dog'. There were also several prison-related songs which in the hands of other artists might have been seen as tasteless or patronising but which Johnny delivered with the right degree of pathos, for example, 'Twenty-Five Minutes To Go', 'The Wall' and 'Green, Green Grass Of Home'. Also included was 'Cocaine Blues' (also known as 'Transfusion Blues') about a man who kills his woman after snorting some cocaine with its unapologetically delivered line, "I can't forget the day I shot that bad bitch down."

The rapport with the audience was at once relaxed, entertaining and edgy, though during some of the songs Johnny allowed his sense of being one of the men to get the better of his professional duties; laughing and bantering during supposedly serious songs. Teresa Ortega, writing in the *South Atlantic Quarterly*, expressed the view that the prisoners and Cash pitted themselves against the authority figures of the guards and CBS (as representatives of big business). At one point, just before going into 'I Still Miss Someone', Johnny announces, "This show is being recorded for an album release on Columbia Records and you can't say 'hell' or 'shit' or anything like that." Turning to producer Bob Johnston, he smirks, "How does that grab you, Bob?" The men loved it. When one of the guards gives him some water, he asks, "You serve everything in tin cups?" to a chorus of cheers. His most risqué line, though, inadvertently snuck out between songs. "Hey, this microphone's got a screw loose here . . . somebody come screw this microphone." Some of the men collapsed in laughter at which point Johnny realised his unintended *double entendre* and joked at his own expense, "What'd I say?"

At the end of the show Johnny was presented with a prisoner's cap and coat and was told that it would make him one of the "in" crowd when he was out, though Johnny enigmatically said that "it just didn't fit . . ." While all around was psychedelic and day-glo in 1968, the troupe dressed conservatively (dark suits for the men, a fur-lined coat for June) and the black and white photographs adorning the resultant album sleeve show Johnny looking timelessly cool. Some mainstream radio stations refused to play songs from the album because of a few profanities and drug references but certain underground stations played the album in its entirety which helped connect Johnny to a younger group of listeners who had little to do with the world of country music.

◆ ◆ ◆ ◆ ◆

There was one other special feature of the show. One of the inmates, Glen Sherley, doing time for armed robberies (with a toy pistol) had given a tape of a song he'd written called 'Greystone Chapel' to the Reverend Gressett a year or so before the show, in the hope that somehow he might get it to Cash, given their pastoral and personal relationship. It would have joined the thousands of others that came Johnny's way, which were either ignored or, on occasion, thrown into the lake. Assuming it was a lost cause, Glen asked for his tape back but the night before the show, Gressett had given it to Johnny in Sacramento. Johnny listened to it this time, realised the relevance of the song (Greystone Chapel was the Folsom Prison church), and stayed up to rehearse it.

Although it was supposed to be a surprise, it seems that word somehow reached Glen because he was given a seat right at the front, enabling him to savour at close quarters Johnny's performance of his song. When Johnny announced 'Greystone Chapel' he observed Glen's reaction. "He grabbed his throat, he tried to laugh and shout, he tried to talk and he couldn't. He was the happiest guy I ever saw in all my life." What did not go through Johnny's mind were the possible consequences for Sherley at the hands of other cons, since in the febrile, hothouse atmosphere of Folsom such exposure might have made him a marked man (though there is no evidence to suggest this happened). In the photograph on the album sleeve, showing him shaking hands with Cash, Sherley avoids eye contact, his head hung low. It was a turning point in the con's life, enriched when Johnny later gave him a deal with his House Of Cash Publishing Company which helped his parole case. After his release he wrote 'Portrait Of My Woman' for Eddy Arnold and enjoyed a modicum of success as a solo artist.

Johnny Cash At Folsom Prison was an immediate hit and went on to enjoy nearly two years in the country charts as well as a lengthy run in the pop charts. Although Cash's recordings had sold consistently well in the mid-Sixties there had not been a spectacular success since 'Ring Of Fire' in 1963. All that changed as the album revitalised his career and somehow symbolised his rebirth as he started to seriously address and overcome the problems in his personal life. The album even won him a Grammy for the six sides of handwritten sleeve notes which were Johnny's attempt to look at the world from a prisoner's perspective. Given his limited experience as an inmate, the words were imbued with artistic licence: "You sit on your cold, steel mattress-less bunk bed and watch a cock-roach crawl out from under the filthy commode, and you don't kill it. You envy the roach as you watch it crawl out under the cell door."

Another unexpected consequence of the show was that Folsom Prison became a most unlikely tourist attraction with thousands of people driving up to the "Stop No Visitors Beyond This Point" sign, eagerly taking snaps and visit-ing the Folsom Prison Museum where they could take a video tour of the facil-ity. Many were disappointed to learn that Johnny Cash had never actually served a sentence there.

◆ ◆ ◆ ◆ ◆

February was to be an eventful month in Johnny's life, starting with several par-ticularly emotional "homecoming" shows in El Dorado, Arkansas, Memphis – where Johnny was given the key to the city – and finally, "Johnny Cash Day" in Dyess. Gridlock ensued as the local population was increased tenfold by incom-ing visitors, and a second show was hastily arranged. The local mayor said Dyess had seen nothing like it since Eleanor Roosevelt's morale boosting visit 36 years previously.

Some of Johnny's fellow performers had been dropping hints about Johnny and June, fuelling matrimonial speculation, and many in the crowd hoped that Johnny would choose the occasion to make an announcement but they were to be disappointed. At a show in Amarillo around this time, a tough looking female with silver-sculpted hair grabbed him by the arms as he came off stage and said, "Hey Johnny, remember me that night in El Paso in 58?" Johnny didn't. She pulled him into a dressing room and when they came out a few minutes later he was blushing. "He remembers now," she crowed. "Wild, wasn't it?" With a boyish grin, he agreed that it was.

At the start of 1968, Vivian's divorce was granted in Ventura, California by a superior court judge on the grounds of Johnny's "extreme cruelty". Johnny did not attend the hearing at which he was ordered to pay $400 per month toward each of the girls as well as any medical costs not covered by insurance. The court also awarded him generous access rights to his four daughters. The catalyst in the divorce proceedings, resisted by Vivian for so long, was a new man in her life, Dick Distin, who was, as Tommy Cash explained, "The detective she hired to look into Johnny's activities." They married soon after the divorce came through and not long afterwards Vivian received an unpleasant parting shot from her old enemies the Ku Klux Klan when it was reported that they burnt a cross on her lawn. Johnny too had a memento of the Klan, a letter from them written in blood which he framed and put up on his wall. The letter included the lines, "You are a traitor to the white people . . . I hope your daughter gives you a nigger grandchild."

Johnny said that he hadn't been a strong enough man to make his first marriage work. "My girls and I are close but I'm glad they're with their mother. She's a fine person and will do a great deal for them." June's comments on Johnny's previous marriage were typically euphemistic, "He didn't have a very happy marriage. His marriage got all mixed up and they separated. Then John was kind of mixed up for a while."

In February, during a live concert in London, Ontario, Johnny proposed to June in front of an audience of 5,000 people, who did not initially twig what was going on. June was embarrassed and flummoxed, hummed a tune and urged him to get on with the show but he persisted and once the audience got the message, they were soon egging June on. When she realised that he was in determined and stubborn mode, she smiled and accepted after which the pair sang 'If I Were A Carpenter'. It was a typically impulsive thing for Johnny to do. A proposal of marriage is usually one of the most intimate utterances a man can make and here he was doing it in front of thousands of people as if his private life had become public property. Did the public setting make it more worthwhile or was it that his life had been spent in the public eye for so long that it seemed a natural setting for such a momentous occasion? Or was Cash just irresistibly drawn to dramatic public gestures?

That same month, having won numerous BMI awards, Johnny was at last honoured with his first Grammy, a joint award for 'Jackson' in the Best Country & Western Performance, Duet, Trio or Group Vocal or Instrumental Category. Johnny used the award ceremony to make an important personal announcement. As he accepted the award, grinning broadly, he told the audience, "This'll be a fine wedding present." The message quickly sank in and though coming as no great surprise, the audience gave the couple a spontaneous standing ovation. Johnny and June were married the very next day, March 1, at a small ceremony in the Methodist church in Franklin, Kentucky attended by family members and The Tennessee Three plus their wives. Merle Kilgore was Johnny's best man and Micki Brooks, one of June's closest friends, was matron of honour.

June had considered waiting longer in order to allow her daughters to complete their school years but both Carlene and Rosey said that now they had made their decision they should get married at the earliest opportunity. The couple did not need any more persuasion. The wedding was followed by a party for about 150 people back at the Hendersonville house. Singer Skeeter Davis no doubt wore a wry smile when she heard of June's marriage because a few years before, she had contemplated getting married to a man who had a child from a previous marriage. June had advised against the idea. A few months after the wedding, on a visit to Israel, Johnny and June bought matching rings, each engraved with "Me to my love and my love to me" in Hebrew.

During a British tour later in the year, an interview June gave to a *Daily Mail* reporter provided an insight into her traditional marriage role. Talking about Johnny she said, "I help him wherever I can. If he wants me to work, I work and if he wants me to wash dishes, I wash dishes." After a discussion with Nat Winston who suggested that June was too independent, she gave up her membership of the *Grand Ole Opry* after 17 years in order to be able to devote herself to serving Johnny better. June's view of married and professional life gave another female country icon, Loretta Lynn, cause for complaint, "Men came first in country music. Men dominated." Soon after their marriage, Johnny and June took up residence in the new house along with June's daughters Carlene and Rosey, the plan being that Johnny's daughters in California would spend part of their vacations in Hendersonville.

Johnny threw himself into touring with renewed vigour in 1968, one of his busiest years for live appearances. In order to capitalise on his popularity in Britain, the Cash troupe toured there twice in 1968 – a two week tour in May (including a sell-out show at London's Royal Albert Hall) and a shorter visit in October to November. Writing in British country music magazine *Opry* (who devoted a regular feature to Cash in the Sixties), Pat and David Deadman were "struck by how well Johnny looked", unlike in 1966, "when he looked terribly tired". Interviewed by the *Daily Mail*, June revealed her disdain for the pop scene in Britain, referring to The Beatles and The Rolling Stones as "them jazzy kind of people". Possibly in an attempt to appear more up to date, The Statler Brothers dropped the American showbiz impersonations and comedy routines from their set.

The troupe did not go to Ireland on this occasion, instead slotting in two American military installations shows in England. During the tour Johnny unveiled, for the first time outside America, the rear screen projection which he used as a backdrop for a medley of train-related songs (usually 'Wreck Of The Old '97', 'Casey Jones', 'Folsom Prison Blues' and 'Orange Blossom Special'), culminating in two trains crashing head on just as the music came to a crescendo. Johnny was one of the first artists to introduce live film to his shows. Jerry Nutting, a lighting technician, had approached several Hollywood studios, eventually coming across footage of two trains colliding dating back to 1919.

In October, June flew home early when news reached her that James Howard, a son of her close friend, singer Jan Howard, had been killed in Vietnam. Mother Maybelle filled in by doing a solo spot.

During the recording of a radio show in London, Johnny found he needed to refer to a copy of the New Testament for a reading during one of his songs from his forthcoming album, *Holy Land,* but even on a Sunday, the BBC studios in Piccadilly were not the most likely place to find a Bible. DJ Murray Kash volunteered to track one down from the nearest church, but despite the fact that it was the Sabbath, the first five churches he came to were closed. No doubt, Johnny made sure he carried his own copy on him after that.

◆ ◆ ◆ ◆ ◆

Johnny's rebirth was overshadowed by a sudden tragedy which shocked and upset everybody connected with him. Luther and Margie Perkins had only just moved into their new lakeside house in Hendersonville, not far from the new Mr and Mrs Cash. Luther joked with Johnny that it would now be easier for him to sail over to visit than to drive. Luther had been working in the studio and was presumably exhausted. The authorities later established that he fell asleep while smoking a cigarette and, in the ensuing fire, suffered third degree burns to 50 per cent of his body.

Margie had been out with one of the children. When she returned to the house and opened the garage door to see smoke, she made frantic efforts to get into the house but Luther was already badly burnt and suffering from severe smoke inhalation. He was rushed to hospital and over the following hours there were some moments of hope when it seemed his condition might improve but when Johnny Cash saw his friend he knew right away that there would be no happy ending. Luther died on August 5, 1968 and was buried in Hendersonville two days later. Ralph Emery spoke for many with his emotional tribute, "It will be hard to adjust to a world without Luther. He was loved by everybody." Johnny, Marshall, Fluke and Carl Perkins were pallbearers at his funeral. Johnny later generously contributed time and money to the establishment of a $2 million specialist burns unit at Nashville's Vanderbilt Hospital – the nearest such facility at the time of Luther's death being in Cincinnati – stressing that he would like the unit to cater for everybody, including those from poorer backgrounds who were unable to meet the cost of treatment.

Johnny's thoughts turned to the issue of finding someone who could "play the boogie strange" like his late friend. Reportedly, certain musicians thoughtlessly offered their services as replacements before Luther had even been buried. "We may find someone to stand in for Luther, but he will never be replaced." At some of the shows soon after Luther's death, some unaware members of the audience yelled out, "Where's Luther?" leaving Johnny with the unhappy task of explaining.

Although Carl Perkins filled in as best he could, Johnny wanted somebody who could give him the "boom-chick-a-boom" sound, though he could not have foreseen the serendipitous circumstances in which this would come about. In September 1968, the troupe were due to play a show in Fayetteville to a crowd of about 10,000 people, one of a number of shows in support of Republican Winthrop Rockerfeller's campaign for governor of Arkansas. Johnny was playing for lower than his usual rates because of his support for Rockerfeller's attempts to get to the bottom of a number of prison scandals in Arkansas involving violence to prisoners and guard corruption. Although never slow to speak out on subjects close to his heart, this was one of the few occasions when Johnny overtly aligned himself with a particular political party.

Bad weather meant that Marshall Grant and Carl Perkins, travelling separately from the rest of the group, were prevented from flying to Fayetteville so that Johnny was faced with the prospect of having no lead guitarist. The running order of the show was rearranged with June doing a lengthier spot, followed by Johnny and Fluke doing a few numbers including 'Orange Blossom Special' with the harmonica parts filling in some of the gaps. The trouble was, by his own admission, Johnny was not a particularly good guitarist and after playing a few songs, he withdrew, unsure as to what he would be able to do for his second spot.

Earlier the same day a man who had been a Johnny Cash fanatic for half of his 26 years had gone to the airport in the hope of meeting Johnny. He waited for hours unaware that Johnny had arrived early and was already at the auditorium. The man in question wasn't just any old fan. Bob Wootton was a small-time guitarist who had a large collection of Cash memorabilia, owned most of Johnny's records and could play along to all of Luther's leads just about note perfect. Born in Paris, Arkansas in 1942, his family had later relocated to California and then Tulsa. Bob had served time in the army as a gunner in Korea and being a fan of country music in general and Johnny Cash in particular, he put together a band called Johnny & The Ramrods. When he came out of the army Bob drove a truck and joined countless other hopefuls trying to carve out a career in music. He was a particular fan of Luther Perkins and one of his most treasured possessions was a backstage photograph of himself and Luther taken in 1966.

Soon after Bob and his girlfriend arrived at the auditorium and became aware that the troupe were two players short, they sent word backstage that Bob was prepared to fill in. June got the message and relayed it to Johnny who was desperate. As he said later, "Well I was ready to try anything, I didn't care if he could play like Luther or not. I needed someone to help me out and I needed him right then." When Bob was introduced to his hero, Johnny was tuning his guitar. Johnny's first impression was favourable. "Well I caught a gleam in his eye, his attitude, his whole attitude was one of confidence." Johnny soon elicited the fact that Bob knew all of his songs and asked if he would be prepared to play the show.

Bob agreed with alacrity and was soon onstage playing his favourite songs to over 7,000 fans. It was, as he put it later, "Every fan's dream come true." Johnny was impressed with Bob's playing, saying later, "He had every one of my songs exactly right. He laid down the Luther beat on everything except maybe 'I Walk The Line' which is a challenge for anybody. I heard a little something in his playing that nobody else has got. If it was close to anybody it was close to Scotty Moore with a Luther beat." By delivering the goods, Bob became the newest member of The Tennessee Three, appearing over the following weeks at the Carnegie Hall and the London Palladium among many other venues. To keep his feet on the ground, his duties also included making sure that Johnny's guitar was always in tune.

Bob Wootton didn't slot in right away. He was taking his place in a family of artists who were bound together by a web of professional and emotional ties. He was also going through a painful divorce and had a lot on his mind, so for a time he tended not to mix with the others; choosing to spend his free time alone by going to the cinema or staying in his room. As time went by, Bob got through his six month trial period without any hitch, settling in as an established member of the Johnny Cash show.

In late-'68, Johnny made up for the disaster of his 1962 Carnegie Hall appearance with a triumphant return which critic Robert Shelton described as "Soul music of a very rare kind – country soul from the concerned and sensitive white south." Johnny broached this theme before the show when he told one reporter, "You don't have to have lived in poverty to be a successful country singer but it helps." A report on the concert in *The Tennessean* confirmed this view of the importance of Johnny's roots. "While admiring the new interest of city pop musicians in country music, Johnny Cash has found no substitute for living in the south, with the influences of Negro music and musicians and white farmers for getting to the heart of country music." In the audience were Janis Joplin and Bob Dylan with whom Johnny had dinner after the show.

◆ ◆ ◆ ◆ ◆

In 1967, Johnny had met with writer John L Smith backstage at a show in Des Moines, Iowa. Smith had become keenly interested in the history of Native Americans so naturally he and Johnny had a lot to talk about. The two remained in touch with the possibility of a benefit show for the Sioux being mooted. Smith was excited and overjoyed to receive a telegram from Saul Holiff saying that Johnny would be able to do a show in December 1968, which duly went ahead at the St Francis Mission on the Rosebud Reservation in South Dakota, with tickets generously priced at 75 cents for adults and 50 cents for children. Indeed it was reported that in order to do this show he turned down the opportunity to earn $10,000 by appearing in a television special with The Rolling Stones.*

Addressing the audience of mainly Native Americans, many dressed in traditional outfits, Johnny skirted around the subject of his own ancestry with skills a political spin-doctor would be proud of. "I've got very little Indian blood in me myself, except in my heart I've got 100 per cent for you tonight." His rendition of 'The Ballad Of Ira Hayes' was a particularly emotional experience for singer and audience alike and following the show there was a ceremony during which

* Namely, *The Rolling Stones Rock'n'Roll Circus*, filmed in London between December 10–12, featuring The Rolling Stones, John Lennon and Yoko Ono, The Who, Marianne Faithfull, Eric Clapton, Taj Mahal, and Jethro Tull. Because of numerous complications, the film and soundtrack weren't released until 1996.

traditional dances were performed and gifts were given to Johnny and the members of his band.

The next day Johnny and June, accompanied by John L Smith, travelled the hundred or so miles to the Wounded Knee community where they were met by Jesse White Lance, William Horn Cloud, Edger Red Cloud and Robert Holy Dance. After a short impromptu performance in a small trading post for some 30 Native American elders who had been unable to attend the show the previous day, they walked to the site of a notorious massacre in 1890 when over 150 Miniconjou men, women and children, including their leader Spotted Elk, better known as Big Foot, were killed by the Seventh United States Cavalry, who still harboured bitter memories of a massacre inflicted on Custer's troops by Native Americans some 14 years before. Johnny was visibly moved as he inspected the site of the mass graves into which the bodies had been unceremoniously dumped. The two-day trip was filmed and segments would later be included in a documentary, *Johnny Cash: The Man, His World, His Music*. On the way back to the airport, in the back of John L Smith's car, as he had done so often in the Fifties, Johnny grabbed a piece of paper having been inspired to write a song, 'Big Foot', which would be featured on a future album.

Commercially, Johnny's position was stronger than it had ever been. The success of *At Folsom Prison* had the knock-on effect of encouraging people to buy his other albums, all of which made good showings in the charts. Significantly, they were being bought by large numbers of people who did not think of themselves as country fans, the sort who were turned off by rhinestones and the bar room mawkishness of more traditional country. Having started the year drug dependent, Johnny was on a roll but there were greater things still to come.

16

"*Come on mothers throughout the land,*
Pack your boys off to Vietnam,
Come on Fathers don't hesitate,
Send your sons off before it's too late,
You can be the first on your block,
To have your boy come home in a box."

('I-Feel-Like-I'm-Fixin'-To-Die Rag' – Country Joe and The Fish)

"*I hear people talkin' bad about the way they have to live here in this country,*
Harpin' on the wars they fight, gripin' 'bout the way things ought to be.
I don't mind them switching sides and standing up for things they believe in,
When they're running down our country man, they're walkin' on the fightin' side of
me."

('The Fightin' Side Of Me' – Merle Haggard)

JOHNNY CASH found himself on the horns of a dilemma over US involvement in Vietnam. Like most people he didn't really understand the history of the conflict which was perceived by many as something of an anti-communist crusade, but he was deeply concerned at the heavy loss of life on both sides, especially the hundreds of deaths of young Americans. He expressed concern to his brother Tommy that "they might be dying for a cause that isn't just". At the same time Johnny was above all a patriot and it would have been unthinkable for him to take an overtly anti-war stance. Generally, his politics allied him more to Merle Haggard than Country Joe, though he was certainly never an enthusiastic supporter of the war *per se*. As he put it in his 1997 autobiography, "I had no really firm convictions about the rightness or wrongness of the war; my mind just wouldn't approach it at that level when my heart hurt so badly."

Johnny queried who was going to extricate America from the war and on one occasion, taking on the role of patriarchal Cash spokesman, he said, "My family stand behind the President in his quest for peace." On the thorny subject of war, he referred to himself as a "dove"; at other times as a "dove with claws", and he maintained that while they were in Vietnam, American troops would have his full support. Writing in the *Village Voice*, Robert Christgau confidently asserted that "Cash was an enthusiastic Nixon supporter," but in his 1997 autobiography Johnny categorically stated that he never voted for Nixon. There has always been something of a smokescreen surrounding Cash's political views. He has referred to himself as "an independent voter", free to support or oppose issues on their merits, regardless of which political party or pressure group happens to be promoting them. Over the years, he has supported both the Liberals and Democrats on issues rather than party lines.

Apart from his independent nature, Johnny has been commercially astute enough to realise that if he were to come down strongly in support of one political party or another he might alienate a large number of potential record buyers. With his conservative views on country, family and religion on the one hand and his support for liberal causes on the other he has always had fans and supporters in a number of camps. He hinted at where his affinities lay when talking about Jimmy Carter, a cousin of June's to whom he became a distant relation by marriage, "He was family by blood, and just about family by heart."

Part of Johnny's response to Vietnam was to play shows for the troops, and at the start of 1969, the troupe embarked on a tour of the Far East which took in visits to American bases including the Long Binh Air Force Base at Saigon, not far from the front line. There, he and June gained first-hand experience of the terrifying reality of being close to war when one morning, after a particularly intense bombardment which had kept them awake for much of the night, they found that the trailer they were sleeping in had been moved a few feet by the shock waves emanating from the blasts.*

Apart from cramming in as many shows as possible, Johnny and June also visited wounded soldiers in army hospitals, taking their details and emotional messages to pass on to families back in America. However, the visit degenerated when Johnny developed a fever following the usual cocktail of air-conditioned rooms, dramatic changes of climate, and smoky venues. Summoning a local doctor, Johnny asked the physician for something to help him through two shows scheduled for the following evening. Presumably June wasn't there when 24 Dexedrine capsules were handed over with the pointless admonition, "Don't take more than one a day."

The shows were wholly substandard thanks to the speed and the large shots of

---

* Johnny and June's experiences during the visit inspired a song, 'Singin' In Vietnam Talking Blues'.

brandy Johnny washed them down with. Characteristic of his former behaviour, Johnny took to hiding the pills in various places like a squirrel depositing chestnuts for the winter. Of course it didn't take long for June to realise what was going on, and she became depressed but resigned, realising that Johnny could be prone to a relapse. Whereas before she might have walked away to save herself further anguish, she had now committed herself to the sanctity of marriage. As the troupe travelled from place to place, June was often found slumped in a corner, quietly sobbing. Johnny was too blocked to be sympathetic; he had a fever, the pills made him feel better, what was the problem? That is roughly how he rationalised it in his head and even the sight of June, unable to raise a smile for the fans during a showstopper like 'Jackson', didn't get through to him. He did get a shock at Saigon airport when he unexpectedly came face to face with the Reverend Jimmy Snow, pastor of Evangel Temple in Nashville, who delivered a sobering reminder of the Christian values Johnny was so blatantly betraying. June tried to cover up for her husband by saying he had pneumonia but Johnny felt ashamed by the Reverend's piercing stare. After they parted, he rushed off to the men's room to alleviate his shame with another pill.

The absolute low point came at Tokyo's Tachikawa Air Force Base. Having arrived two hours late Johnny was hustled onto the stage by an old acquaintance, Takahiro Saito, a Japanese Johnny Cash impersonator, to face a restless, rowdy but adoring crowd. For Johnny, full of pills and brandy, what followed was, "The saddest, most humbling hour of my life." He couldn't sing or stand and was reduced to mumbling an apology by way of an assurance that he wouldn't appear in this state in front of an audience again. Johnny later said that the lesson he learned on the Far East tour was "God is love and God is forgiving," but, as so often, Johnny himself seemed to be more forgiven than forgiving.

◆ ◆ ◆ ◆ ◆

Back in America, at the behest of their mutual producer Bob Johnston, Johnny got together with Bob Dylan who was in Nashville to record his ninth album, *Nashville Skyline*. This was not the first time that Dylan had sought inspiration from the heart of country music, though it was seen as a controversial move by some of his fans and critics. For many, *Nashville Skyline* marked a sea change in relations between the worlds of rock and country. For the session, Bob Johnston set up some mikes, arranged a few stools (including one for Carl Perkins who picked on the session), and let the tapes roll, expecting magic to flow. Unfortunately it didn't. Just as the two greatest football teams in the world can serve up a dull game that never takes off, so Cash and Dylan kicked several songs around to no great effect. The numbers chosen were mainly Cash songs or standards, though the session did produce one Cash–Dylan writing collaboration, the lightweight but catchy 'Wanted Man'. The best moments occurred during two versions of 'One Too Many Mornings' with its nifty key changes, and Johnny sternly reminding Bob of the lyrics to 'That's All Right (Mama)' also has some entertainment value.

Dylan sounds distinctly uneasy singing a country standard like 'You Are My Sunshine', lacking as it does the irony used to such stunning effect in much of his output. As Peter Doggett wrote in *Are You Ready For The Country*: "To the country fan, Dylan's surreal images, allegories and sophisticated language actually sounded dull. Dylan needed the confusing intellectual imagery but Johnny Cash didn't because of the power of his voice and the simplicity, directness and honesty of the message – that's who he was and that's why people liked him." In a similar vein legendary songwriter Harlan Howard said, "That's the beauty of country songs, they don't mystify you," while rural music expert Tom Ashley said, "Country people play their feeling and feel their playing."

None of the songs were of sufficient quality for official release though 'Girl From The North Country', the last song cut at the session, did make it onto *Nashville Skyline*. It's a stilted, lifeless affair with some embarrassing, off-key ad-libbed crooning at the fade, which merely serves to demonstrate how ill at ease they were as a duo. It was not surprising that rumours of a joint album–tour project never amounted to anything. Referring to the session in a 1988 interview with Bill Flanagan, Johnny said, "Musically it's really inferior, it's not up to par for either one of us. I think that he was embarrassed over that and I don't blame him. I regret it. I love Bob Dylan, I really do."

Although the two held each other's creative attention for only a short while, clearly, a bond did develop. George Hamilton IV remembers an occasion when he was on a Toronto television show with Johnny and asked him about his friendship with Dylan. Johnny told Hamilton about the time he and June sent a present to one of Bob's sons on the occasion of his bar mitzvah. They received a scrawled note back simply addressed to "Johnny Cash, Hendersonville, Tennessee," which said, "Dear Johnny Cash, thanks to you and Mom and apple pie and Billy Graham, love Bob." Hamilton asked Johnny what he took from the message. He said, "I have no idea," to which Hamilton replied, "I think that's a really high compliment." Johnny smiled, indicating that he thought so too.*

◆ ◆ ◆ ◆ ◆

Having taken years to sanction an album recorded in a prison, thanks to the success of *Johnny Cash At Folsom Prison,* CBS were not slow in demanding a sequel. The new location was the notoriously tough maximum security prison at San Quentin in California. Johnny had played there before on a number of

---

* Earlier Dylan and Cash had exchanged letters, some of which Johnny wrote on aeroplanes, using "sick bags" as envelopes. He has said that the letters, containing "rambling thoughts", are locked away in a vault and that some time before he dies he will destroy them all.

occasions, including a show in 1958 when Merle Haggard was among the audience.* On this occasion, a Granada television crew from England were on hand to record proceedings in the hangar-like north dining hall, before 1,500 inmates overseen by heavily armed guards. The resultant programme was a powerful document, with talking heads interspersed between songs giving graphic snippets of life on the inside. One prisoner previously on death row spoke affectingly of how he got news of his reprieve hours before he was due to be gassed, though sympathy was balanced by cold horror at his account of strangling a woman and her 12-year-old son because the latter had interrupted their sexual union.

A prison officer gave a minute-by-minute account of the execution process and stated his sincerely held view that none of the men who died felt any physical pain. He also threw light on what lengths men would go to in order to appear tough, such as wrapping toilet paper around their arms to make them look "muscled up". The introduction to the programme featured a short sequence about the settlement of the West; man versus nature, pursuing his religious ideals in the face of adversity and building up many myths in the process. This lead to Johnny's entry when the narration spoke of his affect on the audience, portraying him as "a folk singer who can become the Western hero in their eyes," and "a bit of America people want to look back to."

In a 1973 *Rolling Stone* interview, Cash said that the Folsom show was "closer" to him, partly because of the added tension created by the presence of cameras which made for a less relaxed atmosphere, though he also said that San Quentin felt generally "tighter" than Folsom anyway. Certainly no allowances were made on the security front and, as Johnny went in, a guard stamped his hand with a special dye that would show up under ultra-violet light, telling him, "Remember, on the way out, no glow, no go." The benches and tables were laid out in unbroken rows and as one warder put it, "That way it makes it difficult for them to stand and if it's awkward for a man to rise it's that much harder for him to make trouble." Backstage, Johnny talked about going down among the men during the show but June gave short shrift to that idea. He came over as being particularly fired up by the occasion and when he sang, his lip seemed to curl with even more intensity than usual, though his voice was hoarse at times and his chesty cough bore witness to years of excess.

Johnny used San Quentin to first air the Shel Silverstein novelty song, 'A Boy Named Sue'. Silverstein had first played Johnny the song at a recent musical evening in Hendersonville, to which Johnny responded, "It is the most cleverly written song I have ever heard." It had in fact been inspired by a real-life male

---

* However, while greatly admiring Johnny's prison concerts Haggard said later, "Johnny Cash understands what it's like to be in prison, but he doesn't *know*."

named Sue, one Judge Sue K Hicks of Madisonville. Hicks recalled that Silverstein had been in Gatlinburg when the pair were introduced during a juridical conference.* (Some Native Americans might have initially assumed from hearing the title that Johnny was singing about Sioux Indians!)

According to Ralph Emery, it was pure chance that the song was included in the show at all and it was June who suggested to Johnny that he should take along the lyrics, written on a sheet of yellow paper, at the last minute. Johnny's risk-taking bravado in choosing a song he didn't know for a live recording was as admirable as it was daring. Listening to the released cut, there is a sense of the group winging it with band and singer veering off in separate musical directions at times. Once more Johnny bantered good-naturedly with the crowd though at least one of his lines was off-colour. Just as he was finishing 'I Walk The Line', Johnny started smiling and said to an (out of frame) cameraman, "You better not bend over with that camera like that, man you're in the wrong place to bend over, don't you know it."

Johnny preceded 'Starkville City Jail' with a sanitised and disingenuous account of the time he spent a night in jail and was fined $36 for picking flowers in Starkville. He painted a picture of an ordinary man engaged in an entirely harmless activity not a lawless performer, wired to the hilt, running wild around a strange town in the middle of the night; in the eyes of the police who apprehended him the flower picking activity was doubtless an incidental matter. During his preamble to the song he sarcastically silenced one talkative inmate with, "What? Sorry, I couldn't hear you, I was talking."

As always the troupe were soberly dressed and Marshall Grant's static delivery, matching that of the gaunt looking Bob Wootton, was in marked contrast to the early days when he had bounced about all over his part of the stage. June's entry wearing a girly-frilly white dress looked endearingly out of place, like a pale orchid among a field full of weeds, or as one reviewer put it when talking about June, her mother and sisters, "A little heavenly band thrown before hell's inmates."

Johnny wrote the song 'San Quentin' shortly before the show and with lines like "San Quentin you've been living hell to me" and "San Quentin may you rot and burn in hell", it was bound to be a crowd pleaser. However, when the crowd yelled for a reprise, it nearly incited a riot. Johnny later said he felt the power of having the crowd in his hands (what writer Charlie Gillett referred to as "The Martin Luther King effect"), and that if he had shouted "Break!" at the moment when emotions were highest, the prisoners would have done just that. But was this an act of responsibility? Johnny's emotional support for prison reform was

* After the song was successful, Hicks was sent photographs of Johnny – one of which was autographed, "To Sue, how do you do, from your friend Johnny."

beyond dispute but might it not have been more appropriate to have entertained the men without winding up their adrenaline levels?

Speaking a few years later to *New Musical Express* journalist Mick Farren, Johnny suggested that his anger may have to some extent been put on. When asked about any involvement he had with movements for prisoners' rights he said, "I've never been involved with prisoners' rights as such ... when I recorded those (prison) albums, I had to talk the language of a prison. That's an entertainer's job, to get across to his audience, whoever they are." Judging by the wording of a full-page *Billboard* advertisement to promote the album on its release a few months later, CBS didn't disapprove of Johnny's action, indeed they added fuel to the fire:

" 'San Quentin may you rot and burn in hell.' It only takes one night in San Quentin to feel that way. Not long ago Johnny Cash spent a night in there, singing for the boys. That's what he felt, and that's what he sang. Cash came by his hatred of prisons the hard way. That's why he goes back. First to Folsom Prison, now San Quentin. That's why there's this tremendous affinity with the prisoners. And that's why there's so much feeling in the music . . ."

With advertising blurb like this, it's hardly surprising that many people came to the erroneous belief that Johnny Cash had served time, though perhaps he came closer than many realised, as he later confessed, "There's something inside me. If I weren't playing my guitar, I think I would be a criminal. Man, I came close in that time in the Sixties when I was violent on the amphetamines." Indeed Johnny has conceded that on occasion he broke into drugstores to get large quantities of pills, not because he couldn't afford them but because he didn't want the inconvenience of filling out prescription forms. As he later conceded, "There's a lot of things blamed on me that never happened. But then there's a lot of things that I never got caught at."

◆ ◆ ◆ ◆ ◆

Released in June 1969, *Johnny Cash At San Quentin* was that rarest of beasts, a follow-up which tries to emulate the success of an earlier album and succeeds. Once more the album gave Johnny the opportunity to express himself to the full and both prison albums have stood the test of time. One reviewer, John David Rhodes, put it this way, "Playing to a prison audience seems to have brought out Cash's essence: blunt honesty, gruff compassion and artistic integrity." Another reviewer took the revisionist opportunity to mock the intellectual folk crowd. "While Joan Baez, the Farinas and Pete Seeger were playing protest ditties to liberal audiences, Johnny Cash was bringing the word – cold and hard – to maximum security prisoners. His prison concerts, preserved on a couple of seminal recordings, testify to a social engagement more difficult to classify, and certainly more risky, than preaching to the converted at the Newport Folk

Festival. What's more, these concerts kick ass." The album spent a remarkable 21 weeks at number one in the country charts.

It's not clear whether the inmates who were filmed *en masse* gave their permission to be filmed and it may be that some would have had good reason to maintain privacy.* This issue was addressed at a Tennessee State Prison concert in late-1968, when just before the show began Harry S Abery, Commissioner of the Department of Corrections, appeared before the men, stressing that the show was going to be filmed, saying, "It will be taken for granted by the presence of those who come that they do not have any objections to being included in this film."

Despite Johnny's support for the prisoners' lot, some complained that at a time of seething unrest among black people he never spoke up specifically on their behalf, to which his response was, "I could tell you that I think they're not getting their fair shake. The only reason I haven't written a song about their problem is the inspiration has never come to me and I've never been given any good material on the subject."

By the late Sixties Johnny Cash was at the height of his popularity. The country and pop charts were crowded with his records to the extent that only Barbra Streisand and Johnny Mathis were selling more albums. Even *Holy Land,* inspired by the visit to Israel and featuring tracks with titles such as 'My Wife June At The Sea Of Galilee' and 'Our Guide Jacob At Mt Tabor', made it to number six in the country charts. One track 'Daddy Sang Bass', written by Carl Perkins, became a stalwart of the Johnny Cash show and was spoofed by Ray Stevens as 'Mama Sang Bass' (about the effects on a family of working in a pharmaceutical factory). The song's longevity perhaps owes something to its biographical relevance to Johnny, with the line "Singing seems to help a troubled soul" being particularly apposite. Johnny had heard Carl working on the song and liked it so much that he pushed Carl to quickly finish it, fending off interest from The Statler Brothers who were also keen to record it. Carl had actually considered keeping it for himself but "I guess I came out better by letting John have it."

The prison albums had undoubtedly caught the public's imagination and raised Johnny's profile to new heights. Johnny acknowledges Saul Holiff's contribution saying that if it had not been for Saul's business drive he might simply have continued playing to sell-out crowds at modest American venues. English country singer Frank Yonco recalls Holiff's advice to break free from "Fortress Ernest Tubb", a reference to Nashville and its traditionalism. Johnny was able to command a fee in the region of $5,000 per appearance by the late Sixties, but there was no shortage of promoters who recognised Cash was once more red-hot.

* In an ironic postscript, the co-producer of the Granada film, Michael Darlow, was mugged in a Harlem jazz club a few days later and lost about $500 to the kind of person who might well have ended up in a place like San Quentin.

"The higher he got, the more likely he was to say he was a quarter Cherokee," said Tommy Cash, "but when he was sober it would only be an eighth or less." (*LFI*)

Johnny with his "Junebug". The couple were married on March 1, 1968. (*Mirrorpix*)

With old friend, Carl Perkins. Johnny helped to revive Perkins' flagging fortunes by making him a part of the Cash touring troupe in 1966. (*Corbis*)

The Cash family gathered in the late-60's. L-R: brother Tommy, wife June, JC, brother Roy, sister Joanne, father Ray, and sisters Reba and Louise. Absent is Johnny's mother, Carrie. (*Courtesy of Nashville Public Library*)

Johnny Cash and the Carter Family Show, circa 1967. L-R: The Tennessee Three - Luther Perkins, W.S. "Fluke" Holland, Marshall Grant; The Carter Family – Mother Maybelle, Helen, Anita, June, and The Statler Brothers – Harold Reid, Phil Balsley, Don Reid, and Lew DeWitt. (*The Bill Miller Collection*)

Johnny with The Tennessee Three, 1968. That same year, Johnny's right-hand man, Luther Perkins (left) tragically died in a house fire. (*The Bill Miller Collection*)

Johnny performing at Cummins Prison Farm, Arkansas, April 10, 1969, where he was made an honorary life-term inmate. "I've never been involved with prisoners' rights as such… when I recorded those (prison) albums I had to talk the language of a prison." (*Corbis*)

With guest Bob Dylan on *The Johnny Cash Show*, May 1, 1969. The pair duetted on 'Girl From The North Country' in what was Dylan's first television appearance in five years. (*Redferns*)

With co-star Kirk Douglas in *A Gunfight*, 1970. A critic commented, "(Cash) was looking dour, as if someone had just named him Sue." (*Corbis*)

The proud parents with John Carter Cash, Madison Hospital, Nashville, March 3, 1970. (*Courtesy of Nashville Public Library*)

Johnny and June with Richard and Patricia Nixon after a concert in the East Room
of the White House, April 18, 1970. True to his politically ambiguous views,
in his 1997 autobiography, Johnny claimed that he never voted for "Tricky Dicky". (*Corbis*)

Cash the Patriot. His traditional views managed to
alienate the liberal part of his audience, while the
redneck element of his following were aghast at
certain causes he championed. (*Associated Press*)

Johnny with fellow country legend Tammy Wynette
on *The Johnny Cash Show*. The prime-time ABC
series, taped from Nashville's Ryman Auditorium,
ran for 56 shows between 1969 and 1971. (*Corbis*)

Johnny and June with guests Waylon Jennings, his partner Jessi Colter and Ray Charles during the taping of the CBS television special, *Johnny Cash: Spring Fever*, screened May 7, 1972. (*Hulton Archive*)

Three quarters of the Million Dollar Quartet reform to tape Johnny's 1977 Xmas TV special. Honorary Sun recording artist Roy Orbison stepped in for Elvis Presley (who had died the previous month). The four paid tribute to 'The King' with a version of 'This Train Is Bound For Glory.' (*Rex Features*)

Johnny plants a kiss on his stepdaughter Carlene Carter, watched by Atlantic Records producer, Jerry Wexler (right). Carlene's musical adventures in the late 70's took her to England where she met her third husband, Nick Lowe, who later wrote 'The Beast In Me' for Johnny. (*Redferns*)

Johnny with evangelist Billy Graham, June 1979. Their controversial association started a decade earlier when Graham said, "Johnny Cash has a marvellous communication with the young people of today... he manages to bridge the generation gap, appealing to audiences of all ages." (*Courtesy of Nashville Public Library*)

Johnny, June and six-year old John Carter Cash at the unveiling ceremony of Johnny's star on the Hollywood Walk of Fame, March 9, 1976. Cash was the 1,669th entertainer to be honoured by the Hollywood Chamber of Commerce. (*Corbis*)

In May, Johnny did a show with his 19-year-old friend Hank Williams, Jr, at Detroit's Cobo Arena. In his autobiography *Living Proof*, Hank Williams, Jr made clear his admiration for his older colleague. "Cash was a hard living man . . . There were pills and liquor and there were shows where Cash almost couldn't make it and shows where he didn't turn up at all but when he hit that stage, it was like some automatic pilot demon took over and he went out there and gave those people a show they'd remember." Hank Jr proudly pointed out that there was no opening act, "no lah de dah paraphernalia – it was me and Cash, the two biggest acts in country music, and we were gonna go out there and knock 'em dead."

Some ecstatic reviewers even went so far as to suggest it was one of the greatest shows in the history of country music. Apparently Hank was trying to cut loose from his mother's apron strings and, surprisingly, she had approved of him hooking up with Johnny who she saw as a good and stabilising influence for her wild son. The two sold-out shows in Detroit brought in nearly $100,000 from around 23,000 paying customers – a massively impressive take for a country music show. According to Hank Williams, Jr, it gave the Nashville establishment something of a jolt, thinking that individual performers just didn't bring in that kind of money. In December, Johnny played another sell-out show to 21,000 fans at Madison Square Garden in New York which brought in well over $100,000. Nobody could argue with this kind of success and Nashville had little option but to recognise the appeal of their wayward son even though many still regarded his country music credentials with suspicion.

◆ ◆ ◆ ◆ ◆

Johnny's live albums and the very obvious rapport he had with audiences, attracted the attention of television executives. A number of country singers – including Glen Campbell, Roger Miller and Porter Wagoner – each had their own shows around this time which got good ratings, so it was quite logical that an artist at the top of his game like Johnny should also be offered his own show. The offer of hosting a weekly one hour programme came from ABC though initially it was categorised as a low budget summer replacement programme to feature a selection of currently charting country singers mixed up with some routine comedy talents. Johnny had other ideas and insisted from the start on a degree of control over who appeared, which caused consternation among the executives. Just exactly what the content and style of the show would be was a source of media interest and speculation. In one 1969 interview, Johnny said, "If there is a theme to the show it is to illustrate the contemporary nature of modern country music so the integral part of each week's show will be country music . . . I want to get a real feel, not too slick." *The Tennessean* reported that the show was to feature artists from "the now generation" as well as some of the top exponents of the "standard ballad". The producers and the directors of the show referred to the *Grand Ole Opry* as "hard country" and pointed out that people like Glen Campbell and Johnny Cash were not to be seen there because "they were moving over to the general pop shows." Clearly there were going to be tensions.

Johnny also insisted on the show being broadcast from the Ryman auditorium in Nashville, home of the *Grand Ole Opry*, despite its lack of air-conditioning and modern infrastructure for technical recording equipment. There were early rumours that the producers wanted to move the show to California but Johnny gave short shrift to that idea. "I am not going to do that. It wouldn't be the same show, that's a whole different way of life out there. That's not where I want to be. That's not what I want to be." Johnny also sought to have a say in technical matters and ruffled a few feathers when he took a close interest in many aspects of the show, including the then revolutionary idea of lining up shots from behind the performers. The result was a show which introduced a veritable cornucopia of artists from the fields of country, rock, pop, soul and folk to a large television audience.

The flexible format was such that Johnny was able to flit between solo spots and grab a few lines with his guests. The ratings soared causing Johnny's star to ascend even further and from a commercial point of view the show was a virtuous circle for Cash and his guests. They all benefited from each other's presence, though it has been suggested that one of the executive's main aims for the show was to gain exposure for lesser-known artists on the back of Johnny's super high profile. There is little doubt that the careers of some of the early guests such as Joni Mitchell, Melanie and Charley Pride did benefit substantially from the exposure they received.

The show's atmosphere was compared to that of an old-time revivalist meeting, an impression bolstered by the bustling stage presence of the Carters and The Statler Brothers.

By 1969, Mother Maybelle was not in the best of health and the number of her live appearances diminished but Johnny was keen to maintain her profile and encouraged her to be not just part of the backing singers but to do the odd solo spot as well. In his book on The Carter Family, *Will You Miss Me When I'm Gone?*, Mark Zwonitzer speculates that the country music establishment might have felt a degree of unease about this since Mother Maybelle would have served to remind them that the Carters had been consistently overlooked since the Country Music Hall of Fame was established in 1961.[*] Experienced trouper that she was, Maybelle certainly had a good time during her spot, taking an amused pride in her nickname, "Mother Mothballs", though according to Mark Zwonitzer, at the end of filming one show, one of the Statlers said, "Great show Maybelle," to which she snapped back, "Coulda been, but June ruint it."

---

[*] Whether Maybelle's exposure on the show was a factor is not clear, but the Carters were finally inducted in 1970.

The first show was broadcast in June and featured Doug Kershaw, Joni Mitchell and Bob Dylan. Dylan, his wife Sara and family were staying with the Cash family at Hendersonville and before the taping had occurred in February, a guitar pull was held at the Cash house which has taken on legendary status over the years. The idea of a guitar pull was that a group of musicians sat in a circle with one guitar being passed between them, each recipient being obliged to perform a song or two with visitors to Hendersonville often taking the opportunity to unveil new compositions. Reports of who sang what on this particular evening vary but what seems certain is that Dylan sang 'Lay Lady Lay', Joni Mitchell sang 'Both Sides Now', Graham Nash did 'Marrakesh Express', James Taylor sang 'Sweet Baby James' and Shel Silverstein previewed 'A Boy Named Sue', in advance of the San Quentin concert.

Given the presence of Bob Dylan, the Ryman attracted a far from typical crowd as one local paper put it, "In place of the familiar orderly line of men in sports shirts and women in dresses or pedal pushers, there were clusters of flower children from several states on the steps at the front entrance on Fifth Avenue and in the back alley hoping to catch a glimpse of their idol. Clad in oversize Salvation Army clothes and other colourful garb they sat or lay on the pavement, some strumming guitars." Before filming commenced, Dylan had spent some time in a backstage office at the Ryman watching a discussion about the new left with Johnny and June.

He had been semi-reclusive since suffering serious injuries in a motorbike accident three years before and was still only tentatively making his way back into the public arena. It was clear that his mystique made him temperamentally and socially more of a rock star than a country cousin and the added ingredient of his natural shyness proved awkward for the organisers who felt he upset preparations for the show. He didn't mingle backstage with the other artists and avoided the press. Not content to be fobbed off with only being allowed to submit three written questions through an intermediary, one persistent reporter from the *Nashville Banner* somehow hustled his way into Dylan's presence during the rehearsals. He did manage to put a few questions during a brief exchange but the answers he got were short and hard to fathom. Johnny was keen to protect his friend but equally found it hard to make sense of his standoffishness.

In the event, Dylan got through the rehearsals without mishap, though not before he had succeeded in having the proposed backdrop for his set (a down-home shack exterior) removed. As he complained to Johnny, "My fans are gonna laugh in my face over that thing." The artificial rock which replaced it looked as unconvincing to look at as it appeared uncomfortable to sit on. When Dylan arrived at the Ryman for the actual show, he rushed in through a back entrance, head down, to avoid photographers and fans alike. It may be that his apprehension was not just to do with his reticence, since some of the other out-of-town non-country artists had been on the receiving end of derogatory attacks from locals who didn't approve of longhairs and hippies contaminating *their* part of the American south. Entry to the television taping was free and unsurprisingly the queues formed early, though tickets could also be obtained from various outlets around Nashville including the Ernest Tubb record shop.

Dylan performed 'I Threw It All Away' and 'Living The Blues' before being joined by his host for 'Girl From The North Country'. Some have written of a great chemistry between the pair but it may be that previous reputations have the ability to compromise objective judgement. As Peter Doggett put it, the ground didn't move for the two superstars, neither of whom looked comfortable or relaxed. As Johnny put it, ". . . everybody said it was the most magnetic powerful thing they ever heard in their life. They were just raving about electricity and magnetism. And all I did was just sit there hitting G chords." For all their mutual respect it became apparent that there was a gulf between their artistic worlds which could not be bridged. However, though musically incompatible, they remained good friends without attempting any other joint musical ventures. After the tensions surrounding Dylan's appearance it's hardly surprising that there should have been resistance to the idea of having left-wing folkie Pete Seeger on the show but Johnny held his ground, "I told 'em, it's either my way or the highway." Seeger eventually got to appear but the executives made it clear that he would be "monitored".

When Bob Hope arrived in Nashville as a guest on the show, he received a military escort from the airport to the Ramada Inn where he was quartered during his brief stay. He was also presented with an honorary citizen certificate from the Governor of Tennessee, a key to the city from the mayor of Nashville and the National Guardsman award in recognition of his overseas trips entertaining the troops. During Hope's appearance, Johnny read a personal letter from President Nixon in which the President expressed thanks for Hope's efforts to boost the morals of the nation and also for his stand on vital issues such as the Vietnam War and his opposition to drugs.

Country music was bigger business than it had ever been thanks in no small part to shows such as Johnny's and those of Glen Campbell and Roger Miller, as well as the more hardcore hillbilly, *Hee Haw*. While the shows were spreading the word about country music to a wider audience, they also sanitised it to a great extent. A perceptive view of the changing forces at work for country artists new and old was provided by Teddy Bart and quoted in *The Nashville Sound* by Jol Jensen. "Even though the new breed of performer comes from the same roots as the older, he is a product of the technological change and his values have changed. Where the height of an old country music performer's career might be a full house in every theatre in every small town he plays in for nearly 40 weeks a year and a brand new bus in which to travel, the newer breed of country music performer equates success with appearing on *The Ed Sullivan*

Show, perhaps having his own TV show and most of all getting a hit record that is not only a country hit but a pop hit as well. If having 16 violins and a full horn section to back him up on a recording of a pop song is the way to achieve this success then so be it."

Some critics saw *The Johnny Cash Show* as merely another "variety show" or as one put it rather more cuttingly, "*Rowan and Martin's Laugh-In* set in a barnyard." The cause was not helped by the house orchestra which, when used on songs meant to be played with a bare minimum of instrumentation (such as 'Folsom Prison Blues' or 'Orange Blossom Special'), resulted in the overproduced sound Johnny claimed he disliked. It must have been a ghastly spectacle for the likes of Sam Phillips who, years before, had dismissed criticism of the stripped down sound of 'I Walk The Line' by saying, "Could you imagine that song with fiddle and steel?" While not as full on as the hay bales featured in *Hee Haw*, the set, with its country-style living room replete with fireplace and wooden tables and chairs, was fairly clichéd nonetheless.

The producers had underestimated Johnny's musical integrity and his forcefully expressed desire to feature little known artists of genuine quality alongside the general entertainers and occasional comedians the executives insisted on. Being an established artist with a huge following and plenty of finances, Johnny had the strength of character to take them on. However, while he was a man who didn't like to be told what to do, Johnny did not relish the idea of protracted wrangling and was not always as tough as his gruff exterior had people believe. As Jack Clement puts it, "Cash didn't like to argue much, he would kind of stall." The powers-that-be got their way on quite a few occasions with the dichotomy of the likes of Liza Minnelli and The Monkees on one hand and the regular *Ride This Train* segment – with its hardcore country patriotism – on the other. Monkee Mike Nesmith may have been part of a manufactured pop group but he was a genuinely talented musician who had a high opinion of Johnny Cash and what made him important. Talking about Hank Williams, Jimmie Rodgers and Jerry Lee Lewis, Nesmith said, "Somehow I always get back to them. They, like Dylan, Presley, Cash and The Beatles, have a clearly defined musical position, a pure approach to what they have sung and written, free from euphemisms and alive with their own emotions."

The show threw up unsuccessful juxtapositions when attempts were made to bring different musical styles together, such as Johnny and OC Smith trading verses of 'Yesterday' and 'I Still Miss Someone' respectively, a combination which comes over as jarringly mismatched. There may have been underlying conflicts and disagreements about what ingredients should go into the show but what is undoubtedly true is that it brought Johnny to national prominence and helped transform him from a highly successful country singer into an American icon.

17

WINNING AWARDS and gaining recognition was nothing new for Johnny Cash but 1969 was to be his *annus mirabilis.* The crowning glory came in October at the Country Music Association televised awards ceremony held at the Ryman Auditorium where Johnny took a record five awards including the most prestigious, Male Vocalist Of The Year and Entertainer Of The Year. *Johnny Cash At San Quentin* and 'A Boy Named Sue' picked up album and single of the year respectively and Johnny and June even picked up vocal *group* of the year. In his acceptance speech for the best album award Johnny said, "I would like to thank the men at San Quentin prison because if you've heard the album you'll know that it is the very human sounds of 2,000 men that make this record possible."

Johnny was impressively dressed in a knee-length, tan Lincolnesque coat with dark velvet lapels and shiny black boots. For each visit to the stage to collect his next award, he neatly arranged his increasing haul of awards behind his knees. The host for the evening was Tennessee Ernie Ford, who caused Johnny some embarrassment when he sang a song written by Little Jimmie Dickens, which included the line, "She was so dumb she thought Johnny Cash was money found in a commode." The Record Industry Association of America gave the *San Quentin* album a gold award and at the end of the year 'Daddy Sang Bass' and 'Folsom Prison Blues' received BMI awards to add to the Grammies received for the latter and the *Folsom Prison* sleeve notes. Johnny also received the Metro Metronome award as the individual who contributed most to the development of Music City USA in 1969.

In Las Vegas, Johnny's old Sun label mate Elvis Presley, whom Cash used to imitate back in the Fifties, returned the compliment. "Hello, I'm Johnny Cash," he drawled before launching into pumped-up versions of 'Folsom Prison Blues' and 'I Walk The Line'. Johnny's high profile meant that many organisations unconnected with music wanted to be associated with him. In 1969, Johnny and June were named honorary chairmen of that year's Tennessee Association for

Retarded Children and Adults campaign. Johnny was also in demand as a television guest and appearances with Glen Campbell and Tom Jones were slotted into the last quarter of the year after completion of the first season of his own show – thus keeping Johnny in the living rooms of millions of Americans.

A new series of *The Johnny Cash Show* began in January 1970 and ran through to the early summer. The last show before the summer break featured Johnny duetting with his mother Carrie on 'Uncloudy Day', which was featured on a live album cashing in on the television show released later in the year. ABC executives considered the possibility of a summer replacement show with either Marty Robbins or Merle Haggard but decided against it on the basis that if either host proved to be an instant hit then it might be harder for Johnny to pick up from where he had left off.

During the break after the conclusion of the initial run in September 1969, Johnny's remarks to the media hinted at his continuing behind-the-scenes struggles. He let it be known that some changes would be made to the programme but it seemed he was now seeing things more from the angle of the television executives. "I've learned it's hopeless to try to please everybody. For one thing we're gonna have more comedy. After all, the show's pretty heavy with *Ride This Train* and the closing spiritual and I'm a sad singer anyway. We're gonna have more comedy than we've had but we're gonna try to keep it natural. We're not trying to be *Hee Haw*." Despite the dig at *Hee Haw*, Johnny didn't agree with those who felt the programme gave country music a negative image. "It's a good show, the kind of show that doesn't take itself too seriously and I think we need that sometimes."

However, it seemed the producers of the show had persuaded him that to maintain its success it would be necessary to reduce the country content (despite the fact that the show already included a lot of non-country material). "As I found out, there are a lot of people who do not like country music and I'm not sure I want to limit myself exclusively to that anyway." On another occasion, Cash said there were aspects of the programme he was less than happy with, apologising for the fact that there were too many general entertainers. "We're gonna put more realism, truth and down-to-earth feeling that's in country music into our show. We've already started lining up such guests as Merle Haggard and Charley Pride." There was also unrealised talk of presenting people with "dignity and prestige" such as Hank Snow, Roy Acuff and Ernest Tubb, something Johnny would have, no doubt, loved.

At the start of 1970, it was reported that co-producers Stan Jacobson and Joe Byrn were planning to take a five-year lease on a Nashville office purely to handle administration of the show. In a joint statement to the press they said: "We think Johnny Cash will be a major star for at least that long [five years] and probably much longer. He has the appeal of a Dean Martin, Johnny can go on and on." When the show did resume, some of the underlying tensions rose to the surface, such as the occasion when Johnny was keen to feature a new song called 'Allegheny'. The producers agreed but said they wanted Johnny to include some other new songs as well. At the last minute the song was dropped. Speaking later, Johnny said of such incidents, "That's the way it was. Like all of a sudden, I'm a machine and everybody is pushing the buttons. I didn't like it."

Johnny kept up his acting career with parts in *Wagon Train* and a television film *Trail Of Tears*, narrated by Joseph Cotton, about the forced relocation of the Cherokee tribe from their homelands in northern Georgia to Oklahoma. Johnny had apparently turned down many film offers but accepted *Trail Of Tears* as the subject was close to his heart. The director Lane Slate said of Johnny's acting, "He has the same kind of power about him that John Wayne has, I think. I don't know whether he'll ever be able to play anything but those strong parts but Wayne has certainly been successful at it." Progress was hampered by the fact that Andrew Jackson's residence, The Hermitage, where some scenes were filmed, lay under the main flight path into Nashville airport. Talking about the aims of the film, Slate said, "We're trying to change the image of the eastern Indians. When you say Indian most people think of Jeff Chandler in a loin-cloth but the eastern Indians, particularly the Cherokees had a civilisation like the whites, they lived in houses, owned slaves and schools, had insane asylums and a judicial system. We want to bust this clichéd attitude about Indians."

Johnny was also the subject of a major feature in *Life* magazine whose cover framed him ("The Rough-Cut King of Country Music") against the wheels of a steaming locomotive, strumming his guitar and gazing pensively into the distance. The article, entitled 'Johnny Cash Makes Everyone Like Country Music', tried to analyse Cash's appeal. Dismissing most of Johnny's output to 1969 as "an unpromising mixture of folklore, sentiment and pure corn," the author suggested that Johnny's credibility had changed because he was now able to attract the younger set. "The young like him because he has the ring of authenticity and supports social causes, such as prison reform." Despite displaying an unusual view of what constitutes old age, the author identified another important point. "For old people over 30 he sounds a note of sanity in a mixed-up musical world – they can tap their feet and understand his words." A friend of the author suggested that the success of Johnny Cash and country music had more to do with people being fed up with the pressures of city life and that it might not last. "Last year it was soul. This year everybody is scratching in the soil. That's why Johnny works. He's got soil."

The article featured an intimate photograph of a guitar pull (or to use *Life*'s more sophisticated term, "musicale") and with actor Jack Palance among the guests it's clear that such evenings were open to people from different areas of entertainment. As well as the odd cartoon in the national press, Johnny also received recognition of a different sort when a lady called Lois Williams recorded a "reply" song to 'A Boy Named Sue' called 'A Gal Called Sam'.* Such records, often vehicles for putting across the feminine point of view, were common in country music and 'It Wasn't God Who Made Honky Tonk Angels', a reply to Hank Thompson's hit 'The Wild Side Of Life', had helped to launch the career of Kitty Wells. In the Lois Williams parody Sue marries Sam and their problem is what they should call their baby, in the end plumping for "who".

More Grammies came Johnny's way in March with 'Best Country Vocal Performance, Male', for 'A Boy Named Sue' and 'Best Album Notes (Annotator's Award)' for the rear sleeve notes written for Bob Dylan's *Nashville Skyline*. These notes were at times as impenetrable as the subject's own:

> *This man can rhyme the tick of time*
> *The edge of pain, the what of sane*
> *And comprehend the good in men, the bad in men*
> *Can feel the hate of fight, the love of right*
> *And the creep of blight at the speed of light*
> *The pain of dawn, the gone of gone*
> *The end of friend, the end of end.*

In between delivering weekly television shows, Johnny still maintained a heavy schedule of one-nighters, enjoying particular triumphs at a sell-out show at the Hollywood Bowl and four nights at Albuquerque's New Mexico State Fair, where over a thousand people had to be turned away from the final show. The troupe drew a crowd of over 18,000 people to a minimally advertised show at Toronto's Maple Leaf Gardens, more than The Beatles had managed. An earlier triumph was overshadowed by personal tragedy. The promoter of a show at California's Oakland Coliseum paid Johnny a $5,000 cash bonus for selling out the 14,000 seat venue but as everybody savoured the night's success, a call came through for Helen Carter to tell her that her 16-year-old son had been seriously injured in a motoring accident.

Kenny Carter suffered severe burns after he and four friends crashed a sports car designed for two people. All of Maybelle's grandchildren had music in their genes but Kenny was the most talented, having already released an anti-war song, 'Is This The Way Of The Free?' The $5,000 bonus was used to book airline tickets home with much of the work involved being attended to by Lou Robin, the promoter of the Oakland show. Kenny died of his injuries soon afterwards. Everybody was distraught but for Maybelle, who was especially close to her grandson, the loss was almost unbearable. Johnny played a benefit performance in Jackson with the proceeds going to the burns centre at Vanderbilt Hospital, which Johnny had helped to set up following the death of Luther Perkins.

* 'A Girl Named Johnny Cash' was also a minor hit for Jane Morgan.

Keen to invest some of the money he was earning, and wanting to acquire premises which could serve as offices and studios in Nashville, Johnny acquired the former Plantation Dinner Theater for $225,000. The property, which extended to 14,000 square feet, was situated on the Gallatin Road, not far from Johnny's Hendersonville house on Old Hickory Lake and just across the road from Conway Twitty's theme park "Twitty City". The building was erected in 1968 but the original venture for which it was intended proved to be a failure. Prior to making the purchase, Johnny arranged for the building to be examined by a sound engineer, who reported the acoustics would be perfect for a studio. "The House Of Cash", run by members of Johnny's family, became the centre of Johnny's administrative dealings and proved itself to be an adaptable hub for many other activities.

◆ ◆ ◆ ◆ ◆

Around this time Johnny met Kris Kristofferson, who would become a close friend and important collaborator. A bluff, no-nonsense character with wide-ranging interests and talents, Kristofferson was the son of a US Air Force Major General (apparently one with a bizarre sense of humour since he named his son 'Kristoffer'). In 1958, Kristofferson won a Rhodes Scholarship to Merton College, Oxford, gaining a masters degree in English – his particular passions being English artist and philosopher William Blake and Hank Williams. In 1959, he joined the US Army and learned to fly helicopters, followed by a move to Nashville with the intention of getting into the music scene.

Kris had reportedly met Johnny backstage at a *Grand Ole Opry* show in 1965, fuelling his desire to get into the music business. In Nashville, he did a variety of jobs from working in bars to flying executives and staff back and forth to oilrigs in the Gulf of Mexico. Kris also got work as a janitor at Columbia studios where one of his tasks was to empty the overworked ashtrays. From this vantage point, he was able to observe artists working from time to time. Of Cash, he said, "The atmosphere was electric . . . John paced in the studio like a caged panther." Despite being under strict orders not to approach the studio's clients, Kris passed his tapes to June pleading with her to let Johnny hear them. Given that Johnny was receiving around 10,000 unsolicited tapes a year from amateur and professional musicians,* it's hardly surprising that Kristofferson's songs failed to get the master's attention; in fact, they ended up in Old Hickory Lake. (A few years later, Johnny dragged grappling hooks through the lake in the hope of retrieving the tapes but all he pulled in were telephones he'd hurled into the water when their ringing had annoyed him.)

The breakthrough was engineered by Kris with the most brazen of stunts. He

---

* According to one report, some were even slipped into his pocket when he was kneeling at prayer in his local church.

landed a National Guard helicopter in the grounds of Johnny's house, casually emerging from it, so the story goes, with a beer in one hand and a tape in the other. Johnny had been taking a nap when June woke him in a panic to tell him of what she took to be the latest attempt to see Cash arrested. Johnny could not help but be impressed by this piece of bravado and, deciding to listen to the song the pilot brought, quickly realised 'Sunday Morning Coming Down' was a classic. Kris was invited to the Cash homestead where he got the chance to sing at the regular guitar pulls. As Johnny put it in a 1973 interview, "I heard him sing so many times that it eventually got through my thick head that I should try to do something with some of his songs."

In 1969, Johnny enjoyed a triumphant return to the Newport Folk Festival, delivering a set designed to push all the right buttons, featuring as it did songs by Bob Dylan, The Carter Family and Peter LaFarge, as well as some of his own classics like 'I Still Miss Someone'. He also used the occasion to enhance Kris Kristofferson's reputation by asking him to sing 'Sunday Morning Coming Down' and 'Me And Bobby McGee'. Having had to hitch-hike to the venue, Kris found the experience nerve-racking, so much so that when he was announced he froze and it took a well-aimed kick from June's high-heeled shoe to propel him out onto the stage for what turned out to be a well received set.

The songs of Kris Kristofferson are neither rock nor country but have been hugely influential in both fields. In 1970, Johnny's version of 'Sunday Morning Coming Down' (about the realities of alcoholism) made number one in the country charts and also won Kristofferson Song Of The Year at the Country Music Awards. However, he hardly endeared himself at the ceremony by wearing casual dress, a move bound to infuriate the traditionalists who saw it as disrespectful.

Kris didn't merely provide Johnny with quality new material, he also improved his songwriting.* "Kris made me stop using clichés and think more about the kind of lyrics I should write." This tied in with other changes Johnny made in his songwriting technique at about the same time, as he explained, "I work at the songs much harder. I never let a song rest. I go over every line repeatedly to improve the construction, the dramatic quality of the originality." Kris Kristofferson himself pinpoints one of the reasons for the popularity of his songs, "It's satisfying to express things that you feel and have other people say, 'Right, that's exactly how I feel too.' "

Around this time Johnny talked to his friend Marty Robbins about a simple idea he'd had of playing a selection of old and new favourites, accompanied by just his guitar. Coincidentally, Robbins had thought of a similar idea and recorded such an album shortly afterwards. However seriously Johnny

* Waylon Jennings later claimed in his autobiography that, despite Johnny's sensitive readings, Kristofferson had personally praised Jennings' interpretations.

considered the idea, it's unlikely that CBS would have seen much commercial merit in it, particularly with the massive success of the prison albums fresh in the memory. Not until many years later would Johnny achieve this particular ambition.

◆ ◆ ◆ ◆ ◆

Johnny forged yet another significant friendship in 1969, with the world-famous evangelist Dr Billy Graham.* Graham was said to be particularly interested in keeping up with the young and felt that Johnny Cash would be an ideal contact given his appeal to a wide audience and his firmly held Christian beliefs. At Graham's suggestion, it was arranged that he would visit Johnny and his family for Sunday lunch. The meeting was a source of great interest in the local press and afterwards Graham told reporters, "Johnny Cash has a marvellous communication with the young people of today and that's what we talked about . . . he manages to bridge the generation gap, appealing to audiences of all ages."

This comment overlooked the fact that for many young people Johnny was considered square and Billy Graham, if they had heard of him at all, was a figure to be reviled for his conservative religious views. After their meeting Johnny said, "If there's ever anything I can do to help you any time, I wish you'd let me know." Extolling the virtues of homely religion, June said (after the Graham meeting), "If you felt like you'd been bad you could cry about it in church and you could sing and you had a kind of outlet for the way you felt out there in that little country church. Most kids don't have any outlet like that any more."

In 1970, Johnny released a studio album called *Hello, I'm Johnny Cash*. After the excitement of the live prison albums, it represented something of a resumption of the usual formula. Bob Wootton maintained the spirit of Luther Perkins and a couple of unobtrusive session men filled out the sound on dobro and guitar. There were a couple of love duets with June, one of which, Tim Hardin's 'If I Were A Carpenter', had been a concert favourite for some time (it was the song they performed immediately after Cash's onstage marriage proposal), with the line *"I'd put you above me"* altered by June to *"Don't be above me."* The anti-war 'Route No. 1 Box 144', one of four songs written or co-written by Cash, focused on the death in action of a recently married young man, whose background was remarkably similar to Johnny's. It would be natural to see this song as being aimed against Vietnam, but the lyrics are such that it could apply to any war. Johnny's striking ability to move seamlessly and naturally between singing and speaking was featured, though his description of the nameless victim was, at

* Despite this widely reported meeting in 1969 Johnny stated in his 1997 autobiography that he did not meet Billy Graham until the spring of the following year.

times, verbally clumsy, *"He was thought of as just average, a good boy nothing more, with the average amount of friends."*

With tragic resonance the song which followed, 'Sing A Travelling Song', was written by Helen Carter's late son, Kenny. Two songs, 'The Devil To Pay' and 'See Ruby Fall' displayed sternly conservative moral attitudes toward "fallen" women. Despite the largely unreported shenanigans that occurred on the road Johnny's attitude to women in general was essentially conservative. A career was acceptable so long as it could be fitted round the principal duties involved in being a wife and a mother.*

Although Johnny ensured that a number of new writing talents for the album were involved, he also elicited contributions from old friends, Jack Clement, Merle Travis, early biographer Christopher Wren, and Roy Orbison. Kris Kristofferson's contribution, 'To Beat The Devil', contained a classic Kristofferson line describing a poor itinerant singer-songwriter travelling *"With a stomach full of empty and a pocketful of dreams"*. The Jack Clement contribution, 'I've Got A Thing About Trains' was an unaffected piece of nostalgia, containing lines which Johnny sang with real feeling:

> *When my little boy says Daddy*
> *What was it like to ride a train?*
> *I'll just say it was a good way to travel*
> *When things didn't move so fast.*

By the time the album was recorded June was pregnant with a child conceived, ironically, during a holiday in the Virgin Islands. It was a source of particular joy since her doctors had expressed some doubts as to her ability to conceive again. June decided to take a break from appearing on Johnny's television show. "I'm starting to show a little and I think it would be in bad taste to perform. It's just a little baby after all. The way I feel, June Carter performs but Mrs Johnny Cash ought to just have his baby." This arrangement reflected Johnny's domestic deal with June, agreed on both sides, namely that she give up her performing career (as had, to all intents and purposes, her mother and sisters) to look after the baby and the house; appearing with the travelling show, and making the occasional solo recording from time to time.

Between them Johnny and June had six daughters so they could surely be forgiven for praying, as they did, for a boy. On March 3, 1970, at Madison Hospital, with Johnny present, John Carter Cash was born, weighing in at 7 pounds 10 ounces. June was 41 and Johnny 38. There was never any doubt about the name, which had been previously agreed upon. Had the baby been a girl she

---

* Johnny let slip his prudish attitudes while filming his co-starring role in *A Gunfight* (1971). He refused to do a scene which involved him kissing a semi-nude actress, Karen Black, who was playing the part of a prostitute, until she covered herself up.

would have been named Rachel Carter Cash. June said goodbye to the nurses who lined up to see her off and left the hospital in a black Cadillac, reportedly saying she intended to be back touring with the troupe in about a month's time. Johnny and June later donated $5,000 for refurbishing the paediatrics room at the hospital where the baby was delivered. Johnny said in his 1997 auto-biography, he was "smitten" by his new son, looking toward the kind of parenting he had failed to achieve with his daughters. However, there was still no question that John Carter would have to fit in with his father's lifestyle rather than the other way round.

On a more mundane level, the arrival of John Carter Cash prompted Johnny to stop smoking (albeit temporarily). The baby had been suffering from a chest cold which meant he had to spend time in an oxygen tent while in hospital. There were strict rules against smoking in the ward but showing a typically cava-lier disregard of authority, Johnny lit up in the men's room which he glossed over when talking about the incident at an English press conference in 1971. "Every time I'd cough he'd wake up and cry. He finally got sick and was in the hospital – we had to take him into hospital for a few days – and I just had to stop coughing so I decided I'd stop smoking. He was responsible for that."

Shortly after John Carter was born, Johnny acted as co-chairman of a cere-bral palsy telethon, helped by other stars such as Art Johnston of *Rowan and Martin's Laugh-In* and *Hee Haw*'s Grandpa Jones. The event raised about $250,000 and was a particular pleasure for Johnny because most people who phoned in wanted to know all about his new son, about whom he could talk for hours.

◆ ◆ ◆ ◆ ◆

The public's appetite for Johnny Cash recordings appeared to be insatiable and as a result the charts were saturated with his singles and albums. In 1969, Shelby Singleton, a veteran of the Korean war who had a steel plate in his head as a result of injuries received in the conflict, bought Sun Records from Sam Phillips. Singleton was a shrewd record executive and producer, whose independent label Plantation had enjoyed a number one hit the previous year with the Tom T Hall song 'Harper Valley PTA' sung by Jeannie C Riley. Singleton found himself the owner of over 10,000 hours of tapes by former Sun artists including Carl Perkins, Jerry Lee Lewis and, of course, Johnny Cash, and soon flooded the market with numerous releases.

All of Johnny's Sun singles were issued on the Sun International label as part of a "Summer Cash" campaign and compilation albums – sometimes with thematically combined songs (e.g. *Story Songs Of Trains And Rivers*) – followed. None fared as well as Cash's current CBS releases but with his ubiquitous high profile, sustained by a weekly prime-time advertising slot, they did reasonably brisk business. Singleton even released *Showtime* – an album of studio songs, overdubbed with an audience, perhaps hoping to fool the public into thinking they were buying an album of songs from the television show.*

Recognition of Johnny's status also came from the political world by President Richard Nixon appointing him (along with Bill Cosby) as a member of the Peace Corps National Advisory Council. Johnny was invited to perform for the President at one of his "Evenings At The White House" in April, the day before the Apollo 13 astronauts were due to return to earth. He nearly didn't get in because he forgot his pass and had to sign a special form in order to be admitted to his own concert. While Johnny performed to a select audience, six-week-old John Carter Cash slept upstairs in the Lincoln Bedroom.

Bob Haldeman's office had contacted Johnny's sister Reba at the House Of Cash a few days prior to the performance asking that Johnny play three songs, 'A Boy Named Sue', 'Welfare Cadilac' (sic) and 'Okie From Muskogee'. There was no problem with the first choice but Johnny couldn't perform the other two for, as well as not knowing either, he wouldn't have had time to rehearse them. They were seen as ultra-conservative, anti-liberal songs and the press leapt on the refusal as a case of Johnny snubbing the President for ideological reasons.

Even Nixon understood this was simply untrue. When introducing his guest he said, "Johnny Cash's music speaks to all America." Alluding to the controversy stirred up by the press, he continued, "I'm not an expert on his music – I found that out when I told him what to play. One thing I've learned about Johnny Cash is that you don't tell him what to play. I understand that he owns a Cadillac but won't sing about it."

There had been some confusion because initially Reba indicated that Johnny would perform 'Welfare Cadilac' on the basis that he would play whatever the President wanted to hear. The Tennessee Commissioner of Welfare stepped into the fray saying the song, about a family which used their welfare cheque to make payments on a fancy car, was demeaning to people who found themselves in straitened circumstances. For composer Guy Drake, who up until recently had been painting stripes for supermarket parking areas, the publicity was most welcome.

When Johnny chose to feature the pro-youth, anti-conservative 'What Is Truth', it's hard not to see it as a message to Nixon. In the select audience of 225 people were Roy Acuff, Tex Ritter and a proud as punch Ray Cash. During the hour-long show Johnny talked about his Dyess childhood, saying of the land there, "You'll find it won't grow anything now, it's got too much salt in it from the backs of the Cash family." At the show's finale, Johnny gave emotional support to the man whose office he held in such high regard and who was

---

* When Singleton talked about overdubbing songs from the Million Dollar Quartet, Cash and Carl Perkins instituted legal action to prevent this, though various bootlegs did make it into the public domain.

experiencing such unrest over Vietnam. "We elected our man as President and if you don't stand behind him get the hell out of the way so that I can stand behind him."

He sincerely wanted the President to find a way to get America out of the conflict and on this point he addressed the President directly. "I wish you success in trying to get the war over in Vietnam, and I hope you can get the work done soon so that there will be peace in all the mountains and peace in all the valleys." Later, Nixon admitted he really didn't know much about country music and that the only country stars he could name were Johnny Cash and Glen Campbell, a tribute to the power of prime-time television.

In 1970, Johnny received yet another honour when he beat off stiff competition from the likes of Raymond Burr (*Perry Mason*), Dick Cavett and Bill Cosby to become the critic's choice for 'TV Man Of The Year'. As well as Nixon, Johnny met with one of the President's most visible supporters, Ross Perot, a maverick multi-millionaire who used his wealth and influence to back particular causes (and who later stood for the Presidency as an independent). On a visit to Nashville in support of his "United We Stand" initiative backing Nixon, and more especially his attempts to secure the release and better treatment of prisoners of war in Vietnam, Johnny and June met with Perot. Afterwards June spoke supportively of Perot's aims, saying that she and Johnny were concerned, "As any normal human being would be" and "would like to help if they could."

Not long after the White House appearance, the Johnny Cash show appeared at Leavenworth Prison. As he got into some banter with the inmates, Johnny took an apparent sideswipe at his recent performance by saying, "This is the same show we did for President Nixon but we're gonna try a little harder here." In another introduction, he said, "My mother told me when I was a little boy, be the best you can be at whatever you do. If you're gonna be a baker, bake the best bread in town. If you're gonna pick cotton, pick more than any other man in the county . . . and if you're gonna rob banks, hit First National." Johnny was nothing if not a crowd pleaser.

The windy weather at the outdoor show caused problems for the ladies, in particular Robbie Harden, a singer who occasionally covered for the troupe when any of the female members were indisposed or otherwise unavailable. Her dress kept blowing upwards in the wind and so June, Mother Maybelle, Helen and Anita crowded round in an attempt to provide some protection. One newspaper report described the scene. "They pressed in around her to try to fend off the provocative wind but out there in the chairs and bleachers, facing the stage under white clouds racing in the sky, Robbie was taunted, whistled at, growled over and beckoned to by 2,000 hard-faced Cash partisans." Johnny was most amused by this turn of events, smirking, "They talking to you Robbie." Later, June kicked off a shoe to which one of the inmates pleaded, "Aaaaaw, take it all off." Yet at the end of a heartfelt and pious rendition of 'Peace In The Valley', everyone present was quiet and respectful. Though the audiences at his prison shows were predominantly male, Johnny did perform at such places as Lansing Women's Prison in Kansas.

It was rumoured that one dissenting member of the troupe expressed disquiet about the prison shows, suggesting that there were others, hospital patients for instance, who were far more deserving. It must be said that Johnny lent his support to many worthy causes, such as benefits for the families of murdered or injured police officers as well as prisoners about to be released for good behaviour and, as with the prison shows, he was only paid expenses. In the early Seventies at a time when Johnny's earnings continued to be measured in millions, he and June contributed to many good causes, including their donation of $10,000 towards the $250,000 fund for the construction of a new building for the BC Goodpasture Christian High School, an institution which combined mainstream and religious education. They also gave a grant to Walden House, a school and treatment centre for autistic and emotionally disturbed children as well as a $10,000 grant to the South East and Indian Antiquities Survey to facilitate the purchase of a 100 acre tract of land west of Nashville to be used for the setting up of an archaeology field school for Native American groups.

Johnny accepted an invitation to appear at one of Billy Graham's crusades in Knoxville, and the crowd swelled to over 60,000 as a result of his presence. Graham introduced him as "A man who is as well known as the President." He then went on to say that he was deeply worried about the state of the nation's morals and spoke apocalyptically of the future. "Soon will come the time when people of the world think all is well and there's peace at last, then there will be instant and total destruction." Graham assured the throng that people need not fear the second coming if they had faithfully done the work God had given them. "Everything you do is sacred if it is under God's will. The whole ship is sinking. All we can do is patch it up a little and prepare to meet God by repenting of sins, receiving Jesus Christ by faith and openly acknowledging Him." Such views resonated with those of June Carter. In the course of an interview with Dorothy Gallagher she stated, "If we don't have some kind of spiritual comeback, I think we're going to be in really bad trouble. Our morals are deteriorating to the point where people will just disintegrate." Johnny later referred to the appearance with Billy Graham as "The pinnacle of my career."

◆ ◆ ◆ ◆ ◆

In 1971, Johnny maintained his connections with the movie industry by recording soundtracks for *Little Fauss And Big Halsy*, starring Robert Redford and Michael J Pollard, and *I Walk The Line*, a gritty romance starring Gregory Peck and Tuesday Weld. There were only a few new songs included and some of those featured were spread thin by the additional inclusion of instrumental versions, so there was little in either for anybody other than a Johnny Cash completist. Johnny continued to pursue his spasmodic acting career, accepting the part of Abe Cross in *A Gunfight* – an offbeat Western co-starring Kirk Douglas, with shooting taking place in New Mexico and on location in Spain during the summer of 1970. The simple plot revolved around two ageing gunfighters staging a gunfight which the public pay to watch, with the winner of the gladiatorial spectacle pocketing the proceeds, or as Kirk Douglas' character puts it, "The winner takes all, the loser won't need it." Financial backing for the project (to the tune of $2 million) came from the Jicarilla Apaches of New Mexico. Johnny threw some light on the film's background at a press conference in London the following year.

When asked why the Apache tribe had financed a film which had no connection to the American Indian, he explained, "Well, you see, they said they wanted to support me now that I'd done an album called *Bitter Tears*. And the Chief . . . wanted to support me in a picture. You see the Americans gave them some of this dried up old desert land and what they did was strike oil on it. They had a lot of money lying around that they wanted to invest to make more money. They heard that there was a movie possibility that I might be interested in that they wanted to finance and they did. And I think probably they've got their investment back already." By way of gratitude there was a private preview of the film for an audience made up of Native Americans.

Reviews were predictably mixed. Bob Powel in the British magazine *Country Music People* said that Kirk Douglas was the better actor but that "Johnny Cash came a very creditable second." Another critic said of Cash, "He was looking dour, as if someone had just named him Sue." The *Chicago Tribune* took a dim view of the film saying it was "a solid 30 minute story that runs for 88 minutes", while the *Milwaukee Journal* concluded, "With the clichés flying faster than the bullets the real victims . . . are actors and audience." *Chicago Today*'s film critic Mary Knoblauch was more favourable, even suggesting that Cash had the potential to be a major Western film star. "If the Western is to recover from its current comatose condition, some day they'll look back at *A Gunfight* and say that at least these guys had the right idea." It was never likely that the film would receive Oscar nominations but Johnny could at least claim a few "not bad" reviews for his acting although it was clear his horizons didn't extend much beyond lower level Westerns.

In contrast *Johnny Cash – The Man, His World, His Music* was a creditable attempt at a *cinéma-vérité* type documentary, filmed over a six-month period, which aimed to give an honest picture of Johnny Cash, though naturally what resulted was largely sanitised. However, this didn't mean the film lacked interest and the crudeness of the filming had the quality of a home movie at times, providing fascinating glimpses of life behind the scenes. Informal gatherings with family and friends, forced and awkward though they were, did capture the feel of a family circle where people sat round, sang songs and did a turn. Even Ray Cash was pressurised by Johnny into performing what he could remember of a song learned during the First World War. The film contained footage of a journey back to Dyess as one of its threads and the barrenness of the flat, brightly lit landscape was vividly captured from the inside of the Cashes' Dodge mobile home as it powered along the roads of Johnny's childhood; his excited explanations of places of interest as much for the viewer as for June and the other passengers.

The sense of excitement as they reached the old centre of Dyess was palpable, as was the buzz generated by the arrival of a returning star in a small town of ordinary folk. The visit to the old family home, bleak and deserted, had an eerie feel, as Johnny walked through the dark rooms pointing things out to June, such as the empty paint pots in the middle of the living room which he could still visualise. Early scenes attempted to capture Cash the country boy. In a forest of tall trees he shot a crow, only grazing it, and then walked along holding it in one hand, greatly amused by its attempts to bite him. "I'm gonna charm you yet," he admonished, oblivious to the creature's obvious distress. Was this a mean streak or just the non-sentimental attitude of country folk who have been brought up the hard way?

At times Johnny came over as awkward and ill at ease in front of the camera, away from the stage. Scenes in the studio showed Johnny working on a song from *The Holy Land* with Bob Johnston and also with Bob Dylan during the *Nashville Skyline* sessions. Like an uncertain schoolboy Dylan, not sure if he is near enough to the microphone, asked, "Want me to move in a little closer?" The sight of the two men together struggling to bring life into a song, merely confirmed the lack of artistic chemistry between them. At one point as their attempt to trade vocal licks was losing steam, Johnny burst out laughing as if realising the hopelessness of the job while Bob stuck dourly to the task in hand. There was also a scene filmed at home, of Johnny, accompanying himself on acoustic guitar, singing 'Flesh And Blood' with its line, *"Mother Nature's quite a lady, but you're the one I need."* Johnny delivered the song with a pious air while June looked on demurely. They must have had to work hard to suppress knowing glances as Johnny later revealed that the song was inspired by a particularly fulfilling recent al fresco sexual encounter, so fulfilling that, as Johnny later admitted, he let June drive them home.

In snatches of conversation Johnny provided some insights about music, of which he said love is the most important thing of all and also that there is more sadness in country music and prison audiences. "There is no audience quite like a prison audience, they are not ashamed to show their appreciation." Also well captured were the backstage scenes, with aspiring singers experiencing the excitement of playing a song or two for the star, and fans allowed the privilege of queuing to get his autograph. From the point of view of the star, touring comes over as repetitive and unglamorous; another anonymous, dingy dressing room, another colourless corridor which looks the same as the rest, another group of fans who really don't see him as a real person with everyday hassles, irritations and frustrations. It's striking how many of the women queuing patiently for autographs do so in near total silence, merely issuing a polite "Thank you," a perfunctory smile and a meaningless compliment after having their photograph taken with their hero.

The feature was directed by Robert Elfstrom, who later said of Cash, "This man is America. We have captured him from the time he was a boy to the time he has become a saga in the world of music. He expresses what can happen in America today . . . a rise from a country boy to an internationally known personality." In Britain the film was shown in cinemas for one day only, giving the showings something of the atmosphere of a concert. Advertising for the film (since released on video) overlooked the subtler revelations by proudly describing the film as, "The Warm, Wonderful Full-Length Motion Picture About The Man Who Became A Legend In His Own Time!"

Talk of legendary status, though perhaps a little premature, might have alerted Johnny to the fact that he had now arrived at the stage where, approaching 40, people wanted to know more than just when his next record was coming out. Writers were already starting to look back over his life and career, to assess and explain his contribution to American life and culture, and early in 1971 a man called Ralph Edwards put together a tribute to Johnny which was as public as it was unexpected.

18

"**JOHN, I WANT YOU** to meet a good friend of mine all the way from California. Ralph, would you mind to come on out?" Johnny was startled by this unexpected interruption, as he was in the middle of recording his next television show in front of the usual packed audience, not the best time for social introductions. However, all became clear when Ralph Edwards walked on to the Ryman stage, explaining that he had brought a lot of people with him to "Tell the story of a poet, a troubadour, a musician, a dreamer, a man of great strength, courage and deep faith." The audience erupted as he announced the words, "Johnny Cash, this is your life." A procession of significant people from Johnny's past and present trooped out on to the stage with carefully prepared reminiscences and tributes. These included his high school teacher from Dyess, Mrs Ruby Cooley, two members of the Landsberg Barbarians, Jack Clement, Stu Carnall and Marshall Grant talking about the early musical achievements (glossing over the outrageous vandalism inflicted on countless hotels), Sheriff Ralph Jones and Nat Winston who had contributed to Johnny breaking his drug habit in 1968, and, of course, contributions from members of the Cash and Carter families with young John Carter helping to bring the proceedings to a close. Johnny was tearful on a number of occasions during the show.

Another guest who appeared on *This Is Your Life* was Billy Graham, though his inclusion was perhaps surprising since Johnny had only known him personally a little over a year. It's been suggested that with his recovery from drugs and his marriage to a religious woman (a "prayer warrior" as Johnny affectionately calls June), Johnny became obsessive about religion, anxious to make up for the time he had spent "outside the circle". Waylon Jennings complained that Johnny sold out to religion following his marriage though this might have been a case of sour grapes at the loss of his wild drinking companion. Speaking on The Reverend Jimmy Snow's *Grand Ole Opry Gospel Time* programme, Johnny said, "We've never been what you'd call red-hot Christians, but since John

Carter was born we've really begun to feel it and try to live it. I guess when that little boy entered our house we realised we weren't teenagers anymore."

◆ ◆ ◆ ◆ ◆

It was around May 1971 that Johnny visited a small Pentecostal church, the Evangel Temple just outside Nashville where the Reverend Jimmy Snow was pastor. In response to the altar call to members of the congregation to come forward and "make things right with God," Johnny had got up and rededicated his life to God. According to Charles Paul Conn in his book *The New Johnny Cash*, as Cash got up from his seat the Reverend Snow met him. Johnny told him, "I want to live my life right and the first thing I've got to do is be a spiritual leader in my own home." Members of his family gathered round him as he bent down on his knee in front of Snow. Johnny was an enthusiastic supporter of the church and at a subsequent appearance at the *Grand Ole Opry*, he told the audience, "If you haven't got a particular church to go to I'd like to recommend one that I like awfully well, the Reverend Jimmy Snow's Evangel Temple. A lot of us in the entertainment business go out there. It's a good place to go. It makes you feel good." Speaking about the church, June said, "It's sort of non-denominational, just a good place to go on Sundays."

Johnny had bonded remarkably quickly with Billy Graham, described by George Hamilton IV as "God's man for our time," though Cash has always been keen to stress that Graham didn't ask him for help with his evangelical work. "It was *I* who told *him* that if he ever wanted me to sing at one of his crusades, I'd be there," as he said in his 1997 autobiography. Cash indeed went on to work with Graham on a number of occasions, something he remembers with affection. "We'd walk out on stage and someone would whistle and yell and Billy would turn to me and say, 'That's your audience, those are the ones we're going to preach to tonight.'"

Their association has not always attracted favourable comment. Referring to Graham, Richard Lay, diary editor of the *Daily Mail* wrote (in 1973), "He appeared to have adopted as his pop accompanist the elderly (*sic!*) singer Johnny Cash who flourished in the early Fifties. Still, nostalgia is all the rage these days." This drew a swift response from the then editor of *Country Music People*, Bob Powel who awarded Lay a "Golden raspberry". "It just shows that even journalists on national newspapers don't always know what they're talking about." The event which had provoked this comment was "SPREE '73", a crusade held at Wembley Stadium, which had attracted more than 30,000 converts and non-converts.

However, for all their closeness, Johnny has on occasion been less than overwhelming in his public support for someone perceived to be a controversial figure, even appearing to distance himself from Graham at times. At a press conference in England in 1971, Richard Green of the *New Musical Express* asked,

"Can you tell me something about the work you're doing with Billy Graham? He's on the *Man In Black* album and I gather you're going to do a show with him when you get back home," to which Johnny replied, "Well actually, it's very little work I'm doing with Billy Graham, he was a guest on my show . . . and then after I return I'm simply playing and singing at one Billy Graham crusade in Fort Worth, Texas and then so far as I know, I have no other work I'll do with Billy Graham."

When Cash pledged support for President Nixon over Vietnam it was for Nixon the holder of the highest office in the land, democratically elected and representing the people, not Nixon the Republican. With Billy Graham such a distinction would be harder to make but without compromising his principles Johnny was astute enough ("dumb like a fox" as George Hamilton IV puts it) to avoid a public announcement which would alienate large numbers of potential fans. Once the Watergate scandal hit the news Cash ceased to give Nixon any kind of public endorsement, unlike Graham who said the President was a man of integrity who may have had some bad advice from those close to him. Johnny's support for Graham would certainly have caused difficulties for all concerned if the contents of taped conversations he'd had with Nixon in the early Seventies had been made public at the time. On the tapes, released 30 years later under public disclosure rules, Graham referred to the "stranglehold" Jews had on the country and speculated as to whether a second Nixon administration "might be able to do something."

The potential problems of an affinity to right-wingers such as Graham and Nixon were exemplified in the preamble to an interview by *New Musical Express* rock journalist Mick Farren with Cash in the mid-Seventies. "If I'd never heard of Johnny Cash and someone came up and described him to me, I can't think of any other entertainer, short of Bob Hope maybe, who on the surface would seem more likely to alienate me. He is a personal friend of Billy Graham. He embraces the conservative values of marriage, home and family. He sings duets with his wife while holding hands. He is, on his own admission, a reformed speed freak and drunk who let "Jesus come into his heart" (Farren's contempt here is palpable) and turned his back on the wild life. So far so tacky.

"And this, dearly beloved, is the problem. Despite all his beliefs you just can't help liking Johnny Cash. Also, within his obvious limitations, there's no way you can fault his music." However, perhaps fearing he might offend his predominantly left-of-centre fellow journalists Farren gets in a few more punches, "Being a friend of Billy Graham put Cash only a shot away from Richard Nixon. After all, wasn't it Billy Graham who used to call Richard Nixon every morning with spiritual advice? What was I DOING, keeping this kind of company?" Farren's view of Johnny's live act as a "strange and anachronistic family show" resonated with other writers who referred dismissively to "The family affair known as the Johnny Cash Show." Another complained that, "From being the bitter and effective musical propagandist of the oppressed he is turning into the compere of *Opportunity Knocks* for the Carter Cash family."

With a renewed commitment to God, Johnny apparently toyed with the idea of becoming a preacher in the early Seventies, though the idea of giving up a massively successful musical career to achieve this could never have been a serious prospect. Even the notion of becoming purely a gospel singer would have been too restricting for such a multifaceted entertainer. Such matters were discussed at length with Billy Graham who as Johnny put it, "Advised me to keep singing . . . and put my heart and soul into all my music." According to a report in *Country Music People*, at an appearance in Amsterdam, Pat Boone's wife Shirley said that Johnny (and apparently June) had been filled with the Holy Spirit and performed an altar call, "Johnny surprising himself perhaps as much as his audience, but sensing their spiritual hunger, extended God's great invitation. Like a tent meeting evangelist he urged his listeners to come forward and accept salvation through Christ. And in that foreign city, from among those who'd come to find entertainment rather than Jesus, an estimated 2,000 people responded! . . . because he'd previously asked Christ to take charge of his life, the Lord had used him gloriously."

If this report is accurate it's surprising since Johnny always went out of his way not to proselytise, preferring to answer questions about his beliefs honestly, and to include a few gospel songs in his show. He has certainly never made any secret of his religious beliefs, summing himself up with the adage, "If I'm ever accused of being a Christian, I hope there'll be enough evidence to convict me." It would be a mistake to underestimate the strength of Johnny Cash's religious beliefs, though he appears to have been especially vocal about them in the early Seventies as evidenced by a letter he wrote to singer Pat Boone. "When we met in 1960 at the Steel Pier in Atlantic City, New Jersey, you were finishing a concert and I was about to go on stage. I was already stringing myself out on amphetamines and alcohol and I can remember to this day, how you looked: clear-eyed, clean-cut, I even remember the white sport shirt you had on. How I envied your appearance . . . the meeting with you then had an impact on me spiritually . . . I was still a 'child of God' . . . To me Pat Boone was the man who sang 'A Wonderful Time Up There' (a song Johnny had often sung in child-hood) . . . On that day I made a pledge . . . that at least 10 per cent of whatever I record in my life will be gospel or evangelical in nature (a pledge I have kept to this day).

"In 1967, I won, through God, the victory over drugs, through human anchors that He sent me . . . it was during my television run that I privately and publicly re-affirmed my faith, and re-committed to Christ . . . Adults by the hundred wrote to me for advice on drugs and alcohol problems. During this time, I saw you on a talk show discussing your commitment to Christ, a little later discussing your concert work, and I got a great revelation: a Christian performer, entertainer, cannot turn in a totally secular performance on stage. If Christ is in you, those people in the audience, whether Pat Boone sings a gospel song or not, are going to see and feel the presence of Jesus Christ in His Pat Boone form! So you've really helped me grow." With such powerfully held views, it's surprising that Johnny only saw fit to commit himself to record 10 per cent gospel or evangelical music.

◆ ◆ ◆ ◆ ◆

In February 1971, Johnny was back in the studio recording 'Man In Black', a song intended as a thumbnail sketch of Cash the man and Cash the artist. As well as his trademark habit of regularly appearing in black, Johnny was often asked about his views on issues relating to the various causes he espoused. He got the idea of an answer song to demonstrate a link between them, hence the opening line, "Well you wonder why I always dress in black, why you never see bright colours on my back?"

In the spirit of Hank Williams' 'Men With Broken Hearts', 'Man In Black' mourns for those on the margins of society, "the reckless ones whose bad trip left them cold" (a graphic reference to Janis Joplin), as well as the "lives that could have been", a direct reference to the Vietnam casualties suffered on a daily basis. Also mentioned are those who died believing that *"The Lord was on their side"*, a reference to the countless millions who have died for their beliefs – a criticism of religion or the opposite? In fact, although Native Americans are not mentioned, the song could be taken as a paean to them and just about everyone else whose life is characterised by suffering, oppression or exclusion. The idea was universal enough for Johnny to substitute something topical during live performances.

'Man In Black' has taken on the aura of unofficial Cash anthem and provided his most common epithet, though the wisdom of making such a record was perhaps debatable. For many, it appeared glib and patronising, no matter how worthy the intentions. The song became the title track for Johnny's next studio album which reached number one on the country charts, though its total 22-week run was substantially smaller compared to his recent albums, especially the prison recordings. Johnny's production association with Bob Johnston had ended with the *I Walk The Line* soundtrack. For 'Man In Black' Cash took over production duties himself, though it was not a task he relished, having to concern himself with numerous technical details which left less time to concentrate on singing and playing.

The opening song 'The Preacher Said, "Jesus Said"' – written by Johnny for Billy Graham by way of an introduction to Cash's audience – was surely something of a gamble. Still in the initial throes of his unconditional support for the charismatic evangelist, Johnny saw fit to feature him on the album's opening song in which Graham delivers lines of scripture in between Johnny's opening lines. While it obviously seemed like a good idea to Cash, it was undoubtedly a monumental turn-off for many of the new, largely secular converts he had gained through his television show. Perhaps an independent producer would have seen the potential pitfalls of including such a song.

'I Talk To Jesus Every Day' was co-written by his old drinking partner Glen Tubb, suggesting that he too had been similarly inspired by religion. 'Singin' In Vietnam Talkin' Blues' was an account of experiences in Vietnam which some conservative elements construed to be an anti-war statement. However, it's hard to see how such a conclusion could be arrived at, since there's virtually nothing controversial in the song beyond a strongly expressed sympathy for those suffering and the earnest wish that the war should end soon.

◆ ◆ ◆ ◆ ◆

The Johnny Cash Show put Johnny's career on a level with an elite group of entertainers such as Barbra Streisand and Andy Williams but, behind the glitzy family image, all was not as it seemed. Johnny has said that during the time he made the shows he did little of worth in the studio. The time-consuming filming, with new numbers having to be rehearsed and learned each week, restricted his ability to tour, with concerts revolving around programme schedules. Added to this were the unpalatable pressures and compromises involved, such as the time an executive complained about Johnny saying on air that he was a Christian (in response to queries from viewers).

There was also the time Dan Blocker ('Hoss' in the television Western *Bonanza*) irritated Johnny intensely by making disparaging remarks about the American national anthem containing too many references to war. Not wishing to appear rude to a guest, Johnny turned the other cheek. Cash later bemoaned the fact that, "The ratings are the only thing that is important and ratings mean big name guest stars. Somebody that'll make people turn on the TV set no matter what they're going to do on the show, if they're just going to stand there and pick their nose. All that matters is whether you get Superstar Joe or not. I resented all the dehumanising things that television does to you, the way it has of just sterilising your head. I wouldn't do another weekly show for anything."

With hindsight, his recollections are warmer principally because he got to meet many leading stars of the day, as Lou Robin later put it, "The show opened a lot of doors that wouldn't otherwise have been opened." Clearly the whole experience was one which engendered conflicting emotions. On any level it was a tribute to Johnny that for all its faults, he succeeded in sustaining the show for as long as he did. In total there were 56 shows running from June – September 1969, January – May 1970 and September 1970 – March 1971. Each show featured a concert segment for Johnny and assorted members of the troupe plus a 10-minute slot, *Ride This Train*, when railway themes and travel across America would be explored with guests such as Tex Ritter.

A list of some of the guest artists featured on the show during its lifespan makes for impressive reading and it's hard to imagine another programme which could have showcased such a diverse range of artists: Bob Dylan , Gordon Lightfoot, Linda Ronstadt, Jeannie C Riley, Joni Mitchell, The Monkees, Marty Robbins, Merle Haggard, Pat Boone, Melanie, Roger Miller, Charley Pride, Mama Cass Elliot, Roy Orbison, Jose Feliciano, Kirk Douglas, Tammy Wynette, Ray Charles (of whom Cash said, "He sings the same basics only in a different genre"), Neil Diamond, Jerry Lee Lewis, Kenny Rogers, Bob Hope, Hank Williams, Jr, Jackie DeShannon, Judy Collins, Roy Acuff, Brenda Lee, Dennis Hopper, Bobby Bare, Peggy Lee, Louis Armstrong, Stevie Wonder, Burl Ives, Bill Monroe, The Everly Brothers, Anne Murray, Derek & The Dominoes, James Taylor, Neil Young, Billy Graham (on a show devoted to religious material including the song 'The Preacher Said, "Jesus Said"'), and The Staple Singers. The last two shows of the final season were largely family affairs with Mother Maybelle and The Carter Sisters featured as special guests.

The physical pace of the show encouraged some to speculate that he might be using artificial energy but he retorted that he got through, "Just with God's help, no chemicals." In fact he was becoming so sensible that he even learned to whisper during rehearsals in order to save his voice for the actual performance. Johnny did however use up a tremendous amount of nervous energy and in an echo of remarks made by Kris Kristofferson about Cash in the studio, one commentator who observed Johnny in rehearsals said, "He displayed the same caged animal quality one recalled from concerts at the Newport Folk Festival and Carnegie Hall. He's rarely in repose but rather he writhes in constant nervous motion, his hands whipping like butterflies across his chest, shoulders and face, flicking aside imaginary perspiration and tugging at his nose and ears." An anonymous observer commented that, "He wears out his clothes from the inside out rather than the other way around."

Johnny got word that ABC were not going to renew his television show while touring Australia. His instinctive reaction was one of relief, though he was unhappy with the manner of the announcement, claiming he had already told ABC two weeks previously that he was not going to do another series. Many years later however, speaking candidly on *The Larry King Show*, he admitted, "Oh I didn't give it up, they dropped me." Tommy Cash says that his brother told him that the television work "had been the most exhausting thing he had ever been through."

After news of the cancellation of the show was made public Johnny said, "TV is a man eater. It wears you out mentally and physically. I much prefer performing in person and that's what I'm going to do starting this month and continuing through the late fall or early winter." He resolved that any future television shows would be one-off specials rather than series. On the sleeve of *Man In Black* Johnny gave an indication of the toll the television series had taken by describing himself as 'JCAT' (Johnny Cash after television). The ratings had dropped and for the ABC executives this was the bottom line. Some said the ratings fell because the show was too country, others because it was not country enough, an argument which overlooked the fact that for all the pride in his roots, Johnny never claimed to be a country singer *per se*. Certainly insofar as there was country music on the show, the presence of a house orchestra and some pretty gauche sets contributed to a neutering effect on the music, as had happened with other shows presented by performers such as Glen Campbell and Eddie Arnold.

It was all part of a process of making country-oriented music acceptable to a broad swathe of the white-collar middle classes; being seen by some commentators as "Country music's liberation from its conservative rural southern past," though in the eyes of others, Johnny's image suffered as a result. Writing about the show in *Country Music People* in 1973, Terry Pettigrew said, "Four of his ABC spectaculars, screened over here by the BBC, showed how thoroughly the networks had cropped his strident, beefsteak personality. Despite some major folk talents among his early guests – Dylan, Lightfoot, Kristofferson – the series quickly regressed into a glossy showcase for pop and showbiz personalities."

Johnny's songs suffered under the glutinous production, particularly when accompanied by the house orchestra under the direction of Bill Walker. As he later told Patrick Carr, "All my greatest successes . . . have had that simple Spartan sound." Some critics complained there were too many guests, others that comedy and general variety triumphed over the music. The contrast with Porter Wagoner's show was marked. Wagoner, a country artist through and through, whose show helped launch the career of Dolly Parton (who later wrote 'I Will Always Love You' for him), outlasted the competition by sticking to what he knew best without compromising, in the hope of pulling in more viewers. As other shows briefly hit the heights and then faded, Porter's show marched on year after year.

Johnny's television show can be compared to the commercialisation that blighted Elvis Presley's career. As such, the process proved to be a limited exercise though Cash was not averse to appearing on glitzy mainstream television shows and occasions on a regular basis thereafter. Cash was fortunate in having a stronger personality than someone like Elvis, and was better equipped to take or leave the manipulative tendencies of managers (like Colonel Tom Parker). One retrospective advantage of the television show was that the popularity he gained from it wasn't affected by subsequent fluctuations in his commercial fortunes. Years later Rosanne Cash reflected, "He's given up something for that fame. It's sad but I also think he's handled it better than most people do. Most people go completely behind glass, completely insane in this world of nothing but ego. I think maybe his fame has been his redemption.

It's given him a measure of humility and genuineness he might otherwise have lost."

◆ ◆ ◆ ◆ ◆

When Johnny toured Britain in 1968 he had said he hoped to return later that year. Due to other commitments this didn't occur but the troupe did make it back for a brief visit towards the end of 1971, playing four shows – one in Scotland and three in England. Although only four of the ABC television shows had been shown on British television, the sense of anticipation was considerable, and audiences were not disappointed. Under the heading "The Most Professional Show In Country Music History" *Country Music People* delivered a glowing verdict with two pages of praise interspersed with photographs of the show's various members. The only criticism was that Fluke's exuberant drumming was overly intrusive for the Carters' set and that brushes should have been substituted. A different reviewer found The Statler Brothers hard to take. "The Statler Brothers are a slick polished POP act. Only trouble is they do not belong on the Cash show but at the Copacabana." Clearly not enamoured with their gags, the reviewer concluded, "Actually the Copa might be too sophisticated for their corny humour."

The *Country Music People* review also drew attention to the sheer expense of bringing over such a large troupe. "Let's face it, it would be much more financially beneficial to himself to halve his price, and go on the road with The Tennessee Three, but Mr Cash is a professional and has surrounded himself with professional people." This observation highlighted the contrast between Johnny's approach and that of some other Fifties stars such as Chuck Berry, who toured without their own musicians, hired a cheap pick-up band and delivered a perfunctory show at top prices. Johnny believed in the importance of family values and having a large number of people closely united on stage in a "circle" was symbolic of a united family, an important aspect of how he grew up. Johnny's father Ray had stressed the importance of giving fans a good show because the ticket price might represent a substantial outlay for some people. Many commentators have said of Johnny Cash that "he cares" and "gives a damn" and an example of this occurred at a concert in Glasgow.

Johnny used local crowd-pleasing tactics to throw some light on his early singing experiences. He told the crowd that earlier that day he had visited a place which made him feel "like I was coming home," a place his mother had often sung to him about when he was six years old in a song written by a prisoner to his sweetheart, which had stayed in his memory ever since. With that he launched into a brief a cappella version of 'The Bonnie Banks Of Loch Lomond'. He also related the story of how he first learned songs by his older sister Louise singing a song to him twice in order to make sure he remembered it. Johnny created the image in the audience's mind by having Anita Carter (as Louise) sing some plaintive country melodies while he responded. If nothing else this drew attention once more to the wonderfully pure quality of Anita's voice, technically the best singer in the Cash troupe.*

Johnny's recent recommitment to Jesus was also reflected in a longer gospel section delivered with much fervour and the spoken sections had Johnny sounding like the preacher he had considered becoming. In keeping with such a mood, Johnny let out a howl during 'A Boy Named Sue' rather than inflict "son of a bitch" on his audience, explaining, "I'm not going to say *that* in front of you." At the end of the song he sang, "And if I ever have a boy I think I'm gonna call him . . . John Carter." The 18-month-old boy was present for some of the shows, waving on cue to the crowd from his position in one of the boxes, heading for an inevitable career in the music business.

Some fans who attended the British shows in 1971 complained that Johnny had become far less accessible than on previous visits and that getting backstage was a near impossibility. It was an inevitable consequence of Johnny's higher profile, one which he didn't like since it went against the country tradition of meeting and greeting fans and patiently signing hundreds of autographs for queuing admirers. After threats had been made against Johnny by the likes of the Ku Klux Klan and with a young son as a target, Johnny became less visible to his public. Tommy Cash confirmed that over the years a number of threats were made. "You just never know if one will be the real thing and you can't take chances."

On one occasion in the late Sixties, Johnny was playing a show in Flint, Michigan, when a man, later described as a "fanatic", jumped on the stage and knocked over the microphone before being grabbed by security personnel. On another occasion a telephone threat was made when Johnny attended a cinema in Charlotte, North Carolina. He was escorted out of the building returning an hour later after a suspect had been taken into custody. Speaking years later June Carter talked about the anxiety generated by kidnap threats made against her children, "It can be scary. We travelled with guards all the time. One extortion note asked for $200,000." This was in reference to an attempt by James Earl Joines whose letter read, "Johnny Cash if you want to keep making money and keep your family healthy leave $200,000 in old bills in a plastic bag at interstate 24 at Old Hickory Boulevard Friday night." On another occasion a rock was thrown at a limousine the family were travelling in. Though the glass shattered and everyone was badly shaken, nobody was injured.

◆ ◆ ◆ ◆ ◆

* It's tempting to speculate that with the right promotion and the necessary ambition and single-mindedness on her part, Anita could have been one of the top female country singers of her generation. She later married Bob Wootton, though the marriage did not last.

As the Seventies became established, Johnny Cash was filled with a new serenity, bolstered by religion and a settled home life. However, artistically the question was, what direction to go in next. By the late Sixties Johnny had laid down a body of work that he would find it hard to improve on. Like many artists from Mozart to Van Gogh who had produced their most enduring work while under 30, Johnny had applied his talents to everything from rockabilly and country, through American history and political causes to folk ballads and pop. Ironically, the conquest of his demons and a stable home life served to diminish his creative resources. In fact, if Johnny had succeeded in killing himself at an early age, as had seemed likely, his niche in musical history would have been assured. His challenge in the Seventies was maintaining a centred lifestyle while at the same time rediscovering his creative urge.

19

WITH THE TERMINATION of the television show, Cash went back to his first love, touring, and 1972 saw the troupe making concert appearances during every month except July in places as far afield as Sweden, Germany and Jamaica. In the spring, Johnny followed in the footsteps of Elvis Presley and accepted a lucrative offer to play a series of cabaret style shows at the Hilton Hotel in Las Vegas. On the face of it this was a surprising choice, particularly so soon after Johnny's religious recommitment. Indeed, in the past, he was dead against playing Las Vegas. A recent description in *Frommer's* gives a flavour of his new surroundings, "The lobby glittering with massive chandeliers and gleaming marble is still attention getting . . . there are quite a few terrific restaurants . . . plus the largest hotel convention and meeting facilities in the world."

It was not a municipal concert hall or a prison dining room. However, religion had helped Johnny to look at things differently as he explained to writer Charles Paul Conn. "After I got acquainted with the Lord I began to realise that, now that I have something to give those people, Las Vegas is exactly where I should go. So I agreed to play the Hilton International showroom the week of Easter and, while I was entertaining, tell the people something about Jesus." Indeed, during the last section of the show while the troupe sang gospel songs, images of Jesus Christ were flashed up onto the wall behind the performers. Though some were appalled by an artist using a stage to push religion, the majority gave Cash a tumultuous reception. The *Los Angeles Times* praised him as "A man of deep integrity and purpose . . . unwilling to compromise with the Las Vegas showroom tradition."

Johnny did run into some controversy when it was reported that he had given an altar call at the end of one show with up to 1,500 people coming forward to receive Jesus. Johnny issued a denial saying that the Holy Spirit dwelt in him at all times. "Sometimes it's like a grain of mustard seed but it's there and at times when we sing those gospel songs I think that it does shine through me. That's what happened at Las Vegas and at most of our concerts recently."

Las Vegas was a prestigious city for an entertainer and Johnny knew only too well that the bills had to be paid. He had never wanted to be a businessman but that is exactly what he became. The days of leaving large wads of cash around the house were a thing of the past, and though he retains an aversion to business meetings with lawyers and bankers (and avoids them if possible) the need to keep generating income became his main priority. What's more, there were a few factors which gave cause for minor concern. A second volume of greatest hits, while just making it into the Top 10, did not sell nearly as well as the first and a single, featuring Johnny and June duetting on 'If I Had A Hammer', only scraped into the Top 30 a few months later. The hard fact was that without the regular exposure of the television show, fewer people were buying Johnny Cash records and his overt celebration of religion on record and stage undoubtedly turned potential buyers away.

However, when it came to live shows, the insatiable demand for Johnny's services meant that Johnny was able to do the Las Vegas engagements on his own terms. He refused to have a comedian to open the show (something Elvis had agreed to) and did not use the slick house orchestra which virtually every other artist relied upon. His drawing power was such that he could get away with these demands because the shows sold out and drew nightly standing ovations.

The House Of Cash became centre of operations and a number of personalised touches added to the character of the 30-room building. There was a bedroom with a bed wide enough for four with a sign reading "The Statler Brothers" on the door and another with a bed wide enough for three with "The Tennessee Three" on the door. Johnny's sister Reba took a leading role in the running of the House Of Cash operation while another sister, Joanne, worked as receptionist. In time a Johnny Cash museum was created on the premises featuring artefacts from various stages of Johnny's life including his growing number of awards and gold discs and the bed he and June slept in during their first five years of marriage. When it came to the running of the Cash empire Johnny placed family members in key positions, a practice he defended in an interview with *Cash Box* in the late Seventies. "A lot of people have frowned at the way I do business. I'm always hiring my family or June's family to work for me, but so long as I can afford any of them and things still run fairly smoothly, I intend to do that because I love my family and I love June's family. If there are any of them we can use in any area we will."

Johnny's desire to create an in-house set-up in the working context even included extended family and family friends. "We have a couple of June's old friends working for us, Honey Dickens and Mildred Joyner . . . June's cousin Sue Hensley runs the travel department and souvenirs . . . My mother is the boss of everybody there. She is the grand boss. I am always comfortable when I know the family is around. I have their support and I trust everybody."

◆ ◆ ◆ ◆ ◆

Johnny created a studio in the House Of Cash and started off recording some of the writers he'd signed (including Glen Sherley, the Folsom prisoner whose song 'Greystone Chapel', Cash had performed). By 1973, at 4,000 square feet, the studio expanded to become one of the biggest and best-equipped in Nashville. Not that this impressed Johnny when considering the final product, as he told a journalist, "They can get all the moog synthesisers that they want but nothing will take the place of the human heart." June was not particularly impressed by the technical equipment either. "I don't know if it's the largest or the greatest but I'll bet it's the only studio with expensive antique furniture in it," a reference to her collecting passion.

In 1972, Johnny made another significant business move when he took on a new manager, Lou Robin of Artist Consultants Productions, who would become a close friend and confidant. Saul Holiff wanted to spend more time with his growing family, and had always maintained that he would only be Johnny's manager for a limited time.* Born in Chicago, Robin obtained a degree in economics and international relations and, during his studies, had worked as a disc jockey, promoting jazz concerts. After a spell working in engineering management for a large aerospace company, he progressed to promoting concerts by major artists such as Judy Garland, The Beatles, The Rolling Stones, Bill Cosby and Simon & Garfunkel, among many others. Lou had also promoted shows by Johnny Cash in the late Sixties: "I bought several concert dates around February '69 from Saul Holiff who I met through a mutual friend. Holiff had also asked me to set up the concert for him at San Quentin and the involvement really took off from there when we started promoting most of Johnny's concerts."

Lou was involved in making the necessary arrangements after news of the fatal accident involving Helen Carter's son Kenny was received. A remarkable insight into the business and personal relationship between artist and manager is that Lou has worked for Johnny Cash for more than 30 years without a written contract. When asked about the suggestion that Johnny could have saved money by touring with just The Tennessee Three, Lou agreed that Cash gave more than he needed to. "Sometimes Johnny did more than that but he had a show that everyone enjoyed. There was something for everyone in that show and he was working as much as he wanted and he was able to afford it."

Johnny's first record release of 1972 was the single 'A Thing Called Love' on which he was backed by the choir of the Reverend Jimmy Snow's Evangel Temple. The regular attendance of Cash at the church caused problems to such an extent that it became necessary to put up signs reading, "ABSOLUTELY NO AUTOGRAPHS OR PHOTOGRAPHS TAKEN INSIDE THE SANCTUARY."

* According to one possibly apocryphal story, Holiff said he would quit whenever he had made a million dollars out of managing Johnny Cash.

Pastor Snow also rejected Johnny's offer of financial support for the church, "Man, you'll wreck my whole church if you do that. If the word gets out that you're paying tithes here . . . nobody else will ever give another dime." 'A Thing Called Love' with its typically direct, from-the-heart Cash type message was dismissed by some critics as banal and trite – not worthy of a man who had stood up for prisoners and Native Americans.

A reflection of the domestic and religious fulfilment he was experiencing, it struck a chord with the public, making number two in the country charts and also giving Johnny his biggest hit in Britain since 'A Boy Named Sue'. In March, 'A Thing Called Love' became the title track of a new studio album which performed well though not spectacularly in the charts, reaching a peak position of number two during a 24-week stay. Production duties were handed to ex-radio host Larry Butler who had co-hosted a top live television show before he was old enough to drive.

After moving to Nashville in 1963, Butler was soon in demand as a session musician, playing piano on Conway Twitty's 'Hello Darlin'' and Bobby Goldsboro's 'Honey'. He was later part of a Memphis group called The Gentrys (along with Chips Moman, another man who would produce Cash albums) and had chart success with a number of songs including, 'Every Day I Have To Cry Some' and 'Keep On Dancing'. Returning to Nashville he worked as a producer for Capitol followed by CBS where he hooked up with Johnny Cash, and later helped to convert Kenny Rogers to country music. Butler also achieved a rare honour when winning a Grammy for Producer Of The Year – beating off opposition from the likes of Quincy Jones.

As usual the album contained material with a religious content but as a result of the influence of his new producer, it was more deftly packaged than *Man In Black* and contained nothing as overt as 'The Preacher Said, "Jesus Said"'. The album kicked off with 'Kate', featuring breakneck 'boom-chicka-boom' Perkins-style picking behind a story of murder and a walk to the gallows with a woman to blame. 'Papa Was A Good Man' took a sympathetic view of a helpless alcoholic, mirroring Johnny's own struggles, and 'Arkansas-Lovin' Man' was another slice of up-tempo brash Cash. The resurgence of religious passion and his recent association with Billy Graham led Johnny to more public statements on his religious position.

When asked by writer Charles Paul Conn whether his career might suffer as a result of these pronouncements, he responded, "Well, if what you're talking about is being a man, becoming a Christian doesn't make me one bit less a man than I've ever been. Being a Christian isn't for sissies. It takes a real man to live for God, a lot more than to live for the devil, you know? If you really want to live right these days, you gotta be tough. And as far as that image of me as some kind of mean guy always going around fighting and tearing things up, well that's been exaggerated anyway." In June, he performed with Billy Graham at the Jesus

Musical Festival Explo '72 in Dallas, Texas, a show later broadcast on one of the many American television channels devoted to or prominently featuring evangelical religious services. Billy Graham described it as a "Religious Woodstock" and advertisements for the event tried to appeal to young people by mimicking current advertisements, e.g. "Things go better with Jesus Christ – He's The Real Thing."

The event ran over four days and attracted somewhere between 100,000–200,000 Christians from all over America and beyond. Johnny appeared in the climactic build-up to the appearance of Billy Graham himself. Introduced as "The most exciting man in American music today," Johnny walked onto the stage with his guitar slung across his back to a rapturous reception. The passage of time has not been kind to the stage backdrop chosen for the occasion which looks, frankly, ridiculous, featuring large cut-out stars, a huge hand with the index finger pointing skywards and, inevitably, the word "Jesus" in a zany design prominently placed behind the performers. For the occasion Johnny performed 'A Thing Called Love', 'I See Men Walking As Trees' and the old hymnal song, 'Supper Time'. His high-profile public support for such events continued in the early Seventies with appearances at The Johnny Cash Country & Gospel Festival at the Pocono International Raceway, Pennsylvania, the inaugural First All-Lutheran Youth Gathering, Houston which also featured Paul Simon, and Spree '73 in London.

Released in July, *America: A 200-Year Salute In Story And Song* was a return to the Cash concept-style album which Johnny used to give a sentimental and patriotic overview of modern American history, anticipating bicentennial celebrations by four years. The album resembled a heritage trail – music, historical talk plus anecdotes presented in an easily digestible form and was the end product of Johnny's voracious appetite for the historical and creative literature associated with the emergence of modern America. Though lacking sophisticated intellectual analysis, the album was strong on folksy songs linked by straightforward dialogue (all written by Cash) readily accessible to the man in the street such as this description of the events leading up to the breaking away of the 13 states: "In April of 1775, this great nation started coming alive. Old King George didn't like it one bit so he proceeded to throw him a royal fit. He told his generals better get 'em back in line."

Although accentuating the positive aspects of America's history he didn't shirk from mentioning darker episodes, including (not surprisingly) the treatment of Native Americans. For that topic he revisited the massacre by the Seventh Cavalry at Wounded Knee by including the song 'Big Foot' which he had written following his visit there. The Depression merited only the briefest of mentions, "Well the country went to the poor house all right, but then it got back on its feet to become the most powerful nation in the history of the world." 'Paul Revere', 'The Battle Of New Orleans' (the old Johnny Horton hit),

'Remember The Alamo' and 'Mr Garfield' (about the American President who was assassinated) told their own story.

The music was kept simple, rootsy and melodic and though Carl Perkins and The Tennessee Two contributed, the overriding style of the album was old-time folk and country, emphasised by contributions from pianist Chuck Cochran, harmonica player Charlie McCoy and guitarists Red Lane and Norman Blake, to whom Cash paid a special tribute on the sleeve: "Special thanks to Norman Blake and his guitar for setting the mood for this album." Blake, a self-styled old-time country musician, had played for The Carter Family as well as June's road group and had been one of the session men chosen for Bob Dylan's *Nashville Skyline* album. He was also one of the regular band members for Johnny's television show, picking guitar and dobro.

At times the presence of fluttering harmonica and heart-tugging strings lent the project a down-home feel. Despite its overarching message of American achievement and greatness, the album had a strongly nostalgic and sentimental mood, just the antidote for a nation reeling from the protracted horrors of an Asian war. Johnny's voice was omnipresent – singing, talking, laughing, entertaining, soothing – providing further evidence to support Carl Perkins' dictum about people being happy to hear Johnny talk as well as sing.

Musicologist Henry Pleasants made a similar point when he said, "His commanding voice finds itself in that never-never land midway between speech and song." Some of the songs on the album, including 'Come Take A Ride In My Airship', a song Johnny's mother had apparently first heard in 1912, were originally recorded to provide entertainment for the Apollo 14 astronauts, at least one of whom, Stuart Rosa, had specifically requested material by Johnny Cash. In the event they were not used for this purpose. Commercially *America . . .* was not a major success, continuing a clear pattern of decline in record sales.

◆ ◆ ◆ ◆ ◆

In an eventful 1972, Johnny found time to give evidence at a senate subcommittee hearing dealing with prison reform legislation. With his high-profile prison concerts, he was regarded as a man whose views were worth listening to. Cash started off by countering the impression that he was soft on crime, making it clear that he did not favour the abolition of prison nor the "Pollyanna" treatment of hardened criminals. What he urged was a more humane approach to punishment, with the emphasis on rehabilitation. In evidence he gave examples of incidents which had appalled him. "I've seen things that would chill the blood of the average citizen but the average citizen needs to be chilled." He related the story of a 15-year-old boy who died in an Arkansas prison after being raped by older inmates and another young man in a Virginia prison, who hanged himself after being stripped of his clothing as a punishment. After giving his testimony Johnny met President Nixon and when later asked if he would help CREEP (the campaign to re-elect the President) he said, "If he asked me I would. The dignity of the office should be upheld and respected by all citizens and I will do anything I can for him. President Nixon has done a lot for peace."

When interviewed years later by British music journalist Steven Wells, Johnny displayed diplomatic skills in his response to a hostile question about Nixon. "I guess I think that they needed someone like me giving them another point of view." In 1973 he lent more support to the cause when playing at a formal state dinner for the Republican Governors' conference, along with Mickey Newbury and Bobby Goldsboro. While Johnny lent support to the Republicans on this occasion he maintained his position of doing so without giving his full approval.

Johnny continued to receive or be nominated for many music industry awards, and the 1973 Grammy awards ceremony (covering the eligibility period Oct. 1971 to Oct. 1972) promised to be a very special occasion. Not only was 'If I Had A Hammer' nominated in the Best Country Vocal Performance by a Group or Duo but the ceremony, which had always been held in New York or Los Angeles, was to be broadcast from Nashville. According to Ralph Emery, the decision of the producer Pierre Cossette to stage the event in Nashville went down like a lead balloon with ABC who usually broadcast the event. The network believed people associated Nashville too closely with country so they refused to be involved. When NBC also turned down the television rights, Cossette resorted to desperate measures. He engineered an invitation to stay a weekend with Bob Wood and his wife Lori.

Wood was one of the top programming decision makers at CBS and Emery related how he was eventually persuaded to take the Grammies. "Cossette used the entire weekend as an opportunity to hound Wood to broadcast the Grammy Awards on CBS. Wood wouldn't relent, and on Monday morning, Cossette was still without a medium for the most esteemed program relating to the recording industry. Cossette was walking down a hall in the Wood home at dawn when he noticed the door was ajar to the Woods' bedroom." Apparently he then went back to his room, got his briefcase with all the paperwork relating to the show and returned to the Wood boudoir. He climbed into bed between Wood and his wife and said, "Bob if you don't buy the Grammy show I'm going to do to your wife what ABC did to me." Wood was furious but he agreed to buy the show which remained with CBS thereafter.

There were other problems. Local people were hired to put the show together in the Tennessee Theater but it seems there had never been much call for synthetic smoke in Nashville. This was required for a number by soul singer Curtis Mayfield but the replacement of liquid insect repellent pumped out of smoke machines proved to be a disaster. The spray was allowed to accumulate before being targeted at the stage and when it eventually blew out, Curtis Mayfield as well as those in the front rows of the auditorium, began coughing uncontrollably.

There had been no problem at rehearsals because the back doors had been left open but no one realised what would happen when they were closed. Instead of smooth soul, millions of viewers were treated to a chorus of coughs and the sight of handkerchiefs covering faces. By the time Johnny took to the stage, he was barely visible through the smoke. It would be a long time before Nashville was considered as a location for the Grammies again. To complete a less than perfect night, Johnny and June lost out to their backing singers, The Statler Brothers, who won their category with 'Class Of '57'.

The wide range of organisations which regarded Johnny as a suitable recipient for their awards vividly demonstrated how he was able to garner praise from organisations which had little if anything in common with each other. In 1971, he was given a doctorate of humanities from the Gardner-Webb University of North Carolina in recognition of his good deeds. The institution met with June's approval though her comments sounded more than a little patronising. "This is a great little middle-of-the-road kind of school that still talks about Jesus Christ. It represents the hard-working people of this country." Johnny looked most impressive as he received his award fitted out in gown and mortarboard.

The following year, he received the Audie Murphy Patriotism Award as part of the Spirit of America Festival. A slightly built teenaged orphan from Texas, whose credo was "You lead from the front," Audie Murphy had reputedly dispatched over 200 Germans single-handedly during World War Two. He later went on to a career in clichéd war movies and for many he represented American manhood. The Spirit of America Festival started in the Sixties as a response to the growing protests against America's involvement in the Vietnam War. Citizens of the city of Decatur, Georgia decided to show support for service personnel and to promote American patriotism through the presentation of an annual Fourth of July free event. Previous recipients of the Audie Murphy Patriotism Award had included the Governor of Alabama, George C Wallace.

Johnny also won a Dove Award* in 1972 for the liner notes he wrote to the gospel album *Light* by the Oak Ridge Boys. So it was that in the space of one year, Johnny received prestigious awards for his caring humanity, hard-core patriotism and religious song-writing.

While his purely religious albums hadn't sold anywhere near his more commercial output, Johnny felt the time was right to make a film about Jesus Christ – an idea which originated during Johnny and June's 1966 visit to Israel. The couple were both cinema buffs and had a projector in their house but they complained at being "repelled by many of today's films. Nowadays they make movies full of a lot of four-letter words and they say that nobody is offended by that any more."

* The annual Dove Awards honour the achievements of those in the contemporary Christian and gospel music industry.

Johnny had been keen to create a lasting work of art reflecting his cherished religious beliefs since the days in Memphis when he had told Sam Phillips that he wanted to record gospel songs. Success and the switch to Columbia had enabled him to go some way towards achieving this goal but the project he had in mind was bigger than just an album of religious songs. As he put it in rather grandiose terms to English journalist Tony Byworth in 1973, "There comes a time in every man's life when he says to himself, 'I've got to do something worthwhile for this world.' Every man wants to make that one mark that will say to the world – 'Here's my contribution. This is my something worthwhile.'"

During Johnny and June's Israel visit, June had apparently dreamed she saw Johnny, arms outstretched, atop a mountain with a bible in his hand, talking about Jesus. As Johnny put it later, "Her dream became my vision." In the film to be called *The Gospel Road*, Johnny would sing songs and act as narrator. Making use of her acting experience, June would take a leading role (as Mary Magdalene), and an assortment of songwriters, sympathetic to the basic idea, would write new material for the venture. In 1971, Johnny and June returned to Israel (or the "Holy Land" as they preferred to call it) with a crew of around 30 people and spent most of November recording hours of film under the supervision of Robert Elfstrom (director of *Johnny Cash: The Man, His World, His Music*), who also played the part of Jesus Christ.

The work was arduous with the cast and crew often having to get up in the early hours to make sure they reached particular locations at the optimum time for filming. The schedule was hectic but Johnny still found time to undergo baptism by immersion in the Jordan River as Christ himself had done. Johnny wrote virtually the entire script for the film (which lasted 84 minutes), all of which took up his time in the spaces between touring and recording. The result (completed in 1973) was a piece of work which was an immense source of pride to Johnny and June, for which Johnny was reputed to have put up $500,000 of his own money. Johnny later suggested that divine intervention may have helped to smooth the film's progress. "We got a goodly share of miracles. We got a storm on the Sea of Galilee the day we needed it and a calm sea the days it was demanded by the script."

Speaking in 1973, Johnny set out his thinking about the film. "I'm completely serious about it . . . I believe in what I'm talking about. It's quite a tough job to pull something off like this, to tell the story and still try to entertain people. We have none of the old church hymns in *The Gospel Road*, all the songs are new songs and most of them were especially written for the film by people who are very alert and knowledgeable about what's going on in the music world today." Those "alert and knowledgeable" people included Kris Kristofferson, John Denver, Christopher Wren and Joe South as well as another name who had recently entered Cash's orbit, Larry Gatlin, one of whose ancestors had invented the Gatling gun.

The story of their getting together provides another example of how Cash was quick to help a struggling artist. Gatlin and his wife attended the Evangel Temple in Nashville on a Sunday when June Carter happened to be in the assembly as well. The Reverend Snow asked Gatlin, who was trying to make it as a singer and songwriter in Music City, to step forward and sing his own song, 'Help Me', for the congregation. June was so impressed with Gatlin's singing that she wrote his name down on the back of a blank cheque (appropriate in view of the impact her action would have on Larry's career), pestering Johnny to listen to her new find. A few weeks later Johnny was present when Larry again sang the song in church and, like June, was most impressed by what he heard. It was Gatlin's good fortune that the service took place just when Johnny was looking for contributors to the soundtrack of *The Gospel Road*, editing of which was almost complete.

Gatlin could hardly believe his luck and soon afterwards he found himself, along with the other more established musicians, watching a preview of the film with instructions to come up with suitable complementary music. For the strug- gling songwriter it was the chance of a lifetime not to mention an opportunity to buy decent food. As he said in his autobiography, "But for that chance encoun- ter at the Evangel Temple I think me and my wife might have starved to death." Larry was impressed by the fact that Johnny paid union scale, because he could have taken advantage of the situation by paying much less. Gatlin would have still taken the job.*

Before final editing, Johnny and June held a preview of the film for some of their closest friends and family, including the Reverend Jimmy Snow, Mother Maybelle, Carl Perkins and The Tennessee Three. Their response was positive though the description by writer Charles Paul Conn of the film as being "one of the most memorable pieces of film that ever lit up the silver screen since the dis- covery of celluloid" was way off the mark. Johnny was aware of the financial risk he was taking but his faith appeared to render him calm on this point, saying any profits would be donated to charity. "I've made a lot of big money, and I think God let that happen for a purpose. It's God's money anyway. He's just letting me use it to make a film about Jesus."

After the preview, work began in earnest on the soundtrack. It was Billy Graham, taking the "Why should the devil have all the good tunes?" line who persuaded Johnny to use the best musicians possible. Asked by Johnny to write a song for the last supper scene, Kris Kristofferson came up with 'Jesus Was A Capricorn'. Cash wrote a number of songs himself though the lengthy double album included a lot of repetition, for example, four versions of 'He Turned The Water Into Wine'. *The Gospel Road* was released in April 1973, accompanied by

* Larry Gatlin's song 'The Last Supper' made it onto the *Gospel Road* soundtrack.

a full-page *Billboard* advertisement in which Johnny referred to the album as "My life's proudest work."

Johnny was on hand to meet and greet the public when the film had its first showing in Charlotte, an event attended by Governor Jimmy Carter and his wife. Thereafter it was shown in various cities throughout America close to dates when Johnny and the troupe were playing concerts. For a time, Johnny and Marshall Grant breathlessly criss-crossed the country putting in appearances at opening nights and generally running themselves ragged doing what they could to promote the film. Johnny had organised an invitation-only première a few months earlier in Nashville and had hired the 2,000-seater Tennessee Theater for the purpose. Stars, celebrities and local business people were invited and some tickets were made available to the general public at no charge. The pavements were packed with fans eager to catch a glimpse of the glitterati and the occasion took on the air of a major Hollywood première, in ironic contrast to the life of the leading character. The film received a standing ovation and one local paper spoke of "Many leaving the theatre moist-eyed and moved."

In his book *The New Johnny Cash*, Charles Paul Conn quotes Johnny's view of Christ as expressed in the film. "Lots of people go all their lives thinking Jesus was some kind of pious pushover. He's been portrayed as a sissy and I'm just not buying that concept of Him. He didn't bawl on that cross; I think if you or I had been up there we would have squalled and bawled and tried to get down. Not Jesus. He was a real man. He walked into the seat of authority – Him just a man of the street – and called the Pharisees hypocrites to their faces. That takes a real man too. God was born a human so men could relate to Him, you know? But the problem is that things have been overlooked about Him that should have been emphasised. He was a real human being with great compassion, and a special gentleness toward women and down-and-outers. This film shows Him very much as a human – like He eats boiled eggs and bread with His hands; He gets a rock in His sandal and it hurts Him – that sort of thing."

George Hamilton IV, a committed Christian himself is of the view that when it comes to religion and spirituality Johnny is "very sincere, definitely not a phoney though he has a dark side and a bright side. If there is any contradiction there it is in the human nature of all of us, the fact that we're all sinners; the difference between being just a sinner and being where hopefully I am and where I think Hank Williams was and where Johnny Cash is, is the sinner who loves the Lord. I believe in my heart that Johnny loves the Lord and that he is very sincere about his faith. I also think he is the greatest talent I have come across apart from those that are already up there on the Mount Rushmore of country music with him."

The trouble of course is that such affirmations, while appealing to other believers are less palatable to the non-believer who nonetheless recognises Johnny's outstanding qualities as a man and a musician. Writing some years after the release of *The Gospel Road*, Nick Tosches, a fan of Cash's music, said, "Johnny Cash and his God are a particularly tedious act." (Tosches also complained that fruit punch was the strongest thing served at Johnny's parties – he wasn't the only one to suffer in this way, even the hard-living musicians who frequented the House Of Cash studio had to make do with non-alcoholic beverages.)

Despite the high profile of the scriptwriter, *The Gospel Road* was only a moderate box office draw. However, the film was later acquired by the motion picture division of Billy Graham's Evangelistic Association, at the time the first not to have been produced by his own film company, and has been shown in over 40,000 churches. At the end of the film Billy Graham invites members of the audience to make a commitment to Christ and, according to Cash, many hundreds did just that. However, as with Johnny's other 1973 album, *Any Old Wind That Blows*, sales of the accompanying soundtrack were equally disappointing, with the albums staying in the charts for a mere 14 weeks each; making numbers 5 and 12 respectively. The musical production under the direction of Larry Butler was saccharine and, despite Johnny's oft-stated complaints about overproduction, Butler dubbed on heavy string arrangements for much of the music. Even the singles released from *The Gospel Road* (from which were deleted the many earnest narratives) barely dented the charts.

Inevitably CBS were less than happy. They had supported Johnny's less commercial endeavours in the Sixties but his commercial output had offset any loss. Now even mainstream Johnny Cash albums were only selling moderately well. The coolness of the record company to albums like *The Gospel Road* prompted Johnny to complain, "My record company would rather I'd be in prison than in church." There were vague plans for a follow-up, *The Gospel Ship*, to be made in the Middle East "sometime in the Eighties". The theme of the film, based around the apostle Paul, was that a man can successfully follow the Christian road in everyday life. However, any idea that Johnny would subsequently moderate his religious views was mistaken as he was hard at work on another project which would once more bring his religious experiences and beliefs to the attention of his public.

20

AROUND 1973, JOHNNY set to work on an autobiography, which was to be more than just a catalogue of his life's events. It was an extremely personal kind of testament which flowed from the apparent turning point Johnny had reached in the late Sixties, in particular the regeneration of his spiritual life. The autobiography, which he painstakingly wrote in longhand over a period of almost a year, was called *Man In Black*, a title which neatly coalesced with the song of the same name and of course the whole Johnny Cash image. It was, as Johnny himself put it, "A spiritual odyssey" which traced the key events of his life in the context of his religious experience. Listening to the radio in Dyess wasn't just an introduction to the music that would inspire and make him famous, it was a way of "Getting in touch with something beautiful . . . those songs gave me a taste of heavenly things." The death of his brother Jack is transformed from a miserable and painful loss into a reason to believe. "The memory of Jack's death, his vision of heaven, the effect his life had on the lives of others and the image of Christ he projected have been more of an inspiration to me, I suppose, than anything else that has ever come to me through any man."

As part of their religious regeneration Johnny and June had undertaken extensive Bible studies both via formal correspondence courses leading to official certification, and at home with the aid of an extensive collection of literature on religion which had been greatly enhanced when Johnny inherited Ezra Carter's library of religious and historical books. June emerges as a major influence on Johnny's turnaround, partly through her single-minded determination to keep him from the drugs which threatened to kill him, but also through her relentless determination to keep him on the religious path, and to relate events in everyday life to the workings of a higher power. When Johnny was battling hardest against withdrawal symptoms she would say, "Call on God, John, don't weaken."

A humorous incident occurred while Johnny was at the height of his success during the ABC television season. When playing for a select audience of dignitaries and celebrities at New York's Waldorf-Astoria hotel to honour Mamie Eisenhower, Johnny suffered extreme embarrassment and humiliation when, in the process of bending down to retrieve a plectrum, his trousers tore open from crotch to knee, leaving a sizeable area of flesh exposed. Johnny only just got through his set, aware as he was of sniggers and red faces in the audience. After he finished he rushed off stage and locked himself in the bathroom of his hotel suite. June followed and he could hear her laughing as she waited for him to cool down. "What are you laughing at?" he said. "What can possibly be funny?" and she replied, "John, tonight the Lord busted your britches."

Johnny even suggested that it was the Holy Spirit who caused the jeep his sister Reba was driving, with John Carter and some of his friends on board, to turn over causing injuries to his young son which led to him being kept in intensive care for a short time (though in fact the injuries turned out to be minor). The incident was supposed, in part, to have been visited on Johnny by God because he was pushing himself too hard and not spending enough quality time with his son. When he found Roy Orbison at the hospital waiting to provide comfort and support this was more evidence of divine intervention. "Thank God for sending you at a time like this, Roy Orbison," he cried. Given that the book was aimed at a mainstream audience rather than selected converts, these and other aspects do tend to grate, particularly stories of recovery from drug or alcohol abuse by Carl Perkins, Gordon Terry, Jimmy Snow and of course Johnny himself, the assumption invariably being that recovery was associated with finding God; the idea of people simply using personal willpower to beat their vices without divine intervention is not entertained.

However, what comes through in the book is the essence of Johnny Cash – honest, direct, shooting from the hip, and, following the confessional manner which was a feature of his chosen religious way, brutally frank in his accounts of how he had failed or displayed weakness in his life. Being editor, these incidents were delivered with stark honesty. For instance, without avoidance of shame, he describes the time he travelled from Nashville to California in December 1966 to visit Vivian and their four young daughters. "I tried to go home to see them that year at Christmas time. I left Nashville on December 20, and it was Christmas Eve before I arrived in California. Everywhere the plane stopped, I got off and went to the clubs and honky-tonks, mixing with the kind of people who shared my particular brand of death. I spent two nights in Dallas making all the clubs, sitting in with the musicians, drinking with them and taking pills. Then I made it to Tucson and Phoenix and another whirlwind of clubs and bad company. Only the realisation that it was Christmas Eve got me back on a plane to California. The reaction to my arrival at home was one of surprise. They had given up hope that I'd be home for Christmas. There was no joy in the reunion, no Christmas spirit. I was like a stranger. I felt like one, and I knew I looked like one." Such revelations made the book compulsive reading.

One striking and surprising aspect of the autobiography is the dedication, which reads, "This book is dedicated to Ezra J Carter who taught me to love the Word." While there is no doubt that Johnny spent much time with June's father in the first half of the Sixties, and that the two men became close, to have overlooked his own parents is inexplicable. Ray and Carrie Cash had brought Johnny up, along with all their other children, in a Christian household, with regular church attendance the norm and Johnny maintains he had been a Christian from early on in his life. Johnny had his first major religious experience when he was twelve and his late brother Jack knew before he died that he wanted to be a minister. Ray Cash had even co-written a religious song with Johnny, 'I Call Him', so it's easy to imagine that the dedication must have caused considerable upset.

Johnny Cash's first autobiography went on to sell over a million copies, easily outperforming Johnny's current recorded output. Of the book Ronald Reagan said, "It will help bring about a spiritual awakening in our land," while Billy Graham said, glowingly, "It will surely be a shining witness to all who read it."

Over the years, Johnny has made less favourable comments about the book castigating it for its "sanctimony", and that the overtly religious aspects now strike him as simplistic and naive.

◆ ◆ ◆ ◆ ◆

Around this time Johnny and June became caught up in a pressing matter which touched on the issue of their privacy. The couple had commissioned an interior designer called Patricia Holt to work on their house and, once completed, Holt had sought to publish about 35 photographs in a book she was writing about her experience of working on the Cash house. Johnny and June sought to legally restrain her from doing so on the grounds that they had only agreed to the publication of a small number of photographs in a lofty academic magazine called *Architectural Digest* (published by the American Institute of Architects). Patricia Holt said, "I cannot believe that Johnny Cash is suing me. I feel I have every right to publish the book I have written. It in no way damages Johnny Cash or his family or his home."

Apparently overlooking the agreement made with Johnny and June, Holt's view was that they should not be allowed to place restrictions on where the photographs were published and that in seeking to do so they were depriving Cash fans of something they were somehow entitled to. Johnny and June successfully argued that the relationship was such that there was an implied understanding and agreement that Holt would not make use of the information and photographs obtained by her for any purpose other than the performance of her professional duties, and would not publicise such information for the purpose of private gain. (In the event the photographs which were submitted to *Architectural Digest* were rejected.)

In 1974, Johnny was on holiday in Jamaica with John Rollins, a successful entrepreneur with a diverse range of business interests, who owned a substantial quantity of land in prime locations around Montego Bay. While touring around with Rollins in a four-wheel drive, Johnny came across a semi-derelict house owned by Rollins in an elevated position called Cinnamon Hill. Johnny quickly saw the attraction of the house as a holiday retreat with its beautiful natural scenery, a pleasant all-year climate (warm winters being a particular attraction) and a reasonably short flying time from Nashville. The only trouble was that John Rollins didn't want to sell, as with the case of Braxton Dixon and the house in Hendersonville, where Johnny had his mind set on the very house that the owner-developer had particularly singled out for himself. Initially a deal was struck whereby Johnny renovated the house in return for which John Rollins allowed Johnny to stay there whenever he liked.

As he had done with Braxton, Johnny used all his powers of persuasion, in combination with the offer of a hefty amount, and a deal was eventually struck. Cinnamon Hill was built on a former sugar plantation which was worked for years by thousands of slaves and with his metal detector Johnny has come across artefacts such as nails and chains bearing witness to their presence. The first owners of the house were the Barretts' of Wimpole Street, the family of the lyric poet Elizabeth Barrett Browning, an original creative talent in her own time.*

Rollins and his property holdings in Jamaica later became the focus of a political row. He had originally purchased the land in the mid-Sixties but when Rollins fell into arrears on his loan his bank foreclosed and the lands were then sold to the Jamaican government. Rollins maintained that the taking of his land had been unfair and demanded it back from the government. The ruling party at the time, the JLP was prepared to enter arbitration with a view to selling the land back to Rollins at what they considered a fair price so long as he agreed a suitable development plan for the area, but he was apparently not prepared to enter such negotiations. According to his critics it was only when there was a change of government in 1989 that there was an official change of heart and the land, about 2,700 acres in all, was sold back to Rollins for $1 million at a time when its real commercial value was said to be more like $100 million. Whether and to what extent any of these dealings affected the Cash estate is unclear.

◆ ◆ ◆ ◆ ◆

By the mid-Seventies a commercial pattern of declining record sales coupled with copious live performances started to establish itself for Johnny Cash.

---

* In his 1997 autobiography Johnny unequivocally stated that he has seen ghosts in the house including a woman in her thirties wearing a white dress, whom on one occasion he (along with his houseguests) saw walk through a solid wall.

What's more, as the Seventies progressed about half of his record sales were outside America, thanks to his assiduous touring in far-flung territories; something he later confirmed was a conscious strategy. Referring to his fans outside America he said, "I have really worked hard at building up and maintaining their loyalty. They have country music clubs as well as fan clubs for the individual artists and I work real hard at keeping them happy."

Rockabilly singer Narvel Felts recalled playing a concert in France some years later. At one point in the show, wanting to see which country stars the almost exclusively French speaking audience knew and liked, he shouted out a list of names. There was hardly any reaction until he came to the name of Johnny Cash at which point the audience erupted in whoops and shouts of recognition and appreciation.

Speaking in 1973, Cash said, "Well, when I'm on a stage I feel like I'm a complete person because that's what I feel like I do best and that's what I'm most alive and happy doing, performing." As a man with a wide range of interests and a love of history he appreciated the cultural benefits of broadening his mind by visiting other countries. Not surprisingly, it was to matters religious that he was often drawn, enriching his stock of books on Christianity with purchases made at Foyle's bookshop in London.

Having been in the business for around 20 years, Johnny was seen by the younger generation as someone their parents liked and, of course, to fans of The Beatles, The Rolling Stones, The Doors, Jimi Hendrix or The Who he had never been particularly hip anyway. But a growing number of singer-songwriters were well aware of the debt they owed to an original like Cash. Johnny's touring schedule was heavy – up to 300 shows a year – but according to Lou Robin, it was "not exceptionally punishing when it's what you like doing . . . It was after all a financial necessity and John was probably doing fewer shows than Waylon and Willie and some others much of the time." Johnny himself was always quick to distance himself from those who complained about the rigours of the road, given the privileged position such top artists enjoyed.

It *was* hard at times and Lou Robin saw it as his role to do what he could to ease the stresses and strains on the performers. As he puts it, "I try to work for a common cause with everybody else involved, to do the best shows they could and survive on the road with all the rigours that go with it . . . allowing Johnny to do what he wanted to do, giving the people what they wanted to hear, and still keeping it so that Johnny, June and everyone didn't burn themselves out."

CBS continued to milk their commodity with a compilation, *Sunday Morning, Coming Down*, and an album of duets with June called *Johnny Cash And His Woman* (which included the classic 'City Of New Orleans' by Steve Goodman, a song offered originally to Johnny but passed over because of clashing commitments) but neither album made the country Top 30. An album of children's songs (*Children's Album*) released at the start of 1974, featuring such titles as

'Nasty Dan', 'I Gotta Boy And His Name Is John', 'Miss Tara' and 'Dinosaur Song' didn't chart at all.

In January '74, Johnny took some time out to further his acting pursuits when filming an episode of *Colombo* with Peter Falk in California. In 'Swan Song' (screened in March), Cash played Tommy Brown, a highly successful country music singer whose wife has been raking off his earnings to pursue her own interests. Rather than confront her he drugs his wife and arranges for the small plane he is piloting to crash. While he parachutes to safety, his wife dies in the wreckage. With palpable predictability, Colombo, with his "There's just one other thing" brand of persistence eventually gets his man. Johnny's acting was stilted and his lack of thespian confidence came through. However, an interesting contrast was provided when there were scenes featuring Johnny singing. Although the requirements of television made him smile excessively and in an exaggerated way, Cash nonetheless looked comfortable. This was even more evident when, at the end of the programme, 'Sunday Morning Coming Down' started playing on a car radio. In contrast to Johnny's acting it came over as natural, unforced and authoritative, prompting Colombo to say, "Anybody who can sing like that can't be all bad." Johnny got on well with Peter Falk during the filming though he got irritated at one point as he recalled in his 1997 autobiography. "He was telling me how to deliver a line, and said, 'I'd do it just like this – or however you people say it down there.'"

According to a *Cash Box* report, at the time when Johnny's record sales were declining, there was a serious possibility that the next big thing would be a major career move to cinema, something Cash had of course contemplated in the Fifties when he relocated his family to California. "Johnny Cash could replace John Wayne as a major Western-movie star and symbol of Americana if the career advisers closest to Cash have their way . . . There is a demand . . . for the 'hero-type', manly character in the movies and Cash could easily fit into those shoes."

If such plans had come to fruition it's hard to see that they could have produced as fulfilling a prospect as Johnny found in music. As those around him had worked out for themselves, Johnny could only have aspired to major star status playing the part of a stereotypical cowboy or some other Western-style character. His voice and looks gave him an obvious head start but given the highly limited nature of his acting skills these would have only pulled him through for so long. The trouble also was that Johnny's success on the silver screen would have been tied in to a large extent with the success of his musical career. Since that was in something of a decline, his long-term film prospects weren't promising. Although he continued to make film and TV appearances, plans for a major move into the world of celluloid were quietly put on hold.

◆ ◆ ◆ ◆ ◆

Despite his instinctive support for the President and American soldiers in times of war, Johnny did not have absolute conviction that Vietnam was a just cause and, in conversations with his brother Tommy during the early Seventies, he reiterated his deep unease at the loss of young lives. He had visited Vietnam in an attempt to boost troop morale and now Tommy suggested another contribution he could make. "Why don't you write a patriotic song as a way of expressing support for our boys?" Johnny agreed this was a good idea and a few months later he phoned Tommy from the Plaza Hotel in New York and read out the lyrics to a song which had been partly inspired by America's experiences in Vietnam. On 'Ragged Old Flag' – a recitation set to a moving melody in which Cash used the device of a visitor to a small county courthouse pointing out the run-down state of the flag – "The flag pole is leaned a little bit, and that's a ragged old flag hanging on it" – as a pretext for revisiting one of his favourite subjects, modern American history, with the courthouse being a metaphor for patriotic America and the flag symbolic of the American nation.

An old man explains with a mixture of pride and sadness that the flag had become ragged as a result of the hits it had taken in various conflicts over the years, "You see we got a little hole in that flag there when Washington took it across the Delaware . . . On Flanders Field in World War One she got a big hole from a Bertha gun." As the conflicts came up to date Johnny launched an attack on the lack of patriotism in modern America and in particular those who denigrated the Stars and Stripes as part of an attack on US involvement in Vietnam:

> *And now they've about quit waving her here at home*
> *In her own good land she's been abused*
> *She's been burned, dishonored, denied, refused*
> *And now the government for which it stands*
> *Is scandalised throughout the land*
> *And she's getting threadbare and she's wearing thin*
> *But she's in good shape for the shape she's in*
> *Cause she's been through the fire before*
> *And I believe she can take a whole lot more.*

A few years later, Johnny gave one particularly moving rendition of the song, in the presence of Ronald Reagan, at Ford's Theater, Washington DC, where Abraham Lincoln was assassinated in 1865 by Confederate sympathiser John Wilkes Booth. An American flag was draped over the seat where Lincoln had been sitting. 'Ragged Old Flag' became the title track for a new album of songs which was remarkable for the fact that all 12 were written by Johnny, something of a first for him, when producers of similar artists generally preferred to include songs by a variety of writers.

Although the album has been described in rather grandiose terms as a song cycle about life, family and the American dream, in reality the album, apart from the title track, consisted of fairly ordinary songs without a particularly strong message. 'Don't Go Near The Water' dealt with environmental concerns and included a conversation between father and son, no doubt inspired by the recent arrival of John Carter, about the fact that it was no longer safe to eat fish caught from the river. 'I'm A Worried Man' was inspired by a poor man who approached Johnny in Jamaica to tell him about his long list of personal woes. Ironically, an incident said to have taken place while promoting the album led to Johnny being inadvertently responsible for the very behaviour he complained about in the title track.

An American flag had been bought for promotional purposes but since it was pristine, it did not fit in with the spirit of the song so Bob Wootton and Dave Deadman (then visiting Johnny and the troupe from England) tied it to the back bumper of their car and dragged it through the streets of a small town. However, the local police were far from amused and promptly arrested the pair for this apparently blatant piece of disrespect for the flag and only a personal intervention from Johnny saved the situation. Possibly because the message of the title song chimed so strongly with one side of the public mood at the time, the album fared a little better than Johnny's more recent efforts, reaching 16 in the charts during a run of just under three months. If this represented a revival it was temporary and an album released later in the year, *The Junkie And The Juicehead Minus Me* only just made it into the Top 50. Another live prison album, released in 1974, had been recorded in 1972 at Osteraker prison in Sweden. It was a European-only release but any hopes that the success of Folsom and San Quentin might be repeated were dashed when it failed to make any significant impression on the charts.

◆ ◆ ◆ ◆ ◆

Later in the year Johnny was involved in a project which proved to be a superb vehicle for bringing together his diverse talents and interests. He spent approximately a month recording a film called *Ridin' The Rails* described as "The great American train story." With Johnny acting as narrator, raconteur and singer, the viewer is guided through the history of the railway from its origins, its crucial importance to the development of the American west and the contribution it made during wartime, to its post-war decline and revival. The story is illustrated with re-enactments of famous events such as a race to see which could pull a carriage faster, a horse or a steam train, and an attempt by northern soldiers to steal a train in order to disrupt southern supply lines. Reconstructed railhead towns are brought vividly to life by actors riding into town, guns-a-blazing, with Johnny, in period costume, as merely an observer, who breaks off from watching events to provide some more historical detail. For instance, the "shady ladies" who appeared in the new towns keen to persuade the railroad labourers not to walk the line but rather to part with their hard-earned money.

Johnny may have adhered to a conservative code toward women but this didn't stop him singing with gusto about the men who arrived in town looking for "A shave and a hot bath and a bottle and a woman." Johnny sang a lot of the songs in different settings, sometimes a cappella, sometimes to his own acoustic guitar accompaniment and at other times with the backing of subsequently dubbed instrumentation. Although he didn't take any roles in the historical re-enactments his towering bulk made for an imposing presence, enhanced as it was by appropriate dress, including in one scene a sky blue long-tailed jacket with blue waistcoat, black trousers and a large, floppy, black bow tie. The songs featured were chosen for their relevance to the history of the railway in particular, including 'The Night They Drove Old Dixie Down', 'The Legend Of John Henry's Hammer', 'Casey Jones' (the train driver who crashed attempting to make up lost time), and 'Wreck Of The Old '97'.

Ridin' The Rails is engaging family entertainment, even for those with only a limited interest in trains, though the educational element is part of what makes the film so enjoyable. Even though Johnny didn't write the script (though he is credited with providing "special historical material"), he seemed at ease in the role of narrator/presenter in a way that eluded him in his acting roles. On the cover of the video release, harking back to evocative and romantic images of trains from childhood, Cash states "You know, there's nothing that stirs my imagination like the sound of the steam locomotive." *The Los Angeles Times* described *Ridin' The Rails*, "as rich in historical perspective as it is in entertainment," and the film won a bronze award at the International Film and Television Festival of New York. Johnny also became one of only a few men named a lifetime member of the Brotherhood of Locomotive Engineers, other recipients having included J Edgar Hoover and Harry Truman.

Johnny's iconic status meant that he was in huge demand for all kinds of appearances from live concerts to guest events on television shows. He was an established figure in the eyes of much of the American public and he was not averse to exploiting this by appearing in all manner of advertisements, thus supplementing the falling revenue from record sales. However, when off the road, he continued to spend much of his time in the studio, proving that on occasion he was able to craft a song which could capture the public's imagination.

21

IN 1975 JOHNNY CASH became involved in a promotional deal with a nationwide chain of (now defunct) restaurants called Victoria Station. As part of the deal he recorded an album, *Destination Victoria Station,* containing new versions of old songs such as 'Casey Jones', 'Wabash Cannonball' and 'Orange Blossom Special' which was only available exclusively via the restaurants. The arrangement also involved radio commercials with Johnny singing the restaurant theme song 'Destination Victoria Station'. However, on the album itself, he recorded another version which was loosely based on London's Victoria Station, which he referred to in the liner notes as an "old railroad depot". Johnny was a natural choice to advertise this particular chain because of its railway theme and the liner notes, written to reflect Cash's own straightforward style of delivery, neatly brought together ideas of genuine authenticity while making sure the all important advertising message was delivered.

"Most every Victoria Station Restaurant is a bunch of boxcars and a caboose all stuck together. And inside, the restaurants are decorated with authentic clocks and signs and artefacts and what-have-you from the history of railroading. I grew up living around trains and I've been singing about them for years so when Victoria Station asked me to do their radio commercials and this record album, I thought that it might be an interesting project that would be a lot of fun. However, not until my wife June and my kids had a chance to eat at Victoria Station and give it their approval, did we proceed." The image of Johnny refusing to proceed with the arrangement until he, June and their seven children had sampled the restaurant's wares seems laughable now – present-day celebrity endorsees would be more concerned with the cheque on offer.

Advertising endorsements by famous personalities had long been the norm in America. Johnny had been involved in various campaigns since the late Fifties when he appeared on stage with a laxative advertisement prominently displayed behind him. After gaining national prominence he was mainly involved in television advertisements, for such diverse products as Standard Oil, Hohner harmonicas, Bulova watches, Folger's coffee – "The best part of waking up, is Folger's in your cup", and Lionel Trains – "The big train for small hands." As well as being a locomotive lover, he may well have appreciated this particular product for its slogan, "Kids get something wonderful when they get a Lionel train. They get Dad." There *were* limits to what he would put his name to, regardless of money, and Tommy Cash was amazed when Johnny once turned down an offer of a million dollars to sing a few lines advertising an Australian brand of beer. He wasn't prepared to endorse a product which, as he knew from personal experience, could damage lives (overlooking the fact that the majority of people who drink beer do not become alcoholics). Most of these advertisements weren't seen in Europe, helping to maintain an image of Johnny untainted by commercialism.

Johnny's profile was so high that even a chance remark might be pounced on and turned to commercial advantage. In the course of a private conversation at a function Johnny happened to mention that the best car he had ever owned was a Plymouth Savoy, and he bemoaned how newer cars were not made to the same standards. His remarks were overheard by a Chrysler executive who had the idea of launching a nationwide campaign to find the best surviving example of a Plymouth Savoy in America, using Johnny's name as endorsement for his company. After weeks of searching, a car belonging to a Mrs Ray Hilde was adjudged to be the winner and at a heavily publicised ceremony she handed it over to Johnny and in return received the keys to a brand new car.

Apart from *Destination Victoria Station* Johnny released no less than three other albums in 1975. The first two, *Precious Memories*, an album of religious songs and *John R Cash* made no impact on the charts. The failure of the latter was something of a surprise as the album featured some very strong material gathered from a diverse and chequered posse of top songwriters, 'My Old Kentucky Home' by Randy Newman, 'The Night They Drove Old Dixie Down' by Robbie Robertson, 'Jesus Was Our Saviour (Cotton Was Our King)' by Billy Joe Shaver (the only religion-oriented song on the album) and 'Cocaine Carolina' by the controversial David Allan Coe.

The absence of religious material was almost certainly a reaction against the preaching stance adopted on albums such as *Man In Black* and *A Thing Called Love* which proved a turn-off commercially. *John R Cash* (with a sleeve showing Johnny wearing a blue denim jacket made out of a pair of jeans belonging to TV star John Schneider) suffered from a degree of overproduction, lush strings and other accompaniments, which tended to detract from *that* voice. Though strong in their own right, the material was not the sort Johnny could do credit to – either too pop or too weighty in subject matter.

The choice of songs was largely dictated by CBS chiefs with producer Gary Klein even telling Johnny what key to sing in. The basic tracks were recorded at Johnny's Nashville studio with the additional backings being dubbed on in New

York. Constantly trying out new ideas with different writers overlooked the simpler approach that Johnny Cash (and his audience) felt most comfortable with. However, the unfortunate reality was that the number of Johnny Cash fans wasn't growing and the original converts weren't being replaced. In spite of the attempts by CBS to manipulate the Cash sound into a winning formula, none of Johnny's 1975 releases were successful and Charlie Bragg, who produced the live album *Strawberry Cake* released the following year, addressed the issue with surprising candour in his sleeve notes. "Times change, tastes change, and in order to conform some artists must change. Johnny Cash changed in keeping with the times; but as it turned out, not in keeping with tastes. Many opinions were expressed to John and me, as to what should be done for the sake of conformity. Innovations were tried – new arrangements – different material – engineering gimmicks. . . ." The reference to conformity will no doubt have come as a surprise to many who always regarded Johnny as an independent spirit. Cash found the whole experience frustrating and demoralising and resolved to produce future albums in Nashville his own way.

Another album, *Look At Them Beans*, fared a little better though it only reached number 38. The album featured the edgy Guy Clark train song, 'Texas 1947' and by way of complete contrast, the sickly sentimentality of Harlan Howard's 'No Charge' (a recent crossover hit for Melba Montgomery), as well as typical Cash fare like 'All Around Cowboy' and 'Down The Road I Go'. The tacky sleeve showed proud father Cash lying on his back covered in green beans, with young John Carter sitting astride his stomach. (On the subject of beans, Johnny's 1991 album, *The Mystery Of Life*, included the equally crass 'Beans For Breakfast'. "I wrote that song as a joke, just for fun. I wrote it for Jack Clement when we were in the middle of a session. I wrote it and took it in saying, 'I've got a great new song, I'll sing it for you.' I thought it was the worst song I'd ever written. I was trying to write the worst song I ever wrote and I still may have. June thought it was the worst song I'd ever written but of course Jack wanted to record it.")

The sleeve notes on the *Look At Them Beans* included June's quote: "And even if you've been wrong, and I've known it, you've always been right, because that's God's order." Given its prominence on the album sleeve, Johnny presumably endorsed this conservative view which sat uneasily with his complaint that in American society women ended up getting the "crappy" jobs. He later stated in a discussion with daughter Rosanne that America would see a black President before it saw a woman President.

◆ ◆ ◆ ◆ ◆

In contrast to Johnny's lack of chart success his old roommate Waylon Jennings was scoring hit after hit. A little belatedly perhaps, he and Willie Nelson had grown long hair and sprouted beards; becoming fixtures in the country charts in the mid-Seventies. Willie had even persuaded Columbia to let him produce his own albums though some executives were horrified at the basic, stripped down results. However, the move produced immediate results with Willie's cover of 'Blue Eyes Crying In The Rain' making it to number one and the album *Red Headed Stranger* going platinum. It was Waylon's label, RCA, who supported the idea of an album with Waylon and Willie (with Waylon's wife Jessi Colter and Tompall Glaser also getting in on the act) which would capitalise on their popularity. Supported by a nationwide tour, the album *Wanted: The Outlaws* became a massive hit, went platinum and the concept of the outlaw movement became crystallised.

Johnny, the biggest outlaw of them all, and part of the philosophical inspiration for the outlaw movement, must have allowed himself a wry smile. He was working just as hard on the road and in the studio and yet was lagging miles behind in terms of record sales. Not that he was living on the breadline. With heavy demand for concert and television appearances and steady sales of several of his more popular albums, Johnny Cash was still in the high earnings league, and his advisers (including June, no slouch when it came to business matters) ensured that the money he earned was well invested. Apart from the House Of Cash and Cinnamon Hill in Jamaica, Johnny acquired over a hundred acres of undeveloped land near the House Of Cash in Hendersonville. Though initially he had no clear idea on what to do with it he was confident that the advice to invest money in land was sound.

He also acquired a farm called Bon Aqua about 35 miles west of Nashville. The property had been acquired illegally by Johnny's then accountant along with a number of other Cash assets, after he misappropriated over $300,000 of Johnny's earnings. When the matter came to light and Johnny discovered what had been happening, he forced the man to transfer title in the property. It was a good move as the farm became one of Johnny and June's favourite retreats; highly valued for its peaceful character especially when the pressures of the business got too much for them. As June put it, "Sometimes we get all busted down and we have to have our peace and quiet. It's an old log house and it's really laid back. It's easy and it's fun."

1975 found the Cash troupe once more touring Europe – Austria, Switzerland, Germany, Great Britain and Eire. The visit coincided with a period of terrorist activity on the mainland, motivated by the troubles in Northern Ireland. Johnny got first-hand experience of the constant threat of terrorism when one of his London Palladium shows was interrupted by a bomb scare resulting in the auditorium being evacuated.* Such incidents were unheard of in

---

* The concert was being recorded and the announcements and crowd reactions were included on the 1976 live album *Strawberry Cake*.

America at the time. Later that year, a tour of Japan culminated with a show at the Tokyo Budokan in October. Despite the altar call controversy following his first appearance, Johnny undertook two more week-long engagements in Las Vegas during July and October. While he might have had some reservations about the city's overt materialism, he liked the idea of the audience coming to him, without the need to travel, an arrangement he would come back to.

♦ ♦ ♦ ♦ ♦

In 1976, Johnny recorded 'One Piece At A Time', written by Wayne Kemp, with Johnny narrating the verses; singing only on the chorus. The song told the story of a man working on a Cadillac assembly line who "devised himself a plan" to build his own luxury car by sneaking parts out every day in his lunch box or his "buddy's mobile home". The resulting car was a Heath Robinson affair containing elements of a Cadillac built between 1949 to 1973. Backed by a stripped down Luther-style guitar riff, 'One Piece At A Time' chugged along irresistibly despite the novelty element similar to that other Cash perennial, 'A Boy Named Sue'. The single reached the top of the *Billboard* charts, helped in part by an accompanying promo film which was displayed on a rear stage screen for a time during live performances.

The record inspired one Bill Patch to construct a car like the one described in the song. Patch was a member of the Lions' Club, a good deeds organisation in the small farming and coal-mining town of Welch, Oklahoma, which had recently incurred a substantial amount of debt from building a new civic auditorium. A collector of antique cars, Patch had the idea of building a 'One Piece At A Time' car. Along with his mechanic friends he scavenged scrapyards for Cadillac parts and, from roughly following the instructions in the song, managed to construct a vehicle which could actually be driven. He then had the idea of giving the car to Johnny Cash.

Though initially wary, unsure of what might be expected in return, Cash soon warmed to the car and took it to the House Of Cash museum. Johnny and Bill became friendly and when Johnny heard about the financial stresses associated with the Welch civic auditorium, he and June agreed to play a benefit show there which raised enough money to pay off the outstanding debt, with an amount left over to donate to local causes. The crowd only numbered a thousand but the Cash troupe enjoyed the intimacy of playing to a smaller audience, so much so that they repeated the experience the following year.*

One Piece At A Time was also the title of Johnny's next album which benefited from a return to a more basic Johnny Cash sound, a point the record company

---

* Sadly the association left a bitter aftertaste. Years later when Bill Patch died, Johnny decided it would be a fitting gesture to return the car to Patch's son. Cash's people went to great lengths to make the necessary arrangements but the son sold it to a collector for a reputed $30,000.

emphasised by crediting the album to "Johnny Cash and The Tennessee Three", a claim not deemed necessary before. 'Committed To Parkview', about the musical inmates of a mental hospital, was a tragicomic song inspired no doubt by Johnny's close encounter with such a fate in the Sixties (or perhaps by his friend Merle Travis who was detained in such an institution). 'Let There Be Country' was an excuse for some good-natured name-dropping and 'Mountain Lady' with its simple romantic charm was at once evocative and nostalgic. The obliquely patriotic 'Sold Out Of Flagpoles' was a strange affair musically, with a spring and bounce provided courtesy of a Jew's harp. The fact that Johnny wrote most of the songs on the album probably contributed to the natural ease of his delivery. Though much of the material was an improvement on *John R Cash*, the album is mainly memorable for the title track.

The choice of wording for the advertisements accompanying the album's release suggested that CBS were trying to redress the fall-off in sales of Johnny Cash records. Under the heading 'Good Ol' New Johnny Cash' the advert stated that *One Piece At A Time* is "filled to the brim with the kind of great Johnny Cash songs and music that have made you love him all these years." Johnny pursued a similar theme in his poetic liner notes.

> *Like a favorite old shoe*
> *That you pulled off and threw*
> *In the trash then found your new ones hurt your feet*
> *Wore them new ones all you could*
> *Then shined the old ones up real good*
> *Felt as natural as an old familiar street.*

Clearly helped by the popularity of the title track, *One Piece At A Time* made it to number two in the charts during a run of almost four months, Johnny's most successful album for years. The title track even made it into the lower reaches of the pop charts in Britain where journalists expressed approval of Cash's latest opus. As Bryan Chalker put it in *Country Music Review*, "Some of the past experiments we've enjoyed; others have made us wonder where you were going; the odd one or two have even made us doubt your ability to make it big as a recording star again. But this time you're really back and that's the way it should be."

At the end of 1975 Johnny made some changes to the line-up of his touring troupe following the earlier departure of The Statler Brothers to pursue a highly successful career of their own. He decided, as his brother Tommy puts it, to "lay off" Carl Perkins and Gordon Terry, two men who had, like Johnny, struggled to conquer serious drink and drug problems. Perkins had been part of the show since 1967 and ace fiddler and hellraiser Terry, known by his friends as Mule, had been with Johnny on and off since 1971. It's possible that this was a cost-cutting exercise though in the case of Perkins it could also be said that his pure rockabilly style now didn't fit with the style Johnny was trying to put over. Thankfully, the two remained close.

To replace them, Johnny asked his brother Tommy, who had by this time experienced a fair degree of chart success in his own right, including a number one hit with 'Six White Horses', to open his shows. Tommy was pleased to receive the offer but it did pose a problem because it meant effectively breaking up his regular backing band, The Tomcats, though Johnny agreed to let Tommy bring along his guitarist Wayne Gray. The transformation in the size of the crowds he now played to never ceased to impress Tommy. He recalls a show in British Columbia when he and Fluke were in a room in the auditorium survey-ing the masses pouring in. "I said to Fluke, 'Boy, my brother sure can pull in a crowd,' and quick as a flash he said, 'Yeah, it's like watching a whole bunch of players scrambling for a fumbled football.'"

Tommy also makes the point that Johnny always paid good rates to the people who worked with him. For opening the shows by performing four or five songs, Tommy was paid $1,000 and Wayne Gray received $250. Although the money was good, Tommy Cash & The Tomcats were a reasonably hot act at the time and accepting the proposal from Johnny meant a cut in earnings. Tommy was also conscious that his recruitment had deprived Carl and Gordon of a secure income but the lure of being part of one of the most successful crowd-pulling acts in the business, and the opportunity to work with state of the art sound and lighting, proved an irresistible draw.

1976 was American Bicentennial year and not surprisingly Johnny was part of the action. The troupe played a benefit show in February at the Arizona State University for the American Freedom Train – the brainchild of New York com-modities broker and occasional steam locomotive engineer Ross Rowland, Jr. With America mired in the Watergate crisis and only recently extricated from the Vietnam War, Rowland was concerned that there would not be a nationwide celebration of the Bicentennial as there had been with the exuberantly successful Philadelphia Centennial Exposition. His idea was to set up a travelling exhibi-tion of unique and representative artefacts from various periods of the two hundred year history of the nation. Rowland knew that the steam locomotive was a proven "people magnet", though it was only at the last moment, after many refusals, that corporate sponsorship was secured.

The train, pulled by an enormous steam engine restored for the occasion, featured 12 display cars, 10 that visitors could pass through and 2 to hold large objects which could be viewed from the ground through huge showcase windows. The cars were filled with over 500 precious treasures of American history including George Washington's copy of the constitution, Judy Garland's dress from *The Wizard of Oz*, Joe Frazier's boxing trunks and a piece of rock brought back from the moon. Over a 21 month period from April 1975 until

December 1976 more than 7 million Americans visited the train during its tour of all 48 contiguous states.*

Such a project inevitably appealed to Johnny and apart from playing a benefit concert in support of the venture, he made television public service announcements with a view to raising money to enable it to happen, as had his friend Tennessee Ernie Ford. Johnny was also one of 80 people to receive a special Bicentennial-inspired award given by the Library of Congress to those people who, by their contributions to American life, were deemed to be "living legends". For the actual Fourth of July celebrations, Johnny was in Washington where his concert culminated in him ringing a replica of the Liberty Bell (a gift from Great Britain) 200 times amid a spectacular firework display.

In 1977, Johnny once more hosted the annual Country Music Association Awards show and had the particular pleasure of paying tribute to his old hunting and drinking companion, Merle Travis, who was inducted into the Country Music Hall of Fame. On a less happy note, on January 16, the night before his execution, convicted murderer Gary Gilmore phoned a radio station saying he was a big Johnny Cash fan and that he would like to speak to him before he died. The DJ managed to make contact with Johnny and the two had a brief exchange, with Johnny singing Gilmore an unidentified song. With the amount of songs Johnny had written or sung over the years about prisoners waiting to be executed, it was a case of life imitating art.

◆ ◆ ◆ ◆ ◆

As the years marched on, the deaths of people and friends Johnny had worked with started to mount up. Although Johnny had not been in contact with Elvis Presley for some time his death on August 16, 1977, still came as a shock. He had been aware of the rumours surrounding Presley's health and the evidence of his obesity (such a transformation of the angelic piano player in that iconic Million Dollar Quartet photograph) was plain to see. Johnny had good cause to reflect on how close to death his own addiction to drugs had brought him as he thought, 'There but for the grace of God go I.'

Johnny paid strong tribute to the man whose first Sun record had been released less than a year before his own. "June and I loved and admired Elvis Presley . . . He was the King of us all in country, rock, folk and rhythm and blues. I never knew an entertainer who had his personal magnetism and charisma. The women loved him and the men couldn't help watching him."

In a later interview he reflected on how success had changed Elvis. "I always felt bad that he got so popular and so sought after that he had to close his world

* Lionel Trains for whom Johnny had previously done a series of advertisements, manufactured a limited number of models of the Freedom Train which are now highly prized collectors' items.

in around him and exclude so many people. So I have to say, the Elvis Presley that died, I didn't know him very well." It seems that Elvis pined for the days before fame brought him so low.

A year before his death, during a performance in Lubbock, Texas, he reminisced with feeling about what he referred to as "the good old days" when he would jam with the likes of Johnny, Scotty Moore and others. In October, Johnny recorded his glitzy Christmas special (by now a Cash tradition) and on this occasion, special guests Roy Orbison, Carl Perkins and Jerry Lee Lewis joined Johnny for a reconstituted Million Dollar Quartet to pay tribute to "The King" with a version of 'This Train Is Bound For Glory'.

In May 1978, another death which caused Johnny great sadness was that of Glen Sherley, whose song 'Greystone Chapel' Cash had performed at Folsom Prison. Glen had spent many years in jail for robbery and his subsequent rehabilitation was in many ways a vindication of Johnny's belief that there was good in everyone if the right influences were brought to bear. When Glen was released from prison in 1971 he was paroled into Johnny's custody and when he got married later that year, the ceremony was held at Johnny's lakeside house in Hendersonville. Johnny empathised with Glen's honesty about the fears and uncertainties a prisoner felt, and the tears he cried alone at night while maintaining a tough exterior to make possible his survival in the brutal prison culture. Before he was finally released Glen had recorded, with the support of members of the House Of Cash, a live album at Vacaville prison in California in 1971. A copy of a letter from Johnny was included on the sleeve which gave an insight into his personal philosophy.

After telling Glen that Billy Graham and Jimmy Snow had said prayers for him Cash concluded, "You see Glen, we believe you are a man of destiny. Every man in this world belongs here, and has a right here, but there are a few men who are meant to be a light or a leader, or an example, however you want to put it. You are a symbol of what man can be and do. For one thing . . . the name Glen Sherley . . . is to become a reminder to all men in prison that no matter how low they feel, or how low they go, someone cares for them."

Johnny made representations on behalf of Glen when he came up for parole and after his release he became part of Johnny's show on occasion. He also made a television special called *A Flower Out Of Place* on which Johnny was the star guest, and the pair co-wrote 'Look For Me', included on the *Man In Black* album. Sadly the euphoria surrounding his early successes didn't last and the press reported that Sherley died of a self-inflicted gunshot wound. In commenting on his death Johnny raised the possibility of illness also being a factor. "There are two stories and I don't know enough to tell you which one to believe. It was either suicide or cancer. I know there was a gun involved. The last time I saw him he was back in California working for some big cattle company feeding 10,000 cattle a day. He lived in the cab of a semi truck. He didn't want any more public life, just couldn't handle it." It was a sad end for a man who appeared to have grasped and capitalised on the rare opportunity which had come his way at Folsom Prison.

Later that year Mother Maybelle died and it seemed hard to credit that she was only 69. The black and white images of her primly posing as part of the original Carter Family seemed to be from a long distant past but of course when making those historic recordings in the Twenties she was a young woman. Maybelle had been staying at her house at Port Richey on the Florida coast, unable to enjoy life to the full because of multiple health problems. According to Mark Zwonitzer in *Will You Miss Me When I'm Gone*, her doctors at the Mayo clinic were of the view that she would not last the year out but her daughters decided not to tell her. On October 22 she had gone to bed after watching a re-run of *Bonanza* featuring a guest appearance by her old friend Hoyt Axton and it seems that she died peacefully during the night. Her funeral was held four days later at the Hendersonville cemetery and at the graveside, her many relatives from the world of music sang an a cappella version of 'Will The Circle Be Unbroken?'

Johnny and June cancelled concert appearances scheduled for the early part of November. Johnny felt particularly close to Maybelle and considered that her generous and magnanimous support had helped to save his life during the crazy times he put her (and everybody else) through in the Sixties. He was also acutely aware of her historic musical legacy, as he stated in his 1997 autobiography, "Having her in my show was a powerful confirmation and continuation of the music I loved best. It kept me carrying on the traditions I come from." When Maybelle's health started to fail and she made the occasional mistake on stage she announced that she would no longer appear with the troupe and not even Johnny's powers of persuasion could change her mind.

Known to many as "Mama", Maybelle had been a mother figure not just to Johnny Cash but also to Elvis Presley when they were on package tours together in the Fifties. She had provided sanctuary for Audrey Williams when Hank was drunk and threatening to kill her. Circumstances dictated that she became an integral part of American popular music in the twentieth century. Johnny's 1978 Christmas show, featuring Kris Kristofferson and wife Rita Coolidge, closed with an emotional rendition of 'Silent Night' in her memory.

◆ ◆ ◆ ◆ ◆

George Jones, a good friend of both Johnny and Waylon and another artist with a gargantuan appetite for drink and drugs, ran into overwhelming financial difficulties towards the end of the Seventies and was faced with the prospect of losing everything in order to meet his liabilities. Though Jones was described by one writer as "a charismatic alcoholic so unstable that even Johnny Cash had been advised to steer clear of him," Johnny and Waylon made it possible for him to keep prime assets such as his home, his cars and tour buses. The pair tried to keep it a secret from Jones but he found out through his bank who his benefactors had been. Any protests were rebuffed on the basis that Johnny and Waylon were confident George would have done the same thing for them had the boot been on the other foot. They also helped George through the worst of his problems with alcohol and cocaine, both of which he was ingesting in prodigious quantities, to the extent that his life expectancy was being measured in months. By the time he started getting to grips with his problem, Jones reckoned his IQ was "down to about 72". Johnny and Waylon talked to him and "helped him to see things differently", partly with the aid of readings from the Bible.

Johnny's support of those experiencing oppression or exclusion landed him the B'nai B'rith* Humanitarian Award in 1978. In the studio, Johnny continued to turn out albums at a steady rate. The sleeve of *The Last Gunfighter Ballad* showed Johnny, cowboy hat pulled down below his eyes, pointing a gun at the camera. *The Rambler* followed a few months later but both albums were not particularly distinguished and neither made any significant sales impact.

CBS's promotional blurb for *The Rambler* must have surely been concocted as a case of hope over experience. "*The Rambler* is an entirely new kind of entertainment. It's a story. One that will make you laugh. And feel sad. And it's laced with some of the best music of Johnny Cash's career." When referring to the heady days of touring in the Sixties, Cash wrote, "Some of it's too tough to tell, some of it's too private to tell." The *I Would Like To See You Again* album was spiced up with the inclusion of two duets with Waylon Jennings, including 'There Ain't No Good Chain Gang'.

Towards the end of 1978, Johnny teamed up with his old friend and sparring partner Jack Clement in the hope of once more conjuring up some magic in the studio. Apart from the Clement-composed title song, *Gone Girl*, co-produced by Clement and Larry Butler, featured tracks written by Don Schlitz ('The Gambler') and, more surprisingly, Mick Jagger and Keith Richard ('No Expectations')†. On the one hand such choices demonstrated Johnny's willingness to be adventurous in his choice of writers. On the other they were signs of desperation at declining record sales in a misguided bid to come up with successful material. None of these recent albums performed well – a fact rubbed in by another volume of Cash's greatest hits going gold.

Away from the stage and the recording studio Johnny maintained his interest in acting, with parts in *Little House On The Prairie*, in which he played Caleb Hodgekiss, a con man pretending to be a preacher, who steals money intended

* B'nai B'rith is one of the world's leading Jewish human rights, community action and humanitarian organisations and was founded in 1843 by 12 German-Jewish immigrants on New York's Lower East Side.
† Recorded by The Rolling Stones on their 1968 album *Beggar's Banquet*.

for the victims of a fire, and *Thaddeus, Rose And Eddie,* a television film in which he portrayed a hard drinking womaniser trying to mend his ways. On the evidence of his performance in this dire turkey, he should have stuck exclusively to singing. As with many of the films he appeared in, a part was found for June who at least had some idea how to act. Johnny also put in an appearance on comedian Steve Martin's 1978 television special in the company of such seasoned professionals as Bob Hope, Milton Berle and George Burns. Martin was another artist Johnny had helped in the early stages of his career when he had been a featured artist on a series of summer replacement variety shows Cash hosted in 1976.

While his time was filled by constant touring, studio and television work, awards, and occasional appearances at Billy Graham crusades, after over two turbulent decades in the business, the life of Johnny Cash in the late Seventies had become almost routine.

PART IV

Chicken In Black

"I worry sometimes that I'm just spinning my wheels."

1979 HAD HARDLY STARTED when Johnny and June received the sad but not entirely unexpected news that Sara Carter, the last surviving member of the original Carter Family, had died at the age of 80. Even though she had long since relocated to California it was her wish that she be buried at Mount Vernon cemetery in Maces Springs, Virginia, the place where she had grown up and which had become a shrine to The Carter Family. Her choice meant a complicated day and a half journey for her husband Coy Bayes and her coffin. Though he was prepared to abide by her wish, it saddened him because he felt that her home was in California and he complained to a local reporter that he had already arranged a burial plot for her next to his parents. At the funeral Johnny talked about her talent, her professionalism and her enduring impact on music. "She touched the lives of countless millions of people . . . Sara's voice continues to inspire artists."

A short tour of Great Britain in March included a visit to Belfast which resulted in more first-hand experience of the troubles in Northern Ireland. Johnny's manager, Lou Robin, gave details of the show in the foreword to Peter Lewry's book, *A Johnny Cash Chronicle*, and was evidently able to see the situation from both sides in something approaching a light-hearted vein. "One cold winter night we played a concert in Belfast, Northern Ireland, at a church. The political factions were heavily into the fighting. Somehow the promoter quietly got a truce declared until noon the following day when we would be gone. This way the people would not be going to the sold-out double shows dodging explosions! We also gave tickets on opposite sides of the Church to each faction. So they were all in the same room together for the first time, enjoying an event of common interest. The next morning we went to the currency exchange to make a bank transfer to the US before we left for Dublin on our tour bus. Later that same day we heard that the currency exchange had been blown up that afternoon!"

It was also in 1979 that rumours circulated in some sections of the press that

Johnny's marriage to June was in trouble. Jan Howard, a singer originally from California, had moved to Nashville in the Sixties and had developed a reasonably successful career. In an unbelievably chauvinistic piece of journalism (from 1970), a writer for the British *Country Music People* magazine described her as: "A sincere person, this comes over very clearly in her singing which has a stamp of originality about it which is found only rarely in singers of the opposite sex." Jan had married the songwriter Harlan Howard but, after finding out that he had been unfaithful, they divorced with Jan claiming Harlan cheated her out of her rights to their publishing company.

Later, with ironic timing, one of her sons was killed in Vietnam soon after she had released 'My Son', an emotional recitation in which she expressed the fervent hope that her son would return safely from the war. Four years later another son committed suicide in her house while she was downstairs. Johnny and June (a close friend) helped her to get her life back on track by hiring her to be part of the troupe. It was rumoured that Johnny and Jan had become romantically involved, something Johnny emphatically denied, claiming with a turn of phrase notable for its self-exculpation, "Jan and June are the best of friends. Jan would not do such a thing to June." It would certainly have been a breach of Johnny's religious beliefs.

Jan parted company with the Johnny Cash show in July 1979 and the following year Johnny and June decided to renew their vows at a ceremony attended by their son, John Carter. Whatever the truth of the rumours it appears, at some point, there were problems in Johnny's marriage which he referred to, albeit rather obliquely, in a later interview: "The fighting June and I did and the love affair gone wrong was years ago. Nobody could ever have a truer companion . . ." What appears clear is that they succeeded in putting whatever problems they experienced behind them.

◆ ◆ ◆ ◆ ◆

Early in his career Johnny vowed that no less than 10 per cent of the records he made would be religious music. Johnny easily exceeded that quota and the lack of success of earlier efforts didn't deter him (or indeed CBS) from releasing *A Believer Sings The Truth* in 1979. Originally released as a double album on the Cachet label, the album was later downsized to a single album on CBS, and included a number of standards such as 'What On Earth Will You Do (For Heaven's Sake)', 'I've Got Jesus In My Soul' and 'Oh Come Angel Band'.*

Johnny's next mainstream album, *Silver*, released the same year, commemorated the fact that his career in music had now reached the 25 year mark. This was jumping the gun slightly since his first single was released in 1955 but it

---

* He later recorded another gospel album, *Johnny Cash Sings With BC Goodpasture Christian School*, which included standards such as 'Amazing Grace' and 'The Old Rugged Cross'.

could be argued that to all intents and purposes Johnny's career in music began soon after he left the Air Force in 1954. The album was produced by Brian Ahern (then married to Emmylou Harris) who came up with some strong material such as the powerful opening message song, 'The L&N Don't Stop Here Anymore', about the decline of a formerly prosperous town. Billy Joe Shaver and Jack Clement were once more among the writers and Johnny himself contributed two songs, 'Lonesome To The Bone' and 'I'm Gonna Sit On My Porch And Pick On My Old Guitar', whose virtue lay in their simplicity and directness.

There was also another outing, with a new rhythm arrangement, for 'Cocaine Blues', though the passage of time evidently had a mellowing effect since the line "I can't forget the day I shot that bad bitch down" was modified to "I can't forget the day I shot my woman down." Johnny chose to mark the album's historical timing by including a letter to his mother on the rear sleeve reminiscing about the virtue of the hard work the Cash family did on the farm, and also about the time he had come in from the fields singing in a low register, prompting his mother to say, "God has His hand on you . . . someday you'll be singing on the radio . . . everywhere." The letter finished, "I think maybe my voice is still suitable at times to be played on the radio. You still like it, don't you, Mama? That's what matters to me." He signs the letter with his boyhood name and the one which family members still use, "JR".

Rodney Crowell, the new man in Rosanne Cash's life, contributed 'Bull Rider' which was released as a single. Rodney was still in some awe of Johnny following a visit to Jamaica with Rosanne before they were married, when he was told in no uncertain terms that he would not be sharing a bedroom with his then live-in girlfriend. He felt this to be archaic, not least since he and Rosanne were living together back in America and that for them to sleep apart would be hypocritical. Cash senior was not swayed and, according to Ralph Emery, a bellicose Johnny then delivered a thumping put-down as he towered over Rodney, "Son, I don't know you well enough to miss you when you're gone." They did of course get over this hiccup and went on to have a good personal relationship with Rodney writing a number of songs for his father-in-law.

Although *Silver* only made a perfunctory showing in the charts, a single from the album, 'Ghost Riders In The Sky' spent three months in the US charts and only just missed the number one spot. It was a powerful song strong on cowboys and mysticism, and the inclusion of highly atmospheric French horns and trumpets meant that the music would not have been out of place on the soundtrack of a Sergio Leone spaghetti Western. However the poor commercial showing of the album was a great disappointment because it featured a strong collection of songs, with a sophisticated production.

In sharp contrast to Johnny's first two *Greatest Hits* volumes, a third only just scraped into the charts. Perhaps with this in mind, during an interview in *Country Music People* Johnny was asked if he had considered retiring, a question which received short shrift, "That's stupid," he said contemptuously. "My sound is the same but I'm making it fuller and more acceptable to more music lovers. You see I'm broadening the appeal of my music and working hard on new songs. Because country is my thing I believe that if the songs are recorded properly they will appeal to people who aren't necessarily country fans." He went on to state that there was no question of a crossover to pop, "I would never do that."

In 1980, many of Johnny's friends in the business took part in a television spectacular, broadcast appropriately enough on July 4. There was good reason for celebrating. Johnny Cash was a rare phenomenon, a true original thought of first and foremost as a country artist but whose extensive musical reach and unique vocal sound meant that he crossed over into many areas of music and defied all attempts at categorisation; someone who, despite the recent fall in record sales, had consistently placed records in the charts for most of his career; someone who had concerned himself with, and actively supported, any number of worthwhile causes and been the catalyst to encourage others to do the same; someone from poor beginnings who had gone on to be a guest of American Presidents; someone who had publicly battled with personal demons which had come within an ace of killing him and were still an ever present threat; someone who had made it all the way to being an American icon.

The format of the special had Johnny as presenter and narrator – being like a cross between his ABC television show and *This Is Your Life* – and an impressive array of celebrities popped up to share a memory, present an award or sing a song – in some cases all three. Those appearing had all been significant in Johnny's career – Minnie Pearl who provided such encouragement when he first appeared on the *Grand Ole Opry*, Waylon Jennings (whose son Shooter was born in 1979, with Johnny being one of those providing support at the hospital), Kris Kristofferson, Tom T Hall, George Jones with whom he had appeared on some of those early package tours, Larry Gatlin whose career Johnny had helped to get off the ground, and many more.

As was *de rigueur* on such occasions, the music was considerably softened by the presence of a house orchestra which sounded particularly out of place on an angry message song like 'Man In Black'. Unsurprisingly, none of the songs from *Bitter Tears* were deemed appropriate for the show. In amongst the songs and stories, various film clips were shown, the earliest being a 1959 appearance on *The Ed Sullivan Show* which had a theatrical backdrop representing a nineteenth century American town, with shop fronts and ladies in long period dresses chatting gaily to each other as Johnny, wearing a white jacket, sang 'Don't Take Your Guns To Town'. In another archive clip, Johnny sang a schmaltzy version of the Hank Williams classic 'I'm So Lonesome I Could Cry' with Kate Smith, and succeeded in removing all of its human despair. Such footage served as a reminder that for all his musical and personal authenticity, Johnny was quite prepared to please the mainstream. There were also extracts from his film and television appearances including *Colombo, A Gunfight* and *The Gospel Road.* As had become increasingly the pattern, The Tennessee Three, while introduced and acknowledged, were kept very much in the background, only appearing for a few of the songs and, symbolically perhaps, Johnny stood on a separate stage among the audience.

WS Holland has complained that for all the contribution the group made to the Johnny Cash sound, when it came to shows or documentaries about Johnny Cash they were rarely asked to speak or give interviews even though, as he likes to point out, "We saw it all." In fact there was a brief Marshall Grant interview on this particular special, in which he said no more than a handful of words. The dialogue was carefully scripted which gave the proceedings an unnatural air, with Waylon Jennings appearing particularly edgy when delivering his lines. There was barely a whisper of the bad old days of abuse though Kris Kristofferson, when telling of the time he landed a helicopter in Johnny's yard, did go so far as to say that Johnny was "easily spooked back in those days". Towards the end of the show Johnny sang 'I Walk The Line' with Kris, Waylon and Larry Gatlin.

Another major tribute came from the magazine *Country Music* which published a special edition largely devoted to a quarter century of the Cash phenomenon. Apart from learned articles by top journalists, there was a section devoted to Johnny Cash the photographer, with intimate shots taken in locations such as Jamaica, Bon Aqua and Mother Maybelle's former house in Florida which Johnny and June inherited on her death. Apart from friends and family Johnny captured some excellent close-ups of insects and flowers. There were numerous tributes from family and friends including one from Jerry Jernigan, a prisoner serving 99 years at the Tennessee State Penitentiary where he met Johnny in 1974. Jerry was an aspiring songwriter and gave Johnny a tape of one of his songs, 'It Ain't No Big Thing', which led to a songwriter's contract with the House Of Cash.

Jernigan told of an occasion when, feeling particularly lonely and depressed, he phoned Johnny, asking that he simply be allowed to hear his voice. Johnny and June talked to him for 15 minutes, the maximum allowed under prison rules. "Knowing Johnny Cash has given me self-respect, encouraged me to upgrade my morals, and most of all stand up like a man and be counted." Rosanne Cash, after explaining that her father should not be allowed to drive – "His 12-D foot acts like it's tied to a yo-yo any time it gets near a gas pedal" – went on to say, "I thought the inscription under his senior picture in his high school yearbook was apropos in its foresight. It reads: 'Be a live wire and you won't get stepped on.'"

His friend Ned Joyner recalled an incident when the pair were hunting crocodile in Jamaica. After shooting one beast and pulling it on board, the boat was so heavy that they had to push off from trees at the side of the water. Unfortunately

Johnny pushed so hard that the boat moved off before he could jump on board and he was left hanging from the tree and as Joyner explained, "There he was dangling from the tree with his feet close to the water, when a big crocodile spotted him, started snapping around, coming within an inch of his feet. We just knew he was going to lose both feet." Johnny managed to shimmy up a tree but under his weight the branch started to bend, "and before he knew it that old crocodile started snapping at ole John's 'hiney'." They only just managed to get Johnny back on board before he became a reptile's dinner.

Country Music People had written to many people asking for tributes and reminiscences to mark Johnny's silver anniversary and, as they put it, the response was "exciting". The 24 pages they actually published (out of a total of 54 on Cash) were merely extracts chosen from the pile. Later the full-length originals were presented to Johnny in a bound volume.

The mayor of Hendersonville, T. W. Patterson, declared June 14 Johnny Cash Day and issued a proclamation which spoke for many in paying tribute to Johnny's achievements:

> "WHEREAS, Johnny Cash is internationally known and loved as an entertainer, musician, songwriter, television and motion picture performer; and,
>
> WHEREAS, Johnny Cash and his family have made their home in Hendersonville for many years; and,
>
> WHEREAS, Johnny Cash has established the House Of Cash which brings thousands of visitors each year into our City; and,
>
> WHEREAS, The City of Hendersonville is proud to call Johnny a resident and is grateful for his many contributions to this community; and,
>
> WHEREAS, the June 14th, 1980 issue of *CASH BOX* magazine will pay a special Silver Tribute to Johnny Cash in recognition of his 25 years of service and leadership to the entertainment industry; and,
>
> WHEREAS, the City of Hendersonville and its residents wish to join in this special tribute to their friend and neighbor.
>
> NOW, THEREFORE, I, T. W. PATTERSON, Mayor of the City of Hendersonville, Sumner County, Tennessee, do hereby proclaim June 14, 1980 as JOHNNY CASH DAY in Hendersonville, and do urge my fellow citizens to join me in congratulating Johnny Cash for his 25 years in the entertainment industry, and in paying tribute to him for his many contributions to his profession and his community."

The Governor of Tennessee, Lamar Alexander, (who had also made an appearance on the television tribute show) joined in, stating that "Tennessee is proud to claim Johnny Cash as its own . . . he is a compassionate human being and an inspiration to us all."

◆ ◆ ◆ ◆ ◆

Marshall Grant's appearance with Johnny on the tribute show had seemed amicable in the extreme but within a matter of weeks of the show being taped, Johnny fired Grant by letter, something which caused great offence after all the years they had been together. The precise reasons for the dismissal are not clear. There had been talk that Marshall had reached a certain level in his bass playing and that he didn't make time to learn new songs and, on occasion, would play them poorly on stage. In his 1997 autobiography Johnny was vague about the reasons while alluding to underlying problems. He did say that he regretted dismissing Marshall by letter but as Tommy Cash puts it, "Johnny is a person who makes a decision and does it. I mean if it splits the beans down the middle in the garden he'll still do it. Once he's decided something you can't talk him out of it."

Lou Robin's explanation is similarly vague, though his sudden use of Marshall's surname betrays a sense of his irritation with the situation. "They just came to changes on the road. John went in one direction, Grant went in another." Whatever the reasons, Marshall, who went on to manage The Statler Brothers, followed up his dismissal with a financial claim against Johnny. As Lou Robin economically puts it, "Grant felt that he had some severance money coming to him, or maybe there were some early promises made to him that had to get resolved." The claim was not easily resolved and led to a long drawn-out court case, lasting many years, which eventually resulted in Marshall being awarded a substantial settlement reputed to be in the region of $800,000 with Luther Perkins' widow Margie receiving a comparable amount.

With the departure of Marshall Grant and the start of the Eighties, Johnny took the opportunity to make further changes to the line-up of his touring band. Bob Wootton and WS Holland remained but were augmented by other musicians to provide a fuller live sound: Jerry Hensley on guitar, Earl Ball on piano, Jack Hale and Bob Lewin made up the horn section and Joe Allen replaced Marshall on bass with the multi-talented Marty Stuart also joining in order to complete his musical apprenticeship before going on to a successful solo career. With the change of line-up came a new name, Johnny Cash & The Great Eighties Eight – as cumbersome as The Tennessee Three was memorable.

Later in the year Johnny and his new line-up returned once more to Britain to appear in a three-day country music festival at Portsmouth. It turned out to be a financial disaster for the promoters, though it also provided Johnny with opportunities to demonstrate his well-honed capacity for spontaneous acts of kindness. According to Robin West, a former country music DJ, there had been an extremely popular Southsea Summer Show for about 80 years in Portsmouth and one promoter had the idea of holding a three-day country music festival during its run. Ambitious plans proposed that the festival would be in Portsmouth for two years and then Nashville for two years. West's son-in-law Warren Davies had been head-hunted to work on the festival, the first of a number of events which brought him into contact with Johnny Cash. There was an impressive list of stars booked to appear including Glen Campbell, Hank Williams, Jr, Tom T Hall, Jeannie C Riley, Hoyt Axton and, of course, Johnny Cash.* In addition there was a "Texas Town" with cantinas and Tex-Mex food for sale, a Civil War battle scene and Indian villages.

According to Warren Davies the promoters, Sue Fuller and Michael Moore, were "unknown" and bit off more than they could chew. As he explains, "The deal was that each major star was to get the same money, $100,000, and of course there were lots of additional costs on top for the other artists, hotels, plane tickets and so on. The payments to the major stars were scheduled, in other words they were payable in regular instalments starting well before the festival was due to take place. The first serious problem arose when Fuller and Moore were unable to meet one of the instalments. In terms of the contract the agency acting for Johnny and the other artists was entitled to demand all monies due in terms of the contract or declare the contract null and void."

Those acting on behalf of Johnny and Glen Campbell duly demanded that all outstanding money be paid right away. In desperation Michael Moore went to his backers, managed to extract the necessary money from them and, as Davies puts it, "In an act of bravado Moore flew to America and laid the money on the agent's table, thus ensuring that the festival could go ahead." According to Davies the essential problem was that insufficient money was spent on promotion with even some of the locals being unaware of the festival until it had almost begun, and his advice on this point was not followed. Despite an impressive artist roster and perfect weather, of the 100,000 people needed to ensure the event's success only about 20,000 turned up.

The country music press pointed out that there were a number of other festivals occurring around this time and *Country Music People* editor Tony Byworth described "A climate of too many festivals chasing too few fans." The net result was that there was insufficient money to pay many of the people involved, including Warren Davies, who was left to negotiate with hotel owners and angry musicians and crews. When Johnny got back to America and heard about the problems, he and Lou Robin discussed the situation as Robin recalls, "Yes the whole thing was a financial disaster. A lot of people think Johnny agreed to forego some of his fee but what actually happened was that we paid some of the sound and light people directly. They weren't going to get paid. They might have gone bankrupt and it wasn't their fault. The trouble with the festival was it was a

* Dolly Parton was also originally booked to appear but it was written into her contract that if a film offer came up she could withdraw.

case of two young people who had this great idea but not the necessary experience nor the people around them to do it properly."

Naturally a lot of media people were in attendance at the festival including the BBC's David Allan, one of the leading country music broadcasters and commentators in Britain and someone who had helped to promote the Cash cause in Britain. The timing was tight but it had been agreed that David would be able to record a short interview with Johnny just before he went on stage soon after the Cash entourage arrived in a fleet of limousines. There were also representatives from hospital radio keen to have an interview but according to Warren Davies, "Lou Robin was not so keen on the idea of the hospital radio people. However when I went to Johnny's trailer he said he had heard there were some hospital radio people and that he'd like to see them first. This caused some real panic for David Allan who got more and more twitched up. He went around saying, 'We are the BBC you know,' rather loudly."

He got his interview but only just, because there was another small delay, again resulting from an act of consideration, spontaneously and randomly given to a long-time fan of Johnny's, a disabled woman who was a friend of Warren Davies. She had asked if he could possibly arrange for her to just say hello to Johnny. "I arranged for her to be sitting in an area between the Johnny Cash trailer and the press marquee. In fact instead of just saying hello, he actually spent about five minutes chatting to her which of course made her very happy indeed."

Davies tells of another experience he had with Johnny in Britain in the course of a subsequent visit. "I found myself alone in a room with Johnny Cash for about four hours and I can tell you it was not an easy experience, very uncomfortable. It was all to do with logistics. Johnny was doing *The Terry Wogan Show* and the BBC people want their artists there early to practise positioning, and it would not have been practical to get back to the hotel for a break before his slot on the show. So basically he just had to kill four hours at the studio and it was my job to look after him. I found him shy and nervous and very poor at small talk. It was about the longest four hours of my life." The fact that Davies was not particularly knowledgeable about Johnny's career probably didn't help but given Johnny's well-known aversion to the superficiality of cocktail parties, his unwillingness or inability to get into social chit-chat was hardly surprising.

On another occasion Davies was involved in setting up a press conference for Johnny. Lou Robin, initially unenthusiastic, agreed when remembering the work Warren had put into trying to sort out the Portsmouth fiasco. As Davies recollects, "The press conference should have been a spectacular event. I had noticed at Harvey Nichols there was some American promotion going on and they had a number of very large model eagles with wingspans of about five feet. I persuaded the shop to let me borrow one and I set this up in the press-room with a large Stars and Stripes, it was a terrific backdrop. However, the whole thing had to be cancelled at the last minute because Johnny's flight was delayed and as it turned out he was so late he didn't even have time to do a soundcheck before the show."

Johnny was well known for spontaneous acts of kindness as the disabled lady at Portsmouth discovered. Back in Nashville another such gesture helped to inspire some fellow citizens to follow suit. Johnny donated $10,000 to help provide treatment for a kidney patient by the name of Alfonso Braden. It was reported that his donation triggered off a wave of community spirit, leading to a group of North Nashville residents starting up a city wide drive to assist patients with kidney disease, with the emphasis on poorer areas where money for complex medical treatments was in short supply. Johnny did not know Mr Braden personally but as he put later, "I just knew of a human problem."

◆ ◆ ◆ ◆ ◆

The words "legend" and "legendary" were by now finding their way into sentences featuring the name Johnny Cash with increasing regularity. As far back as 1966, with his career only just over 10 years old, and with equal measures of bravado and immodesty, the annual publication of the Johnny Cash Society was called *The Legend*. Even by 1980 the term was being overused in the context of popular music but the definition in Chambers Dictionary provides unequivocal support: "A person having a special place in public esteem because of striking qualities or deeds, real or fictitious: the body of fact and fiction gathered round such a person."

Certainly the country music powers-that-be were in no doubt and, with past misdemeanours apparently forgiven or forgotten, it was announced that Johnny was to receive country music's highest honour by being inducted into the Country Music Hall of Fame at the CMA awards ceremony in October. At 48, he was the youngest person ever to receive the honour, bestowed on the vote of 200 anonymous key figures in the country music scene. The presentation was made by Kenny Rogers, and many family members and friends were in the audience for the occasion. In a lengthy acceptance speech Johnny paid tribute to his parents and gave thanks for the wonderful times he had experienced travelling all over the world. He also acknowledged that he did not meet with universal approval at first. "It was at times a struggle starting out and there was not always acceptance in the country music community in Nashville for a long haired hill-billy from Memphis. But a lot of you welcomed us with open arms, a lot of you took us in as one of your own, and a lot of you did not know what to do with us."

With an eye to tradition, Johnny also had some advice for the newcomers; advice which many would say has not been heeded. "I'd like to say to all the new entertainers that are coming on the scene, to the young artists and singers, don't let yourself get caught in a bag because it's the stylists like Kenny Rogers and some of the great ones of our time . . . Waylon Jennings . . . that have made country music what it is . . . have built the excitement for us all to enjoy. It's given country music a great shot in the arm when the so-called rebels came along . . . people just doing it their own way." In closing Johnny also made it clear that retirement was definitely not on the agenda. "I'd like to say this also, to all new artists, that if you're concerned about competition, don't write me off yet, cause my dad Ray Cash, is sitting here tonight. He's 83 years old and if God lets me live that long, that's 35 more years that I'm gonna be out there singing country songs."

To mark the event June presented Johnny with a new Mercedes 450 SLC. Johnny's plaque in the Hall of Fame, featuring a rather unflattering likeness, has the following citation, "Songwriter, historian, fighter of causes; friend to the deprived and the troubled, friend of great men; a leader in the temporal world, and follower in the spiritual world, Johnny Cash is the total entertainer. An internationally famous performer he carries his love for his country, and for country music around the world. The man in black retains his roots in the soil as he grows in conscience and integrity. He is one of the world's most beloved and honoured stars." The award was all the more impressive considering that he received it only one year after his hero Hank Snow (one of a select few artists whose photographs hang in Johnny's private office) received the same honour. Not only that but he was one year ahead of Vernon Dalhart, now largely forgotten but who in 1924 became the first million seller with 'The Prisoner's Song'. Johnny Cash's living legend status was now official.

Whether enjoying his newly conferred legendary status or that of a senior figure of country music, Johnny still needed to work. In June 1980, he released his major album of the year, *Rockabilly Blues*. Once more he demonstrated his enthusiasm for learning from younger talent by featuring a track written and produced by Nick Lowe, a versatile singer, songwriter and musician who had emerged to become part of the "new wave" rock scene of the late Seventies in Britain. Johnny recorded the basic track for the song, 'Without Love', in Nick Lowe's studio in late 1979 during a private London visit and Dave Edmunds, Elvis Costello and Martin Belmont were also present for the session. By working with Lowe he was also following another of his own favourite principles, keeping it in the family, since "Basher" (as Lowe was nicknamed) was by now married to Johnny's stepdaughter, Carlene.

The rear sleeve featured a superb early black and white photograph of Johnny live in concert in which he is standing next to Luther, singing, or at least with mouth agape, holding his guitar high up to the microphone. Closer inspection of the picture reveals that Johnny was doing this for a reason other than showmanship because while Luther's guitar is amplified, Johnny's is not. He may well have been playing 'Big River'. The album, featuring Johnny playing "rockabilly rhythm guitar" and Earl Poole Ball on "rockabilly piano", was unusual in that it lacked most of the big themes featured in so much of Johnny's work. On *Rockabilly Blues* he seemed quite content to churn out songs celebrating love, women and lust. The album had something of a back to basics feel which delighted many fans who despaired of the earnest overproduced sound of much of his recent CBS output. As Johnny said of the album, "I was looking to my roots, if only briefly. I didn't want one of those super producers who slicks everything up. I wanted it a little grittier."

The serious, earnest side of Johnny's character took something of a battering when he indulged his playful sense of fun with an appearance on *The Muppet Show*. As well as doing battle with Kermit, who had arranged a special hoedown for the occasion, Johnny sang a selection of his best-known hits. In similar, though slightly more serious vein, Johnny accepted an assignment from *Country Music* to interview Waylon Jennings. He did so with alacrity by saying, "I'll get out my guns and go find him." The result was a rambling conversation covering nine pages of print with a series of informal photographs taken by June and Jessi Colter, which caught Johnny looking unusually relaxed in the agreeable surroundings of his Bon Aqua farm. The lack of formality resulted in some playful exchanges between the two old hands, for instance when talking about George Jones:

WAYLON: "I think he's getting fat now."

CASH: "Yeah probably is. He can't get any uglier, so maybe he is."

On drugs:

WAYLON: "Your body has all the strength that you ever will need. It's actually a weakness, drugs . . ."

CASH: "There's no denying the fact that the drugs make you feel good. So you think, 'How could this be wrong if it feels so good.' But in my case, you know what happened to me. Deception set in. Instead of me taking the pills, the pills started taking me."

1981 promised the usual round of live performances and the prospect of working with yet another producer and a film which would help to raise awareness of a largely unpublicised social problem. However, the year would also hold some unpleasant surprises.

23

BILLY SHERRILL was in many ways a strange choice of producer for Johnny Cash. Although he had worked for Sam Phillips and been brought up as a southern Baptist, for those who favoured more traditional forms of country, he was responsible for sweetening the music into more bland, palatable forms, often with Mantovani-style string arrangements which led to successful cross-over hits like 'Stand By Your Man' by Tammy Wynette and 'The Most Beautiful Girl' by Charlie Rich. Sherrill had been producing CBS artists for nearly 20 years but given their differing musical philosophies, it was not surprising that it had taken so long for him and Cash to work together.

Greatly concerned at Johnny's consistent commercial failure, it was the CBS bosses who brought them together. Most of the regular Cash writers were sidelined for the resultant album, *The Baron*, and musically the album featured a lot of easy listening country, verging at times on slick adult oriented rock,[*] Sherrill also tried to include all the Johnny Cash ingredients such as storytelling in doom-laden tones on the title track, offbeat comedy to a "boom chicka boom" rhythm on 'Chattanooga City Limit Sign', the story of a lift from hell with a group of hard-drinking, long-haired country boys, and patriotism on 'The Greatest Love Affair', which Sherrill co-wrote. The latter was particularly sentimental, with a man thinking he has been abandoned by his woman. The woman is a metaphor for America and the point was that he hadn't been abandoned – it was all a dream.

> *I love you America*
> *I love you America*
> *And if I sail a stormy sea please be there to shelter me*
> *So just keep holding me close and I won't care*
> *And will show the world that what we share*
> *Is still the greatest love affair.*
> *And I love you America.*

---

[*] The album spawned a low budget, low quality film of the same name in 1983.

A sophisticated string section competes with a heavenly choir to up the saccharine ante even more. Despite being well advertised in the music press and two singles modestly charting, the album only just made it into the Top 30. This marked CBS's last serious effort on Johnny's behalf while most fans and critics regarded the teaming of Johnny with Billy Sherrill as a mistake. The disappointing performance of the album provided evidence that Johnny had become the victim of demographics and that the efforts of record companies should be directed towards younger audiences with the most spending power. It was hardly surprising that Cash lost energy and enthusiasm for much of the material he was asked to record. As he put it in his 1997 autobiography, "If you were a little too old and your anatomy not quite 'hot', it didn't matter how good your songs or your records were or how many fans you'd had for how long: you weren't going to get played on the radio." This was a common complaint among many older artists but one that overlooked the hard realities of the music business.

Johnny was certainly not alone in his scathing comments regarding the "Urban Cowboy" craze which swept parts of America in the early Eighties.* What passed for country at this time was often slick, overproduced muzak and it seemed that much of Nashville was trying to cross over to the pop charts, where bigger financial returns beckoned.

In April 1981, Johnny was playing a show in Stuttgart which up to the interval had been unexceptional. He was aware that his old friends Carl Perkins and Jerry Lee Lewis were working in the same part of the world but was nonetheless taken aback when June gave him a message to say that both men were backstage. During the break, after much handshaking and backslapping, Johnny said, "I'd really like it if you guys came out and sang some songs with me in the second half."

Persuasion was not required and with no rehearsal whatsoever the audience were treated to an impromptu performance which was recorded, later edited and mixed by Rodney Crowell, and released as *The Survivors* in 1982. The title pretty much chose itself, a recognition of the years of self-abuse that the trio inflicted on themselves, which somehow had failed to claim them. On the subject of Carl's drinking (which Perkins reportedly gave up after throwing his last bottle into the Californian sea during a tour with the Cash road-show in 1968), Johnny did not spare his friend when writing the album's liner notes. He remembered particular problems when touring Canada in the Fifties. "Sundays were unusually bad days for Carl. The stores were closed and if he had forgotten to get a double supply on Saturday, he would tremble and sweat backstage. Once

---

* A reference to a brief craze that the film of the same name spawned, with people in urban cities wearing cowboy boots and going to countrified nightclubs with coin-operated bucking broncos and the like.

on stage, the audience never knew he was suffering." During a television inter-view, Perkins recalled an incident when the religious spirit moved within him while he was travelling on the tour bus. He immediately demanded that the driver stop so that he could get down on his knees to pray. Actually he was so drunk he wanted the driver to stop so that he could get down on his knees and throw up.

Johnny's tribute to Jerry Lee Lewis attempted to get a handle on the man. "You hear him praise God on this record, but you also hear him doing a lot of shaking in a frenzy, caught up in his own talent. I am not sure I can separate the two: his God-given talent and the shaking."

The album sleeve revealed the surviving members of the Million Dollar Quartet showing their age and the music is a record of three old friends having a lot of fun jamming and making music together. It's entertaining but hardly revelatory and though the evening began life as the Johnny Cash show the high point is a particularly lascivious version of Jerry Lee's 'Whole Lotta Shakin' Going On'.

◆ ◆ ◆ ◆ ◆

Still in demand for film parts, Johnny could afford the luxury of rejecting scripts which didn't appeal to him. One that struck a chord was *The Pride Of Jesse Hallam* which told the story of a recently widowed 45-year-old farmer who is forced to confront his illiteracy when his daughter is taken ill. Jesse moves from Kentucky to Cincinatti in order to have her treated but is unable to complete the simplest of forms. Overcoming his shame and embarrassment, he attends classes with his son and gradually succeeds in learning to read and write.

The film, in which Eli Wallach co-starred, mirrored Johnny's instinctive support for those less fortunate and prompted over a thousand people to write to him expressing gratitude for publicising the very real problems of adult illit-eracy, which had given them courage to address the issue in their own lives. Johnny was proud of the fact that the film was endorsed by the National Educa-tion Association, which led to him being given the Pride Of Tennessee Award for his contribution to a state campaign against illiteracy. Although respectful of the director's role Johnny was not averse to suggesting changes. For instance, instead of telling his son to "run fast" he urged him to "run like a deer" which gained the approval of one of the film executives who considered it to be "more lyrical". Funnily enough, the same line was to be found in the rollicking 'One Way Rider', written by Rodney Crowell which was featured on the album *Rockabilly Blues*. Johnny, June and his band arranged and performed the music for the soundtrack of the film.

Given his interest in history it was not surprising that Johnny wanted to find out more about the Cash ancestry. Although, in the early part of his career, he had often spoken about Native American and Irish ancestry, subsequent inquiries pointed to a Scottish connection. In 1981, when visiting Scotland along with Andy Williams to record a Christmas special, Johnny took the opportunity to carry out further research, check local records and speak to local experts, all of which helped to confirm his Scottish line of descent. A week was set aside for filming location shots for inclusion in the Christmas special: some in Edinburgh, others in and around Falkland Palace and yet more in coastal villages in the East Neuk of Fife.

During one section of the show, recorded at Edinburgh's Playhouse Theatre, the audience were forced to endure a five hour wait while sound and lighting arrangements were sorted out. Johnny appeared at intervals to reassure the audience that they would eventually be getting a show. At least one person who attended the concert, long-time Cash fan Murdoch Nicolson, found the whole experience fascinating, despite the many retakes needed to satisfy the technical perfection demanded by American television. Murdoch was particularly amused by a man holding a large sign with "Clap" written on it – feeling he didn't need to be told when to applaud.

Unaware that Johnny was in Edinburgh, another fan, Ed Dixon chanced upon him near the Scott Monument on Princes Street. "I'm normally a pretty together sort of guy but I was transformed into a gibbering idiot. All I could think to say was, 'You're Johnny Cash,' to which he replied, 'Yes I am.' I introduced my wife and young daughter Lynn and we chatted for a while. Johnny was extremely courteous to us all but he didn't have a lot of time to talk. He did stay for a while longer talking to what I took to be members of the production team. We saw his limousine pulling away later. As it did, Johnny lowered the window and said, 'Bye Lynn.' I was very impressed that he'd remembered my daughter's name."

Though they were only together for a short while, Ed's wife was struck by Johnny's awkwardness. "It seemed that Johnny found it easier to speak to my daughter Lynn, who was two and a half, than to adults." Ian Boughton, then editor of a Scottish country music newspaper, received a tip that Johnny and June were going to be filming scenes in a church in the little fishing village of St Monans in the East Neuk of Fife. "I phoned up the nonplussed minister to see if the tip was correct. He confirmed it was and that 'Mr Cash' would be coming up the next day." Apparently Andy Williams had asked to film his segment on a Saturday but this had been ruled out due to the activity involved in getting the church ready for its Sunday service.

Despite a complete lack of publicity, when Ian got to the church it was almost full. "I managed to get a seat and found myself next to what turned out to be an American tourist who said, 'I always watch the Johnny Cash Christmas special,' and then added perfectly seriously, 'In the States we have so many Christmas specials we have to start showing them in November to get them all in.'" Johnny arrived soon afterwards with June and John Carter. "He was wearing a jacket which would have been just like a road worker's if it were not so expensively cut. He shook every hand near him whether it wanted to be shaken or not, and then took his place in front of a choir from the local school who had been waiting patiently for their big moment. What happened next was quite wonderful. They had to do 15 takes of a carol because Cash messed up halfway through each one, while the kids, who could have been no more than 10 years old, got every single take perfect."

◆ ◆ ◆ ◆ ◆

Not long after the Scottish Christmas special was broadcast, Johnny and June were on holiday at Cinnamon Hill in Jamaica with various family members on Christmas Day, 1981.* Just as they were starting dinner, three masked, armed robbers suddenly burst into the house, terrifying the occupants with their words of introduction, "Somebody's going to die here tonight." What followed was a terrifying two hour ordeal as the intruders moved from room to room of the luxury mansion, robbing valuables worth over $30,000. For much of the time a gun was held to young John Carter's head. Before scurrying, the intruders locked the whole household in the basement, and as an afterthought served up a plate of Christmas dinner to their terrified victims.

According to Johnny the police response was brutal. The Jamaican authorities understood that having a temporary resident of Johnny Cash's stature was good for tourism and local business, so making an example of the offenders made sense. According to Johnny the ringleader died resisting arrest and the other offenders were caught following another robbery and apparently died trying to escape from prison.† In his 1997 autobiography, Johnny didn't criticise the actions of the police directly "So what do I think about it all? What's my stance on unofficially sanctioned summary justice in the Third World? I don't know. What's yours? . . . I'm out of answers. My only certainties are that I grieve for desperate young men and the societies that produce and suffer so many of them, and I felt that I knew those boys." Johnny got involved in supporting local causes in Jamaica and became one of the sponsors of the SOS Childrens Village – a home for needy children.

Johnny and June were naive in not having any security around the house, particularly in view of the previous threats which had been made against them in America, which led to them regularly employing security guards. Considering Jamaica's high crime rate, the robbery could have forced Johnny to find a luxury

---

* Others have dated the incident that followed as occurring earlier but Johnny, who was there when it happened, insists the date is correct.
† Confusingly, Johnny gave a different account of the intruders' fates in a 1988 interview, claiming one was killed during a subsequent robbery, one was in jail for an unrelated offence and the third was alive and living in Kingston.

holiday home elsewhere. It didn't, though the house was soon encircled with 24-hour professional security.*

◆ ◆ ◆ ◆ ◆

In 1982, Johnny took on the role of a small town sheriff in the film *Murder In Coweta County*. CBS produced the film at a cost of $3 million after Johnny's efforts to interest other companies in the project were thwarted. The film concerned a murder committed just inside the boundary of Coweta County and the subsequent capture of the murderer, a well-known character from a nearby town. Johnny's acting was once more awkward and unconvincing, his macho, almost mincing walk being a particular weakness. He may have been the thinking man's John Wayne but Cash certainly lacked the presence and charisma in front of a camera which the Duke so effortlessly exuded.

Johnny's acting was ham and when delivering his lines, his voice often came across as uncertain and tremulous.† There was talk of a sequel to be called *Revenge Of Coweta County* but this did not materialise. Another Cash acting venture was a Japanese film called *Kairei*, a religious tale bankrolled by the Billy Graham organisation, with Johnny's lines being dubbed later. When acting, Johnny was away from his natural environment in front of an audience, a setting that was so right for him he often appeared impatient to start, having little time for formal musical introductions, regularly beginning a song before the applause for the previous one had died down.

Despite his popularity as a presenter of programmes such as the annual Country Music Association awards which he enlivened with his charismatic presence, Johnny came over as ill at ease on such occasions. One year, when making a presentation with Dolly Parton, the two delivered a carefully scripted comic exchange full of double entendres inspired by Dolly's well-known attributes. Dolly delivered her lines with natural verve, but Johnny was conspicuously uncomfortable.

During the making of *Murder in Coweta County*, in which a white man is convicted of murder partly on the testimony of a black man, Johnny was once more the subject of attacks which he took to be from his old enemies the Ku Klux Klan. Apart from the incident arising from the "negress" photograph of Vivian years before, the Klan had apparently never forgiven Johnny for having black artists on his television shows and hugging Charley Pride. In a later article in the *Sunday Mirror* magazine, Johnny said, "They shot arrows in the tyres of the crews' trucks, and they put sand in the gasoline tank of the car I was driving

---

* Cinnamon Hill has remained one of Johnny's most favoured hideaways, though his sister Reba, shocked and traumatised by the incident, vowed never to return to the island.
† He did however get into the part to the extent that on at least one occasion he remained in character by returning home to Nashville still dressed as the sheriff.

in the movie, it went down the highway about two miles and then it quit. These people have to be taken seriously."*

◆ ◆ ◆ ◆ ◆

The dangers to Johnny from attacks by the Klan and Jamaican bandits were very real but not as potentially lethal as his own continuing self-abuse. In 1981, Johnny underwent eye surgery following which he was over-prescribed pain-killers, which triggered another relapse. It was not until two years later that his problems became serious again, thanks to a freak accident.

Johnny and June owned a large area of undeveloped woodland across the road from their house in Hendersonville, which they kept as a kind of wilderness populated with a menagerie of animals which included wild boar and buffalo and on which they built a log cabin which became another of Johnny and June's bolt holes and subsequently a recording studio. June liked the idea of having a piece of real country so close to their house because she thought it would be good for John Carter to experience country life and to "shovel a bit of chicken manure". Ostriches are usually a docile bird and Johnny had never experienced difficulties with the small flock he kept until one large male became disturbed when his mate died.

On a cold winter's day, Johnny was walking across his land when he was confronted by the male ostrich acting in a hostile manner, hissing and spreading its wings. Johnny walked past without incident but some quirk of his character made it necessary for him to get his own back on a dumb animal. When the ostrich repeated its behaviour on the walk back, Johnny launched himself at it with a sharp stick. However, he had not reckoned on the speed of his adversary's response as the ostrich leapt up, leaving Johnny helplessly swinging at thin air until seconds later he was hit by the animal as it plummeted to the ground. The ostrich's foot-long claw ripped into Johnny's stomach; according to different reports "partly disembowelling" or "gutting" him. Two ribs were broken in an instant as well as a further three as he fell back onto some rocks from where he managed to strike a blow which scared the ostrich off. The incident had uncanny echoes of the fatal injuries suffered by Jack Cash nearly 40 years previously. Only the fact that Johnny was wearing a heavy leather belt saved him from worse injuries.

Johnny was rushed to hospital where his wounds were stitched but with the agony of five broken ribs, he was prescribed medicinal drugs. Conveniently forgetting his vows and good intentions of the recent past he was soon overwhelmed by the craving to satisfy his addiction. His amphetamine use spiralled

* When asked about these events, Johnny's manager Lou Robin had no knowledge of them and speculated that Cash might have been merely looking for publicity.

out of control, exacerbated by washing the pills down with wine. Their side effects deceived him into thinking he was having a good time. On an English tour, Johnny really started going crazy, trying to find a non-existent Murphy bed in the wood panelled walls of his hotel, tearing at the wood with his bare hands, cutting himself on splinters which caused his hand to swell up dramatically with infection. Cash made up a story about being bitten by a poisonous spider (in England, in winter?) which some sections of the press actually swallowed. By the time he got home to Nashville he had to be admitted to hospital for treatment to his hand, which was twice its normal size.

The drugs aggravated his other ailments – ulcers, internal bleeding and intestinal damage – which demanded surgical attention. As well as the hospital regulation, he had his own secret supply (a card of Valium) which he hid among the bandages covering the incision made when removing his duodenum and parts of his stomach, spleen and intestine. The staff realised there was a problem when they found it difficult to wake Johnny. Some active spark of self-preservation made him realise the danger he was in and through the drugged haze, he managed to alert nursing staff to what he had done. They managed to save him, though it was later reported that at one stage his heart stopped beating for almost a minute. Johnny moved seamlessly from frying pan to fire as he lapped up the morphine given for his post-surgical pain. He began to have hallucinations again including one with a commando holding a gun to John Carter's head.

Johnny's family were faced with a similar situation to when Nat Winston co-ordinated efforts to save Johnny in 1967. Once more, they despairingly sought help, this time from the Betty Ford Center, whose treatment programmes "assist men, women and their families in starting the process of recovery from alcoholism and other drug dependency."* The Betty Ford Center is now world famous having treated thousands of people, including many celebrities, over the years. Working on the assumption that Johnny wouldn't voluntarily attend, the family went straight on to the next stage – a family intervention for which a trained professional works with the family to arrange a structured meeting with the addict. The theory is that the intervention begins the process of recovery for the whole family which usually includes facilitating admission of the addicted person into an appropriate treatment programme.

The objective of the exercise is that a person is brought face to face with family and friends, each of whom has some carefully prepared words about how the person's addiction has affected him or her, while at the same time giving a message of love and support. In Johnny's case, about 25 people participated, consisting of close family, band members and a few other long-time friends. The

* The Betty Ford Center was co-founded in California in 1982 by the wife of President Gerald Ford following her successful treatment for an addiction to painkillers.

contribution from John Carter had the most effect. He told of an occasion when Johnny had caused him dreadful embarrassment by stumbling around drunk in front of some of his friends. Despite the intrusive presence of an intravenous drip, Johnny put his arm round his son from his hospital bed to help him speak through tears, a dreadful ordeal for a 13-year-old boy and a source of deep sorrow and shame for his father. June was furious at being put through such an experience again, not least because it was not long since she had undergone the physical trauma of a hysterectomy. She told him that the family would break up if he couldn't overcome his addiction. Daughter Rosanne spoke of her own problems with drugs and the effect they had had on her life.

The Betty Ford option was not cheap.* Johnny remained at the Center for 43 days and has written positively of the regime's efficacy, closely related to the Alcoholics Anonymous 12-step programme, and its tough love principle – he even had to dress his not yet healed surgical wound. Johnny has talked of his addiction problems being a disease which he has to face each day, with God's help. He also openly spoke of it being a family disease. In answer to a question from a fan he admitted, "All six of my daughters have been in treatment as have two of my sisters and two of my brothers." Not all have conquered their problems with Carlene Carter's recent experiences being well-publicised examples of the difficulties in staying clean.

The origins of addiction in human beings are argued over by laymen and experts alike but the tendency of people such as Johnny Cash to talk of a family disease suggests that the condition (like, for example, Huntingdon's Disease) is in the genes and thus virtually inevitable. The problem is how to deal with it if or when it strikes. Both Johnny and June pursued their careers assiduously and all seven of their children suffered, to a greater or lesser degree, from a simple lack of parental involvement. June chose to go on the road with Johnny, when there was no financial imperative for her to do so. It was her choice but one which meant that she was not around much of the time to provide her children with the kind of support and involvement that most children are fortunate to take for granted. It's hard to avoid the conclusion that this contributed to the children's adolescent problems.

Perhaps June's motives were mixed. Apart from the excitement of touring and performing, her presence on the road meant that she was in the best possible position to keep an eye on Johnny, particularly in the early days. She would no doubt have been aware of the problems in resuming a career after taking time away to look after her family. While Johnny was helped by his time at the Betty Ford Center, the benefits were not permanent and he returned for further treatment on a number of subsequent occasions. Though patients are told not to

---

* The current charges are $1,175 per day (for the first six days), with every additional day of in-patient treatment costing $525.

disclose the names of other residents, it's known that Johnny made the acquaintance of Ozzy Osbourne during his time at the Betty Ford Center.

After his release Johnny was inspired to help Waylon Jennings who was heavily into cocaine at the time, having reputedly spent half a million dollars on the drug during the previous year and, in his own words, "weighed 135 pounds soaking wet." Waylon managed to quit and for a time Johnny was in touch by phone every day to ensure that he wasn't backsliding.

◆ ◆ ◆ ◆ ◆

While Johnny was at the Betty Ford Center he wrote to tell his musical team that if they wanted to work for him, drink and drug use were out. As he put it, "I had to clean up my playground and my playmates." This seemed hypocritical given Johnny's own track record, but it didn't pose a problem for the teetotal WS Holland.

Prior to his stay at the Betty Ford Center, Johnny had gone back into the studio with his old sparring partner, Jack Clement, to make *The Adventures Of Johnny Cash*, with Johnny sporting a cowboy hat on the sleeve photo taken by Marty Stuart ("The Boy In Black") who, in 1983, became Johnny's son-in-law when he married Cindy Cash. The album had such pleasant but inconsequential numbers as 'Georgia On A Fast Train' and 'Ain't Gonna Hobo No More' but lacked anything to raise it above the ordinary. The following year Johnny came up with *Johnny 99*, which was more edgy and R&B influenced. Once more he opened himself up to the influence of younger star writers with both the title track and 'Highway Patrolman' being written by Bruce Springsteen (and featured on his own 1982 album, *Nebraska*).

Johnny now resorted to a routine of using a group of top session men when cutting albums. Bob Wootton, formerly a pivotal element, is merely mentioned as one of four guitarists and Fluke wasn't featured at all. The days of the crude Tennessee Three sound were long gone but by contrast June's out of tune singing was still present, all the more incongruous in view of the high quality of the instrumental backing. Even by her standards, June's vocal on 'Brand New Dance' was dreadful. One American journalist commented, "On the rare occasions that she manages to grab hold of a note she rapes it until it peels the paint off the wall." It must have been hard for Anita and Helen, both of whom were highly accomplished singers, to spend most of their time singing back-up to their less vocally talented sister.

During one show June made light of the issue after a song performed with her sisters. "If we're on the piano and you're (indicating one sister) on the black notes and you're (indicating the other sister) on the white ones, I'm in the cracks somewhere." As a probable result of the extremely close personal and professional relationship between Johnny and June, Johnny rarely performed and recorded duets with top female country singers. A collaboration between

Johnny and Dolly Parton, for example, would have had the potential to create a particularly memorable union.

Touring had continued unabated until Johnny's drug problem became unmanageable, with some appearances having to be cancelled. Johnny had been asked to take part in a series of Billy Graham crusades in England but told Graham that he did not feel it was right for him to appear until he had got himself sorted out. (George Hamilton IV replaced him.) Later Johnny did appear with Graham at Little Rock and he spoke frankly to the spellbound crowd about his ongoing battles with drugs. "It was the most powerful testimony I had ever heard," said George Hamilton IV, "and by the end I was in tears." The cancellation of concerts in the Soviet Union at the tail end of 1983 had nothing to do with Johnny's problems with drugs, however.

These shows were due to take place shortly after the shooting down of Korean Airlines Flight 007 by Soviet Mig fighters. Apart from the general horror Johnny felt about the incident, June's doctor and his wife had been passengers on the flight. As Johnny put it, "I don't feel like singing and dancing for the Soviets right now." It was also around this time that Johnny performed his last prison concert. Despite the nature of the many prisons he had played in over the years, he had rarely encountered any hostility. However he had a bad experience when playing a show in Vacaville Prison when the troupe was poorly received amid a generally tense and hostile atmosphere. On the way out some yelled threats were directed at Johnny who felt the time had come to call a halt to playing such venues in future. Apart from anything else, he made no profit from the prison benefits. In general, Johnny felt gloomy about the failure of successive administrations to effect any meaningful prison reforms. Though he remained an advocate of an overhaul of the system with a view to introducing more humanitarian regimes, he ceased to be actively involved.

For his 1983 Christmas special, Johnny and some of the troupe (along with guests including Merle Haggard and Ricky Skaggs) went to the Carter Fold in Virginia. As June explained, "We were trying to remember what Christmas was like when we were young, the love that this valley generates." Now aged 13, John Carter Cash was a seasoned regular at such events, encouraged by his parents to become part of the musical family. Although John Carter was involved in his father's professional life from an early age, Johnny cleared space in his schedule to spend time alone with his son without the pressures of producers, technicians and businessmen, and on one occasion took him to Alaska on a fishing trip.

Johnny and June made another property investment when they bought an eighth-floor suite at the Berkeley-Carteret Hotel on the ocean-front at Asbury Park, New Jersey. The building had lain derelict before developer Henry Vaccaro lavishly restored the property, creating a total of 259 suites. For Johnny and June it was their "cabin in the sky", providing a comfortable base when they were in the east. June lavishly furnished the apartment with items from her large collection of antiques. John Carter Cash became friendly with the Vaccaros' son and it's a sad indictment on his upbringing that the time he spent with the Vaccaro family was among the few occasions that bodyguards weren't hovering in the background.

The disaffection between Johnny and CBS was becoming more and more pronounced. The company were restricting the budget available for each new album. While still recording some songs of which he felt proud, Johnny in turn found it hard to get enthusiastic when he sensed that he was not getting any meaningful support. Perhaps he was working with the wrong producers, or was bringing out too much product, or had run out of the kind of creative energy needed to produce music that was vital and had something significant to say, and that would sell. No doubt all of these explanations had some validity but the combined effect was demoralising for Johnny who got to the stage where he was almost past caring about what came out of the studio. In 1984, he cut a record which he himself later described as "intentionally atrocious".

24

"**I WAS BURLESQUING MYSELF** and forcing CBS to go along with it," Johnny wrote in 1997 when recalling 'Chicken In Black' – one of the last records he made for the label. Describing it as "intentionally atrocious", he added, "I hated it from the first day and I refuse to admit that I even know the words to it anymore." Despite such scorn it turned out to be Johnny's most successful single in two years, reaching number 45. Produced by Billy Sherrill, the song told the crazy tale of a head transplant with Johnny getting the head of a bank robber with his own head going to a chicken. It was accompanied by an equally tacky video featuring shots of Johnny dressed up in a garish yellow and blue superhero type costume, prancing about the streets of Nashville; even tainting the hallowed ground of the Ryman auditorium.

This was not the first time Johnny had publicly dressed up in an outlandish costume. When introducing Elton John on *Saturday Night Live* in 1982 he wore goggle-like glasses, a large cape, chaps covered in glitter and a long, brightly coloured boa. Though not nearly as good as 'One Piece At A Time', 'Chicken In Black' had a similar madcap feel which made it moderately engaging. Surprisingly, in view of Johnny's comments, he occasionally featured it in live perform- ances. The song was a surprising choice given the massive repertoire Cash could select from but the intractable situation with CBS forced his hand. With two years of his contract to go, there seemed little prospect of a revival in record sales, although the demand for live performances was constant. However, an unexpected revival in Johnny's commercial fortunes sprang from a get-together in December 1984.

Johnny was recording his Christmas show in the picturesque Swiss setting of Montreux in Switzerland with invited guests Willie Nelson, Kris Kristofferson and Waylon Jennings. At a press conference to publicise the show, when asked why Montreux had been chosen for the Christmas location, Waylon replied, "'Cos that's where the baby Jesus was born," which the journalist solemnly noted down. During the making of the show the idea emerged of the four renegades getting together to form a kind of country supergroup for occasional recording and touring. Jennings explained how the idea came about: "We started trading songs in the hotel after we worked on the special, and someone said, like they always do, we ought to cut an album . . . Usually everyone goes their separate ways after that but the idea took hold."

The four got to talking about some of the duet albums they had done and Johnny said, "Yeah, well, we don't want to stand in line to get a duet album released with you, Willie, so why don't we all do it together?" Talking about the logistics of putting together a band, Kristofferson said, "I can remember not too long ago when just one of us was too many to handle in the studio. Getting us in here together and working smoothly is pretty remarkable." Willie Nelson saw other potential problems but believed they could be overcome. "You'd think as many egos that are involved here, and large ones, including mine, would have problems but it doesn't seem to be any problem. We all seem to know a good song when we hear it."

Lou Robin remembers the group having a great time together in Switzerland and the rationale behind the idea: "They said why don't we just go out on tour together once in a while when we're all just looking for a change of scenery from the regular touring." Such a project would have been unimaginable 20 years earlier when egos rendered them less amenable to sharing the limelight but they had all mellowed, had learned from various setbacks and lean times, and between them brought over a century of collective musical experience to stage and studio. Some of the logistical problems were eased by the way the project was organised.

Lou Robin: "There was one studio band for the records with each member of the quartet being allowed to bring one of their own musicians along. Otherwise there was a common band for everybody. It was the same with the technicians, they were drawn from each of the artists' groups, so there was a nucleus of people and then the tours were planned far enough ahead so that the artists could block out the dates. Billing was not an issue. There was equal billing alphabetically. They were all friends and they shared the money equally even though what they got was not consistent with their normal prices." There may have been talk of equality and sharing musically, but as Jack Clement points out, "They all still had their own tour buses and entourages."

Chips Moman, who had produced 'Suspicious Minds' and 'In The Ghetto' for Elvis Presley, was sound engineer for the 1984 Christmas special and became yet another producer hired by Columbia to work with Johnny. In Nashville, he was recording a duet by Johnny and Willie Nelson when Waylon and Kris dropped by. "We remembered a Jimmy Webb song called 'Highwayman' that we had all liked in Switzerland," remembered Jennings, "and since we were in the same place at the same time, we did a track on it. Then another, and another. The album was underway without us even knowing it." Johnny reckoned it was a good deal, "Four for the price of one." The song, 'Highwayman', was supposed to be on a Cash solo album but, instead, it became the banner song for the album and provided the quartet with a name.

Like the country equivalent of Crosby, Stills, Nash & Young, it was understood from the outset that the four were free to honour other commitments, being an arrangement among friends, albeit with a major commercial component, which they would return to from time to time. It suited them all because, as Jack Clement points out, "They didn't have to carry the whole show so there was less pressure on each one of them." The fact that the album became a commercial success didn't hurt either. All of the tracks for the début *Highwaymen* album were recorded in December and released in May 1985. The single, 'Highwayman' reached number one and the album also reached pole position, spending over a year on the charts, eventually going gold.

The album was successful partly because of the heavyweight names involved, who between them were able to generate a large groundswell of interest, and partly that, unlike *The Survivors*, the album sounded like a rebirth of each of their careers. While not an outstanding album there were some quality songs included such as 'Highwayman', Guy Clark's 'Desperadoes Waiting For a Train', and, with a touch of knowing humour, the Cash song, 'Committed To Parkview'. Even some of the more ordinary songs were enlivened by the individual contributions, though Kris Kristofferson came over as the weakest link vocally.

Part of the attraction of touring was the camaraderie which it allowed. With their individual commitments these old friends didn't get to see each other as often as they would have liked and being on the road gave them the perfect opportunity. For Johnny it was also a chance to get to know Willie, their paths having crossed only rarely in the past. In Waylon's view there were problems with the live concerts at the beginning. Writing in 1996 he said, "When we first took the Highwaymen out live, it looked like four shy rednecks trying to be nice to each other. It almost ruined it . . . it was really bothering me how different we were on stage than we were sitting around in the dressing room."

Jennings was even ready to quit. Johnny felt the same way and told him, "I don't want to look like I'm trying to steal your thunder." As Waylon put it, "We were boring each other and the audience." The answer lay in loosening up on stage, helping each other out, making a joke, adding a harmony here and some ad libs. It worked and soon Waylon felt the atmosphere onstage change, "We were a group," though all four spent lengthy periods of time offstage during each solo turn. There were also some tensions backstage. Jack Clement was brought in as musical director for one of the tours but succeeded in getting on the wrong side of Willie by criticising his vocal timing. The worse for wear for drink, Clement told him, "You're really fucking 'Good Hearted Woman' up. You're doing it twice as fast as you're supposed to." Cash and Jennings informed

Clement about his possible early departure from the tour. "Willie tried to have me fired, but he got over it. He came down to see me next morning and brought me some weed." Clement was much more circumspect in his comments thereafter.

Unfortunately, in their enthusiasm to put together the new outfit, nobody connected with the team realised that The Highwaymen was not an original name. Even though they had disbanded years before, there was a threat of legal action from the Sixties group who had first used the name.* The issue was amicably resolved when the original Highwaymen opened a charity show for their successors.

♦ ♦ ♦ ♦ ♦

The exhilarating success of The Highwaymen project was in marked contrast to Johnny's studio work. To little fanfare, the album *Rainbow* was released in October 1985. Produced by Chips Moman, it contained one or two passable songs but the overall feel was poppy and lightweight. Johnny wrote the sardonic sleeve notes:

> "We've just finished a take on one of the songs. It sounds good. Everyone is excited, saying things like, 'That's a hit,' 'That's a single,' 'It's a monster.'
>
> "I said, 'What do you think Chips?'
>
> "A long pause . . .
>
> " 'It could sell hundreds,' says Chips."
>
> There is a hint of defiance in his final words:
>
> "I don't think about sales and promotion when I record a song . . . I record a song because I can love it and let it become a part of me. And even a blind pig gets a grain of corn once in awhile. So who knows, maybe I'll sell hundreds."

Without promotion by CBS and with Johnny's fortunes as a solo recording artist at an all-time low, it didn't achieve a great deal more than that estimation. Moman wasn't even aware that the album had made it into the record shops, and in an interview some years later, when asked if he had any particular favourite Johnny Cash songs, he mentioned the John Prine co-write, 'Unwed Fathers' (included on *Rainbow*), saying it was a pity that it hadn't been released.

When Bob Wootton was unable to play a trio of Toronto dates for family reasons, Cash asked Waylon Jennings if he could suggest anyone who was able to fill in at short notice. After saying he would see what he could do, Waylon got back to him and said, "I've got a guitarist for you – me." Johnny was taken aback, saying he couldn't possibly have a star of equal stature playing behind him but Waylon pointed out that if the roles were reversed Johnny would do the

---

* 'Michael (Row The Boat Ashore)' was a *Billboard* number one in July 1961.

same for him, a proposition he found hard to argue with. Jennings duly appeared for three nights giving the audiences an unexpected bonus. In the summer The Highwaymen played a short set at the annual Willie Nelson Picnic. Having never been able to meet up much because of their conflicting schedules it seemed now that the gang were hardly ever apart.

CBS realised the possibility of capitalising on the runaway success of The Highwaymen by signing all four members to appear in a remake of the John Ford classic, *Stagecoach*. The film was released early in 1986 and as well as the four Highwaymen the extended Cash family was heavily involved. There were small parts for June (by now, a well established tradition), a chubby John Carter Cash, Jessi Colter, Billy Swan and David Allan Coe. On the production side, Anita Carter was credited as "Talent co-ordinator" with WS Holland as "Assistant to Mr Cash".

The film was not an improvement on the previous efforts Cash had been involved with. While the performing load was spread so that the spotlight was not solely on Johnny, his primitive acting ability was still shown up by those with real talent. Waylon Jennings had a certain cool presence and Kris Kristofferson looked relaxed and natural as the Ringo Kid; it was not surprising that Hollywood had beckoned him. For the real pros like Tony Franciosa, it seemed a case of enjoying the company and taking the money. The film was a lacklustre vehicle for famous names and hangers-on or, as Tony Byworth put it, "a case of home movies for the boys".

It was surprising that Cash agreed to appear in a film which negatively portrayed American Indians as savages. There were a few lines, particularly from Willie Nelson as Doc Holliday, which put across the Native American point of view, but overall the film was similar to countless other low-budget Westerns. Despite having the upper hand, the Indians suffer many casualties while inflicting only one death in return, the clichéd villain on the stagecoach. Another unrelated incident had the potential to cause a degree of tension between Johnny and his brother on the subject.

Tommy Cash played a show in Washington at which a very drunk Native American kept on shouting out for Johnny Cash songs. Tommy politely informed him that this wasn't going to happen but the heckler, who was at the front of the stage, persisted and started grabbing onto Tommy's leg. As Tommy explained, "I repeatedly warned him to let go of my leg but he ignored me and eventually I kicked out at him. I just meant to push him away but I actually connected quite hard and jerked his head right back. It was all rather ugly, though it did eventually die down without any serious injury being caused." By coincidence Tommy met his brother on a connecting flight back to Nashville and told him about the incident. "I got the strong feeling he was not overly pleased."

Towards the end of 1985 Johnny also played the part of Frank James in the film *The Last Days Of Frank And Jesse James* with Kris Kristofferson and Waylon

Jennings also having roles.* Johnny was honoured to be permitted to wear Western gear from the collection of John Wayne which was normally stored in a temperature controlled vault.

◆ ◆ ◆ ◆ ◆

As if recognising his importance as part of popular music history, Johnny took part in a series of recording sessions at Sun in Memphis for the first time since 1958. Under the overall control of Chips Moman, Johnny, Carl Perkins, Jerry Lee Lewis and Roy Orbison teamed up with an assortment of newer admirers such as Marty Stuart, The Judds, John Fogerty (of Creedence Clearwater Revival) and Dave Edmunds. Sam Phillips and Jack Clement even got in on the act so there was something of a reunion feel to the whole venture. Indeed the album which resulted was called *Class Of '55: Memphis Rock & Roll Homecoming*. Unfortunately it was a disappointment, being another attempt to resurrect the Million Dollar Quartet template.

The music was, in the main, loose, second-rate rock'n'roll with a soupçon of pop and gospel thrown in; fun for a one-off gathering, but not strong enough for a commercial release. The final track, 'Big Train (From Memphis)' was eight minutes of repetitive tedium with a large cast joining in. Even the sleeve notes traded on past glories while ignoring present realities:

> "What this music is about is a refusal to let the best of our American past – our best music, deepest traditions and truest friendships – simply slip out of our lives."

1985 ended on a sad note for the Cash family. Ray Cash had been ill for some time and it became clear that he would not last out the year. Despite his condition, he was still able to provide the family with some moments of poignant amusement. Ray had a prized white dog called Snowball, but even though he and Carrie had lived in comfortable houses in towns and cities for years, Carrie still followed the country rule that the dog lived outside and was forbidden from entering the house, much to Ray's chagrin. As he lay on his deathbed he motioned to Carrie and whispered in her ear. The family was intrigued to know what final words of wisdom Ray might have imparted to his wife. He'd asked Carrie to allow Snowball into the house when the weather got bad.

Ray died on December 23, 1985 at the age of 88, thus dampening the spirit of the Cash Christmas celebrations. Johnny and June were in fact en route for Jamaica for a holiday when they received the news. Ray was buried at Hendersonville Cemetery on Boxing Day and, in accordance with his last wishes, 'Amazing

---

* For this and his many other appearances, Johnny went on to win a Golden Boot Award in 1989 for his contribution to the Western genre. Other recipients included Robert Mitchum and Angie Dickinson.

Grace' was sung at his funeral. Many family members and close friends attended the ceremony and the American flag was draped over the coffin, something which for Ray, an ex-serviceman and patriot, was particularly important. Johnny has written of a dream he had the night before his father was buried in which he saw Ray appearing out of a long silver car looking fit and happy but clearly on the other side of an unbridgeable chasm. In the dream he says to Johnny, "Tell your mother that I just couldn't come back. I'm so comfortable and so happy where I am." He told Carrie about the dream at the funeral. Her tears turned into laughter, when she said, "God still has his hand on you."

◆ ◆ ◆ ◆ ◆

Although Johnny Cash continued to receive regular honours from a wide range of charity organisations – including cerebral palsy, autistic children and battered women refuges – his musical career was lagging. As part of The Highwaymen, he was nominated for a Grammy (his first in a decade) though 'Highwayman' lost out to 'Why Not Me' by The Judds.*

The success of The Highwaymen provided a timely boost. However, the unhappy situation at CBS came to a head when Rick Blackburn, Columbia's man in Nashville, decided against renewing Johnny's recording contract after 28 years. In fact, Johnny had briefly been out of contract during that time when the original agreement with Don Law expired. There were a number of factors contributing to CBS's decision. Although Johnny's loyal following enabled CBS to shift 30,000 to 40,000 copies per album, it wasn't enough for the company to justify their investment.

By 1986 country sales had declined and the profits of most companies had fallen significantly. Like Johnny, a number of big-name artists with long-standing label relationships, including Dolly Parton and Waylon Jennings, suddenly found themselves out in the cold. The reaction of fans, musicians and certain industry people was a combination of outrage and disbelief. Blackburn became an unpopular figure with his assertion that dropping Johnny Cash had been "the hardest decision I've ever had to make in my life" evoking little sympathy. Dwight Yoakam,† a rising star with a strong sense of country music's history, was particularly outspoken (as Johnny himself had been when CBS had their doubts about Bob Dylan). "What kind of decency is that?" Yoakam raged. "The man's been there 30 fuckin' years makin' them money. He paid for the son of a bitch's office that the prick sits in and lets him leave the label. He built the building, man."

---

* The blow was softened by his daughter Rosanne winning the Grammy for Best Female Country Performance for 'I Don't Know Why You Don't Want Me'.
† Johnny rated Yoakam as one of the brightest of the "new country" stars. When asked if anyone reminded him of his younger self, he said, "Well, Dwight Yoakam twitches like I did."

There were two sides to Yoakam's argument. Johnny had earned huge amounts of money for CBS and helped to maintain their major league status. However, the company stayed loyal for longer than they needed to when the sales returns became increasingly threadbare. The reality Johnny came up against was the same as any artist has to deal with, the need for continuing commercial success. It was a blow to his pride but it did not come as a shock. Johnny was aware that, through a mutual lack of effort, the arrangement had resulted in a growing disaffection on both sides. He later wrote, "People were going into Rick's office, pounding on his desk and calling him names – but I understood. I called him and told him, 'Well, you did what you thought you were supposed to do. I've always enjoyed working with you, and I like you.'" Lou Robin confirmed Johnny's feelings on the matter. "Johnny felt Rick wasn't totally unjustified, given the product he was getting." Robin also expressed frustration at the fact that the producers Johnny worked with were unable to come up with the right sound and material for renewed chart success – though this overlooked the fact that Johnny was no longer a commercial proposition.*

While Johnny waxed philosophical Carlene Carter revealed another side. "All Nashville wants is new, new, new. They basically turn their backs on a lot of these performers . . . I think they've been pretty ungracious particularly to John. He built that town in lots of ways. He definitely opened doors for a lot of these kids that are big stars now, and to be treated the way he was, I think it's pretty fine for him to have the taste in his mouth that he does, which is pretty bitter."

◆ ◆ ◆ ◆ ◆

1986 also saw a project Johnny had struggled with for the best part of a decade come to fruition. In the mid-Seventies, Johnny and June successfully completed a three-year Bible study course with Johnny taking a particular interest in the apostle Paul. Johnny's novel, *Man In White*, was based on Paul's life, and much has been made of the parallel with Johnny's own life, particularly the Damascus-like experience in Nickajack Cave in 1967 which inspired Johnny to effect a major change in his life.

In an interview with the *Denver Post* Johnny provided some insight as to why he wrote the book. "Well I decided that if theologians can do so much speculating and make it interesting, I might throw in my two cent's worth. After all, Paul had become my hero, he was invincible, he made it his life's mission to conquer and convert the idolatrous pagan world over to Jesus." The considerable task of writing a full-length novel almost proved too much for Johnny. To do it justice it was necessary for him to study many weighty religious tomes but work commitments and health problems meant that, for long spells, his

---

* Jack Clement is on record as saying that a top CBS official he later spoke to said the company subsequently regretted its decision to drop Cash.

manuscript lay untouched. He did receive encouragement from various friends and associates, including Billy Graham, who told his congregation that the book was written when in fact it was only half finished. Johnny's relapse into drug use after the ostrich incident meant that his head was not in the right place to get down to serious writing, though it was during his stay at the Betty Ford Center that the project was largely completed.

The novel starts with a lengthy introduction in which Johnny explains the book's origins as well as providing an insight into his Christian beliefs – all the while resisting attempts at narrow categorisation. Irritated by a reporter's constant attempts to tie down his religious creed and the specific religious angle the book was coming from, Cash "settled on a fundamental answer." He said, "I, as a believer that Jesus of Nazareth, a Jew, the Christ of the Greeks, was the Anointed One of God (born of the seed of David, upon faith as Abraham had faith, and it was accounted to him for righteousness), am grafted onto the true vine, and am one of the heirs of God's covenant with Israel." To which the confused reporter responded, "Uh! What was that?" Johnny then delivered the point of his message. "I'm a Christian. Don't put me in another box."

In the introduction he states, "I believe the Bible, the whole Bible, to be the infallible, indisputable Word of God . . . Where the Word is silent and for my story's sake, I have at times followed traditional views. Other things, some characters, some conversations, and some occurrences, are products of my broad and at times strange imagination." Louise Cash Garrett's daughter Margaret said of the book, "I think it was a case of Johnny daydreaming, writing a novel based on his own thoughts and fantasies arising out of the situation with St Paul." It cannot be said that the book is an easy read. At times, the style is heavy and plodding with much of the content being of principal interest only to Christians with a historical fascination. "I did try to read it a number of times," says Tommy Cash, "but I always found my mind wandering off after a while." However the book garnered some favourable comment from the religious press. Johnny's own assessment was measured. "It has its moments. I'm satisfied with it but that don't make me no novelist." In what might have been an act of atonement for the *Man In Black* dedication, *Man In White* was "dedicated to my father RAY CASH 1897–1985. Veteran of World War I. Discharge: Honorable. Conduct: Good."

In 1986, Johnny released *Heroes*, an album of duets recorded with Waylon Jennings, during the time Waylon filled in for Bob Wootton. For the two participants it was a welcome opportunity to spend more time together, as Waylon said, "There's no one I'd rather hang out with than Johnny Cash." The cover was a still taken from the film *Stagecoach*, showing Johnny and his ex roommate looking older and heavier, kitted out in full Western gear – hats, long black trench coats, guns, holsters, etc.

The rear sleeve showed both facing Lash La Rue who had appeared in a number of Westerns including *The Law Of The Lash* and *Song Of Wyoming*. Produced by Chips Moman, *Heroes* was another example of unsympathetic production with heavy orchestrations and brass sections ladled onto what were fairly simple songs. Moman appeared intent on accentuating the sentimental aspects of each song, particularly Kris Kristofferson's 'Love Is The Way' and 'I'll Always Love You (In My Own Crazy Way)'. The worst mismatch between song and production was reserved for Bob Dylan's 'One Too Many Mornings', featuring a light, orchestrated backing of strings set against a jaunty beat. It made the crude version Cash and Dylan had recorded back in 1969 sound inspired by comparison.

Frustratingly, on the occasions when Cash and Jennings played a simple country song in a straightforward way the results were far better, as on 'Even Cowgirls Get The Blues', Tom T Hall's 'The Ballad Of Forty Dollars' and 'Field Of Diamonds'. As with the *Class Of '55* album *Heroes* only made a modest dent on the charts. These albums were a case of Johnny "spinning his wheels" (to use his own expression) and he looked toward the rewards of a new recording contract, assuming that anyone wanted to take him on.

Also during this period Johnny narrated an entertaining networked series of 500 three-minute programmes dealing with an aspect of America's folklore, written by the academic folklorist Dr John Oldani. *Johnny Cash At Folsom Prison*, by now nearly 20 years old, went double platinum (selling more than 2 million copies), an achievement matched by *Johnny Cash At San Quentin* and *Johnny Cash's Greatest Hits*.

At the age of 54 and without a recording contract, Johnny was perceived as a figure from the past (albeit a legendary one) whose modern recordings had been of little or no relevance to all but his diehard fans of whom there were a significant number in America and elsewhere. With a guaranteed fan base he could continue touring if he desired, albeit at smaller venues. Given the vast number of songs he'd recorded over the years the set list could vary from show to show and he could save money by reducing the size of his troupe. His substantial property investments and the constant demand for television appearances had generated a substantial secondary income. He could devote more time to his many hobbies and interests such as coin collecting, Bible studies, fishing, visiting Civil War sites as well as staying in touch with the many friends he'd made during his career. Then, there was the appeal of one-off projects like *Come To America*, the only Statue of Liberty Centennial album officially sanctioned by the Statue of Liberty/Ellis Island Foundation on which Johnny sang 'Let America Be America'.

However, Johnny Cash was not one for retirement. Speaking to writer Nicholas Dawidoff, June Carter said: "He finds it nearly impossible to stay in one place. We'll come home for one or two days and he'll say, 'Let's go to the cabin, let's go to Jamaica, let's go to the farm, let's go to Florida.'" His priority was gaining a new recording contract and Johnny humbly approached several record companies. He received a rebuff from Jimmy Bowen, then one of the main men on Music Row. Johnny ran through some songs in Bowen's office but didn't receive a reply.

One industry contact, Dick Asher, president and CEO of Mercury/Polygram, offered a deal, albeit on less favourable terms than Cash was used to. Steve Popovich, senior vice president of Nashville operations, was happy for Johnny to hook up with Jack Clement once more. As always on such occasions, warm words were exchanged. "We're very pleased to be given this new association with a man of Johnny Cash's stature," said Asher. "His talents speak for themselves." Popovich added, "The world awaits great music from him." A new album on a new label with a favoured producer was certainly a prospect Cash fans relished.

25

IN THE SPRING OF 1987, Johnny experienced an alarming health scare during a show in Council Bluffs, Iowa. He hadn't felt well prior to the show, and stumbled as he took the stage. His right hand shook so much that he had to hold the microphone with two hands, and was unable to plug in his guitar lead. By the second song it was obvious he could not continue. Though wearing her dressing gown, June went out on stage and under the pretence of giving Johnny a hug, she felt his pulse which was "flying". The show was cancelled with long-time Cash fan and organiser Dennis Devine asking the audience to say their prayers for Johnny who spent the night in hospital under observation. Johnny later explained that he had stopped taking his blood pressure medication. The show went ahead a few months later and on this occasion it was briefly interrupted by a bomb hoax.

That same year, a brief European tour opened in Gdansk, Poland. Though technically a trade union representing the interests of the workforce, Solidarity, led by former shipyard electrician Lech Walesa, grew to be far more than that: a vehicle for political change in a country desperate for freedom from communist oppression. Though somewhat more liberal than certain Eastern Bloc countries, visitors were still treated with suspicion and were not expected to behave in a way that might give rise to controversy. Enter Johnny Cash.

"We went to play in Gdansk," explains Lou Robin, "and I was approached by this disc jockey who was prominent in the music world but who was also involved in the underground movement. He came to me on a Friday I think, the day before the concert on Saturday night, and he said that Walesa would love to meet with Johnny in a church in Gdansk on Sunday. He stressed that it was all very hush hush and that the government people who were sponsoring the tour must on no account get to hear about it. He said we would be guaranteed to have a photograph of Johnny and Lech on the front page of the *New York Times* on the Monday morning.

"This guy said that it would help Lech with his political moves to unseat the communist regime and would generally increase the credibility of Solidarity in the outside world. We tried to arrange it so the disc jockey would take us to meet Lech and then afterwards take us to the airport where a government plane was going to fly us all back to Warsaw. Unfortunately the government people got wind of the meeting and they came to me and said, 'We know what you're doing and if you do it, we'll never have another American entertainer come here.' Coincidentally George Bush, not long before he became President, was scheduled to visit Poland soon afterwards."

Lou found himself in a sensitive position to put it mildly. "I gave John the alternatives as I saw them. One of the big factors was that we were stuck in Gdansk and dependent on the government people to get us back to Warsaw to continue the tour. It wasn't as if we could jump in the car and go home. John was particularly worried because it wasn't just him – the whole troupe was there. If they wanted to get tough there wasn't anything I could do about it. I couldn't reach any of the US Embassy people on the Sunday morning to get advice on what to do so we just sent our regrets to Lech and went on to Warsaw, much to our chagrin. It was an intimidating experience, especially when you're stuck there and you're at their disposal.

"Later that Sunday we went to a reception at the US ambassador's home in Warsaw and told him what had happened and he reckoned we had probably done the right thing. With a concert to play in Belgium in two days' time there was nothing more Johnny could do and he had to settle for writing a personal letter to Lech which the Embassy people made sure was delivered to him."

It was a sign of his international fame that Johnny featured in a joke which did the rounds in Soviet Russia during this time. A Russian official is talking to an American official. "You have Ronald Reagan, Bob Hope and Johnny Cash. We have Mikhail Gorbachev, but no hope and no cash."

As if his Iron Curtain visit didn't generate enough controversy Johnny also travelled to the American air base at Guantanamo Bay in Cuba to play for the servicemen there. Now on the other side of the argument so to speak, he hardly endeared himself to the American authorities by accepting Fidel Castro's invitation of an officially guided tour of the island.*

◆ ◆ ◆ ◆ ◆

The title of Johnny's first Mercury album, *Johnny Cash Is Coming To Town* (released in 1987) was doubly appropriate. Apart from signifying new product from a new label, it was also the phrase Jack Clement invariably used when people asked what he was working on (if that work involved Cash). For the liner notes, Mercury hired noted writer and historian John Lomax III to trumpet Cash's past glories:

* Cash was the first American entertainer to visit the base since Bob Hope in 1971.

"The pundits in Nashville pass around the plaudit 'superstar' like others pass around the potatoes but when Johnny Cash's achievements are measured against others claiming the title Cash towers above those poseurs like Godzilla over a Toyota!" Glossing over Johnny's prolonged lean spell, Lomax reeled off a dazzling list of statistics regarding historical sales, awards and achievements, even taking a sideswipe at some modern American success stories. "It's ironic that many rock writers have spent the last few years glorifying such artists as Bruce Springsteen, John Cougar Mellencamp and Bob Seger for their 'blue-collar' concerns – music they wrote with the working class in mind. Who do they think Johnny Cash has been writing about and singing to for the last 32 years?"

While the sleeve shots caught Johnny looking strangely stilted – chastened even – the album proved that musically, Johnny Cash had barely changed in 32 years, containing as it did a selection of simple, accessible songs. Religion and other dominant issues were usurped by love, human failure, trains and the working man. An edgy arrangement of Merle Travis' 'Sixteen Tons', and 'Let Him Roll', about "a wino who fell in love with a Dallas whore," were particularly strong; the latter accompanied by a video featuring Waylon Jennings and the song's writer, Guy Clark. Despite John Lomax's dismissive comments regarding contemporary artists, the album's lead-off track (written by Elvis Costello), 'The Big Light', was a song Johnny regarded as prime material, its vicious hangover subject matter being something he could relate to. "It's important to be aware of what's going on. You can get locked in your own little bayou of the river," he said in summing up working with newer songwriters.

"I've always believed that traditional music is the backbone . . ." said Johnny at the time of the album's release, singling out Reba McEntire, Randy Travis and George Strait for particularly favourable mention. "Trends and fads come and go but every few years the pendulum swings back to traditional." *Johnny Cash Is Coming To Town* was produced by Jack Clement thus continuing the paradoxical relationship between two men. Cash always maintained that he sounded best with minimal musical accompaniment yet going back to 'Ballad Of A Teenage Queen' Clement took every opportunity to fill out the Cash sound. While conceding that the backing vocals on that particular track were used effectively, in an interview with *USA Today* Johnny claimed, "I never liked the vocal overdubs on 'Guess Things Happen That Way' (written and produced by Clement). So many producers wanted to overproduce me like they've overproduced everyone else. My best records like 'Folsom Prison Blues' and 'I Walk The Line' have had maybe three or four instruments on them."

Speaking (in 1988) to Bill Flanagan, Cash said the vocal overdubs on 'Guess Things Happen That Way', "ruined it for me. I never saw the singing group. They overdubbed it after I thought the song was finished." How Johnny regarded the overdubs on 'Ballad Of A Teenage Queen' as perfectly acceptable when those on 'Guess Things Happen That Way' apparently ruined the song is difficult to fathom.

"All my greatest successes have had that simple Spartan sound," he confirmed to Patrick Carr, which makes the attraction of Jack Clement the more surprising. When Carr challenged Cash as to why the majority of his albums over the previous 15 years had been anything but Spartan sounding, he responded, "You know, when you've been working with people for months on a project, you tend to go along with their ideas." This lame rationalisation conflicts with the hardened image of Cash as an artist who knows what he wants and how to get it. However it does tally with the shy, uncertain character encountered on a one-to-one basis. As Clement points out, "Johnny always liked to do things that were different. I know it's not the greatest song I ever wrote but 'Dirty Old Egg Sucking Dog' is an example. I worked a lot on 'Everybody Loves A Nut'. We had a lot of fun making that album."

Their relationship in the studio seemed to suit Johnny. Some producers, notably the late Don Law, would let him coast whereas Clement pushed him. "I would make him sing till he was blue in the face to get it right." In an interview with the *Chicago Sun Times*, Cash commented, "He's the kind of guy who sees through all the plastic and the glitter, then he lets you see through it to the reality of the situation, musically speaking. He's not a yes man and I've gotta have people around me who are going to be that way." "I call him Captain Decibel because he's got the loudest recording voice I've ever heard," said Clement. "As far as being able to cram a lot of other stuff in there under it, drums, horns, banging guitars, you can hardly cover him up, he's just a very loud level voice."

Inevitably sparks flew in the studio. With a sly grin Jack remembers such instances. "We had our differences. I'm bad for making people sing until they drop. We usually got along pretty good but there were a few times when we didn't. It's not like we were screaming at each other in the studio but there was one time when we had a disagreement and I'd had enough. I headed off. There weren't nobody knew where I went. I just got in my car and took off. They were calling all over the place asking, 'Where the hell's Cowboy?' Then I came back. Cash left a jar of syrup or molasses or something hanging on my door as a kind of peace offering."

Despite the odd moment of dissent and indifference to some of Johnny's more critically acclaimed work, for a man who has worked with Louis Armstrong, Jim Reeves and Waylon Jennings, Clement's affection for Cash is undiminished. "He's one of my all-time favourites. I think the world of him. Of all the people I've worked with he's the king."

It helped that Johnny and Jack shared a similar sense of bizarre humour. Clement recalls an occasion when the two visited the graves of members of The Carter Family in Virginia. "When we got to old AP's grave Johnny was serious for a while then he says, 'You know what? I'm gonna have me one last smoke with old AP,' and with that he gets down on the ground and lies flat out right there next to AP's grave and lights up a cigarette. He even offered AP a puff." On a more ordinary level Jack is eternally grateful to Johnny for introducing him to a brand of nose spray ("Four-Way"), which Jack has found to be particularly efficacious.

♦ ♦ ♦ ♦ ♦

Given that there was nothing radically new about *Johnny Cash Is Coming To Town*, the predictable outcome saw only loyal fans subscribing. In concluding his liner notes, John Lomax III encouraged people to "cherish" the album when exhorting people to "play, enjoy and tell all your friends" might have been a better sales pitch. Though the album remained in the charts for six months its top position was 36 – not a great commercial success, and certainly not the start that Mercury hoped for. Shortly after the album was released Johnny made an appearance on Ralph Emery's television show *Nashville Now* during which he experienced a bitter-sweet moment when Rick Blackburn, the man who had recently dropped him from CBS, presented him with double platinum awards for *Johnny Cash At Folsom Prison, Johnny Cash At San Quentin* and *Greatest Hits.*

Johnny had never been gung ho about America's involvement in war, despite his partisan support for Nixon and a premature end to the Vietnam conflict. However, by 1987, his views became more hardline, which may well have been due to the fact that John Carter was now 17 and approaching draft age. Johnny went on record as saying he felt less comfortable with Ronald Reagan in the White House than he had with Jimmy Carter, a relative of June's and a personal friend. When speaking about 'Ragged Old Flag', Johnny told Robert Oermann, "I wrote the song to remind myself how many and how often this country's been involved in wars. It seems to me like the politicians and the military just can't wait for another one and that really bothers me. It bothers me that we're going to have 50,000 on manoeuvres off the coast of Central America and at the same time the Russians are getting into war games on their eastern border."

Johnny agreed with Kris Kristofferson's condemnation of Reagan's policy of supporting the Contras in Nicaragua, and the two appeared at New York's Bottom Line to duet on Dylan's 'Masters Of War'. "I'm totally against funding the Contra war in Nicaragua. These politicians standing up saying they don't want a communist country in the western hemisphere . . . that's a bunch of crap. People are going to go with anybody who'll feed 'em." In another interview, Cash drew on his historical readings to deliver further condemnation of US foreign policy. "There are a lot of dangerous things happening now that have parallels with the Roman Empire, like a big country, the US, jumping on little countries like Rome did. I think we're in a lot of unhealthy situations right now, being involved militarily around the world. History is repeating itself."

Though remaining strongly patriotic, Johnny's views on specific American foreign policy issues, as revealed by numerous interviews over the years, have at times given out conflicting signals. Johnny looked at each situation on its own merits and tried to avoid knee-jerk reactions dictated by the policies of a particular party or interest group. While having the highest respect for the office of President he will not support whatever government is in power, believing in the maxim that a patriot must be prepared to defend his country against its government. Whatever the truth of his innermost feelings the patriotic bit is beyond doubt. Indeed, for many years, there was a clause written into his performance contract which demanded: "An American Flag on a pole stand (typical size 3′ by 5′) is required on stage in full view of the audience throughout the show. For outdoor shows the flag may be on a fixed pole but must be in full view of the entire audience."

In 1987, Johnny signed up enthusiastically for *The Johnny Cash Freedom Train*, a series of rallies and concerts in 10 cities aimed at raising money for war veterans and their families. "It's good to be able to wave the flag again," he said. "I come from a long line of flag wavers." Times had changed and in stark contrast to its predecessor's triumphant progress, sponsorship for the venture was not forthcoming and all but one of the proposed concerts was cancelled. The following year, Cash took part in an experimental tour, something quite different from the large-scale packages he had presented since the Sixties. The Affordable Art Tour featured a handful of dates at universities featuring Johnny, June, Waylon and his wife Jessi Colter backed by five musicians including Bob Wootton and WS Holland.

The stage set was informal and shouted audience requests were encouraged. In a newspaper interview from the time, Johnny explained the thinking behind the tour: "We are dropping prices to a level we believe the fans can afford (tickets were $9.50). The prices for most country music shows have gone out of the ceiling and I believe that the average fan can't afford to take their family to a show. The show's going back to basics. We're gonna do the songs people want to hear but without the high tech schmaltz." It may well have been that Johnny, acting on the professional advice of his financial team, wanted to see if he could present a show in a more cost-effective way. For all his comments about getting back to basics the idea did not take hold at this time. Within days of the last Affordable Art show he was back on the road with his usual band in the manner to which they had become accustomed.

◆ ◆ ◆ ◆ ◆

While Johnny's fortunes had been declining, those of his daughter Rosanne continued to soar. His stepdaughter, Carlene Carter was also making a name for herself. Both women had experienced the privations of being born to celebrity parents though in Rosanne's case there was the comfort of having a mother who was not part of the entertainment business, though the strictures of Vivian's devout Catholicism added to Rosanne's rebelliousness. Rosanne also had to contend with her father's absence, as well as his unpredictable behaviour when he *was* around. She recalled various family traumas in dealing with Johnny's drug-ravaged behaviour, including the acute embarrassment of being the centre of attention when Johnny set speakers on top of their Californian house to blast out Christmas songs to the neighbourhood. One advantage was that Rosanne learned a huge amount about being a performer from her father, who gave her a list of a hundred essential country songs to learn, such as 'The Battle Of New Orleans', 'I'm So Lonesome I Could Cry' and 'Wildwood Flower'.

Rosanne became a rebel at school and endlessly found herself in conflict with the authorities. By her mid-teens she was lonely, moody and already using a variety of drugs. *Village Voice* writer Jan Hoffman described her as "a champion bad-Catholic-girl troublemaker". In 1973, to the relief of her teachers, she left high school and hooked up with her father's road show. Carlene too put in some appearances around this time. Not unnaturally Vivian had concerns about this development in view of what she had been through with Johnny. Rosanne started out as a general dogsbody and her duties included taking care of the laundry. She went on to become a backing singer and despite a strong degree of competitiveness between them, she and Carlene were eventually allowed to do the odd solo spot with 'Silver Threads and Golden Needles' being their showcase.

Rosanne enjoyed a sojourn in London, mainly at her father's expense, though she did some "play-working" at the CBS office. Although disparaging about her work, Tony Byworth remembers her being efficient in helping to organise the annual Wembley Festival. Johnny eventually put a stop to her time in England by withdrawing financial support when it seemed that Rosanne was partying too hard. In search of a direction, Rosanne spent some time at Hollywood's Lee Strasberg Theater Institute. Through Carlene, Rosanne met Rodney Crowell (whom Carlene had previously been involved with) and they married in 1979. It seemed a great match not least because of their shared passion for music.

In an interview with *Country Rhythms* in 1982, Rosanne admitted to having told Rodney that, in his place, she would have had second thoughts. "My family is so intense, they all are – all of them. I can't explain to you how intense all of the little back and forth is, the little things that go on." She claimed that marrying Rodney was part of a process of putting distance between her and her family. Rosanne became successful with Crowell producing some of her most popular material. "It gave me a real boost without me really knowing it. It's just that if you believe in yourself others will believe in you too." However all was not well.

"Rosanne achieved a stardom that she could hardly abide and that her husband desired with a desperate passion," journalist Laurence Leamer wrote.

"Among the things they had in common was a drug problem." It took Rosanne various spells in rehab to conquer the "family disease". Since most of her family took to prescription drugs like ducks to water, it was hardly surprising that she would follow suit. "Cocaine is an insidious drug. It's like a snake. It's really awful. My God, the time you waste with drugs. Getting 'em, doing 'em, recovering from 'em." In total contrast to her father, Rosanne detested life on the road, claiming she would only agree to tour because her record company threatened to pull her tongue out.

Rebecca Carlene Smith, better known as Carlene Carter, took the world on from an early age. Having learnt piano at the age of six and guitar at 10, taking lessons from Carl Perkins, she performed with Mother Maybelle and The Carter Sisters – her showstopper being 'Charlie Brown'. Strikingly attractive with long blonde hair and intense eyes, in 1971, at the age of 15, Carlene married Joe Simpkins (an engineer at the House of Cash recording studio) at Hendersonville Baptist Church with the Reverend Jimmy Snow officiating while Johnny sang 'I Promise You'. As she said later, "You get married then either because you're stupid or you're pregnant. Unfortunately I was both." The couple had a daughter, but the marriage soon ended and, at the age of 19, Carlene married Jack Routh, a producer who became a member of the extended Cash musical family, working on a number of albums with Johnny. The union produced a son, John Jackson Routh.

Apart from being part of the Johnny Cash show Carlene appeared and recorded with Mother Maybelle and The Carter Sisters. Despite her country roots, Carlene looked to the rock scene for inspiration. In 1977 she moved to London with then-boyfriend Rodney Crowell to cut an album blending new wave rock with country elements, backed by Graham Parker & The Rumour, and acquired a third husband, the multi-talented British artist, songwriter and producer, Nick Lowe. Carlene was no shrinking violet but even by her own standards, a club appearance at The Bottom Line in New York produced some jaw-dropping stuff. After a rousing rendition of 'Swap-Meat Rag' (from 1979's *Two Sides To Every Woman*), she exclaimed with wicked glee, "that one ought to put the cunt back into country." What her highly conservative mother would have made of that remark can only be guessed at. The most risqué remark June Carter made publicly was in admonishing the leering gents who whistled at her and her sisters when they took to the stage in smart, matching dresses, "Now don't go gettin' all excited boys, this is as sexy as it's gonna git."

After the break-up of her marriage to Lowe, Carlene returned to America, bruised from failed relationships and ongoing drug and alcohol problems. She appeared with the Johnny Cash road show on occasion, and June welcomed her back to the fold. For all the craziness of growing up with successful country music singers as family, Carlene praised the fact that June brought her up to think she could "be anything she wanted to be, to be real comfortable about being myself." She later attracted some adverse comments in the American press who saw her moves as opportunistic. After taking in a show, one journalist described her as, "Recently de-programmed and re-countrified after an eight-year flopped attempt at rock'n'roll stardom in Europe." Carlene gave the lie to her time of experimentation in Europe having failed when a few years later she released several country rock albums which briefly achieved critical and commercial success.

◆ ◆ ◆ ◆ ◆

The realisation dawned early for both Rosanne and Carlene that, to establish themselves artistically, they would have to escape the shadow of their famous father/stepfather. While both women would use the association from time to time, they did so on their own terms.

With growing approval from both fans and critics, Rosanne came to be seen as one of the leading figures of young country. Her spiky hair and modern clothing gave off a rock'n'roll appearance, leading one journalist to describe her as "the queen of country's hip parade". On the suggestion of Rodney Crowell, she recorded 'Tennessee Flat-Top Box' for her highly successful album *King's Record Shop* (1988). The single made number one in the charts, though amazingly Rosanne was unaware that the song had been written by her father, assuming it was public domain.* Johnny responded by writing her a letter and then bought space in *Billboard* to tell not just Rosanne, but the whole world, about the feelings that the discovery evoked in him. The letters published about Bob Dylan and Ira Hayes in the Sixties had a clear logic to them but the reasons behind this personal correspondence were harder to fathom. Johnny possibly needed to use a grand gesture to make the kind of paternal statement of love and approval he had failed to give when his daughter was growing up. Or like his public proposal to June, it perhaps felt natural for him to think in terms of a performance that would garner the approval of an audience. "I think you always loved me almost as much as I loved you, if that's possible. But you had your own dreams, your own goals, your own hopes and cares . . . your success with 'Tennessee Flat-Top Box' is one of my greatest fulfillments."

Like Johnny, Rosanne has made public stands on issues she feels strongly about, such as nuclear power, child abuse and artistic censorship while speaking out in favour of the preservation of the environment and world peace. When her father was awarded the newly renamed Johnny Cash Americanism Award for humanitarianism by the B'nai B'rith's Anti-Defamation League in 1989, she paid a heartfelt compliment to her father when saying, "You sparked something in me. It was tolerance. And that's what I love about you."

Possibly as an act of defiant individuality to test others' tolerance, she altered

* 'Tennessee Flat-Top Box' was a hit for Johnny in 1962.

the spelling of her name from Rosanne to Roseanne. Sadly, though perhaps not surprisingly, she also suffered from depression and the material she recorded after the breakdown of her marriage to Rodney Crowell makes for difficult listening, such is the intensity of her personal pain.

◆ ◆ ◆ ◆ ◆

One of the more recent causes to which Johnny lent his name was support for the victims of AIDS. An unlikely assortment of alternative rock musicians including Michelle Shocked, Marc Almond and The Mekons got together to make 'Til Things Are Brighter, an album of Johnny Cash covers with proceeds going to the Terrence Higgins Trust, a leading AIDS charity. The sleeve notes took a typically revisionist line by claiming that "Johnny Cash was the only country and western singer to make a stand against the Vietnam War" – another example of the left reworking Johnny's past to fit their own agenda. *Country Music People* were a little surprised at the choice of country music as a vehicle for supporting an AIDS charity, concluding that Johnny had been chosen as "a well-known crusader on behalf of freedom." After pointing out that "many Christians abhor homosexuality which is (rightly or wrongly) generally considered to be a major cause of AIDS," the reviewer queried whether Cash was aware that the album was a "fund-raiser for a controversial disease's victims."

Johnny was outraged at the suggestion that a Christian might not want to help AIDS sufferers and was fully aware of where the proceeds from the album were destined. What the artists featured on the album made of Johnny's leanings to the right is unknown, though they would almost certainly have disagreed with June's feelings on another controversial subject, abortion. In a 1989 interview with a journalist from the *Roanoke Times*, she said, "There are instances where there is a rape or incest, where I would take to my knees and ask God's help. I'm feminist enough to have compassion for women who have these problems, but because of my faith, I'm not in favour of abortion."

'Til Things Are Brighter resulted from Johnny's initiative to set up the Music Business Foundation for AIDS Research with June, Waylon Jennings and Jessi Colter. The aim was to raise funds in helping the medical establishment find a cure for the disease, of which (at the time) very little was known. In a letter to Waylon Jennings, Johnny wrote that, according to his calculations (on the basis of information given to him by "experts") there could be 185,000,000 deaths from the disease in America alone by the year 2000. "That is only if the number doubles each year. Some experts suggest that deaths could triple or quadruple." Despite these sensational figures Johnny adopted a reassuring tone, "I'm not trying to be a modern day prophet Jeremiah, and I'm not crying 'doom' and I'm not trying to scare anyone . . ."

Two years later, as part of a UK tour marking his 35th anniversary in the business, Johnny was in Liverpool. "He had a sprained ankle, it was nothing serious but he called a doctor to the hotel," said journalist and broadcaster Spencer Leigh. "He told me that he realised it was an expensive way of dealing with a minor ailment but he was worried that if he went to hospital there would be speculation he had AIDS." This enigmatic comment provides an insight into both Johnny's relationship with the press and the impact of the disease. He may have appeared sensitive on the subject but has never evinced any ill will toward homosexuality (not necessarily a typical attitude in the southern states of America). In a lengthy article entitled 'My Name Is Sue! How Do You Do: Johnny Cash As Lesbian Icon', feminist writer Teresa Ortega gave a remarkable thesis on how Johnny Cash provided valuable solace to lesbian teenagers.

Religion, prison and crime featured strongly in his songs with elements of nonconformity and escapism characterised by "gender covering" clothes. Ortega argues that like many lesbians, Cash struggled against the odds in his early life and that his persona of succeeding-in-the-face-of-adversity came to fruition in 'A Boy Named Sue' – "a natural point of identification for a butch lesbian child." The fact that the hero was given a female name helps this theory, though it's unlikely that Shel Silverstein wrote the song from a lesbian angle. Ortega also uses Cash's trademark black dress to support her argument, partly because wearing black helps to hide hips and feminine curves and add height. "Cash's Everyman look also appeals to lesbians because of how easily his style can be adapted and transformed into the fashionable habit of Everydyke." Saving her best shot until last, Ortega claimed that by being a lesbian icon, Johnny Cash had reduced the suicide rates amongst teenage lesbians.

◆ ◆ ◆ ◆ ◆

1988 saw yet another honour being bestowed on Johnny Cash when the Country Music Foundation put on a $70,000 exhibition, sponsored by Holiday Inns, based on his life and career.* Bill Ivey of the Country Music Foundation said, "This collection provides unprecedented documentation of country music's most distinguished career. It is extraordinarily rich due to Cash's unusual level of co-operation and interest and the availability of his extensive personal archives." The *Daily News* of New York described it as "the most ambitious historical display ever undertaken by the museum."

The exhibition followed the various stages of Johnny's life and career from his humble origins in Dyess, Arkansas, his time in the Air Force and Sun Records, to his steady rise to fame in the worlds of music and film, with space being reserved for Johnny's many interests beyond music. Among the diverse artefacts on display were school report cards, his Air Force uniform, the steel bars he used during performances of 'The Legend Of John Henry's Hammer', log books of recording sessions, a Colt revolver, fishing tackle and many private photographs

* Such an event had only been previously staged for Dolly Parton and Willie Nelson.

from Johnny's extensive collection as well as posters and clips from numerous film and television appearances. At Johnny's suggestion all graphics were uniformly black, white and silver which made for a striking effect. The exhibition ran through to the end of 1989 and attracted around a million visitors.

Also, in 1988, Johnny submitted plans for a mixed development on some 95 acres of his land near the House of Cash in Nashville which would have resulted in the construction of 219 family homes, a shopping centre and an office complex. The proposals aroused much hostility among the Hendersonville locals and as a result there were public meetings and a flood of angry letters to the press. In the end the plans did not proceed because Johnny's request for re-zoning the land was turned down. Years later, he made a tidy profit by selling off much of the land for housing development. It was also reported that Johnny was interested in becoming part of a consortium of investors, along with June, Waylon and Jessi, in building a major $30 million complex on Music Row. The development was to include a 200 room hotel, office and retail space, two restaurants, musical production facilities, a radio station and childcare and recreational facilities but Johnny lost interest in the project.

Johnny lent support to his sister Joanne's ambition of recording a live video album of Christian music at the church where she worshipped in Kernersville, North Carolina. Despite a heavy cold, Johnny appeared at the event and contributed some performances for the album. Joanne followed through with her passion and together with her husband, pastor Harry Yates, she founded the charitable Nashville Cowboy Church. A less happy event in 1988 was the divorce of Cindy from Marty Stuart. Their marriage had lasted less than five years and was but the latest in a long line of Cash-Carter marital failures.

As usual, Johnny and the troupe spent most of the year on the road. Johnny showed that he had lost none of his knack for crowd pleasing, remarking at one show, "We're gonna do some old ones, but if you enjoy 'em they're brand new to me." Press reviews were not always favourable. A show in Orange County, southern California, was performed against a backdrop of the opera *Aida* (set in ancient Egypt) which prompted one critic to comment that, while the religious material was "spirited not preachy," Cash should "retire one overly biased film clip he has used in the gospel set in which a blond bearded man dressed as Christ wanders the countryside anointing, amongst others, June Carter . . .* This cheap attempt at conveying spirituality lacks the integrity of some of the other film segments which illustrate songs by showing prison inmates and locomotives. Except for that one missed step however integrity reigns throughout the evening."

One audience member at this show felt the venue, which had previously played host to the likes of the New York City Ballet, was inappropriate for a country boy like Johnny Cash. "You'd think he'd be playing at a honky-tonk

* A reference to a much used clip from *Gospel Road*.

somewhere." Johnny had to interrupt another show, mid-song, due to an attack of hiccups, confiding to his audience that it was the first time this had happened to him. The attack lasted six hours. There were other tour calamities to contend with, such as Carlene Carter being left behind in hospital to recover following excessive vodka consumption – not long after she had rejoined the troupe claiming she "wanted to be part of the Carter family again." Early on during a show in North Carolina, Anita had a rheumatoid arthritis attack so severe that her throat closed, causing her to pass out. June, being a trouper who had got through countless backstage dramas before, managed to appear on time for her slot, though now minus two parts of the four part harmony. She ended up singing ballads with Helen. "This has been an unusual night," June told the crowd by way of explanation. "It hasn't gone exactly the way we planned it. I don't know how to explain it except to say I have one daughter in the hospital and one sister who's fainted."

Not for the first time, June came in for criticism. In one review of a show also featuring Conway Twitty, she was referred to as "June Hurricane Carter" (a reference to the boxer Rubin "Hurricane" Carter), with her voice being described as "ravaged". The critic obviously liked her comedy routine though. "She kicked off her shoes, pulled up her sequined dress to reveal red drawers, and did a spirited buck and wing right into the heart of the enthusiastic crowd." June was playing Aunt Polly, a character she had featured during past shows but had dropped, only to revive her at Johnny's urging in the Eighties. Perhaps this was a polite indication that comedy was where June's real strength as a performer lay. For some, the Carters' detracted from Johnny's impact: "The Carter Family broke the mood and spell created by Johnny earlier on," being one complaint. In Pennsylvania a reviewer complained that "June was taking up too much of the programme and was plugging her books and records." Even Johnny did not earn his usual plaudits. "Johnny was warm and friendly if not inspired, his band was competent." Still, the devotion of some fans was remarkable. At one show long-time admirer, Francis Gauthier, presented Johnny and June with a bust of the pair of them which had taken him 75 hours to carve.

People appreciated Johnny's direct and witty banter. "I don't dance, tell jokes or wear my pants too tight like other entertainers do, but I do know about a thousand songs." "The Cash style of performance crosses social and racial boundaries," wrote one journalist. "Old and young alike identify with him, whether successful or downtrodden, and Christians know him as a brother. JC is a dynamic eagle figure displaying truth and honesty and in a perceptive way, the human condition good and bad." "He has one of those voices which hit that elusive spot of pure truth," wrote the *Sunday Independent*. "No explanation is needed, you can feel it in your bones."

As the Eighties moved towards the Nineties the Cash troupe played smaller venues which reflected Johnny's reduced audience pulling power – a fact highlighted in a number of concert reviews. Guitarist Jim Soldi recalls a fairground show where after a few songs, the power went down. The problem could not be sorted but rather than cancelling the show Johnny simply played an acoustic set, with people holding battery operated flashlights to illuminate the stage. Given the limitations on the volume he was able to generate without amplification, the crowd were told to keep quiet during the songs. The proceeds from a benefit show at Virginia's Handley High School went to Shalom et Benedictus, a 28-bed treatment centre which helped young people in trouble. Its stated aims related to the worst aspects of Johnny's own life: "Preventing, treating and ameliorating the tremendous physical, psychological, spiritual, family and societal damage done by the harmful use of drugs and alcohol."

The community was open to teenagers between the ages of 13 and 18 with admission charges varying according to income. The show had been set up by Max Mandel who got to know Johnny while he was a college student involved in concert promotion. "John always felt a very close kinship with those having a hard time in their lives," Mandel said. Before the show Johnny spent some time talking to the youngsters, telling them, "I know a lot about Shalom et Benedictus. I learned the hard way." Also appearing with Johnny was June's old actor friend, Robert Duvall, who sang a couple of songs including 'I Overlooked An Orchid (While Searching For A Rose)'.*

1988 saw the release of two Johnny Cash albums, though the first, *Classic Cash*, was Mercury's attempt to trade on past glories. The double album featuring Johnny's most famous songs – from 'I Walk The Line' to 'Sunday Morning Coming Down' – was re-recorded in the Reverend Jimmy Snow's church studio. Johnny was proud of the fact that the album was produced with the remarkably small budget of $35,000. "I asked for a budget that low because I think if you spend much more on a Johnny Cash album, you're doing something wrong," he told Patrick Carr.

Despite his comments in support of low budgets producing good results, none of the remakes eclipsed their originals. The other album release, *Water From The Wells Of Home*, featured a proverbial kitchen sink of well-known guests including Paul and Linda McCartney, Hank Williams, Jr, Emmylou Harris, The Everly Brothers, Roy Acuff, Tom T Hall and Waylon Jennings. Representing the immediate family were Rosanne Cash, Cindy Cash and John Carter Cash. Jack Clement was particularly pleased that the opening track was a remake of his maligned 'Ballad Of A Teenage Queen', as the lyrics which had been deleted from the original hit were reinstated and sung by Rosanne Cash.

---

* During her time at acting school June had met a number of famous or soon to be famous actors including James Dean, though she remained tight-lipped about the extent of their involvement. "He once gave me a rose and that's all I'm ever going to say about it."

Like the Cash family, the McCartneys had a holiday home in Jamaica. Both families were visiting the island at the same time which resulted in the collaboration, 'New Moon Over Jamaica', on which Paul reportedly played nine guitar parts. Johnny was delighted to be playing with the ex-Beatle, as he confirmed in an interview at the time, "A guitar pull with Paul is really a trip. He's the only singer I've ever sat with across a porch who plays a guitar left-handed and upside down." The song was light but catchy, though at least one reviewer felt the backing vocals detracted from the song. "It's Johnny and Paul singing with their wives crooning off key in the background." As well as music, family was important to both Cash and McCartney. As Johnny put it, "We identify with them because they travel like a bunch of gypsies with their kids and that's the way we've done it too."

'That Old Wheel' was remarkable because it had been sent in, entirely unsolicited, to Mercury's office by one Jennifer Pierce. It was released as a single and only just missed the Top 20. The album's nadir came with the execrable 'A Croft In Clachan (The Ballad Of Rob MacDunn)', written by Johnny and Glen Campbell. As is often the case when Americans sing about their Celtic roots, their imagination gets carried away by visions of a mythical land that exists as some kind of Walt Disney creation. There can be little doubt that a good time was had by all in making the album. However, it only just made it into the Top 50.

Already there were signs that the honeymoon period with Mercury was over. In October, Johnny played a show at the Ritz in New York which attracted a pitifully low turnout from the record company personnel. As one commentator put it, "Guess the chieftains were too busy celebrating the new Bon Jovi LP to participate in greatness." Johnny's complaint about Mercury's lack of understanding was equally blunt. "The thing is if you got it, you always got it, you know?"

Towards the end of the year Johnny received an unwelcome shock that overshadowed the problems with his record company.

26

FOR JOHNNY AND HIS FAMILY the end of 1988 was an anxious time. He had been experiencing more health complaints including a "sick fainting spell", and during a subsequent medical check-up it emerged that a coronary artery was severely clogged and that he would have to undergo immediate heart bypass surgery. The fact that family friend Roy Orbison had died of a heart attack, aged 52, two weeks previously only added to their concerns. Heavy smoking, drug abuse and a bad diet for food that was rich and fatty had resulted in severe blockages in Johnny's coronary arteries.

By a remarkable coincidence Waylon Jennings was also in the same hospital undergoing triple bypass surgery. He had fallen ill a short time before on his way to appear as a guest at a Johnny Cash "Holiday Homecoming" show in Bristol, Tennessee. Given the pair's fame, the local press followed every twist and turn of their progress with a hawk's eye, quizzing members of Johnny's medical team at the Nashville Baptist Hospital at every opportunity. The Orbison angle helped to intensify the feeding frenzy. Was there going to be a hat trick of deaths in the same month?

One sobering aspect was how young they were to have inflicted such damage on themselves. Jennings was 51 and Cash – 56. After a short delay to allow Johnny's smoke saturated lungs to be cleared, the operation took place on December 19. Doctor Robert Hardin, chief of surgery at the hospital, said afterwards that the procedure had been straightforward, the patient being listed as "critical but stable". The blockage had been in a "critical location" and speedy surgical intervention had been essential. The four-hour procedure, estimated to have cost between $18,000 and $21,000, involved taking unblocked vessels from Johnny's thigh and chest and implanting them around his heart to bypass the blocked up part of the coronary arteries. Apart from this, given his history of drug abuse, Johnny was in surprisingly good health.

However, the doctor spoke too soon when shortly after the double bypass surgery, Johnny succumbed to a near lethal bout of pneumonia, though the immediate presence of a team of medical experts helped to ensure that he recovered reasonably quickly. Johnny revealed that during the battle with pneumonia he had an out-of-body experience where he saw "the light of God" which was "too beautiful to explain in earthly terms," as he put it to Neil McCormick in the *Daily Telegraph*. In fact when he came round and realised that he was not in the hereafter, he kicked up quite a fuss, pulling out tubes and wrestling with medical staff.

Under the headline, "Hard to be a saint under medication," the *Nashville Banner* reported that Cash had caused upset and concern to the medical and nursing staff with his volatile behaviour. The newspaper mounted a defence, saying that, "When you're on lots of drugs you really don't know what you're doing." The last thing Johnny needed was to be pumped full of drugs with all the attendant dangers of a relapse into his old ways. Because Johnny reacted badly to many of the drugs, the doctors had to come up with different combinations which would not bring on adverse reactions. These decisions were made under extreme pressure when he additionally developed pneumonia.

By December 28, local newspapers were reporting that Johnny was making good progress and that "the nurses were having a little trouble keeping up with him." The fact that Johnny and Waylon were in the hospital at the same time prompted fans, encouraged by disc jockey Johnny Western (who had previously been on the road with Johnny), to arrange for the display of a massive combined Christmas/Get Well card signed by over 4,000 people, which was clearly visible from inside the hospital. (Western had done the same thing for Barbara Mandrell when she was recovering from horrific injuries sustained in a car crash.)

Needless to say, the pair spent much time together during their recuperation and soon after Johnny's admission Waylon amused him with stories illustrating the levelling effect of hospital. "When they get you up to walk, you can hardly stand up, and they put that little gown on you. You're about halfway down the hall, and you feel the draft from behind. You know you ain't got no back, and you got no shorts on, and people are looking at your ass. That superstar shit goes right out the window."

Not surprisingly, Johnny and Waylon discussed possible future collaborations, one idea being a spoken word album of Robert Service poems. Service, born in England to Scottish parents, was a man that both could identify with – a writer with a distinctive line in simple unpretentious story poetry who had travelled the world, identifying best with those at the lower end of the social scale. He died in 1958 at the age of 84 and part of one obituary read, "He was not a poet's poet. Fancy-Dan dilettantes will dispute the description 'great'. He was a people's poet. To the people he was great. They understood him, and knew that any verse carrying the by-line of Robert W Service would be a lilting thing, clear, clean and power-packed, beating out a story with a dramatic intensity that made the nerves tingle." As always Johnny was looking for new creative outlets, though it appears that this particular idea never amounted to anything.

◆ ◆ ◆ ◆ ◆

Eventually, Johnny was discharged from hospital. Doctor Charles E Mayes, a cardiologist, told a reporter, "I think he will need to change his lifestyle some and I believe he will." Johnny was going to have to make radical changes to his intake: no alcohol, no cigarettes, no fried food, no sweets, no rich desserts. His response was predictably gloomy. "It was like telling a man that in order to live he's got to die." Just after his release from hospital he expressed a resolve to change his ways. The operation had been a "soul-searching" experience. "There's going to be no more alcohol, no more smoking and all that stuff. I'm 56 now and I don't ever want to have to do that again."

Speaking at the same press conference June, wearing a fox fur hat and a full-length mink coat, said Johnny was "committed to life", but she expressed doubts about the new regime prescribed by the doctors saying with resignation, "I've never seen anybody keep Johnny Cash to anything." Johnny had in fact been allowed out of hospital briefly the day before his final release in order to attend a New Year's lunch with friends. As he put it, "I'm probably the only person who's gone out of intensive care, gone out to lunch and then gone back to intensive care."

The adverse effects of years of smoking were clear to see. Johnny often had to fight that bit harder for breath and his shoulders hunched up from the increased effort. After John Carter was born, he had tried to give up on a number of occasions, all to no avail. The *Nashville Banner* reported that he smoked his final cigarette just half an hour before his emergency surgery. Approximately three months after the operation, Johnny was back on the road. As he took the stage to rapturous applause at Jackson Community College, he told the audience that it was good to be back but he now intended to cut back the number of shows he did each year to around 60.

Johnny's respect for the younger set put him at odds with the views of various acquaintances. Johnny and June got on well with Al and Tipper Gore and indeed Johnny performed at Gore rallies on occasion but he had little empathy with Tipper's crusade to censor rock music. Tipper was greatly concerned by some of the lyrics contained in the music of artists such as Prince and Judas Priest whose song 'Eat Me Alive', so she claimed, was about forced oral sex at gunpoint. Along with some well-connected "Washington Wives", members of the Parents Music Resource Center led a major campaign to have music rated, pressurising broadcasters to exercise voluntary restraint.

For Johnny such attitudes were anachronistic and unrealistic. "Radio and TV stations are wasting their time in bleeping out what they consider rough rock'n' roll lyrics. It's pretty silly to think they're gonna protect our youth by censoring three minutes of the dialogue they hear all day long from their friends, from TV, books and magazines. It doesn't give parents too much credit nor their teachers . . . If a parent hasn't been close enough to his kids to let them make their own decisions, then it's too late by the time they're ready to rock'n' roll."

Some of his more conservative supporters might have been surprised by such a statement but, throughout his career, Johnny had sung lyrics with the power to move and shock, only rarely resorting to bad language which was in any event invariably tame. How many of the artists in Tipper Gore's sights produced such memorably chilling lines as "But I shot a man in Reno, just to watch him die." Johnny also expressed an interest in what his son was listening to. While in Toronto to play a show, he took the opportunity to visit an auditorium where Iron Maiden were rehearsing, "just to feel the music". He was flattered that the band recognised him and he obtained some autographed pictures for John Carter, who was a big fan. Later he dropped in on the band's concert and approved of what he saw. "What I observed was a lot of teenagers and young adults just letting loose and having a good time. 'Course there was grass smoking, but there's grass smoking in people's houses everywhere."

In 1989, it was a more conservative aspect of Johnny's character that sprung him into action. In the case of Texas v Johnson, the American Supreme Court decided that burning the American flag was "expressive conduct" and "symbolic speech" protected by the first amendment and as such a law prohibiting flag-burning would violate free speech and breach the American constitution. The case went back to 1984 when Gregory Lee Johnson had taken part in a protest rally at the Republican National Convention in Dallas against the policies of the Reagan administration and some Dallas based corporations. An American flag was burnt while protestors chanted, "America, the red, white and blue, we spit on you." Johnson was convicted of desecration of a venerated object in violation of a Texas statute and sentenced to a year in jail.

A series of appeals followed culminating in the Supreme Court decision. Predictably, the decision was hugely controversial and outraged patriots and conservatives alike who pointed to previous Supreme Court rulings which had consistently upheld the right to protect the flag from public gestures of disrespect. They were not mollified by the judges' reasoning, one of whom, the late Justice William Brennan, said, "We do not consecrate the flag by punishing its desecration, for in doing so we dilute the freedom that this cherished emblem represents." His colleague Justice Anthony Kennedy said with resignation, "It is poignant but fundamental that the flag protects those who hold it in contempt." Rather than jump into the debate, Johnny re-released 'Ragged Old Flag' by way of restating his own brand of patriotism.

The following year the first full-scale Highwaymen tour gave Johnny an opportunity to drive home his patriotic message and respond to the Supreme Court ruling even though it was, to some extent, a case of preaching to the converted. Soon after Kris Kristofferson's 'They Killed Him', a song illustrative of

Waylon Jennings' observation that "Politically Kris swings us to the left," which may have raised Johnny's hackles at that sensitive time, Cash took to the stage. With sentimental tones lilting in the background, he talked about his feelings for America, the freedoms people enjoy, and how, as much as he enjoyed touring, he was always glad to get back home. In a thinly veiled reference to the Texas v Johnson case, he said that people in America even had the right to burn the flag. The audience appeared puzzled with what seemed to suggest his compliance, before he delivered a final denouement, "But don't forget, I've got the right to bear arms so if you burn the flag I'll shoot you."

With the audience firmly on his side he launched into 'Ragged Old Flag', leaving no doubt that he was stressing his patriotism rather than his concerns about the warlike tendencies of some American governments, an aspect from the song highlighted in an earlier interview. This treatment of the recitation became a regular part of Johnny's segment thereafter. Surprisingly, such robustly stated reactionary views didn't seem to affect Johnny's standing with musicians, whose political leanings could be generally described as liberal. Para-doxically, it seemed that because Cash was vocal on worthy causes, the left were prepared to overlook the views and beliefs they found unpalatable.

Johnny's standing among his peers was illustrated by Kris Kristofferson naming his son John Cash Kristofferson, while Larry Gatlin called his, Joshua Cash Gatlin. Another of the many compliments paid was Kellye Cash, a former Miss America and Johnny's great-niece, announcing that at her forthcoming wedding, the five attendants "will be wearing the traditional Cash black."*

Johnny's well-publicised drug problems made him a sought-after personality for those in the business of treating people with dependency problems. In June 1989, he was guest of honour at a conference organised by the University of Arkansas where he spoke frankly about his lifelong history of drug use. The conference was led by Dr Martha Morrison, described as an "addictionologist". A few months later, it was reported that Johnny had entered the Cumberland Heights Alcohol and Drug Treatment Center for a two-week stay to guard against the possibility of a relapse.

"I came in sober and I came in straight," he said. "Anyone who has under-gone drug treatment has the chance of a relapse and I am wise enough to know that. I enjoy my life too much to do that." Lou Robin simply said that Johnny began the treatment on the advice of his doctors, given that he had received strong painkillers during his recent heart bypass surgery.

◆ ◆ ◆ ◆ ◆

* After Kellye had won her Miss America title she appeared with Johnny to sing 'Jackson' at a celebratory dinner.

A Cash visit to Belfast brought about a transformation in the fortunes of one Irish singer. In 1989, Sandy Kelly released a cover of Patsy Cline's 'Crazy', which made number two in the Irish charts. Initially reluctant to record the song, it turned out to be a fortunate choice for Sandy when Johnny heard the song on the radio. At the time, Sandy was driving about in a battered old car doing interviews when a phone call came through for her. "Hi, I'm Johnny Cash, is that Sandy Kelly?" Sandy thought it was a joke. "No, it's Dolly Parton, pull the other one, it's got bells on." She soon realised it really was Cash. As Sandy explained, "He said he and June had heard 'Crazy' on the radio and wanted to meet me. He arranged for me to go to their concert that night in Belfast. Apparently Waylon Jennings had mentioned my name so I think maybe Johnny was looking out for me." Johnny asked Sandy to get to the venue early. "I didn't have time to change and so I was in the same pair of jeans I'd been wearing for weeks but what could I do?"

Their actual meeting had a farcical element to it. Sandy thought she might only have a few moments with Johnny and wanted a memento of the occasion. She arranged for a photographer friend to be on hand. "I told him to take a shot just as Johnny stepped out of the dressing room door. What I didn't know was that Johnny was his all-time hero so when Johnny stepped outside the door this guy fainted flat out." Despite such an introduction, Johnny invited Sandy into his dressing room where they played Patsy Cline songs with the Cash band. "It was like a dream but then he said to me, 'You're gonna be on stage tonight and you're gonna sing some of these songs.' So there I was on stage with Johnny Cash singing Patsy Cline songs. It had all happened so fast I could hardly take it in." Although a thrill for Sandy, Johnny was astute in having a popular Irish singer appear with him in front of her home crowd.

Sandy assumed it would be a case of goodbye and good luck, even when Johnny gave her his number and told her to call him in Nashville the following summer when Sandy would be in town for the annual Fan Fair extravaganza. She didn't help her cause by losing Johnny's phone number. "I was frantic about losing his number and didn't know how I would manage to get hold of him but then lo and behold three days later the Country Music Association phoned me saying Johnny had been in touch with them because he wanted to get hold of me. I must admit I felt a little bit triumphant."

Sandy was invited to a party at Johnny's house to launch a book which June had put together called *Mother Maybelle's Cookbook: A Kitchen Visit With America's First Family Of Song*. A feast of dishes from the book was laid on for the 250 guests who included 84-year-old Carrie Cash and the newest addition to the clan, Rosanne's baby daughter, also called Carrie. Barbecued beef, chicken and pork, a variety of vegetables, salads and gourmet desserts were available for the guests who sat at tables laid with sparkling crystal and silver and decorated with miniature orchids. After the feast there was an impromptu concert with

"It's important to be aware of what's going on," said Johnny. "You can get locked in your own little bayou of the river." (*Alan Messer/Star File*)

Johnny (with June and John Carter Cash) after being inducted into the
Country Music Hall Of Fame, Nashville, October 13, 1980. (*Corbis*)

The Cash homestead on Old Hickory Lake, Hendersonville, Tennessee, pictured in 1982.
(*Courtesy of Nashville Public Library*)

Everybody Loves A Nut - introducing Elton John on *Saturday Night Live*, 1982. (*Photofest*)

Country "supergroup" The Highwaymen – JC, Willie Nelson, Kris Kristofferson, and Waylon Jennings – toured and recorded three well-received albums between 1985 - 95. (*Courtesy of Nashville Public Library*)

June and Johnny with their closest friends, Waylon Jennings and Jessi Colter. In 1989, the four set up the Music Business Foundation for AIDS Research to raise funds toward helping the medical establishment find a cure for the disease. (*Redferns*)

At the 1994 Grammy Awards. L-R: John Carter Cash, June, JC, Rosanne Cash, and Rodney Crowell. *American Recordings* received the Grammy for Best Contemporary Folk Album and a NAMMIE (Nashville Music Awards) for Best Folk Album. (*Retna*)

American Recordings producer Rick Rubin and Johnny listen to play backs of their second collaboration, *Unchained*, Van Nuys, California, 1996. Rubin re-energised Cash's career, bringing his music and image to a new, younger audience. (*Retna*)

American Recordings and Johnny Cash would like to acknowledge the Nashville music establishment and country radio for your support.

The shot that shocked Nashville. The picture (taken in 1969 during a show at San Quentin Prison) appeared as a full-page ad in the industry bible *Billboard* in March 1998. (*Jim Marshall*)

The 'I Walk The Line' finale of the TNT special: *An All-Star Tribute To Johnny Cash*, April 1999.
L-R: Trisha Yearwood, Chris Isaak, John Carter Cash, Willie Nelson, W.S. Holland, June, JC,
Bob Wootton, Sheryl Crow, Kris Kristofferson and Wyclef Jean. (*Associated Press*)

Johnny being awarded with the National Medal of the Arts by President George W. Bush,
April 22, 2002, in a ceremony at Constitution Hall, Washington, D.C.
The award recipients are first nominated by the public, decided upon by the Council of the
National Endowment of the Arts and then finally by the President. (*Associated Press*)

Inseparable partners – Johnny and June Carter Cash approaching old age. Ironically, not long after Johnny was discharged from hospital after another life-threatening operation, June unexpectedly passed away on May 15, 2003 - a month before her 74th birthday. (*Alan Messer/Star File*)

A frail Johnny at June's memorial service, held at Hendersonville Memorial Gardens, outside Nashville, May 18, 2003. At Johnny's request, the ceremony was opened to the public, with approximately 2,500 people attending. "My daddy has lost his soul mate," said Rosanne Cash on behalf of her tearful, wheelchair-bound father. (*Associated Press*)

Johnny making a special appearance at the Carter Family Fold, in the Virginian mountains, June 21, 2003. Johnny was helped on stage by family members and held his guitar (although he did not play) as he sang six songs in tribute to June. (*Retna*)

"I don't carry any guilt about anything, including the hell I might have given people when I was using and abusing… God has forgiven me and it's drive on now." (*Corbis*)

songs from Rosanne, Rodney Crowell and Dottie West. At Johnny's urging, Sandy also sang.

After the party Johnny asked Sandy to stay for a while. "We went into his house and he sat in a big rocking chair in the kitchen. He took out a tape and played a song called 'Woodcarver' and said it was a song he'd had for some years. He'd been waiting to record it but he needed the right voice. He said he wanted a folky voice and I nearly died when he said he had thought about Emmylou Harris. I went back to my hotel and listened to it and just knew that my life was going to change.

"He was honest in a business with lots of false promises. I never asked for a contract but the whole thing really did happen. Three months later I was back in Nashville with Harold Bradley producing and it was quite a scene at his studio because there were film and news crews there. I was so nervous I stayed in the bathroom for half an hour. Eventually Harold came to the door and said, 'You can stay in there all day or you can come out here and cut this record.' When I came out Johnny was there eating yoghurt. I still have the carton and the spoon. It was the best day of my life."

Johnny gave Sandy the choice of what to record as the B-side. When she suggested 'Ring Of Fire' he winced and laughed, saying he was "kind of sick of that record". However, both 'Woodcarver' and 'Ring Of Fire' achieved gold status and the success of the record led to Sandy becoming one of Ireland's top singers, with her own television show.

◆ ◆ ◆ ◆ ◆

1990 once more saw America involved in war following the invasion of Kuwait by Iraqi forces led by Saddam Hussein. Although it was 20 years since their trip to Vietnam, the memories of the young lives lost and appalling injuries suffered were fresh in Johnny and June's memories. Prior to the launch of Desert Storm, they decided to use what influence they had in an attempt to impose restraint on American President George Bush, asking, in a letter, that the sanctions imposed be given more time to produce results, "Negotiate and re-negotiate and try to work it out without anybody dying."

In an interview from the following year, Johnny said, "I think a concerned, responsible citizen in a position of influence should tell the President of the United States what he thinks. He's got enough yes men around him, telling him how great he is. If I see something that I don't agree with or that I feel is unjust, I speak out." Having said that, once American troops were committed Johnny accepted the position and patriotically supported their endeavours. Indeed, he played at the Operation Desert Star benefit show for the families of personnel serving in the gulf.

In the first few months of 1990, two albums were released which enjoyed mixed fortunes. *Highwayman II*, another collection of mature, adult oriented, countrified rock songs, skilfully blended the talents of all four. As before there was a kind of mystical air to some of the material with Johnny, Willie, Waylon and Kris waxing lyrical about a farmer, a river boat gambler, a preacher, a murderer and a good woman who loves a bad man among others. Johnny managed to get in a rather self-congratulatory number, 'Songs That Make A Difference', based on the legendary guitar pull at his house in 1969 featuring Bob Dylan, Shel Silverstein, Joni Mitchell, Graham Nash, as well as "a few who came in off the street". There was real-life drama during one of the recording sessions for the album when Johnny and Kris Kristofferson heard gunshots out in the street. It turned out that an employee of *Cashbox* had been shot to death, his body being discovered by Candy Parton, a distant cousin of Dolly.

"Like the original record," wrote *Stereo Review*, "*Highwayman II* pays tribute to the spirit of the American hero throughout history as well as to the good brotherhood that bound the fraternities of the nineteenth-century settlers and vagabonds. Somehow, like mythic horsemen riding through time, the singers realise that they are moving into the roles of country music's elder statesmen." Though not scaling the heights achieved by the début album, *Highwayman II* still attained respectable critical and commercial success, reaching number four in the charts during a run of almost a year.

There was speculation that The Highwaymen project might have caused friction in certain areas. Writing in *Country Music People*, Spencer Leigh said, "Given the performers, I'm sure they don't care, but they have managers who . . . are obliged to do the best for their clients and so I suspect there are boardroom squabbles over the billing." Lou Robin suggests otherwise. "It was agreed that billing would be alphabetical so it really wasn't an issue. In concert they did the same number of songs, though they all sang back-up on other people's songs as well. They were all close friends. There were no ego problems."

In reality the billing varied and was certainly not alphabetical consistently. Waylon Jennings light-heartedly said that at times Johnny and Willie were competitive, "like Truman and MacArthur". While Kris Kristofferson was an outstanding songwriter, to the public he was the least familiar of the four, something he readily acknowledged. "I still don't know what I'm doing in this thing. It's like waking up and seeing your face on Mount Rushmore." None of this prevented some good banter on stage. On one occasion Kris told Willie he was losing his voice, to which Willie replied, "How can you tell?" One time, when Willie was singing 'Always On My Mind', Kristofferson told the audience he was doing it for the IRS.

In March, Johnny released *Boom Chicka Boom* – promoted as a "back to basics" album (the title being a giveaway). "Cash manages to re-create the stark backings which rocketed him to fame in the Fifties and sustained his top position for the following two decades," praised *Country Music People*. "It is not quite as austere as it was back then, but it is a return to basics." To emphasise the point, the photograph on the back sleeve shows Johnny's guitar with a piece of paper threaded through the strings to illustrate the way his percussive Sun sound was created. Appropriately enough, Johnny's mother Carrie sang on 'Family Bible'.

Boom Chicka Boom was a strong album featuring quality songs with an authentic Johnny Cash feel but, already, the relationship with Mercury had lost energy. The record was poorly promoted, becoming another statistic in a long line of Cash commercial failures. "I would get excited about my recording projects but nobody would share that," said Johnny, "and I kept hearing demographics until it was coming out of my ears." Johnny recalls talking to a record executive around this time. When asked what he was involved in, the man said, "We're looking for the new Randy Travis," to which Johnny exasperatedly shot back, "What's wrong with the old one?"

In a *Billboard* tribute to Cash, Robert K Oermann wrote, "For 35 years Cash has been the voice of those who have no voice of their own, the forgotten prisoner, the taken for granted labourer, the ignored homemaker, the exploited miner, the viciously cheated Native American, the oppressed migrant worker, the victims of racism, the downtrodden poor. Using his music, his celebrity status and the example he sets with his life, Cash has tried to give these Americans back the dignity society has tried to take away."

More recognition followed with a Grammy Living Legends Award – which had only been given to a few other major figures in popular music such as Quincy Jones and Aretha Franklin – which recognised Johnny's contribution went far beyond the confines of country music.

The release of the second Highwaymen album was followed by a two-week American tour to promote it. The opening show in Houston attracted more than 50,000 people, but, for Johnny, the tour was overshadowed by yet more health problems, with him experiencing excruciating pain for much of the time.

Lou Robin takes up the story. "John had gone for dental treatment to have a cyst and also a wisdom tooth removed from the same side of his mouth at the same time. The guy damaged his jaw. It was very painful but John was told that it was just the effects of the treatment and it would wear off. Two days later, when John bit on a piece of steak, he heard something crack and that was when his jaw broke fully. The trouble was he didn't realise the full scale of the problem and so he did all The Highwaymen shows before he realised it was something more serious and then he had to go and get it sorted out.

"He could have sued the dentist but he didn't want to destroy the dentist's livelihood. I said, 'John, you're suing insurance companies not the dentist. Someday it'll disable you and you'll be sorry that you didn't sue.' However, he wouldn't do it and it did lead to disability."

Johnny claimed he got through the shows with God's help, though his doctors told him it was because the adrenaline rush of performing temporarily blanked out the pain. During The Highwaymen tour, Johnny appeared on the television programme *Nashville Now*, applying an ice pack to his jaw when not on stage. It was reported that due to his previous drug problems Cash had refused to take any medication for the pain. As a result of remedial dental surgery and the insertion of a platinum plate for which Johnny required hospitalisation, a European tour set for March and April had to be cancelled. Of the shows that he did perform, one report from a concert in Joliet, Illinois said that his "rumbling bass baritone" trailed over some of the songs like a "shaky freight train". It was also suggested that old favourites such as 'I Walk The Line' were omitted because Johnny lacked the strength to do them justice – there being only a few flashes of "the old Cash".

As if the dental problems weren't enough, Johnny also suffered from herniated discs, which caused him much discomfort. Though he intended to have surgery it would have meant losing time from his busy schedule, so he chose to live with the pain. Just possibly, the words of Sam Phillips, talking about Gladys Presley's reluctance to see doctors, had some relevance, "You've got to remember with poor southern folk, it's a tradition not to go to the doctor until you're really sick."

◆ ◆ ◆ ◆ ◆

In March 1991 a tragedy struck Nashville which had a particularly chilling resonance for Johnny and June given their anxiety about flying. A plane carrying seven members of Reba McEntire's band as well as her tour manager crashed with the loss of all on board. It had a ghastly resonance for many in Nashville as Ralph Emery explained, "Almost everybody in the doomed band had played in other Nashville bands. Those eight people therefore were known by hundreds of other musicians who dot Nashville's spectacular Music Row. One could physically feel the collective grief along the Row, as well as the foreboding realisation among the living, touring musicians who thought that any one of them could have been on that plane. Each had jetted through darkness to still another show hundreds of times. There is no telling how many millions of miles Nashville entertainers ride and fly annually. Life hangs gingerly in the balance, dependent on tyres that don't blow out at high speed or planes that don't go down in foul weather."

Reba took a personal hand in organising the memorial service at Christ Church in Brentwood, Tennessee and asked Johnny to give a eulogy. It was a particularly dreadful ordeal because five days before the incident, his mother Carrie died at the age of 86. Johnny was still upset by his mother's passing and the contrast between her long and fulfilled life and those lives cut short was depressingly jarring. "Closing my mother's coffin was the hardest thing I ever had to do," he told Ralph Emery. The service was full and mourners had to be accommodated in the parking lot where the service was relayed by loudspeakers.

Drained and dispirited, Johnny felt emotionally ill-equipped to deliver a eulogy but nevertheless, he managed it. While performing the song 'Jim I Wore A Tie Today', Johnny substituted the names of those who had died.

The Cash family were shocked by the plane crash and it reminded them of their own mortality (June described the crashes which claimed the lives of Patsy Cline and three of her other friends, Cowboy Copas, Hawkshaw Hawkins and Randy Hughes as a case of Satan finding her weak spot), but as Lou Robin puts it, "For Johnny and the troupe, flying was a matter of necessity." In the early Seventies, the troupe had a scare when their plane had to abort a landing when it came in too steeply, making a second approach necessary. They were so shaken following the ordeal that they cancelled their connecting flight back to Nashville and took a bus. On another occasion, the troupe was diverted from Pittsburgh to Erie. On the first landing attempt, one wing brushed the runway before the pilot took the plane off the ground and circled until successfully landing at the second attempt to the great relief of those on board.

However, for Johnny performing was the single most important aspect of the music business and to give up flying (and therefore touring) would have been unthinkable. One writer described him as a "road addict", and no setback, whether it was drug withdrawal, open-heart surgery, or the responsibility of children, kept him away (though if it wasn't possible to take John Carter on tours, oversees tours were restricted to no more than 10 days). They might cause a temporary disruption but dealing with such inconveniences was merely a question of management and logistics. Some artists might have felt ready to quit the road after treading the boards for so many years, but for Johnny this was out of the question.

By the early Nineties, Johnny's shows were often in places he had previously played but on one occasion he performed at an unusual and unfamiliar town. Regal, Minnesota had a population of about 60 souls – two bars, a grain elevator, a church and a baseball field. As one resident put it, "It's the kind of place where you better put on your brakes a mile ahead if you don't want to miss it." It was not the kind of place Johnny Cash would be expected to play.

The show was set up by Mike Kampsen, whose father Herman was a country music fan in general and a Johnny Cash devotee in particular. Regal was transformed from a handful of houses to a town of almost 5,000, with people arriving 12 hours before show time to get good positions. Police had to mount quite an operation to deal with the cars which provided Regal with its first and last traffic jam, something of a novelty for the locals. According to press reports, some townsfolk revelled in the attention, though a few "let the greed come out", charging $8 for a backyard parking spot and $5 for a cheap pair of sunglasses. Disappointingly, Johnny was not in good voice as a result of a severe chest cold, but the reception he got was enthusiastic nonetheless, especially when Herman Kampsen got up on stage and sang with his hero. During the show Johnny said,

"Twenty years ago they had Woodstock, welcome to Cornstalk." Though there was talk of an annual event at Regal, this failed to materialise.

Around this time Johnny gave a helping hand to another struggling musician trying to make a name for himself in Nashville. Ronnie Dunn, a former psychology and theology student from Texas, had tried his luck at singing and songwriting with limited success and after his first marriage broke up, he and his new wife Janine moved to Nashville. Dunn had won a talent competition, and gotten to know a Music Row producer who introduced him to Johnny. Realising that Ronnie and his wife were struggling, he offered to let them stay in his Hendersonville cabin. Johnny visited one day and gave Ronnie one of his Man In Black stage suits, a gift of emotional as well as financial value, but reportedly told Dunn, "Don't tell June about it."

Ronnie and his writing partner Kix Brooks released their first album, *Brand New Man*, and, for the cover shot, Ronnie wore the suit Johnny had given him. For some time, Johnny's black outfits had been designed by Nudie Cohn, the man whose brightly patterned rhinestone suits, worn by such country singers as Webb Pierce and Porter Wagoner, had helped to define the image of country music for many people.

Beyond the major assets of property and cars, expenditure on luxury items was not something Johnny craved. The same could not be said for June who was passionate about shopping – particularly antique furniture, as well as glass and silverware – the kind of things which assisted nest building with her "Husband, lover, friend and brother in Christ", as she described Johnny in the dedication to her autobiography, *Among My Klediments*. Most of her purchases ended up at the lakeside house in Hendersonville, where visitors were impressed by the $50,000 chandelier in the master bedroom, various Norman Rockwell lithographs, Ming dynasty ornaments, animal skins and a ceramic washstand commemorating the marriage of Charles and Diana.

These nestled amid items Johnny brought to the house, such as numerous award plaques, antique pistols and sprays of cotton from Dyess. When asked what he thought was the secret to a long and happy marriage, Johnny quipped "Separate bathrooms." According to a feature in the *New York Times* magazine, June's bathroom was "Pure country diva" with "A wall of gold-veined mirrors and a bathtub the size of Tennessee ... and gilded girly furniture vying for attention with framed photographs of family, friends and celebrities like Paul and Linda McCartney and James Dean."

Journalist Adam Sweeting provided more vivid details of the way the house was furnished. Talking about the busily fitted out downstairs toilet, he said it "Looked as though it had been designed by a drunken surrealist with washbasins made from the halves of an enormous clam shell ... little leftover spaces were filled with statues of an elephant and a replica of Rodin's *The Thinker*."

One project Johnny had been working on for some time (which he had told

Waylon Jennings about in hospital) was the *New Testament*, a mammoth project with the resultant works covering no less than 14 cassettes. For Johnny it was a labour of love, as he explained in the footnotes. "To turn the word into the spoken word has long been my dream but little did I dream that speaking the New Testament aloud in its entirety would so much further enrich my spiritual life . . . I have strived against reading any personal interpretation into the scripture. The most powerful, uniquely dramatic words ever written do not need any special attempt on my part to sell them. I chose the new King James version because it retains much of the beauty and classic prose and poetry of the original King James version yet it is easily understood by those who might have said, 'I've read the Bible but I don't understand it.' "

The collection was honoured in 1991 when it won Album Of The Year at the annual Angel International Awards[*] in Beverly Hills. Not long before, Johnny had received another award to add to his groaning sideboard from the London based *Country Music People* magazine, which acknowledged his loyal following in Britain. The Heritage Award was voted on by punters not pundits, a condition being that the recipient had to have given at least 25 years service to country music.

The award, presented at the House Of Cash by the late Wally Whyton, was given at a time when Johnny was recuperating from dental surgery and the enforced rest and inability to tour was frustrating for him. "I love performing and being kept indoors like this is giving me cabin fever." June took the opportunity to comment on the ever-present issue of the problems associated with drugs. "John, being a chemically dependent person, has had to deal with pain and what he can and can't have to fight it. He's probably the strongest man I know. He's a survivor."

When Johnny got back to Europe in spring 1991 the audience figures for his shows were something of a disappointment. An economic recession was biting hard, but in addition, the demand for what were perceived as old country acts was steadily diminishing. Along with Tammy Wynette and Crystal Gayle, Johnny headlined the Wembley Festival, Britain's première country music event, which provided a joyful meeting for at least one of the performers. In 1989, George Hamilton V (son of IV) had been invited to sing 'I Walk The Line' at an awards ceremony at Nashville's Vanderbilt Plaza Hotel. "I arranged a slow, folky ballad version of the song accompanied by my guitar and a fiddle. I sang the song staring straight into the eyes of Johnny Cash and June Carter who were seated in the front row about 15 feet away.

"You can't imagine how hard it is to sing someone their own hit signature song or how ridiculous you're going to feel doing it until you're actually doing

---

[*] The Angel International Awards are given to honour productions of outstanding moral, spiritual and social impact.

it." George had intended getting Johnny to autograph a copy of his 1975 auto-biography *Man In Black* after the show but was so "freaked" by the experience that he decided against it. In 1991, having fully recovered from his ordeal, George was at Wembley and decided that he would like to meet Johnny. He waited near his limousine after the show and, "as Johnny and June headed out of the dressing room and walked towards the car, I introduced myself and they both said in unison, 'We loved how you sang "I Walk The Line",' an endorse-ment which is a real source of pride to me." What George did not know was that back in 1956 Johnny had conceived the song as a slow number and was origin-ally unhappy with the Sam Phillips-inspired up-tempo version which went on to become a hit.

The Wembley Festival had been a fixture for over 20 years, but audience numbers declined to the extent that 1991 proved to be the last one. New hat acts like Garth Brooks and Clint Black cut a swathe through the country music scene which would change it forever by bringing rock elements to the fore, both in terms of the music and the staging of shows. More traditional acts were rele-gated to the fringes and pure country became even more of a minority taste than it had been before. It was a pattern which continued throughout the Nineties, affecting country music strongholds all over the world. Against this background Johnny's latest single, 'Goin' By The Book', only struggled to number 70 in the *Billboard* chart. This was not to say that there was any shortage of recognition of Johnny's body of work. Indeed, at the start of 1992 he received an award which placed him in an elite category few could aspire to.

27

THOUGH JOHNNY CASH is generally referred to as a country singer, it would be wrong to define his style as country. It has encompassed many styles – opera and jazz being notable exceptions – and created some new ones along the way. Recognition of his importance to rock music came at the start of 1992 when he was inducted into the Rock And Roll Hall of Fame based in Cleveland, Ohio. Fellow inductees were The Yardbirds, Sam and Dave, Booker T. & The M.G.s, the Jimi Hendrix Experience, The Isley Brothers and Bobby "Blue" Bland. Johnny's induction reunited him with some of the people he had worked closely with over the years. Sam Phillips (a "non-performer inductee") was one of the first to be admitted at the Hall of Fame's inception in 1986 and others who followed included Elvis Presley, Roy Orbison, Carl Perkins, Bob Dylan, and much later, Pete Seeger. Jimmie Rodgers, Hank Williams and Bill Monroe were admitted as "early influence inductees".

The Hall of Fame biography for Cash stressed the breadth and importance of his music. "What Cash and his group The Tennessee Two brought to the Sun sound was a Spartan mix of guitar, stand-up bass and vocals that served as an early example of rockabilly . . . he straddled the country, folk and rockabilly idioms . . . a prototype for the black-clad rebel rocker." Referring to the late Sixties it went on, "The rugged simplicity and uncut honesty of Cash's approach was steadily seeping into rock'n'roll by way of the burgeoning country rock scene." Johnny would dispute the reference to the Million Dollar Quartet session taking place, "*sans* Cash who stays only briefly." Johnny maintained that he was heavily involved in the event though it's hard to find two accounts of that legendary afternoon which tally.

The honour was bestowed on Johnny at a star-studded ceremony at New York's Waldorf-Astoria, with such luminaries as Keith Richards, Jeff Beck, John Fogerty and Jimmy Page in attendance. Rumour has it that when Keith Richards found himself in the men's room with Johnny he started singing 'Loading Coal' (from the *Ride This Train* album) and suggested a photograph to commemorate them meeting in such a remarkable location. Johnny declined. At the end of the show there was the bizarre sight of Johnny taking part in the closing jam featuring such "classic rock" songs as 'Purple Haze' and 'Green Onions'. It's a sign of the immense reach of Johnny Cash's art that he is the only musician to have been inducted into the Country Music Hall of Fame, the Rock And Roll Hall of Fame and the Songwriter's Hall of Fame. As a sign of the highly variable nature of his career, the day after receiving his Rock And Roll Hall of Fame award, he recorded an appearance on the children's television programme *Sesame Street.* Projects for children appealed to Johnny and he narrated stories such as *The Good, The Bad, And The Two Cookie Kid* for a series of audio tapes accompanying the hardback books.

◆ ◆ ◆ ◆ ◆

Despite smoking contributing to Johnny's heart problems and an avowed intention never to touch another cigarette, June's doubts about his ability to kick the habit proved to be well founded. Newspaper and magazine interviewers regularly commented upon Johnny's addiction, often in the context of his nervous, edgy demeanour. The introduction to a 1991 *Q* magazine article referred to Johnny's tendency to twitch and blink. "His hands are restless and his eyes sometimes seem about to roll over with exhaustion. Johnny Cash's legend . . . doesn't stop his knee from bobbing restlessly beneath the table or his hands from reaching for yet another Winston." In the early Nineties, Johnny claimed that he had given up smoking, having had his last cigarette in England some years before. Yet in an interview for the *Sunday Express* in 1991, he conceded that he still smoked but the interviewer was told firmly by Cash and his manager that there were to be no photographs of their man with cigarette in hand.

"I love smoking," Johnny sheepishly explained, "and I know I shouldn't but I always stop two to three hours before a concert." In effect he was turning his back on the potentially serious consequences, preferring to risk damage to his health rather than kicking cigarettes. It was further evidence of his addictive personality. "I have a disease called chemical dependency and I've had it all my life, which means I'm in recovery now because I don't use drugs or drink . . . and it's a great life without drugs and alcohol." In an interview with the *Daily Mirror* at the tail end of 1988, he said, "It's great to be able to go on stage and enjoy myself for a couple of hours and remember every minute of what I did. In the past I was cheating my audience." Johnny made this statement not long before his heart surgery, and continued to make similar claims, yet by 1992 he was back in treatment for drug dependency.

True to form, when Johnny was struck by ill health he found it impossible to exercise self-control by restricting himself to taking medication in the doses and time periods prescribed by his doctors. Cash reportedly sought counselling from his friend Billy Graham, admitting, "I've had to take far too many painkillers and flirted with disaster." In July, he booked himself under an assumed name into the Loma Linda Behavioral Medical Center in California, staying there for three weeks during which he received therapy for alternative pain management. Cash himself described it as "a fascinating system of mind games and self-hypnosis. With God's help and the continued support of my family, friends and fans I know I'll be able to end this nightmare." By August he was back on the road again.

Journalist Tom Zucco effectively contrasted Johnny's still impressive appearance with the inevitable and poignant signs of ageing. "He reminds you of a photograph of Abraham Lincoln in his later years. He has a presence about him, but he also looks tired and worn. His silver and black hair was brushed back and he was wearing what he always does, black coat, black pants, black shirt, black boots. A silver conchos was hung around his neck and a hearing aid was carefully tucked in his right ear. His face was weathered. His eyes were red." Whatever his condition, Johnny remained instantly recognisable and, in a 1992 *Rolling Stone* interview, he admitted to occasionally disguising himself. Once he donned a blonde wig, some sunglasses and a yellow shirt but was recognised almost immediately.

During a summer vacation on his tour bus, he pulled into the small town of Lonoke in the early afternoon. Word quickly spread and Johnny was soon surrounded by people, posing for photographs and signing autographs which turned the simple act of buying two scoops of ice cream into a day to remember for the people of Lonoke and another reminder for Johnny of the price of fame. Examining the countless interviews Johnny Cash has given over the years it's clear that some journalists got more out of him than others. This was attributable to either a jaded lack of interest on his part or on the limited skills of a particular journalist. Writing for the *Daily Telegraph*, journalist Tony Parsons was concerned that, being one of several people granted an audience, he might simply be treated to a few blandishments. Knowing that Cash was a collector of coins he started the interview by giving him a Churchill crown. The strategy succeeded and Parsons was allowed more than the allotted 15 minutes.

◆ ◆ ◆ ◆ ◆

In 1992, Johnny became interested in a venture proposed by businessman David Green of a 2,500-seat theatre and theme park, inspired by and dedicated to Cash, built on a 140 acre site in Branson, Missouri. This would become the principal venue for his live concerts, providing 300 full-time and 450 seasonal jobs with an annual payroll of around $7 million. There was to be a Johnny Cash museum on the site and long-time Cash fan and collector Jan Flederus entered talks with Lou Robin who was interested in buying part of his collection for the project.

Branson has something of a negative image among some sections of the music industry who perceive it as a place where artists past their sell-by date are put out to pasture. Others argue its merits as an outstanding holiday destination, where visitors can visit the beautiful Ozark Mountains and take in a highly polished evening show. Though the rapid expansion has at times been chaotic, all year round theatres dedicated to artists such as Roy Clark, Andy Williams and Moe Bandy continue to do good business, and a well organised commercial operation brings many thousands of visitors on package holidays throughout the year.

This might all sound rather tame for the man in black but in fact the shows his troupe had been putting on for years could have been easily categorised as family entertainment. For nearly four decades Johnny Cash had spent each year undergoing the rigours of travelling all over America and beyond. He wasn't getting any younger and was increasingly dogged by health problems. While he didn't want to stop performing live, Branson had a definite appeal in that the people could come to him rather than vice versa. The idea was for two daily shows, five days a week, two weeks per month.

Tommy Cash was hired for promotion but after a while he became aware of the venture's pitfalls.

"It was originally going to be called the Johnny Cash Theater but the final plans were for the whole thing to be called Cash Country. David Green hired me to work as a PR director and to promote the project. He sent me to TV stations all around the Midwest within several hundred miles of Branson. The theatre was about 80 per cent complete when we began to hear that David Green was in financial trouble and wasn't paying all the bills and was being saturated with claims from people who were working on the theatre and weren't getting paid. It wasn't long after that, he filed for bankruptcy. He had already booked several hundred thousand dollars worth of talent for the opening weeks and months of the theatre."

At this stage Johnny had no direct financial interest in the venture but with Green's problems this became a possibility and as Tommy Cash explains, "I think David, possibly in conjunction with the court, offered to sell the whole thing to Johnny and June. I seem to remember the figure asked was in the region of $4 million but by that time they had decided that doing over 200 shows a year in the same place would kill them so they passed on buying him out. A lot of us were disappointed. I would have done a spot in the afternoons with my band and Sandy Kelly from Ireland was going to be part of the show and as a matter of fact she spent six months or so over in Branson rehearsing before it all collapsed."

Johnny subsequently played shows at Branson's Wayne Newton Theater but after the David Green deal fell apart the appeal of the idea of a permanent performing base in Branson wore off. The theatre was eventually sold with the approval of a federal bankruptcy judge for $4.1 million. Some fans who'd bought tickets, unfairly felt that Johnny had let them down. Cash did what he could to ensure that where possible ticket money was refunded. Though disappointed by the outcome Sandy Kelly had a great experience during her time in Branson. As well as getting to know Johnny, she developed a close friendship with Helen and Anita Carter, who were very supportive of a young Irish "colleen" (as the press dubbed her) so far from home but Sandy took a little longer to get to know June. "At the beginning I was a little scared of her but of course she always looked out for him."

Sandy particularly appreciated the consideration and kindness shown to her at a time when Johnny was experiencing health and business problems. "I worked with Johnny in Branson and because it turned out to be a financial disaster he felt responsible because it was his name, but none of it was his fault. I had a really nice condo and Johnny phoned quite often to see how I was. There was one time when Johnny went to Dublin with The Highwaymen, so he was in Dublin where my family were and I was in Branson. He arranged for my husband and children to go backstage and get priority seating. It was really thoughtful."

Lou Robin also witnessed many random acts of Cash kindness over the years. "We were in the car one time in Nashville and we saw this one legged man at the side of the road. Johnny stopped the car and it turned out the guy was on his way to Vanderbilt Hospital for some treatment. It wasn't that far away but Johnny picked him up and took him to a hotel and confirmed that he would be responsible for his bill right up until the time he had to be in the hospital for his operation. The guy was overwhelmed, it was like a fairy tale, but though he thought Johnny looked familiar he didn't actually know who he was. He was from the mountains where even Johnny's fame may not have reached."

On another occasion Johnny sought to help a child at a school where he was playing a show. The school locker rooms were being used as the dressing room and Lou Robin found Johnny walking along the lockers, looking through the gratings of each one. "He said he was trying to figure out which shoes looked like they were the rattiest and he pushed a $20 bill through the gratings so that that particular kid could buy a new pair of trainers."

Writing for the *Cape Cod Times*, Dan McCullough reported another act of kindness by which he was greatly moved, even though by McCullough's own admission, he had "never been a big fan of country and western music". However, he had two friends – Bobby, a Down's syndrome adult and Gordon, a congenitally brain-damaged adult – who were rabid Cash fans. When Dan read that Johnny Cash was coming to his hometown of Boston he tried pulling a few strings to arrange for his friends to meet Johnny. His efforts bore fruit when he was told that he and his friends should be at a certain stage door at a certain time on the night of the concert. Dan decided not to tell his friends for fear of disappointing them in the event (likely in his view) that it might not happen.

The trio duly turned up at the appointed place and time but after waiting for some minutes and with the concert due to begin, Dan was relieved he had done the right thing in not telling Bobby and Gordon about the rendezvous. "My back is to a dressing room area. My two pals are facing me, and they're not having a good time. They're bored and confused. A minute later I'm reviewing my first-aid training, because it's clear that both Bobby and Gordon have gone into some sort of aphasiac seizure at the same time. Their eyeballs are frozen on an object behind me. I turn around. The object says, 'Hi Dan, I'm Johnny Cash.'"

For the next half hour Johnny chatted away with Dan, Bobby and Gordon "as if they were just three guys back in their neighbourhood." When it came time for Johnny to go, Dan was especially moved by what followed. "Bobby said, 'I say a prayer for you every night Johnny.' Cash looked like someone had punched him in the stomach. Then Gordon hit him with a left hook: 'I don't pray for you every night, but just on Sunday when I go with my mom.' Johnny was visibly moved but he had to go because it was show time." The trio only just made it into their seats in time to catch the start of the first song, 'Ring Of Fire' played especially for them. "So, country and western music?" Dan mused. "Naah, doesn't do much for me. But Johnny Cash? Well, let's just say I'm a big fan."

Sandy Kelly's involvement with Johnny Cash was to last, on and off, for about five years, during which she appeared on some shows during his European tours. On one British tour, she slept on the coach next to Helen. Sandy recalled an example of Johnny's childlike sense of humour when she woke up to a sudden flash of light to find that Johnny was taking pictures of everybody while they were asleep. She also recalls how he passed time on the bus. "He sewed a lot. He had a box with lots of buttons that he had collected from various places and would sew them onto his jacket. He also makes things out of leather and suede. I asked him to make something for me and later a package arrived in Ireland which was a replica of a spirit mantle he wears around his neck."

Sandy is in no doubt that her involvement with Johnny boosted her own career tremendously. When she was given her own prime-time Sunday night television show in Ireland, Johnny was the first guest. In order to give the initial show a memorable launch, the producers decided to record it on location. The experience gave Sandy another opportunity to observe Johnny at close quarters. "We went to a lovely old castle in the west of the island and stayed there over the weekend with Johnny and the family. We had a party and everybody dressed up, Johnny as an Indian and June as a page 3 model – really. She looked fabulous. We had the castle for the whole weekend and it was great fun. Johnny was behind the bar doing the drinks." Sandy remembers the pleasure Johnny took in connecting with the surroundings. "I remember looking out of the window of that medieval castle and seeing him walking around the grounds on his own and the freedom he had, nobody bothered him, and he seemed to really love that."

She also got a taste of the blacker side of Johnny's humour. "I was in Nashville visiting the House Of Cash and Johnny started clowning around. He got down on one knee and he started singing to me. It was all really rather ridiculous. Then suddenly he said in alarm, 'God what is that, what is that terrible smell.' And you know, like a woman does, I was wanting to smell good and be perfect and he's talking about this terrible smell. Then he says he thinks it's cat shit and tells me to look at the bottom of my shoes. So I took off my shoe and then he started roaring with laughter. I was really annoyed and said I didn't think that was very nice. He started asking me to forgive him but I said no. It was all in fun really but I kept it up for a while but then eventually my manager said, 'Sandy, whatever it was, FORGIVE him.' That Christmas I sent Johnny a bar of soap to get rid of the smell.

"One thing that kind of upset him was when I said it was very hard to be his friend because there are so many layers you have to get through to get to him. I think it hurt his feelings and yet once you're there he's great. At times he seemed so lonely. He had everything but there was this little boy in him that wanted to do things like get in a jeep and drive all round Ireland."

Overall, Sandy Kelly's assessment is positive. "I spent a lot of time with Johnny and the family. I found him very motivated with a great sense of humour, modest and humble and really kind. I remember I was hosting a radio show in Ireland one time and the producer automatically thought that I would be able to interview Johnny on the show. It was all stupid really but they kind of put me into a corner about it. I phoned Reba at the House of Cash and within 10 minutes he was on the phone and did the interview.

"There was another time I was with him when he was going to be playing at the Wembley Festival where I had never appeared before. He just decided there and then that I would appear with him that night and we sang 'Woodcarver' together." The consideration shown to Sandy went well beyond her professional career. "When my daughter was ill, they phoned to see if I wanted her to be flown to the USA to be treated by their doctors. I feel I've always got somewhere I could go for help."

Though from different religious backgrounds, Johnny and Sandy share a belief in the power of God. "I believe that God brought me to Johnny Cash. A night or two before I met Johnny I was at an all-time low. I had recorded 'Crazy' and I remember talking to Patsy Cline. I'm not a craw thumper but I looked up and asked her to let me have the song for six months. I went to a prayer meeting and queued up to get a blessing. Something happened that night, I felt woozy, all a bit strange and then the next day or so I got the call from Cash."

◆ ◆ ◆ ◆ ◆

While Johnny had enjoyed a number of high-profile industry celebrations of his own career, the roles were reversed when he was invited to be a guest at a

Madison Square Garden concert on October 16, to mark the 30th anniversary of Bob Dylan's first release on CBS. To get in the mood, Johnny sang 'Blowin' In The Wind' on *The David Letterman Show* the night before the concert. The surviving members of Booker T. & The M.G.s formed the nucleus of the backing band for an eclectic roll-call of stars, including Neil Young, George Harrison, Eric Clapton, Roger McGuinn, Lou Reed, Tracy Chapman, The Clancy Brothers with Tommy Makem, Willie Nelson and Kris Kristofferson, who performed in front of a sell-out 18,000 audience. Rosanne Cash joined with Shawn Colvin and Mary Chapin Carpenter to do a swinging countrified version of 'You Ain't Goin' Nowhere'.

Johnny and June performed a celebratory, down-home version of 'It Ain't Me Babe', then joined in a rousing finale of 'Knockin' On Heaven's Door' with the other guests. Dylan reappeared on his own to close the show with 'Girl From The North Country'. Because this served as a personal farewell, Cash did not join him for the song.

Early in 1993, the Johnny Cash show set off on yet another European tour but, bizarrely, British performances were confined to two shows at Butlin's Southcoast World at Bognor Regis. *Q* magazine described it as "Surely one of the least likely bookings in the history of popular music."* The package included a chalet for three nights, meals and a ticket to see Johnny Cash, all for £61. From his interview with *Q* it was clear that Johnny didn't get what made Butlin's such a terrible step-down for an artist of his stature. (The weekend after, it was the turn of Rolf Harris to entertain the troops.) With a hint of defiance, Cash said, "I'll play anywhere the demand is and where they can afford to bring us . . .† I'd liken (Butlin's) to Asbury Park, New Jersey in its heyday, games on the boardwalk, Ferris wheels, stuff for kids and shows for adults. Everyone enjoys getting away to the ocean." The affair may have been decidedly low-rent but the audience response, especially for the second show, was wildly enthusiastic and a total of around 4,000 fans went home happy.

In contrast to the brief stopover in Britain, Johnny played seven concerts in Ireland. The show in Dublin was attended by three members of U2, all longtime Cash devotees, and Johnny invited Bono up to duet with him on 'Big River'. Cash bass player Dave Roe, who had only joined the band at the tail end of 1992, remembers it well. "When Bono came out he knelt down on the stage in an act of supplication in front of each member of the band which was a new experience for me. He didn't know the lyrics of 'Big River' though, because he had them neatly written on his forearm."

Sandy Kelly, who also appeared that night, recollected that Bono actually kissed Johnny's feet and on an earlier occasion when U2 had gone to one of

---

* Butlin's being a popular (and cheap) British holiday camp.
† The price of booking Johnny Cash at this time was said to be $50,000.

Johnny's shows in Dublin, they had to stand at the back because the show was a sell-out. The shows in provincial Ireland were staged in smaller venues but were invariably packed. For the locals, "it was sort of like the Pope had come to town," Roe described. In an interview with the *Dublin Evening Herald* Johnny detailed the pressures he had to contend with on a daily basis. "People pull me from so many directions, so many different angles. Some are good, some are ridiculous, some are insulting, some take up a lot of time and some are important, like folks that care about human rights." Tommy Cash recalls similar comments from Johnny when family or friends asked for favours or help. "Johnny often complained that people came to him asking for help, money, whatever. He'd say, 'Just because they're having a crisis doesn't necessarily mean I'm not having one.' Lots of people saw him as this godfather kind of figure who could sort out people's problems."

If the Butlin's show represented some kind of career low, an event that occurred on the Irish tour triggered a reversal of Johnny's artistic fortunes. Before the Dublin show Johnny teamed up with U2 at their Windmill Lane studio. The group were in the middle of recording their new album *Zooropa* and were experiencing some difficulties as Bono explained, "You know Johnny Cash was in town. We had this song ('The Wanderer') that we were working on and it wasn't working out. We got this new melody but I couldn't sing it so we wrote lyrics because Johnny Cash was in town. He was a hero of ours, somebody that we were in awe of." It was put to Bono that the new album had an expansive vista and that the addition of Johnny Cash was a surreal touch. Bono agreed. "Well, he's the antidote to 'Zooropa'. You're quite right. He is the other side of that song. He's the end of it. It's the same song really, it's just about going out there and Johnny Cash has been out there. That's why we dig him. That guy is hard. He's as hard, he's as tough-minded, he's as tender, he's as wise, he's as surreal as you would hope. Listen, Johnny Cash – we were following him around for years. He's a badass. He's the real McCoy. We're all just little fucking apprentices.

"You know, myself and Adam (Clayton – U2 bassist), at the end of the Joshua Tree tour we drove across America just rootin' through the rubble. We got to Nashville and we met up with this guy called Cowboy Jack (Clement). He brought us to Johnny Cash's house and Johnny Cash was really cool about it, he looked after us really well. He even took me to a zoo – you know that Johnny Cash has a zoo?" Johnny laid on dinner and Bono recalled his wry sense of humour. "We bowed our heads and John spoke this beautiful poetic grace and we were all humbled and moved. Then he looked up afterwards and said, 'Sure do miss the drugs though.'"

Johnny's voice provided what Bono felt was missing from U2's previous efforts. "He is the Wanderer and he's kind of in character in the song." Consideration of one line from the song provides strong evidence for this view: "I went out there to taste and to touch and to feel as much as a man can before he repents." Despite his iconic status, Johnny was in the commercial doldrums. The association with U2 contributed to the process of raising his profile, and of reaching a new audience with renewed credibility. As one writer put it, "Almost overnight a new generation was exposed to the low growl, the real raw danger of Johnny Cash."

In a way it was payback time. Johnny benefited from a lifelong readiness to make common cause with artists of all ages from all musical styles. Just as he had helped out by featuring them on his television shows or recording their songs, he was not too proud to accept a reciprocal favour. While Johnny was hardly struggling, he had, to use one of his own sayings, been "spinning his wheels" for some time. The relationship with Mercury proved unproductive, with his five albums for the company selling a little over 200,000 copies. Johnny claimed that only 500 copies were pressed of his last 1991 album, *The Mystery Of Life* (featuring the prophetically titled 'I'll Go Somewhere And Sing My Songs Again'). As *Country Music International* put it, "A lot of the Mercury material had noxious studio tweakery layered on in a desperate sop to country radio which didn't care anyway."

In considering the other options available, acting had already been ruled out ("They are not exactly beating my door down bringing me offers for movies any more you know"), and a record company desk job certainly did not appeal, nor did becoming an ageing TV celeb. The association with U2 was undoubtedly helpful but the creative catalyst for the transition to the next phase of Johnny's career was to come from what was, on the face of it, the least likely source imaginable.

Long-haired and bearded rock and rap producer Rick Rubin had co-founded Def Jam Records in New York in the early Eighties, associated with such pioneering groups as Run DMC and The Beastie Boys, as well as dark metal acts like Slayer. He produced the successful rock album *Bloodsugarsexmajik* for Red Hot Chili Peppers, so why he would be interested in taking on an ageing legend was a curiosity (though he had just finished work on Mick Jagger's third solo album *Wandering Spirit*). It was very much Rubin who took the initiative, having to reach a financial settlement with Mercury to buy Johnny out of the remainder of his contract. Johnny had initially been sceptical when Lou Robin informed him that Rick Rubin requested a meeting.

According to Lou, "When the two men did meet for the first time they just stared at each other for a while to sum each other up." In a series of meetings which started soon after the European tour ended, Johnny gradually became convinced that Rubin had the kind of broad vision that would allow him the artistic freedom in the studio he had craved for so long. Johnny explained their union. "He heard I wanted to cut ties with Mercury Records because it had been an unsuccessful venture, on their part and my part. So Rick called my manager and said he'd like to sign me. He didn't say he'd like to talk about it, he said he'd like to sign me. So when we met I asked him, 'What kind of album would you like me to record?' And he said, 'Whatever Johnny Cash is, that's what I want on a record.' He made me feel like Sam Phillips made me feel."

There were other parallels between Rubin and Phillips. Each man was at the cutting edge of popular music innovation, blending styles and concocting new sounds, while at the same time respecting and building on what had gone before. Most importantly, like Phillips, Rubin made it clear that there would be no time constraints in the studio. Johnny was particularly excited at the prospect of recording an unplugged album comprising just him, his guitar and some of his favourite songs, a project he had discussed a quarter of a century previously with Marty Robbins.

The irony was that Rubin knew very little about country music. To help him do his homework, Johnny bought Rick a box set of one of his all-time favourite artists, Hank Snow. Some cynics thought that Rubin knew nothing about Cash other than that he was cool, his contract was about to run out, and that the choice of Cash was really just pragmatic opportunism. In an interview with the *Daily Texan* given after he had started working with Cash, Rubin didn't totally reject this view but insisted that he could get the best out of his new signing. "I had mainly worked with young artists on my label, young new artists and I thought it would be really interesting to try to work with a legendary classic guy. I tried to think of who was like that, who really wasn't in the best place or wasn't treated so well at the label they were at. John came to mind, he was the first one that came to my mind you know, the quintessential icon artist in America. It just didn't seem like he was cherished. He's a great man.

"I always had a vision of who he was and I think that sometimes it was harder for him to see how people saw him, so I would always try to direct it back. You know he'd play me some songs he liked and I'd say that's a nice song but I don't think that's what people expect from Johnny Cash, people want something more serious whether it be religious or political or scary or life and death or whatever it is. There's a certain amount of weight that you want from Johnny Cash that is clearly part of his vocabulary but he really didn't focus on it. I tried to focus on it more."

Soon Johnny and Rick were hard at work laying down songs as part of their musical and personal bonding. What Johnny came to call his "third career" was now underway.

PART V

The Road Goes On Forever

"Like a shark, gotta keep moving."

28

DURING THE SUMMER and early winter of 1993 Johnny and Rick spent long hours in Cedar Hill Refuge Recording Cabin (Johnny's comfortable and well-equipped studio in the Hendersonville wilderness) and the living room of Rubin's apartment in Los Angeles. Some songs were well known to Johnny, the more recent came from the pens of Leonard Cohen, Tom Waits and Kris Kristofferson, as well as the less obvious choice of heavy rock artist, Glenn Danzig. In all, they recorded around 120 songs, far more than the usual 30 or so Johnny was used to laying down. When Johnny signed to Rubin's American Recordings label both men instinctively recognised that a wide range of songs should be worthy of consideration.

It wasn't only in his choice of record label that Johnny was prepared to toe an unconventional line. In 1992, he was looking for a new bass player when the name of Dave Roe was suggested by one of Dave's friends who told Johnny that Dave could play slap bass. Without an audition Johnny hired him. "After I got the gig," said Roe, "I said to Johnny that I would see him at the rehearsal before the first show I was going to play. Johnny said there wouldn't be a rehearsal and that I should just turn up backstage. I said in that case I'd just see him at the soundcheck. No soundcheck either, so I just turned up in time for the actual show." After the show Johnny took Dave aside. "You can't play slap bass, can you?" to which Dave confessed that he couldn't. When asked why he had taken the job, he said, "I just wanted to say I'd played with Johnny Cash."

Roe assumed he'd blown it but Johnny roared with laughter and confirmed the job was his. It was the start of an association which has resulted in Dave's respect for Johnny growing ever greater. "I've worked for about 12 major artists over the years and of them all Johnny Cash is my favourite. He's the most interesting and the most intellectual. He can talk about a wide variety of subjects and is generally well informed. And he knows so much about so many kinds of music. I've heard him say he knows about a thousand songs and Jack Clement said on one of his albums Johnny knew about two thousand. I reckon the truth is nearer five thousand."

Johnny continued to play shows all over America (including several at Branson) and made television appearances, singing 'Don't Take Your Guns To Town' on *The David Letterman Show*, and an extended cameo appearance as Kid Cole in *Dr Quinn Medicine Woman*. The latter (starring Jane Seymour) fitted in well with Johnny's character since it was strong on old-style family values and the pioneering spirit which had forged modern America. In advance of the release of his first Rubin-produced album, Johnny played a show at The Viper Room, a rock nightclub in West Hollywood owned by Johnny Depp, star of such cult films as *Edward Scissorhands*. Although it hadn't been open long, the venue had already become notorious, thanks, in part, to another hip young actor, River Phoenix, dying of a drugs overdose on Halloween night in 1993.

The small venue only held about 250 people and in early December, introduced by Depp, Johnny played his first solo concert in some 30 years. The invitation only audience of around 250 included Hollywood insiders and stars such as Dwight Yoakam, Sean Penn, Juliette Lewis, and Barbara Orbison who came forward to hug Johnny after his version of her late husband's hit, 'Ooby Dooby'. That Johnny's performance was so ecstatically received was another sign of his growing recognition as a true pioneer. After the show Johnny said, "I noticed the young people responding wildly to things where I hadn't had the same response since maybe the Fifties and Sixties. It was a real kick for me."

Early in 1994, Johnny played some shows in New Zealand and was amused to come across Ian Signal, a retired horse breeder and racer who had a whole stable of horses named after country music singers; naturally one was called Johnny Cash which had apparently won 11 races in the course of its career. In March, sporting a shamrock, Johnny appeared at the annual SXSW (South by Southwest) conference, an important trade fair for all aspects of the music and film industry. Johnny gave a speech in which he talked about the first hillbilly folk record he ever heard, 'Hobo Bill's Last Ride', and the music which fired his imagination, The Carter Family, Jimmie Rodgers and Gene Autry, "real basic stuff, just voice and guitar," indicating that's what he had returned to with Rick Rubin and American Recordings. Johnny interspersed his speech with songs from the new album *American Recordings*, which was now due for release.

Entertainment Weekly was full of praise for Johnny's performance saying he "balanced humour and portentousness and the rockabilly back-up band transformed the elder statesman into a whooping cow punk playing the jaded yet rapt crowd like a revivalist preacher." Johnny also played a set at Emo's, a grungy, partially open-air punk club with room for about 500 people with many turned away. This plus the Viper Room appearance, as well as a show at the Fez Club, a hip New York venue frequented by showbiz types, further established Cash in territory previously unfamiliar to a country music icon. Kris Kristofferson added his voice to the chorus of approval, "He stands out in any bunch just by his reality, just by the heart and soul of his music. It's like watching an old coyote walk through a poodle party."

The mayor of Austin presented Johnny with the key to the city and named March 17, 1994, Johnny Cash Day. Even for such a seasoned entertainer, appearing in front of new audiences with just his guitar was quite daunting, as he revealed in an interview with *You* magazine when asking, "What will people think of me?"

Although critics had been interested in the changes taking place in Johnny's career, it seems that nothing had quite prepared them for *American Recordings*, released in April. *Country Music*'s reviewer described it as "utterly unanticipated".

The album was exactly what Johnny had wanted it to be, namely a collection of old and new songs, with the only accompaniment being Johnny's own guitar. It was so stripped down he didn't even use a pick. Although there were one or two lighter moments, it did not make for easy listening and was in marked contrast to so much of the lightweight pop/country coming out of Nashville. Writing in *Country Music People*, Al Moir said, "It is a serious, often dark and menacing collection, frightfully stark, awesomely commanding and, in a sense, like scrutinising another man's soul, staring fascinated at his battle scars and almost eavesdropping on his confessions and prayers to himself and his maker." In the same magazine another writer talked of Johnny's "master storytelling".

Country Music was inspired to compare the album with *The Night Of The Hunter*, in which Robert Mitchum played a psychotic man of God roaming the southern countryside with the words "love" and "hate" tattooed across his knuckles, trying to find buried bank money. "Both music and movie take place in a landscape where everything seems to be governed by ancient, inexplicable forces that keep playing out, over and over, the big questions – life and worthiness, death and redemption." Another writer stressed that the album was one Johnny had been itching to do for years. "From Memphis to Nashville to Branson, Mr Cash has given the folks what they wanted. Now it's his turn." It has been suggested that the album was in part inspired by Bruce Springsteen's stark 1982 masterpiece *Nebraska*. If so, it was a fair exchange since Springsteen's raw hard hitting sound owes a considerable debt to Cash.

The opening song 'Delia's Gone' described in graphic detail a premeditated crime of passion in which a man ties a woman, who was "low down and travelling" to a chair. In lines possessing the same ability to shock as 'Folsom Prison Blues', there is an attempt to evoke a degree of understanding or even empathy for the killer:

> *First time I shot her, shot her in the side,*
> *Hard to watch her suffer, but with the second shot she died.*

Johnny had previously recorded this song in 1962, when the composers were given as K Silbersdorf and D Toops.* A comparison of the two versions provides powerful support for the proposition that Johnny should have been following his instincts and producing a far more basic sound years before. Luther's bouncy guitar riff and the female backing singers on the earlier version merely serve to trivialise the song's story. The Rick Rubin produced version comes across like an old painting in all its original glory after the layers of dirt had been skilfully removed. Some of the lines in Nick Lowe's 'The Beast In Me' – which found disfavour with some feminist commentators – were so apposite that he actually slipped them into an interview with *Country Music International*, "I've been so screwed up that I didn't know if it was New York or New Year."

'Drive On' was based on something Johnny had heard from soldiers who had fought in Vietnam. If a group was moving through the jungle and one of their number was hit, any attempt to go to his aid was liable to be rebuffed with a curt, "Drive on, it don't mean nothing." Kris Kristofferson's 'Why Me Lord' contained reflections on feelings of unworthiness in being the beneficiary of God's mercy. Kristofferson claimed that he was almost embarrassed to talk about the song. "It was one of those songs when I was just holding the pen. It followed a profound religious experience in a church, John's church actually, which is not exactly common behaviour for me. The song was just a personal expression and it struck a chord with a lot of people but it's also led people to want me to talk about a lot of organised religion which I don't have much to do with but I try to lead a spiritual life and that's what the song's about."

'Thirteen' by Glenn Danzig (originally recorded with his eponymous band, Danzig – perhaps an unusual choice for Cash given Danzig's reported interest in the occult) was a mournful dialogue of a life blighted by bad luck and misery which resulted in repayment in kind – another example of Johnny speaking up on behalf of those at the bottom of the ladder. Two songs recorded at the Viper Room gig provided light relief – Jimmy Driftwood's 'Tennessee Stud' and Loudon Wainright III's 'The Man Who Couldn't Cry', which had some members of the audience laughing enthusiastically as Johnny sang of the man being "bullied and buggered". Each song (some are more like spoken meditations) touches on something profound in the human experience and condition but the philosophy is one that anybody could grasp.

The album sleeve harmonised perfectly with the songs. In a change of branding, "Johnny" was dropped and the word "Cash" appeared in bold capitals above a black and white picture of a frowning Johnny standing at the edge of a wheat field, wearing a great black coat which almost renders invisible the guitar case he is resting his hands on. The frown fitted the mood of much of the album,

* For this 1994 outing Cash claimed the composing credit, though when a later video was made all three were given credit.

though it would surely not be fanciful to think it might have been a result of the ongoing dental-facial surgery which left one side of his face swollen. His timeless appearance may not have looked dissimilar to his grandfather, William Henry Cash, himself a travelling preacher. Johnny undoubtedly looked every one of his 62 years despite his dyed black hair. (As he told a *Sunday Express* reporter, "I like my hair dyed black but then I like it grey as well and sometimes I let the colour wash out.")

Cash described *American Recordings* as "an album of sin and redemption." On the sleeve a white dog and a black dog symbolically sit to either side of him. To emphasise the point the black dog has some white in it while the white dog has a little black. The sleeve also featured Johnny's lengthy handwritten notes which, in keeping with the album's back to basics quality, were penned on sheets of cheap lined paper torn out of a student pad. Johnny used the words – some scored out and changed – to reflect on his earliest experiences of music, such as mother Carrie singing 'What Would You Give In Exchange For Your Soul?', as he went to sleep under a tarpaulin on the journey to Dyess in 1935 when JR was three years old. Then there was the pure magic of the wireless of which he says, "The most amazing thing to me about the songs on the radio was the number of them. They just kept coming, one after another and I seemed to know them all after hearing them once or twice."

Talking about one of his favourite Jimmie Rodgers songs he explained that, " 'Hobo Bill's Last Ride' became 'my' song and the neighbours started coming over to hear me sing it." At night, as he walked along dark moonlit roads he sang all the songs he'd heard on the radio and learned from his friend Jesse Barnhill, the boy who had suffered from polio but was still able to inspire young JR as he beat a perfect rhythm with his tiny right hand. "I decided that that kind of music was going to be my magic to take me through all the dark places." Johnny explained how he learned to play the guitar and how he came to realise that it wouldn't be necessary for him to be able to play like Chet Atkins.

"I think I am more proud of this than anything I've ever done in my life," Cash said of *American Recordings*. "This is me. Whatever I've got to offer as an artist, it's here." As an artist, and indeed to some extent as a man, he was exposed before the microphone, and not found wanting. Rick Rubin gave his own take on what contributed to the album's quality, "He's striving for a less produced and more personal and spare sounding record. Cash's metaphoric step away from Nashville brings him that much closer to the Doc Marten-ised masses. He's the quintessential image of rock'n'roll really. The outsider."

Speaking to Adam Sweeting, Johnny admitted that it had been some time since his work in the studio had inspired or excited his independent spirit. "Around 1972 or 3, the excitement went out of my recording career. I really lost interest in what was being cranked out as country music in this town. I was never a serious part of this town or any town from the time I started on Sun records in Memphis. We kinda cut our own path, cast our own shadows." Making the album must surely have been a cathartic experience after the latter CBS years and the empty experience at Mercury. As Johnny put it, "It's like in Camelot when old King Arthur said Merlin stole all the pink. That happened in my life and in the Seventies and Eighties somebody stole the pink, but now the music and the magic has come back."

By its very nature it was never likely to be a big selling album but the critics immediately realised that Johnny had produced a major work. *Billboard* were not alone in suggesting that *American Recordings* might just be his best ever album and *Rolling Stone* suggested that Johnny's voice sounded better than it had done for over 30 years. *The Los Angeles Times* described it as "A milestone work for this legendary singer." *New Country News* said, "*American Recordings* will sound as good a hundred years from now as it does today. For that matter it would have made just as much sense in 1894 had the recording technology existed. Got a better definition of a classic?"

The fact that the album was not an outstanding commercial success and that country radio largely ignored it bothered Johnny less than might have been the case in the past. Hit collections and reissues of old albums sold consistently and with television and film appearances and property interests, Johnny was less concerned with financial gain – the critical acclaim and the sense of self-fulfilment being satisfying rewards in themselves. "I don't know what station is going to play an album of Johnny Cash and his guitar, maybe there are a few of 'em," he said. "But what I've got on this album is the real me. It's as far from rock'n'roll as Brahms. It's as far from mainstream country as anything could be."

A video made for 'Delia's Gone', the first single from the album, provoked howls of protest from some television executives, enhancing Johnny's outlaw image. Twenty-year-old supermodel Kate Moss (a "waif goddess" as some in the media dubbed her) played the part of Delia who is tied to a chair and shot through the head, with Johnny shovelling dirt on her face as she lies in a shallow grave. Though pretty tame by the standards of much cinematic and television violence it was nonetheless graphic and went beyond what was normally accept-able for music clips. As a result the scenes deemed most offensive were cut by MTV, though some that were left in, such as Johnny carrying Delia's lifeless corpse from the boot of his car to her grave, were still pretty strong stuff. The fact that Delia's lover was more than three times her age escaped mention. Feminists were doubtless unconvinced by Johnny's remark at a concert soon afterwards that he was "not anti-woman, just anti-Delia."

Johnny was vocal on the subject of women's rights. "Women are still treated like second-class citizens in a lot of areas of our society," complaining they often had to do the "crappy" jobs in society. Then again if his views on the place of women in marriage coincided with those of his "dependent" wife, he could hardly be shocked that women were doing such jobs.

Johnny's excursion into the world of MTV and his involvement with Rick Rubin were factors in bringing him to the attention of a younger rock audience. He also started receiving endorsements from what were, on the face of it, unlikely quarters. Speaking in *The New York Times* in 1994, Chuck D of rap group Public Enemy said, "Country music and rap are diametrically opposed to each other but rebels like Johnny Cash are the exception to the rule." Others went even further by saying that the violent imagery in songs like 'Folsom Prison Blues' and 'Cocaine Blues' anticipated gangsta rap, a view his new record label boss concurred with. Speaking in a *Rolling Stone* interview Rubin said, "He's a timeless presence. From the beginning of rock'n'roll there's always been a dark figure who never really fits. He's still the quintessential outsider. In the hip hop world you see all these bad boy artists who are juggling being on MTV and running from the law. Johnny was the originator of that."

Cash played down the significance of violence in his lyrics. "I wrote 'I shot a man in Reno' and all that over 40 years ago and I don't know anyone who's gone out and done that just because I sang about it. Maybe gangsta rap does have some influence on people but I think the six o'clock news is probably the most violent thing we hear today." Journalist Barney Hoskyns was in no doubt about Johnny's relevance beyond his usual following. "The man has become a trans-generational icon, a godfather of American gothic, a *tabula rasa* for people who prefer mythology to reality. All we need now is for Johnny Depp and Kate Moss to have a baby and ask Cash to be the godfather."

◆ ◆ ◆ ◆ ◆

However, for all the renewed interest, Johnny's general popularity was of a partisan nature. At the end of 1993, the Cash international fan club magazine reported that due to lack of numbers there would be no booth at Fan Fair the following year and members were also given the bad news that there was to be no club get-together, being frostily reminded that only 27 members had taken the trouble to turn up for the club breakfast the previous year. Tours of the stars' houses no longer included Johnny's lakeside mansion; the days of him coming out to meet and greet fans were long gone, though a large US flag remained proudly on display.

To mark the silver anniversary of the original legendary event, Johnny was approached to take part in the Woodstock festival being held over three days in summer 1994. Lou Robin as always handled the negotiations. "It turned out that there were two stages, one for what they reckoned were the major artists and another for smaller artists and that's where they wanted John to perform. I made it plain that John had played on the main stage at concerts and festivals all over the world and he was not going to start to do it differently at Woodstock. That was the end of the discussion."

From a commercial point of view, Woodstock would have put Johnny in front of a broad-based audience at a time when *American Recordings* was still receiving a lot of publicity. Approximately 300,000 people attended and enjoyed music from a wide variety of artists, such as Nine Inch Nails and Sheryl Crow to old stalwarts such as Peter Gabriel, Joe Cocker and Bob Dylan. In the autumn of 1994, Johnny played in Branson but this time there was a poor turnout. "Branson is a tourist town," Dave Roe pointed out. "The amount of people at any given show is directly proportionate to the amount of tourists in town overall. The weekend shows were always capacity and if we were drawing 800 people a show during the early part of the week, or during the off season, that meant we were still the biggest draw in the city."

However for Johnny the love affair with Branson was over. "I have no plans to come back at all. I don't think I'm doing myself or my fans a favour by being here." Reports in the British press suggested that for some shows the audiences were as low as 300 in an auditorium (the Shenandoah South Theater) capable of holding 3,000. It was a different story when Johnny was a surprise choice for the annual musical festival at Glastonbury, England, featuring Jackson Browne and Peter Gabriel, as well as hip newcomers such as Radiohead, Oasis and Chumbawamba. For this festival Johnny got to play on the big stage, though for some of the younger members of the audience the inevitable, "Hello, I'm Johnny Cash," introduction was probably necessary. Johnny and band played a selection of his best-known hits shot through with a selection from *American Recordings* – a part of the show he referred to as "the most unforgiving".

Critics and fans alike were bowled over by his performance despite the fact that his voice, as so often, sounded ragged. Paul Moody, writing in the *New Musical Express*, said, "Here is a man so capable of putting on a show that we simply fall into the palm of his hand and let him take control . . . it's a legend come to life before our eyes. 'Ring Of Fire' and a rabble-rousing 'A Boy Named Sue' get the biggest cheers." *Melody Maker* described Cash as "absolutely brilliant" but also gave a sobering assessment of the Sunday afternoon slot, describing it as a Glastonbury tradition which provided space for the "highly ironic and oh-so-post-modern rehabilitation of a veteran mainstream artist."

The Sunday Times: "Despite having spent large stretches of the Eighties in twilit, cabaret tinged obscurity – fighting addictions, falling out with increasingly negligent record companies and undergoing open-heart surgery – this year saw Cash invited onto the Lollapalooza tour." Lollapalooza was a transatlantic touring version of Glastonbury put together by a group of people including in 1991, American Recordings executive Marc Geiger, featuring a variety of alternative rock acts such as Ministry, Jane's Addiction and Throbbing Gristle. Despite his successes at venues like the Viper Room, Johnny felt this was a step too far and declined the offer, much to the chagrin of John Carter Cash who thought Lollapalooza's cutting edge would have suited his father.

The only other English date was a well-received concert at the Shepherd's

Bush Empire. Johnny took the stage with his tight little band of players: Dave Roe on bass, Bob Wootton on guitar and WS Holland, in his 35th year of drumming for Cash. Two days earlier, Carlene Carter had played London wearing a tight black miniskirt which may or may not have been a tribute to her stepfather, though her full-on version of 'Get Rhythm' certainly was. The more country elements of the Cash show alienated some of his new-found rock audience, leading one reviewer to complain that June's presence imposed a "country-lite" feel that spoiled the mood.

The potential tensions between old and new was of concern to Lou Robin. Referring to the Rick Rubin material he said, "I think the older fans will enjoy it and hopefully younger fans will see that he's not an interloper, he's always had integrity no matter what he's done." A Carnegie Hall show in September 1994 was lauded by critics, but for Johnny it was successful for a far more personal reason. Though he had tried his best to make amends for the neglect of his daughters as they grew up, it had been a source of regret for many years. In a later interview Rosanne ("the brain" as he affectionately referred to her) revealed that their coming together at Carnegie Hall had a curative effect on their relationship. "I brought up some old grievance which he listened to gracefully."

Johnny asked if Rosanne would sing 'I Still Miss Someone' with him. Initially non-committal, she eventually decided to make their communion public. "As we sang together, all the old pain dissolved and the old longing to connect was completely satisfied under the lights and the safety of a few thousand people who loved us, thus achieving something I'd been trying to get since I was about six years old. It was truly magic for both of us. I don't think we've ever been so close." In April 1994, Johnny connected with his roots when he went back to the place of his birth, Kingsland, Arkansas to play a homecoming show. There had long been a statue of Johnny in the local park and to commemorate his visit the town's post office was renamed in his honour.

◆ ◆ ◆ ◆ ◆

In October, Johnny spent a week in Hollywood with the other Highwaymen laying down tracks for the band's third album, *The Road Goes On Forever* (released at the start of 1995) with new producer Don Was, who had previously worked with Kris, Willie and Waylon.

"They may be old, they may be grizzled, but, unlike most superstar collaborations, Kris Kristofferson, Johnny Cash, Willie Nelson and Waylon Jennings still pack a mighty punch," wrote *Country Music People*. "The playing has a loose, gritty spontaneity that contrasts with the glossy sterility of most contemporary Nashville product, and the album has a proud mixture of free spirited rebellion and deep-seated integrity that recalls the best work of all four men . . . God bless you, boys, for keeping the true spirit of country music alive." The album's title was tinged with irony since it was to be the last Highwaymen project.

In February 1995, *American Recordings* received the Grammy for Best Contemporary Folk Album and a NAMMIE (Nashville Music Awards) for Best Folk Album. Although the folk category might have been debatable it was one that pleased Johnny. "I've always loved folk music, it's the backbone of country, or it used to be. It's where country came from and I think if country ever looks again to its roots and draws on that tradition it'll be in good shape." *American Recordings* also received the award for best country guitar album from *Guitar Player* magazine, quite a feat for a man who, by his own admission, was no great shakes as a guitarist. "I know about four chords and they've always worked for me: C, F, G7 and A minor; or if you're in G, that's G, C, D7 and A minor. Since I've been with American, I've had to learn a few more. I think there were seven chords in Nick Lowe's song 'The Beast In Me'."

Following the release of The Highwaymen album, the four musicians took to the road to promote it. There was talk of calling the excursion the "Teetotal Tour" to reflect the abstemious condition the quartet now found themselves in. However, the tour was jeopardised because Johnny had to undergo surgery for the removal of a facial nerve in an attempt to get rid of the pain which, despite numerous attempts at remedial surgery and treatment, had been plaguing him ever since his dental surgery had gone badly wrong. Cash had been due to undertake a European tour in early May but in the event only managed to struggle his way through one show at the Royal Albert Hall where one commentator said, "He looks sepulchral, like a voice from the tomb." After the show he apparently flew to California to a "pain management clinic".

The Highwaymen tour of America eventually got underway at the end of May and one fan of "real" country music, eccentric comedic country talent Kinky Friedman took in one of the shows. "Watching the four of them is like watching Mount Rushmore. It was great, very poignant and inspirational – I don't mind admitting that the Kinkster had a tear in his eye. But these guys can't keep jumping through their assholes for America. They're getting O L D." The Highwaymen subsequently undertook a tour of Australia, New Zealand and Asia towards the end of 1995, during which Lou Robin had the opportunity to perform one of his key functions namely, "working out the best economics". He had hoped to set up a show in Hong Kong but there wasn't a suitable venue available at the right time. He did however hear of a group of well-to-do American businessmen who were in town at the time and arranged for the group to play a private concert for them. He hadn't realised until they were actually "getting into the show" that the audience would number less than 200 but as he says, "The show was not typical but it still made financial sense."

Despite the opportunity to see four such famous figures in concert together (for the last time), the ticket demand was generally disappointing. At the outset it was apparently Kristofferson who was most keen in taking the band on lengthy tours but by the end, Jennings was pushing for more and more engagements. There was disagreement among the four and their advisers on a compromise and a feeling among some that Waylon's desire to do longer tours was economically unrealistic. His apparent reluctance to see other people's points of view was said to cause tensions amongst the four. "I have no interest in doing another Highwayman album," said Jennings. "We did enough of that." Willie Nelson expressed similar sentiments.

On an early summer day in 1995, 25-year-old John Carter Cash married model Mary Ann Joska, a native of Massachusetts, in the grounds of the sonville house. For the wedding, Johnny took the unusual step of wearing an all-white suit with a white bow tie, though his Mickey Mouse socks rather spoiled the effect. Waylon Jennings quipped, "Damn, Johnny looks good. He's been wearing the wrong colour all these years." As a present Waylon gave the couple a 1940 Ford coupe saying, "If you can't make out in that car you can't make out in anything." His ribbing of John Carter didn't stop there. "We're going to get rid of this red-headed freckle-faced kid of John's today. I never thought that kid would get married, anybody with freckles that big." The wedding was attended by 300 guests including many of Johnny and June's friends, including Chet Atkins, Jack Clement, The Oak Ridge Boys and Ronnie Dunn. The couple honeymooned in Israel.*

It was inevitable that John Carter Cash should go into the music business given his provenance. Johnny has said he figured this from an early age because his son used to sleep with his guitar. Determined to make up for past parental inadequacies Johnny and June went out of their way to ensure that his need to be with his parents was met by taking him on the road with them when younger. They also ensured that there was a reliable nanny figure to look after him when they were working. It's clear from an interview Johnny gave to Good Morning America shortly after John Carter's birth that he had high expectations of what his son would bring to his life.

"I want someone to pitch a baseball with, to sit beside a flickering fire with and share my deepest feelings; someone to walk in the woods with amongst the giant oaks and pines and tell how fortunate he is to have the opportunity to walk amongst such ornate creations by God. I want someone to tell that life is a splendid experience if we perceive it the way that God intended us to see it, which I believe is the continual exploration of every experience no matter how small or large each may seem as it comes our way. I want someone I can teach to fly a kite on a windy day, to pick up a simple stick and imagine it as a priceless toy, to tie a hook on a fishing line, bait it and toss it into a rattling creek." While there can be no doubt of Johnny's love for his son his vision placed a heavy burden of expectation on the child.

---

* In line with family tradition, John Carter Cash's marriage ended in divorce. In July 2000, he married musician Laura Lynn Weber who had appeared in June Carter's band.

Country-music writer and publicist, Tony Byworth recalls an early Seventies appearance in London when a very young John Carter, wearing an electric guitar, appeared on stage with his father. "He was only two or thereabouts so of course he couldn't play anything and all he was doing was making a noise. The musicians kept on unplugging the leads but then Johnny plugged them back in. John Carter was part of the show right from the start. In the best traditions of the American south, it was a family affair." In his teenage years John Carter developed a taste for heavy metal music but he continued to be involved with his father. By the late Eighties, he regularly appeared as a guitarist in Johnny's band. Many critics have suggested that in supporting his son's musical progress, Johnny allowed his love to blind him to the reality that his son possessed a very ordinary talent. Such a view was confirmed in 1997 when Johnny's second autobiography was published. The dedication reads, "To John Carter Cash. The Gift. You have it. Never forget."

A press review from 1988 was not untypical. "Something of a disappointment, his singing and songwriting skills show promise but his guitar playing is in need of work. During 'Big River' and several other tunes his acoustic guitar was so prominent in the mix that his aggressively awkward rhythm lines nearly drowned out his father's vocals." Around the same time New Jersey's *Home News* said, "John Carter Cash introduced an element of rock'n'roll to the repertoire but at times could not carry a tune . . . he sounded like Bob Dylan trying to impersonate Elvis." Other comments such as "looked ill at ease on stage", and "having a limited range and merely adequate" were common. In his defence, George Hamilton V, who co-headlined a number of shows with John Carter, says, "There is an aura, a stage presence about him that's very reminiscent of Johnny Cash. He is hauntingly like his father with equal conviction, intensity and authenticity in his song delivery."

John Carter also had the example of a talented stepsister but Rosanne succeeded because she was able to escape the constraints of working in her father's shadow. John has carved out a modest career in the music business (including producing a band known as The Bastard Sons Of Johnny Cash) but as a live performer and songwriter he remains unconfident and unconvincing. Many feel that unless John Carter ("a bit of a lost soul" as one described him) is prepared to make a similar move to that made by Rosanne, then any talent he has will not be allowed to develop properly.

◆ ◆ ◆ ◆ ◆

In 1995, the House Of Cash Museum in Hendersonville closed as a result of falling visitors and declining sales. The antiques and paraphernalia collected by Johnny and June over the years were contained in an old railway building of the L & N line not far from the main building. The artefacts on display included a letter from Andrew Jackson, a desk set once belonging to Chiang Kai-shek, John

Wayne's Pacemaker, Buddy Holly's motor cycle and props from the film *Gospel Road*. An important part of the project went when Johnny's mother died in 1991. Carrie had spent years greeting all-comers, sometimes from her rocking chair, and patiently answering all sorts of questions about her famous son. Johnny said he didn't want to be in the tourist business any more.

29

ALTHOUGH HIS CAREER now encompassed a broader rock audience Johnny was not forgetful of his original fanbase. As journalist Barney Hoskyns summed up, "He needs to move forward as much he needs to oblige diehard fans with songs he's been singing for 40 years." In September 1995, Johnny appeared at the inaugural concert to open the brand new $92 million Rock And Roll Hall Of Fame And Museum in Cleveland. The building – designed by world famous architect I. M. Pei and positioned on the edge of Lake Erie – was described by *The New York Times* as "a soaring open space, a transcendent greenhouse." Nearly 60,000 people attended the show which also featured Aretha Franklin, David Bowie, James Brown, Chuck Berry, The Kinks, and Bruce Springsteen, among others. Being the only country-oriented representative Johnny sang 'Folsom Prison Blues'.

Though *American Recordings* had been an unqualified success on every level, when it came time to return to the studio to cut a new album with Rubin, Johnny resisted the temptation to repeat a winning formula. Although an album's worth of usable material was left over from those initial Rubin sessions, for their second collaboration *Unchained*, Cash and Rubin opted for a full band sound with Tom Petty and The Heartbreakers providing the nucleus. Johnny had already worked with Petty earlier in the year when the band backed him on several songs during a show at LA's House of Blues. Some other rock names were roped in too including Flea of Red Hot Chili Peppers, Fleetwood Mac's Mick Fleetwood and Lindsay Buckingham, and Marty Stuart who played bass on half the tracks.

The album had a raw, earthy feel and was enhanced by some great instrumental work especially from the guitar of Marty Stuart whom Johnny referred to (on the sleeve) as "the energiser". Johnny's road musicians were conspicuous by their absence. This was no surprise to Dave Roe who claims Rick Rubin "reckoned we were too old-fashioned and too hillbilly."* Roe recalls another incident

---

* Roe actually played on the album but Rubin later wiped all his contributions.

which occurred backstage after a show at New York's Irving Plaza around the time *Unchained* was released. "During the show we'd done a new song. Rick said in a loud voice so that everyone could hear, 'Dave, what you're playing, I don't like it. Listen to the record and try and get to play it that way.' Cash heard this and he said in an equally loud voice, 'Dave, do you like what you're playing on this,' to which I said, 'Yes.' So Cash said, 'Well that's fine you just play it the way you like.' He will not put up with people throwing their weight around like that." Roe and the rest of the Cash band generally enjoyed working for Johnny; his pay rates were generous, hire cars were provided during tours and they got to stay in good hotels. Dave also appreciated the fact that Johnny liked to hang in the band room and chat with his musicians until show time.

Unchained covered a broader spectrum than *American Recordings*, containing a wide range of material encompassing folk, country, pop and rock. The song selection spanned 50 years from Jimmie Rodgers' 'The One Rose' to Beck's 'Rowboat', the suitably authoritative opening track. Originally rejected by Cash it stood out as one of the album's strongest songs. The poppy 'Memories Are Made Of This' (partly the inspiration for Jack Clement's 'Guess Things Happen That Way') was a surprise inclusion as was the menacing 'Rusty Cage', originally recorded by Seattle grunge metal band, Soundgarden. The title of 'Meet Me In Heaven' was taken from the words on brother Jack's tombstone, while 'Spiritual' was a long meditative prayer on the subject of death.

Johnny revelled in the free rein Rubin gave him as is evident from the sheer *joie de vivre* that pervades many of the tracks. Although his voice showed signs of age, Johnny's rumbling baritone still delivered with impressive ease. "*American Recordings* was harder," Cash told *MOJO*. "There was nothing to hide behind and that was scary. With this album I had more fun because I was with a bunch of people making music together. It's a more musical record. The sessions felt a lot like the Memphis days . . . that kind of freedom, sitting around and talking, 'What do you wanna do now?' No clock on the wall, no pressure. I'd been doing 'Country Boy' in concert and so we got into that and boy it felt good. 'Mean Eyed Cat' was originally written 40 years ago but never finished."

For most of his career Johnny had churned out two or three or more albums each year. *Unchained* was released more than two and a half years after its predecessor. For the cover of the album Johnny chose an atypical image of him leaning against his log cabin, his hair showing its natural grey. By way of contrast, an inner photograph of Johnny as a young boy served to represent the journey he had travelled. While not receiving the same amount of rapture that greeted its predecessor, *Unchained* attracted favourable comment. "It has Cash's history in its favour but this album is far from a piece of history," reviewed Scott Byron. "It's a beautiful blend of the classic and the timeless with the contemporary and the new, a potent reminder of how where we've been is a part of where we're going."

On the other hand Q's David Hepworth felt that a 64-year-old country singer doing young people's rock songs was like Alec Guinness reading *Trainspotting*, although he praised some of the older songs on the album. In *Rolling Stone* David Fricke said, "Cash brings equal helpings of spirituality and *savoir-faire*." There's little doubt that many of Johnny's long-time blue-collar following found the new material unfathomable. Around this time, Barney Hoskyns attended a show in Kansas and during 'Rusty Cage' he looked around at the rows of conservative farming families to see what they made of it. "I see only blank incomprehension," he wrote, "and then huge relief as the band segues seamlessly into 'Ring Of Fire'." In early 1998, *Unchained* won another Grammy for Best Country Album, and was also named Country Album of The Year by NARAS (the National Academy of Recording Arts and Sciences). Ironically the album garnered more airplay on alternative rock stations than country stations.

The Grammy award inspired Johnny and Rubin to ruffle a few feathers by publishing an advertisement in *Billboard* (dated 14/3/1998), showing an old photo of Cash flipping the bird (making an obscene gesture with his middle finger), with the words "American Recordings and Johnny Cash would like to acknowledge the Nashville music establishment and country radio for your support," above the upwards finger. The picture had been taken during the recording of the San Quentin concert when Johnny lost his cool after tripping over the television camera cables. Once more Johnny went public with his anger at the country music establishment failing to support older artists. With a reputed price tag of $20,000, it was an expensive way of making his point.

"We hope it will open the eyes of the country community," Rick Rubin explained, "and hopefully they'll say, 'He's making records considered the best in country and maybe we should readdress the situation.'" Willie Nelson commented, "John speaks for all of us," and hung a copy of the photograph in a prominent place on his tour bus. George Jones was also supportive, saying, "Well if no one's going to stick up for us we'll have to do it ourselves." Whereas, in the past, musicians such as Chet Atkins had held key positions in record companies, "now they have lawyers and accountants and that's why the music sucks so bad."

Many industry people, including some on Music Row, found the stunt amusing but not everyone had the same sense of humour. "Radio is not dumb," wrote *Radio And Records* magazine. "Programmers and corporations do a lot of testing to find out what kind of music they should play . . . if there was a huge demand for their music it would get played." Leroy Van Dyke, who had a major hit in 1961 with 'Walk On By', and had appeared with Cash the following year as part of a Hollywood Bowl package, was openly critical. Van Dyke said that older performers should learn to bow out gracefully, pointedly reminding Cash that he had been one of the newcomers who had edged out the likes of Webb Pierce,

Carl Smith and Faron Young in the Fifties. "We need to be grateful not vindictive," Van Dyke reasoned. "We should not harpoon the media that made us what we are. I don't recall people like Roy Acuff, Red Foley or Ernest Tubb meeting the challenge of change with anything but dignity and composure."

There was irony in Van Dyke's reference to Roy Acuff, the legendary elder statesman of the Grand Ole Opry. George Hamilton IV was told that when Acuff's health was failing (he died in 1992) he personally called Johnny. "He asked if (Johnny) would come back to the Opry and pick up that mantle and be kind of the patriarch figure. Roy Acuff would have had the clout to get that done if Johnny had agreed but he turned it down because his touring commitments wouldn't allow it. I think he would have made an ideal person to replace Mr Acuff as the father figure of the Opry, a spiritual leader to whom other artists would have deferred."

The conflicting views filled the letters pages of *The Tennessean* for a time. One journalist illustrated the polarity within the country music world with traditionalists on one side and modernists on the other. "I, like many others, did not get a chuckle out of Johnny Cash's ad in *Billboard* – I applaud it. As a writer for *Vintage Guitar Magazine* I see first hand what the industry's done to many artists whose time has come and gone. I do not think the question is whether they have saved up for a rainy day; it's that a lot of people running Music Row simply don't know or care who they are. Garth Brooks did not invent country music, in my opinion he does not even play it. I don't like Billy Joel and I certainly don't like some cheap imitation of him with a cowboy hat.

"I think Mr Cash's whole point was that he did sell records despite being misdiagnosed as a has-been by the powers that be in Nashville. Mr Van Dyke who to my knowledge has not had a record in about 20 years or so may just want to get in on a little of the limelight that the media are finally shining on Johnny Cash again. I would like to join Mr Cash in his bird flipping and add that the music industry here may kindly kiss off."

◆ ◆ ◆ ◆ ◆

In late 1996, Johnny was honoured by the John F Kennedy Center for the Performing Arts – an award which elevated him above being a mere country singer, as most people perceived him. With fellow recipients including playwright Edward Albee, actor Jack Lemmon, and ballerina Maria Tallchief, Johnny was in outstanding company. Chairman of the trustees, James A Johnson referred to "The unique and invaluable contribution the recipients had made to the cultural life of our nation." The primary criterion for the selection process is excellence. The honours are not designated by art form or category of artistic achievement, though over the years the selection process is said to have provided a balance among the various arts and artistic disciplines. Vice President Al

Gore had recommended the honour, saying that Johnny's music covered "The entire range of existence, failure and recovery, entrapment and escape, weakness and strength, loss and redemption, life and death." President Bill Clinton presented the award during a ceremony at the White House, saying, "Johnny Cash made country music not just for our country but for the whole world."

Naturally Johnny was honoured but conversation with the President failed to flow easily. When the two men found themselves alone at one point, they ran out of things to say and ended up comparing shoe sizes. Johnny had spent time with each President since Richard Nixon. Though he found them all to be men of great charm it appears he had the least warmth for Clinton. As Cash said, "He is a great *politician* . . . and that's it."

As if to demonstrate that his enthusiasm and energy remained undiminished, shortly after his 65th birthday, Johnny embarked on yet another tour of Europe, taking in Czechoslovakia, Germany, Norway, Sweden, France, Austria, Switzerland, and England. At the Albert Hall, reviewer Douglas McPherson found Cash to be in good voice. "Amazing shape considering the punishment his body has endured over the years. His notes were as deep and true as ever, his throat still plated with gold. His assured involved delivery tempered by an underlying good humour still had the magic." McPherson was less charitable to his immediate family, feeling that June's inclusion in the line-up was justified by "a respect for history", pointing out that many in the audience took the opportunity "to go to the loo" when she took the stage. McPherson's comments about John Carter Cash were particularly barbed. "There is no justifying the presence of their useless tub of lard of a son . . . did he do five songs or was it 55? I know it was too many. But Cash loves him so we have to put up with him."

In 1997, *Johnny Cash The Autobiography* was published. Written with the journalist Patrick Carr, who interviewed Cash many times over the years and had become a personal friend, the style was far removed from the 1975 autobiography, *Man In Black*, which Johnny himself had criticised for being too "sanctimonious". While not in any way retracting his religious beliefs, Johnny claimed that he no longer regularly attended church, preferring to worship in the private chapel built in the grounds of his Hendersonville house. The style of the book was more breezy and anecdotal than *Man In Black*, with scant regard for chronology. The reader is suddenly brought up to date with details of which town Johnny's beloved tour bus, "Unit One", happens to be passing through as he writes. Johnny talked with great candour particularly about his drug abuse, the full horrors of which were once more starkly portrayed.

Though many of the events in his life and career had been written about before, there were new anecdotes and opinions. His detailed recollection of the robbery at the house in Jamaica and a rebuttal of the suggestion that working with The Carter Family had been detrimental to his career had not been publicly aired before. Johnny also painted a far less idealised picture of his father

351

than he had done in his first autobiography. Apart from the fear caused by his father's drinking, Johnny bemoaned the fact that Ray never told him he loved him or gave him any real praise until he became a successful singer. *Johnny Cash The Autobiography* made compulsive reading and sold as well as its predecessor.

◆ ◆ ◆ ◆ ◆

Though he had some initial misgivings about the exposed nature of the event, Johnny agreed to take part in a television show with Willie Nelson in the *VH1 Storytellers* series. As Johnny said of it afterwards, "We pick yet we know not what we pick . . . just like a guitar pull at my house." Apart from The Highwaymen albums and tours, Johnny had rarely worked with Nelson, indicating in his autobiography that he had never felt able to get particularly close to him. The format was just the pair, as one reviewer put it, "armed with only their acoustic guitars and their million dollar voices," sitting on stools on a small square stage, surrounded by footlights, in the middle of a small audience. To a backdrop of a redesigned American flag with wavy lines, they traded tunes and reminiscences. For the most part the songs were past classics such as 'Folsom Prison Blues', 'I Still Miss Someone', 'Crazy', and 'Night Life'.

Though the results (also released on album) were pleasingly informal, a few more duets (apart from the sole 'Ghost Riders In The Sky') would have spiced up proceedings. Johnny was the more loquacious of the two, with stories about the provenance of songs. There were moments of jocularity. Willie, noticing that the only drinks available were water, coffee and hot chocolate, wondered if the lack of alcohol would harm their image. Johnny shot back, "As long as we keep wearing black, I think we might be all right." To help maintain this image, Johnny's grey hair was dyed black for the occasion. Though sounding relaxed and on good form, the effects of years of heavy smoking were only too evident in the way he struggled for breath. In 'Drive On' he was unable to reach the high note in, "*And I got a woman who knows her man,*" which he sang lower. The show gave Johnny a chance to take a closer look at Willie Nelson and he approved of what he saw. "I watch Willie's hands as he takes a guitar lead . . . I've seen hands like that on the cotton field. Rough, gnarly, dextrous, determined, precise, concise, fascinating."

In September, Johnny went back to Washington in order to make a personal appearance of a different kind. He had become increasingly concerned at how new technology allowed people to obtain copyrighted music via the internet. This went against the basic principle he had learned as a boy growing up in Dyess, i.e. you get paid for the cotton you produce. Imposingly dressed in black, Johnny addressed the House Judiciary sub-committee on Courts and Intellectual Property in support of legislation intended to protect copyright holders. "Our laws respect what we create with our heads as much as what we build with our hands." Members of the committee listened attentively as he continued, "That's true in real life and it ought to be true in cyberspace too."*

Critics said the legislation might well go too far by outlawing household fixtures like audio tape, video recorders and personal computers. Cash insisted that recording artists faced major rip-offs if the laws were not enforced.† After doing a web search on his name he found that 'Ring Of Fire' was being offered on a website in Slovenia without his permission. "Maybe I should be flattered that someone in Slovenia likes my song but when he or she makes it available to millions of people this hardly seems fair. The music and the artist that create and perform it deserve protection whether it's an old 45 or a song we've yet to hear from an artist who's still waiting for a break."

In October 1997, Johnny was playing a show at Flint, Michigan when he dropped his pick. Bassist Dave Roe explains what happened next. "Cash staggered quite badly when he tried to pick up the plectrum. Some people laughed and a woman in the audience shouted out, 'You're drunk.' He went up to the microphone and said, 'No, I'm not drunk, I'm suffering from a form of Parkinson's disease. But I refuse to give it some ground in my life.'" (Johnny's paternal grandfather, William Henry Cash, suffered from Parkinson's disease and died at the age of 52 in 1912.)

The press reported that Johnny's timing appeared to be off during another show a few days earlier. Somebody close to the tour said that Johnny had looked unwell before the Flint show, and that he was half-supported by two helpers as he waited to go on. They took his coat off and "sort of gave him a little shove and he went out to the microphone and that's where he stood the whole night except when he turned round to ask June to come up and sing. He wasn't very mobile and clearly wasn't in the best of health. His banter with the audience was limited and nothing like it had been in the old days. He seemed to be on a lot of drugs."

Johnny got through the show but the rest of the tour was cancelled, as was a series of personal appearances to promote his autobiography. Johnny had been aware of his condition for some months following a medical check-up but felt able to honour his performing commitments particularly since the effect of Parkinson's disease was not totally debilitating to sufferers, particularly in its early stages.

The inescapable conclusion was that all the years of drug abuse and unhealthy living had finally caught up with Johnny. What was remarkable was how long it

* The proposed legislation had been introduced by President Clinton in the House of Representatives and the Senate with the intention of implementing December 1996's world intellectual property organisation treaties on copyrights, performances and recordings.
† Ironically, in a 1988 interview, Cash admitted to autographing bootlegs of the 1969 material he cut with Bob Dylan.

had taken. Lou Robin released a press statement. "He's faced a lot of challenges in his life. He thrives on challenges. Johnny feels confident that once the disease is medically stabilised he will resume his normal schedule." The news of Johnny's illness soon spread, with the press being quick to assume that the problem was serious enough for his days to be numbered. They weren't far off the mark. While walking in New York around the end of October, Johnny suffered some kind of attack which affected his ability to walk. He was rushed to hospital suffering from double pneumonia and blood poisoning. For 10 days, he lay unconscious and was only kept alive with the aid of a ventilator.

During this critical time, Johnny received a visit from his long-time friend, Merle Haggard. A quote from Johnny about the experience appeared on the sleeve of Haggard's 1999 album, *For The Record*. "I was lying in the hospital slipping in and out of the coma of death. A man walked quietly into my room. He did not say a word. He walked to my bedside, leaned down and put his arms around me. I lay there for a while feeling his arms gripping me as if he was afraid he would have to let go. I slightly opened my eyes and said, 'Is that you Hag?' He just nodded his head. He was only allowed to stay one minute but that one moment is more precious to me than any time of my life."

Johnny thought he was going to die. Though he wasn't ready, it did not hold any great fear for him. As he told Patrick Carr, "I thought of it in Christian terms – that I would be there with God in eternal bliss. Ecstasy. I was kinda disappointed when I realised I wasn't going to die – you know – more of this pain." After the eleventh day Johnny made a dramatic recovery, something he attributed to divine intervention. In the postscript to his 1997 autobiography, Johnny explained that by the tenth night his doctor had run out of strategies for keeping him alive. "She told God that she and medicine had done all they could, it was in His hands now, and she spent the whole night praying." While it might be wondered what the good doctor's other needy patients made of this, family members formed a prayer circle around Johnny. By the eleventh morning, Johnny was sitting up in bed drinking coffee.

However, the prognosis was not good. Johnny was told that he was suffering from an uncommon variant of Parkinson's disease known as Shy-Drager syndrome, a progressive and incurable neurological disorder characterised by the progressive failure of the nervous system. The condition affects key body functions such as heart rate, blood pressure and bowel and bladder control. In addition to medical treatment, it was imperative that Johnny got plenty of rest. He and the family spent the next weeks and months in and out of hospital and recuperating in Nashville and Jamaica.

In an interview with *Country Music*, Johnny described the simple charms of a typical day at Cinnamon Hill. "I'm up every morning at five. I get up and make the coffee before everybody else gets up in the house. I sit in the breakfast room and I do a lot of peaceful, calm, very beautiful, early morning reading. Then June gets up and we'll watch the morning news. After breakfast we'll jump in the golf cart and go all the way to the sea. We'll sit down there on the beach for a while. Usually late morning I'll do a little work on my songs. After dinner, and after we watch a little television, I'll work on a song some more." One of the hardest things for Johnny to come to terms with was the fact that his touring days were over, there being no way that his constitution could handle such activity. It was a sad end to his live career, particularly as he had intended to stay on the road as long as there was breath in his body. As he told a *Winston Salem Journal* reporter in 1987, "When I finally go, people can say that I bopped till I dropped."

Rosanne was frank about the general effect on her father. "It depresses him. He's not used to sitting around. He's a very powerful person and to not feel well, that's really hard for him. He spent over 40 years on the road and suddenly he's not out there. When that energy comes to a screeching halt there's a lot to deal with just inside yourself." In January 1998, press reports suggested that the Cash family was planning to sell off various properties in order to meet mounting medical expenses. According to one report they were asking $795,000 for the House Of Cash, $75,000 for the old railroad building which had housed June's antiques and $1.8 million for two 7-acre plots belonging to John Carter Cash. There was never any question of selling the family home in Hendersonville.*

There were also suggestions that Johnny was helping other members of the family with medical bills and that Johnny and June's children were "squabbling" over their inheritance. As the *Star* of Tarrytown, New York put it, "Johnny has a lot of property but he doesn't have a lot of cash. Other members of his family have also been seriously ill recently, and it has really rocked him financially." The same report suggested that it was clear that John Carter Cash was the "chosen child" which made his daughters bitter. It was also suggested that certain family members had chronic money problems and sold personal items of Johnny's. One dealer was quoted as saying, "There is a lot of Johnny Cash stuff flying about. There are items so personal you wonder why anyone would sell them." The items apparently included a Man In Black outfit and a recent driving licence. The unnamed source pointed the finger at one of Johnny's daughters who was described as a memorabilia dealer. Tommy Cash dismissed the reports about family splits as "a lot of bull dreamt up by the newspapers."

That same month, another of Johnny's long-time friends, Carl Perkins, died after suffering a series of strokes. Sadly Johnny was not well enough to attend the funeral at which George Harrison, himself suffering from throat cancer at the time, was persuaded by Wynonna Judd to sing 'Your True Love'.† According to

---

* With a premium for the celebrity connection, the house would now be worth $3–$4 million.
† In 1985, Harrison was one of the star musical guests (including Rosanne Cash) paying tribute to Carl in *Blue Suede Shoes*, a television special to mark the song's thirtieth anniversary. Johnny paid tribute to his old friend via an opening video message.

Tommy Cash, "Johnny liked having people on stage with him that he really looked up to, like Carl." Johnny said that though he was, at times, uncomfortable about having someone as talented as Carl in his shadow, he was in no doubt about Carl's place in history. "I'm not well enough acquainted with the field to know whether music historians and rock'n'roll fans celebrate Carl the way they should today, but if a hundred years from now he's not recognised as a great master and prime mover, somebody will have messed up badly." In early summer, June's sister Helen died, aged 70, after a long period of poor health which had seen her hospitalised with stomach problems for the year leading up to her death. She was buried at the First Baptist Church in Hendersonville.

It was a strange period for Johnny with most of his normal activities being denied him. For the first time since the mid-Fifties, life did not revolve around the next concert or recording session, though song ideas continued to pour forth. As he said, "Being idle, my brain still wouldn't slow down. I was always thinking about those songs." Johnny managed the occasional appearance and caused a real stir when he emerged unexpectedly onto the stage of the Ryman Auditorium as Kris Kristofferson was performing 'Sunday Morning Coming Down'. There was wild cheering as he walked out and finished the song. Kristofferson looked on, visibly moved at this unexpected bonus. In recognition of the many hundreds of get well cards he had received Johnny thanked his fans for helping him pull through. One newspaper report noted, "He looked thinner than he had, walked a little slower, but still had the Johnny Cash arrogance that has made him one of the legends of country music."

◆ ◆ ◆ ◆ ◆

The legend received yet more awards and tributes as the millennium started to draw to a close as some institutions perhaps sensed that Johnny's life might be heading the same way. At the end of 1998, the National Academy of Songwriters honoured him with their Lifetime Achievement Award and early in 1999 he received a similar honour at the annual Grammies ceremony. In March, it was the turn of the National Academy of Recording Arts & Sciences who selected Johnny for their Governor's Award, which was in fact collected by John Carter Cash since Johnny's health problems prevented him from appearing in person.

In April, a spectacular TNT (Turner Network Television) *All-Star Tribute To Johnny Cash* special was recorded at Manhattan's Hammerstein Ballroom, with appearances from Bob Dylan, Bruce Springsteen, Willie Nelson, Sheryl Crow, Brooks & Dunn, Wyclef Jean and many other artists from different genres illustrating the truth of Charlie Gillett's comment that Johnny Cash was "outside the category of country music." The Mavericks were the house band for the evening and actor Jon Voight acted as MC. June performed a moving version of 'Ring Of Fire' and spoke of how the song described her feelings when she first met Johnny – "He was kinda scary then."

It was not clear until after the show had started whether Johnny's health would permit him sufficient energy to make an appearance but this was one party he didn't want to miss. Towards the end of the show the lights dimmed and actor Tim Robbins read an essay about life in prison. When the lights came up again they revealed Cash on stage, waiting to deliver the lines that everybody hoped they would hear, "Hello, I'm Johnny Cash." Overcoming his palpable weakness, he went straight into 'Folsom Prison Blues' and 'I Walk The Line', with the black-clad guests joining in. One notable aspect of the show was the public reconciliation of Johnny with Marshall Grant. According to Tommy Cash, despite suing Johnny in the Eighties, Grant had never lost affection for Johnny and had phoned from time to time to express his concern at press reports of his health problems.

Paying tribute to the star of the show prior to performing 'Give My Love To Rose', Bruce Springsteen said, "You took the social consciousness of folk music, the gravity and humour of country music and the rebellion of rock'n'roll and told all us young guys that not only was it all right to tear up those lines and boundaries but it was important." Marty Stuart said Johnny was the kind of guy "who could take your hand and walk you into the cowboy world or the Indian world or the prison world or the Jesus world. He is a communicator between a lot of worlds . . . I really do think he's the guy concerning what we do – playing country music – most qualified to shut out the lights on the twentieth century around here."

At their 82nd General Assembly, Johnny's home state of Arkansas passed a resolution declaring February 26, 1999 and each February 26 thereafter as Johnny Cash Day. The accompanying citation read, "Johnny Cash is an Arkansan who is better known in the world than in his home state and is truly representative of the spirit and ideals which have made our state great." Though there was no question of Johnny being strong enough to play a full-length concert, he did put in a couple of appearances with June as she played a series of dates to promote her first solo album in almost 25 years, *Press On*. The title was pure June, being her invariable response to the countless setbacks and false dawns she had dealt with over the years, "We've just got to press on, press on." A kind of musical autobiography, the album featured songs reflecting the history of The Carter Family, her love of Johnny and also celebrated the newer generations carrying the traditions of country music forward to the next century.

In May, Johnny and June opened their house to 150 friends for a musical evening to launch the album which went on to win a Grammy for Best Traditional Folk Album. Johnny's indisposition gave June something of an opportunity, for the first time since she joined the Johnny Cash road show in 1961, to be an artist in her own right. One of the songs, 'I Used To Be Somebody', acknowledged that once June became involved with Johnny she lost some of her own identity, not that she was complaining. "I have no regrets about not becoming an actress or whatever. I'm proud to be walking in the wake of Johnny's fame." At one of two shows at New York's Bottom Line, June joked that because Marty Stuart and Rodney Crowell played on the album, she was thinking of calling herself June Carter and Her Ex-Sons-in-Law. If Nick Lowe had been present, perhaps she would have done.

Johnny continued to be reminded of his mortality when just over a year after the death of Helen Carter, Anita Carter died, again after a long illness. Despite his own poor health, Johnny read the eulogy at her funeral as she was laid to rest beside her sister.

30

THE SUDDEN END to Johnny's touring career held implications for many –
not least his band and crew who now found themselves out of work. Although
WS Holland was quoted as saying, "Hey, the man is sick and can't travel, what's
he supposed to do?", the rock steady beat of the Johnny Cash sound for almost
40 years felt that in recognition of his loyalty he was entitled to a severance
payment, not only due to the time factor but on the strength of specific
assurances he believed had been given over the years. As time went by without
any word from Johnny or his advisers, Fluke became more aggrieved and
eventually decided that he had no other option but to resort to court action,
although given the amount he sued for, reputedly $50,000, it appeared his
action was more a matter of principle than a serious financial reward for his
time with Cash.

For Lou Robin, there was no merit in Fluke's case. "Holland was suing Cash
because he said that Cash promised Holland that he would always have food
on his table. There was never anything in writing and nobody else ever heard
Johnny say that. Whenever Johnny got sick, Holland said, 'Well Johnny will
take care of me,' and we all said, 'Well why is he going to take care of you and
no one else?' Finally the action was thrown out of court in March 2001. The
judge wouldn't even let it go to trial . . . He was shooting at ghosts. It's unfortunate that he got desperate when this ended because he had nothing else to do
in my opinion. He did make some investments but he wanted to be real sure
that he didn't end up the way he started at whatever cost. It let John know
what he was really like. Some lawyers, if you pay them, they'll do anything. I
think they figured John would prefer to settle with them but there was no
merit in it. If John did it for Holland he'd have to do it for everybody."

Once Fluke raised his grievances Bob Wootton indicated that he too might
follow suit. Lou Robin again: "Wootton was going to do it if Holland had been
successful. He was just tagging along on Holland's coat strings without putting
up any money. Wootton worked for John after the band broke up, he was head

of security for a while until he didn't want to do that any more and then he left. Johnny was very good to them. The court scene was really bad, milking the thing, but some people think that's OK. Not everybody's like Johnny. They were just trying to take advantage of the situation."

Tommy Cash expressed surprise at the court action. "My understanding of why Fluke sued Johnny was that when they were successful in a big way at first, Fluke said Johnny told him things like, 'I will take care of you.' I think that though some of them invested well and some of them have lots of money and are well off, I think some of them were just a little greedy. They still wanted a piece of the pie even though Johnny was not doing concerts anymore. I don't agree with that and Johnny certainly doesn't. I was surprised when I heard about it because Fluke has always been a loving member of our inner circle. We've all loved him since we first met him back in the Fifties. Johnny has suggested to me that it was like kicking someone when he's down."

Tommy, however, accepts that Fluke was on the road with Johnny for years and that he doesn't know everything that was said and done or what might have been promised. He also acknowledges the difficult times the band had to go through with Johnny on occasion in order to keep the show on the road. Sandy Kelly too expressed surprise at the court action. She had gotten to know Fluke quite well and saw him as Johnny's right-hand man, always protective of his boss. Once Johnny signed to American Recordings, Fluke and Bob Wootton simply became his road musicians. Because he was no longer able to perform in concert, there was some logic to the view that they could hardly expect Johnny to go on supporting them and to many it appeared callous to raise a court action against a man who was in such patently bad health. Many would also point out that being on the road around the world with Johnny Cash for years provided an unforgettable experience very few were privy to.

The opposite viewpoint sees Fluke contributing to the distinctive Johnny Cash sound for nearly 40 years. Regardless of whether anything was put in writing, under American law, an employee working for a company for the same length of time would receive a substantial severance or redundancy pay. There were other, less tangible factors to consider. In the Sixties, when Johnny failed to turn up for shows, the rest of the troupe were put in the unenviable position of having to somehow fill in on the occasions that the show was not cancelled altogether. Either way the troupe lost money. Then there was the stress involved in dealing with his drug habit and the emotional support provided while he was going through withdrawal. According to this argument, regardless of what was said (and clearly some things were said), Johnny was under a *moral* obligation to ensure his loyal sidemen were taken care of. There were thus people who very much supported this position.

Despite this, Fluke did not pursue the matter after a judgement went against him, even though there were appeal procedures open to him which some confidently predicted would have brought eventual victory. It appeared that Fluke simply didn't have the will to pursue the matter to a final conclusion and that he now feels disillusioned with the whole business.* Whatever the rights and wrongs it was a sad end to such a long and fruitful partnership, though despite it all Fluke clearly retains affection and admiration for his former boss. "He's got it all as a personality and character, the good, the bad and the ugly."

◆ ◆ ◆ ◆ ◆

In trying to make light of his new situation – in particular the end of touring – Johnny told *Rolling Stone*, "I have had 43 years of that. That's enough. I can direct my energies more to recording now. I intend to keep recording as long as I'm able. It's what I do. It's what I feel." Though recording was now the only option, Johnny was still determined to sing in front of an audience from time to time, preferably when his appearance was uncertain or unannounced. In June 2000, he appeared at the Carter Fold with June and John Carter Cash where he received a prolonged standing ovation from the 1,200 strong audience. The *Bristol Herald Courier* reported that Johnny was in good voice, singing about 12 songs and even when others were singing, he never left the stage despite his frail appearance. "The music," wrote the correspondent, "really played second fiddle to the emotional tug underscoring Saturday's show." Johnny told the audience, "From now on if I can only squeeze out one show a year it's going to be at the Carter Fold."

True to his word Johnny was back there the following year in the company of family members, including Rosanne. June said that they were "hoping to retire" to Maces Springs, back to the home where she was brought up, and that she had acquired some 12 years previously. Johnny had actually started work on his third Rick Rubin-produced album not long after *Unchained* was released but as a result of his intervening health nightmares it took three years to bring to fruition. *American III: Solitary Man* was eventually released in October 2001. The by-now trademark black and white sleeve shot showed Johnny (with guitar) standing in the shadows of a nondescript corridor, hunched, pensive and alone. The irony was that he appeared to be waiting to go out on stage.

It was immediately apparent that the great booming baritone of old was gone forever, replaced by a tremulous substitute whose delivery betrayed the need for a considerable effort on the part of the singer which had rarely been evident before. The change in Johnny's voice was particularly noticeable on the "s" and "sh" sounds at the start of words, the new configuration of his articulators (tongue, roof of the mouth) allowing through too much air and distorting the sound. None of this meant that Johnny was incapable of producing the goods;

---

* At the time, it was alleged that Fluke suspected the judge might have been bought, though there is no hard evidence for this.

on the contrary the new offering was another triumph. One critic, Robert L Doerschuk, found virtue in the songs as "intimate sessions in which even the singer's flaws grow beautiful."

The production was considerably more stripped down than on *Unchained*, with a predominantly acoustic sound that provided little in the way of cover for Johnny's vocal shortcomings. Guests included Norman Blake and Marty Stuart on guitars, Tom Petty on vocals and organ and Sheryl Crow who, apart from providing distinctive backing vocals, also played haunting accordion on two old folk songs, 'Wayfaring Stranger' and 'Mary Of The Wild Moor'. 'Nobody' was a 100-year-old comic vaudeville song with a nice line in self-pity of the kind Johnny might understandably have given in to during the previous three years.

Once more Cash and Rubin looked to well-known names in the rock field for the album's songs – U2 ('One'), Neil Diamond ('Solitary Man'), and Tom Petty ('I Won't Back Down'). Undoubtedly the most powerful performance was Nick Cave's 'The Mercy Seat' (first recorded by Cave and his band, the Bad Seeds on the 1988 album *Tender Prey*), about the vivid thoughts of life and death, guilt and innocence swirling wildly around in a man's head as he is about to be put to death in the electric chair. Johnny connected with the song right away. "I did a show at the Tennessee State Prison one time and I walked by the electric chair and a chill came over me. I thought about that feeling when I first heard that song." 'I'm Leavin' Now', a duet with Merle Haggard and perhaps a thank you for his hospital visit, was inspired by thoughts of Johnny's first wife Vivian, a possible sign that the guilt he felt had never been fully exorcised. Johnny strummed chords in his usual loose fashion while Marty Stuart played "Hank Snow style guitar".

One critic insisted that if Johnny were to make a great album ever again he would need to recover his legendary voice. However, in *PopMatters*, Wilson Neate spoke for many. "While his is, more than ever before, the voice of an ageing man and while some of the strength may be gone, on this batch of songs of love, God and murder, Johnny Cash still communicates his faith, wisdom and experience with a simple power that few living artists can match."

In the conclusion to his sleeve notes, Johnny gave an upbeat picture of the future. "The Master of Life's been good to me. He gives me good health now and helps me to continue doing what I love. He has given me strength to face past illnesses, and victory in the face of defeat. He has given me life and joy where others saw oblivion. He has given new purpose to live for. New services to render and old wounds to heal. Life and love go on. Let the music play." The Cash-Rubin partnership made it three Grammies in a row when 'Solitary Man' received the award for Best Male Country Vocal Performance. The respected British rock magazine *MOJO* chose *American III: Solitary Man* as its album of the year.

The optimistic note Johnny sounded in the album's sleeve notes was due in no small part to the welcome news that the Shy-Drager syndrome diagnosis had been cast into doubt. If it had been correct then Johnny would have been in much worse shape than he actually was. "I suppose I've got this disease, they keep saying I do, but I don't have the symptoms you're supposed to have when you have Shy-Drager, whatever it is. I don't have any debilitating symptoms that keep me from doing the things I want to do. I walk up and down stairs, I don't shuffle, I don't have trouble swallowing, I don't have the common maladies you're supposed to have."

The term the doctors now ascribed to his cluster of symptoms was autonomic neuropathy – another way of saying that he had something wrong with his nervous system but it was not exactly clear what that was. The wide range of symptoms associated with autonomic neuropathy included constipation, excessive perspiration, dizziness and diarrhoea, among many others. What was clear, however, was that the condition did not affect the intellect. It's believed that the possible causes include damage to the nervous system brought about by alcohol or drugs, diabetes and Parkinson's disease. Johnny was puzzled by a diagnosis of diabetes since he regularly checked his blood sugar level and it was always within normal limits.

In October 2001, a particularly severe bout of pneumonia left him in a coma for eight days. Once more his powerful will to live and an ox-like constitution pulled Johnny through. As soon as the temperature levels in Nashville dropped, Johnny headed to Cinnamon Hill. However, the medical facilities in Jamaica were limited and a deterioration in his condition resulted in him being urgently airlifted back to Nashville. Journalists who have visited Cash in recent years comment on the large array of pills and medicine that surround him. "Drugs, they'll sneak up on you," Johnny told *Rolling Stone*. "All of a sudden there'll be a beautiful little Percodan lying there and you'll want it."

The ironic consequence of Johnny's frequent bouts of ill health brought renewed interest in the form of increased record sales. A veritable outpouring competed for space in the CD racks including three themed career-spanning compilations, *Love, God* and *Murder* being released in 2000 (*Murder* inevitably proving the biggest commercial success). Noted film director, Quentin Tarantino, contributed sleeve notes for the album and provided some thoughts on crime and Johnny Cash music. "Unlike most gangsta rap, Cash's criminal life songs rarely take place during the high time but after the cell door has slammed shut." A number of Johnny's old albums, including *Ride This Train* (one of his personal favourites) and *Orange Blossom Special* were re-released and Columbia put out a 2 CD retrospective, *Man In Black: The Very Best Of Johnny Cash*, with 40 tracks taking in much of the best of the Sun, Columbia, and Mercury years (though not the American Recordings material).

The collection was notable for the liner notes which featured words of praise and reminiscences. Keith Richards defined two vital aspects of the Cash appeal.

"He had real, real stuff . . . What he had going on in the early days was what other guys like Muddy Waters were doing. It was really roots music, but they conveyed it through electricity, and the judicial use of it. The music was so true to the roots and at the same time so modern. Another attraction for me was the way he slung his guitar so very low." In addition Marty Stuart and Dave Roe were involved in producing tribute albums, *Kindred Spirits* and *Dressed In Black* respectively, with the albums featuring a wide range of artists from many strands of rock and country. Stuart laid down a rule for *Kindred Spirits*, that the songs chosen had to have been written by Johnny Cash, so songs such as 'Ring Of Fire' and 'The Ballad Of Ira Hayes' were not eligible for inclusion. Bob Dylan performed 'Train Of Love' and Bruce Springsteen reprised 'Give My Love To Rose' (from the TNT tribute programme).

Other artists included Little Richard, Dwight Yoakam and Rosanne Cash whose quote about her father on the sleeve was typically perceptive. "He's an original, timeless . . . he could be a medieval minstrel or he could be someone from the future . . . drop him down in any century and he'd work." Marty also presented a television spectacular about Johnny's life which featured performances of songs from the album.

The artists on Roe's album were less well known but some outstanding talent such as Rodney Crowell, Raul Malo and Mandy Barnett featured nonetheless. Robbie Fulks quote about Johnny was playfully risqué. "I discovered *Johnny Cash At San Quentin* and *Playboy* magazine in 1970 while visiting my seven-year-old girlfriend at her trailer. I took a childish liking to both, not realising at the time which was the nakeder." Rodney Crowell also featured his ex-father-in-law on his own 2001 album, *The Houston Kid*, cheekily asking him to duet on a revised and revamped version of 'I Walk The Line', a daring move which Crowell himself compared to "getting da Vinci to paint a moustache on the Mona Lisa."

While Johnny was of course flattered by the respect implicit in the releases, in truth they were of no great interest to him. "It's kind of an edited version of my life," he told Neil McCormick of the *Daily Telegraph*. "I suppose I'm happy with it but it's for others to look back over my life. I gotta focus on today . . . Every year gets better because I get more and more grateful for having another year. I suppose it's good to be alive and still be around doing what I love to do. I wouldn't trade my future for anyone's I know."

◆ ◆ ◆ ◆ ◆

Johnny was in Jamaica when the attacks on the World Trade Center took place on September 11, 2001 and like millions of people around the world, he watched in numb disbelief as the enormity of the atrocity unfolded. "I watched it on television and I guess I wanted to kill someone myself. I do love this country and I saw somebody take a really good shot at it. It was a striking blow at our morale but I've recovered from that, just as this country is recovering. I believe this country will prevail." He was not well enough to take part in any of the fundraising events which subsequently took place, though he was there in spirit. The reissue of 'Ragged Old Flag' three months to the day after the attack took on a new meaning, as the flag on the cover evoked the tattered one recovered from the World Trade Center.

Waylon Jennings had been in poor health for some time with complications arising from diabetes and in December 2001 his left foot had to be amputated. Johnny spoke to him afterwards by phone and though some people said he would get better and even go back on the road with the aid of a wheelchair, Johnny didn't share that impression. Waylon died about six weeks later in February 2002, less than a year after he had been inducted into the Country Music Hall of Fame. Unlike Johnny for whom it had been his proudest achievement, Waylon was unmoved by the honour. "It meant absolutely nothing to tell you the truth."

Despite his long friendship with Waylon, Johnny was unable to attend the funeral as he had managed when Chet Atkins died the previous summer. Lou Robin explains, "Johnny didn't go to Waylon's funeral. He wanted to really but he did not want a media circus. Also he wasn't well and he would have had to go all the way to Phoenix, Arizona. Johnny was the first one the family called when Waylon died." Johnny's ill health also prevented him from attending a memorial service for Waylon at the Ryman Auditorium where he had been scheduled to appear first. Shooter Jennings explained to the audience that Cash was in Jamaica and his doctors had advised him against travelling. He read a brief message from Johnny to the crowd. "Enjoy yourselves and honour Waylon." While he appreciated the general fuss made to mark the event, when Johnny's 70th birthday came around on February 26, 2002, he spent the evening quietly having dinner with friends.

In March 2002, Johnny met George W Bush who presented him with the National Medal Of Arts. Like the Kennedy Center award this is given to people from all artistic disciplines and is accordingly all the more prestigious. It seems Johnny's opinion of the new President was not much better than the previous incumbent. He had followed the 2000 Presidential campaign and, after watching one of the debates between Gore and Bush, he told a reporter for *The Tennessean*, "I thought Gore stomped him . . . I thought Gore was so much better." The ceremony also gave Johnny an opportunity to be reunited with fellow honouree Kirk Douglas. (The two had starred together in *A Gunfight* 31 years previously.) The citation for the award read, "Johnny Cash for his contributions to the music and entertainment industry; for his remarkable musical innovations that drew from folk, country and rock'n'roll styles; and for setting an extraordinary standard in American music." For those who had not seen Johnny for some time the pictures from the ceremony came as something of a shock, the ravages of illness made him appear much older than his years: red-faced, white haired and wrinkled, his jaw misshapen from all the surgery he had endured over the years. These images were offset to a degree by his still upright posture and imposing presence.

Johnny continued undertaking more recording projects – an album of acoustic gospel songs, a duet with Dave Matthews, 'For You', which was featured on the soundtrack of the Vietnam war film, *We Were Soldiers* starring Mel Gibson, and a maudlin yet dignified recitation of 'I Dreamed About Mama Last Night' on the Hank Williams tribute album, *Timeless,* which went on to receive a Grammy for Best Country Album. His main focus was on his work with Rick Rubin and roughly two years after *American III: Solitary Man* he was ready to release his fourth album, *American IV: The Man Comes Around.*

From the outset it looked as though the project might never be completed. There were days when Johnny was simply incapable of producing a vocal sound of sufficient quality, and sessions had to be cancelled or postponed. Johnny's voice had deteriorated since the previous album and no amount of engineering wizardry could disguise the smacks and clicks of extraneous mouth noise. Cash and Rubin chose a group of songs which some considered inspired and others found unfathomable. 'Bridge Over Troubled Water', 'The First Time Ever I Saw Your Face', 'In My Life' and 'Desperado' mingled with old standards like 'Danny Boy', 'I'm So Lonesome I Could Cry' and 'We'll Meet Again'. The old Vera Lynn classic featured Jack Clement on dobro and backing vocals. Although he and Johnny had remained close, they had hardly worked together since Johnny signed with Rick Rubin's American Recordings label. Clement said he liked some of the material but "it's not the kind of stuff I'd record myself."*

The new album also featured contributions from young, cutting-edge artists, such as 'Hurt' by Trent Reznor of Nine Inch Nails. "That sounds like something I could have written in the Sixties." Johnny said. "There's more heart, soul and pain in that song than any I've heard in a long time. I love it." A video was made for the song which delivered a powerful anti-drug message, especially poignant in Johnny's case. The effect of the video – showing Johnny exactly as he looked with no cosmetic retouching – was nothing short of dramatic. In certain shots, he had the countenance of an embalmed corpse, with his skin drawn tightly over his bones. The juxtaposition of these recent images, interspersed with numerous fast edit clips of a young and attractive Cash throughout his career is painful to behold, as are the shots of the House of Cash with its "Closed to the public" sign – the symbolism all the more powerful since the property is now in an extremely run-down condition, having suffered recent flood damage.

The director, Mark Romanek, only had a couple of days to put the video

---

* Clement had not been impressed with the sound on the widely acclaimed *American Recordings* début, complaining that it didn't suit Johnny's voice because of the lack of echo.

together before Johnny headed off to Jamaica. "This concept is completely and utterly alien to what videos are supposed to be," he said. "They're supposed to be eye candy – hip and cool and all of that youth and energy stuff. This one is about someone moving towards the twilight of his career. It's about reality." The innovative video received substantial airplay on Country Music Television (CMT) and MTV.

What seemed to be common to the songs was their deep personal resonance with many aspects of Johnny's life, which made the omission of 'You'll Never Walk Alone' from the final selection surprising. There were only a few Cash originals and Johnny conceded that as he got older his power to compose had diminished.

In the liner notes he claimed that more time was spent on 'The Man Comes Around' than any other song he had ever written. The inspirational spark for the song came from a dream Johnny experienced seven years previously in England. "I dreamed that I walked into Buckingham Palace . . . she (Queen Elizabeth II) had a basket of fabric and lace. Another woman sat beside her, and they were talking and laughing. As I approached, the Queen looked up at me and said, 'Johnny Cash! You're like a thorn tree in a whirlwind.' "

Johnny found this expression in the book of Job, followed his thoughts into the book of Revelation and eventually wrote the song. The album also included Sting's 'I Hung My Head' which, with its themes of killing, innocence and guilt, punishment and the hereafter, was made-to-order from the Johnny Cash school of songwriting. Johnny reaffirmed his strong religious beliefs by including in the CD insert a close-up photograph of his left hand, showing a gold ring with Christ on the cross in relief on his wedding ring finger. The instrumental and vocal work came from a diverse collection of artists including Benmont Tench, Fiona Apple, Nick Cave and Randy Scruggs, just the kind of people Cash preferred since they were not involved in what he now referred to as the "over-plasticisation of music". As with the previous album, John Carter Cash was heavily involved, receiving an associate producer's credit.

The album divided the critics. For some, including a number of younger reviewers unfamiliar with much of Johnny's back catalogue, the album was a breath of fresh air in a world of artificial product. However, there were those who took the view that Johnny's obvious vocal frailty meant it really was time for him to bow out gracefully; others reckoned he had completely lost the plot. One reviewer, Dan Aquilante, felt that Johnny's versions of other people's songs did not work nearly as well as his own. "Cash should have trusted himself more on this record instead of rolling on a bed of wrinkled covers." On the other hand, Nick Reynolds found much to commend. "Only his Creator knows how he does it. We should just be grateful that Cash is still around to make records as uplifting and entertaining as this." *Rolling Stone* reviewer Mark Kemp was scathing. "Hearing him warble through Depeche Mode's 'Personal Jesus' you feel embarrassed for Cash and angry with Rubin for bleeding the life out of this experiment."

The end of year "Critics Choice" in *Country Music People* made it hard to believe that the contributors had been listening to the same album. Douglas McPherson was full of praise. "The man in black celebrates his 70th birthday on a career high with an album of devastating power." Dave Hastings took a diametrically opposed view. "Love Johnny Cash but this is just the pits. Poor guy has lost his voice, and the choice of songs is dreadful." Chris Bolton took a similar line. "Sad to think it's come to this for JC. The voice is gone and the song selection is incomprehensible."

On any view of it Johnny's achievements with Rick Rubin were remarkable and a whole new generation of fans, as well as many older ones, can perhaps be grateful that the Branson idea did not work out. Publicity surrounding Johnny's birthday helped to boost sales of his albums and it was reported in early 2002 that *Sixteen Biggest Hits* had shipped 600,000 copies since February 1999 and, within the same time, 150,000 copies of *Johnny Cash At Folsom Prison* were sold.

Despite the infrequency of Johnny's live performances it was reported that he might attend a festival planned to take place in London to celebrate his 70th birthday – similar to the Manhattan TNT spectacular. A deal was apparently agreed with Lou Robin, subject to the proviso that Johnny could pull out for health reasons. The ambitious project never got off the ground, ostensibly due to a lack of financial sponsorship but in reality Johnny's health precluded his involvement. However, he did manage a small number of personal appearances in 2002. During a holiday in Jamaica he sang 'The Ballad Of Annie Palmer' at a banquet for the Horatio Alger* Awards Committee. Johnny said it felt good to sing in front of an audience again and that he wanted to perform on a limited basis if his health continued to improve.

In September 2002, Johnny made a surprise appearance at the Americana Music Association's inaugural awards show in Nashville – his mere presence drawing the loudest applause of the night. He was presented with the inaugural Spirit of Americana Free Speech Award but, rather than making an acceptance speech, he recited 'Ragged Old Flag' with the lyrics updated to include references to Desert Storm, September 11 and the war in Afghanistan. June made a short speech during which she made the half-jesting remark, "He's always wanted to be a Carter brother." In similar vein she had previously referred to Johnny as "Brother Maybelle".

◆ ◆ ◆ ◆ ◆

---

* In the latter half of the nineteenth century, Alger had written novels of courage, faith and hard honest work which captured the imaginations of generations of young Americans and gave them a model of hope and promise in the face of hardship.

After completion of *American IV: The Man Comes Around*, Johnny was quick to scotch any idea that he might be calling it a day. "We're not into stopping and polishing milestones. We look forward to the next one." As 2003 neared, he told *Rolling Stone* that he would like to do an album called *Grass Roots*, featuring folk and country songs going all the way back to the early part of the twentieth century. When asked about retirement, he snapped back, "No no no no no. I'd die if I retired. Like a shark, gotta keep moving." In February, 'Give My Love To Rose' won the award for Best Male Country Vocal Performance, Johnny's twelfth Grammy. The ageing grandfather took the opportunity to praise controversial rapper Eminem, even though he was not familiar with his music. "If he's making the records he wants to make and people like them then that's what it's all about." Indefatigable as ever, he could have been talking about himself.

EPILOGUE

As a result of years of abuse, Johnny Cash's body gave out long ago. His physical condition deteriorated to the extent that towards the end, his life revolved around hospital admissions and medical consultations. Glaucoma robbed him of the ability to read the literature from which he drew so much inspiration. However, unlike others less fortunate, his success and position enabled him to have a loyal and dedicated group of retainers on call to look after his daily needs and to deal with the inevitable health crises as and when they arose. He had many friends with whom mutual empathy brought comfort. Though his professional life was, to all intents and purposes, virtually over by the mid-Nineties, an open recording arrangement enabled him the creative freedom he always wanted, resulting in some of the best albums of his career. Though he said he preferred to look forward, his massive contribution to music and other walks of life will always be recognised.

At the time of writing, a long-mooted Hollywood biopic, tentatively titled *Walk The Line* (with Reese Witherspoon playing June Carter and Joaquin Phoenix appearing as Johnny), is in the pipeline.

In March 2003 Johnny was readmitted to Nashville's Baptist Hospital, again suffering from pneumonia that seemed destined to claim him in the end. After weeks on a ventilator he was eventually released from hospital in such a weak condition that he had to learn to walk again. However the saddest blow of all was dealt just a month after his discharge. June was admitted to the same hospital for a routine operation to replace a heart valve. The surgery appeared to go well, but 48 hours after the operation June suffered a massive heart attack. She remained on life support for a short time but, bowing to the inevitable, Johnny took the deeply distressing decision to have the machine switched off on May 15, 2003.

Through all his health problems and brushes with death, Johnny could always rely on the strong and unwavering support of his beloved wife of 35 years. It was hard to imagine that his ability to (in June's words) "press on" in the face of adversity would be unaffected by her loss. Perhaps her death was an indicator that his own time was drawing near and that their enforced separation would not be for long.

June was laid to rest at Henderson Memorial Gardens, outside Nashville. The funeral service held at the First Baptist Church in Hendersonville (which was opened to the public at Johnny's request) was attended by approximately 2,500 people, including such Cash friends and associates as Lou Robin, Jack Clement, Jane Seymour, Robert Duvall and Rick Rubin. Musician friends paying their respects included Kris Kristofferson, Emmylou Harris, Hank Williams Jnr, Larry Gatlin and Sheryl Crow (who sang 'On the Sea Of Galilee'). The Jamaican prime minister sent a representative. Rosanne Cash spoke for her tearful, wheelchair-bound father by saying, "Her life was art, as much as her art was her life. There were two kinds of people in her world; those she knew and loved and those she didn't know and loved."

To mark what would have been June's 74th birthday, on June 21, Johnny appeared at the Carter Fold, in the Virginia Mountains. He was helped on stage by family members and held his guitar (although he did not play). It was a monumental effort on Johnny's part and he was only able to manage a few songs before being taken home to rest.

Despite everything, Johnny continued to record new material most days. He was taken the short distance from his house to his studio across the road by an ever-present medical aide, where he sang until he tired. Some 40 songs were believed to have been recorded during these final sessions. Tommy Cash felt that his brother appeared to have found an inner strength during the last few months of his life. "Johnny is sad and grieving but trying to accept things he has to accept and go on with his life."

That life ended on September 12.

SELECTIVE DISCOGRAPHY

Ask the average Johnny Cash fan to name all the Cash songs they can think of and they'd probably run out of titles after the first twenty or thirty. This isn't a criticism but rather a comment on how only a small proportion of songs recorded by an artist make it into the person's long-term memory. Other artists are lucky if even *one* of their songs makes it this far.

As a solo artist and in the company of others, Johnny Cash has recorded thousands of songs in his long and distinguished career – enough to fill a book of their own. For those who have such an interest, John L Smith, a personal friend of Johnny Cash, has painstakingly put together various books detailing most of the songs Cash has ever recorded, including production and musician information. For the Cash obsessive Smith's body of work is a goldmine.

In similar vein, the German record label Bear Family has produced compilations featuring much previously unreleased Cash material. Their first album, *The Unissued Johnny Cash*, was released in 1978 since when a number of other sets have followed. As with Smith's books these collections are for the enthusiast only, featuring aborted takes and unreleased versions. For those with only a general interest in Johnny Cash's music many representative compilations have been released over the years containing most of his well-known songs. One particularly good compilation, released around the time of Cash's 70th birthday, is the Columbia 2 CD set, *Man In Black: The Very Best Of Johnny Cash*, which features a well-chosen cross section of 40 songs from 1955 up until 1993 (excluding the material recorded for Rick Rubin's American Recordings label post-1994).

The problem with compilations is that certain material inevitably gets omitted. In my view, the essence of Johnny Cash's music lies beyond a compilation, though naturally which albums best capture that essence is a matter of opinion. For what it's worth, in my view the following albums (all currently available) define Johnny Cash at his best:

Up Through The Years (Bear Family) featuring the Sun singles.
Ride This Train.
Johnny Cash At Folsom Prison.
America – A 200 Year Salute In Story And Song.
American Recordings.

What follows is a selective but representative list of Johnny Cash's albums (to 2003):

With His Hot And Blue Guitar (1957) (Sun): 'Rock Island Line', 'I Heard That Lonesome Whistle', 'Country Boy', 'If The Good Lord's Willing', 'Cry! Cry! Cry!', 'Remember Me', 'So Doggone Lonesome', 'I Was There When It Happened', 'I Walk The Line', 'Wreck Of The Old '97', 'Folsom Prison Blues', 'Doin' My Time'

The Fabulous Johnny Cash (1958) (Columbia): 'Run Softly, Blue River', 'Frankie's Man, Johnny', 'That's All Over', 'The Troubadour', 'One More Ride', 'That's Enough', 'I Still Miss Someone', 'Don't Take Your Guns To Town', 'I'd Rather Die Young', 'Pickin' Time', 'Shepherd Of My Heart', 'Suppertime'

Hymns By Johnny Cash (1959) (Columbia): 'It Was Jesus', 'I Saw A Man', 'Are All The Children In?', 'The Old Account', 'Lead Me Gently Home', 'Swing Low Sweet Chariot', 'Snow In His Hair', 'Lead Me Father', 'I Call Him', 'These Things Shall Pass', 'He'll Be A Friend', 'God Will'

Songs Of Our Soil (1959) (Columbia): 'Drink To Me', 'Five Feet High And Rising', 'The Man On The Hill', 'Hank And Joe And Me', 'Clementine', 'Great Speckled Bird', 'I Want To Go Home', 'The Caretaker', 'Old Apache Squaw', 'Don't Step On Mother's Roses', 'My Grandfather's Clock', 'It Could Be You (Instead Of Him)'

Ride This Train (1960) (Columbia): 'Loading Coal', 'Slow Rider', 'Lumberjack', 'Dorraine Of Ponchartrain', 'Going To Memphis', 'When Papa Played The Dobro', 'Boss Jack', 'Old Doc Brown'

Now, There Was A Song! (1960) (Columbia): 'Seasons Of My Heart', 'I Feel Better All Over', 'I Couldn't Keep From Crying', 'Time Changes Everything', 'My Shoes Keep Walking Back To You', 'I'd Just Be Fool Enough (To Fall)', 'Transfusion Blues', 'Why Do You Punish Me (For Loving You)', 'I Will Miss You When You Go', 'I'm So Lonesome I Could Cry', 'Just One More', 'Honky-Tonk Girl'

Hymns From The Heart (1962) (Columbia): 'He'll Understand And Say Well Done', 'God Must Have My Fortune Laid Away', 'When I've Learned', 'I Got Shoes', 'Let The Lower Lights Be Burning', 'If We Never Meet Again', 'When I

Take My Vacation In Heaven', 'When He Reached Down His Hand For Me', 'Taller Than Trees', 'I Won't Have To Cross Jordan Alone', 'My God Is Real', 'These Hands'

The Sound Of Johnny Cash (1962) (Columbia): 'Lost On The Desert', 'Accidentally On Purpose', 'In The Jailhouse Now', 'Mr Lonesome', 'You Won't Have Far To Go', 'In Them Old Cottonfields Back Home', 'Delia's Gone', 'I Forgot More Than You'll Ever Know', 'You Remembered Me', 'I'm Free From The Chain Gang Now', 'Let Me Down Easy', 'Sing It Pretty Sue'

Blood Sweat And Tears (1963) (Columbia): 'The Legend Of John Henry's Hammer', 'Tell Him I'm Gone', 'Another Man Done Gone', 'Busted', 'Casey Jones', 'Nine Pound Hammer', 'Chain Gang', 'Waiting For A Train', 'Roughneck'

Ring Of Fire (1963) (Columbia): 'Ring Of Fire', 'I'd Still Be There', 'What Do I Care?', 'I Still Miss Someone', 'Forty Shades Of Green', 'Were You There (When They Crucified My Lord)', 'The Rebel – Johnny Yuma', 'Bonanza', 'The Big Battle', 'Remember The Alamo', 'Tennessee Flat-Top Box', 'Peace In The Valley'

Bitter Tears (1964) (Columbia): 'As Long As The Grass Shall Grow', 'Apache Tears', 'Custer', 'The Talking Leaves', 'The Ballad Of Ira Hayes', 'Drums', 'White Girl', 'The Vanishing Race'

Orange Blossom Special (1965) (Columbia): 'Orange Blossom Special', 'Long Black Veil', 'It Ain't Me Babe', 'The Wall', 'Don't Think Twice, It's Alright', 'You Wild Colorado', 'Mama, You've Been On My Mind', 'When It's Springtime In Alaska', 'All Of God's Children Ain't Free', 'Danny Boy', 'Wildwood Flower', 'Amen'

Ballads Of The True West (1965) (Columbia): 'Hiawatha's Vision', 'Road To Kaintuck', 'Shifting, Whispering Sands (Part 1)', 'Narration', 'Ballad Of Boot Hill', 'I Ride An Old Paint', 'Narration', 'Hardin Wouldn't Run', 'Narration', 'Mister Garfield', 'Streets Of Laredo', 'Narration', 'Johnny Reb', 'A Letter From Home', 'Bury Me Not On The Lone Prairie', 'Mean As Hell', 'Sam Hall', 'Twenty Five Minutes To Go', 'The Blizzard', 'Narration', 'Sweet Betsy From Pike', Green Grow The Lilacs', 'Narration', 'Stampede', 'Shifting, Whispering Sands (Part 2)', 'Reflections'

Everybody Loves A Nut (1966) (Columbia): 'Everybody Loves A Nut', 'The One On The Right Is On The Left', 'A Cup Of Coffee', 'The Bug That Tried To Crawl Around The World', 'Singing Star's Queen', 'Austin Prison', 'Dirty Old Egg Sucking Dog', 'Take Me Home', 'Please Don't Play Red River Valley', 'Boa Constrictor', 'Joe Bean'

Happiness Is You (1966) (Columbia): 'Happiness Is You', 'Guess Things Happen

That Way', 'Ancient History', 'You Comb Her Hair', 'She Came From The Mountains', 'For Lovin' Me', 'No One Will Ever Know', 'Is This My Destiny', 'A Wound Time Can't Erase', 'Happy To Be With You', 'Wabash Cannonball'

From Sea To Shining Sea (1967) (Columbia): 'From Sea To Shining Sea', 'The Whirl And The Suck', 'Call Daddy From The Mine', 'The Frozen Four-Hundred-Pound Fair-To-Middlin' Cotton Picker', 'The Walls Of A Prison', 'The Masterpiece', 'You And Tennessee', 'Another Song To Sing', 'Flint Arrowhead', 'Cisco Clifton's Fillin' Station', 'Shrimpin' Sailin'', 'From Sea To Shining Sea'

Carryin' On With Johnny Cash And June Carter (1967) (Columbia): 'Long-Legged Guitar Pickin' Man', 'Shantytown', 'It Ain't Me, Babe', 'Fast Boat To Sydney', 'Pack Up Your Sorrows', 'I Got A Woman', 'Jackson', 'Oh, What A Good Thing We Had', 'You'll Be All Right', 'No, No, No', 'What'd I Say'

Johnny Cash At Folsom Prison (1968) (Columbia): 'Folsom Prison Blues', 'Dark As a Dungeon', 'I Still Miss Someone', 'Cocaine Blues', 'Twenty-Five Minutes To Go', 'Orange Blossom Special', 'Long Black Veil', 'Send A Picture Of Mother', 'The Wall', 'Dirty Old Egg Sucking Dog', 'Flushed From The Bathroom Of Your Heart', 'Jackson', 'Give My Love To Rose', 'I Got Stripes', 'Green, Green Grass Of Home', 'Greystone Chapel' (*Re-released in 1999 with the addition of three previously unreleased tracks,* 'Busted', 'Joe Bean', *and* 'The Legend Of John Henry's Hammer')

Johnny Cash At San Quentin (1969) (Columbia): 'Wanted Man', 'Wreck Of The Old '97', 'I Walk The Line', 'Darling Companion', 'Starkville City Jail', 'San Quentin No. 1', 'San Quentin No. 2', 'A Boy Named Sue', 'Peace In The Valley', 'Folsom Prison Blues' (*Re-released in 2000 with the addition of eight previously unreleased tracks,* 'Big River', 'I Still Miss Someone', 'I Don't Know Where I'm Bound', 'Ring Of Fire', 'He Turned The Water Into Wine', 'Daddy Sang Bass', 'The Old Account Was Settled Long Ago', 'Closing Medley')

Hello, I'm Johnny Cash (1970) (Columbia): 'Southwind', 'The Devil To Pay', 'Cause I Love You', 'See Ruby Fall', 'Route No. 1 Box 144', 'Sing A Travelling Song', 'If I Were A Carpenter', 'To Beat The Devil', 'Blistered', 'Wrinkled, Crinkled, Wadded Dollar Bill', 'I've Got A Thing About Trains', 'Jesus Was A Carpenter'

Man In Black (1971) (Columbia): 'The Preacher Said, "Jesus Said"', 'Orphan Of The Road', 'You've Got A New Light Shining', 'If Not For Love', 'Man In Black', 'Singin' In Vietnam Talkin' Blues', 'Ned Kelly', 'Look For Me', 'Dear Mrs', 'I Talk To Jesus Every Day'

A Thing Called Love (1972) (Columbia): 'Kate', 'Melva's Wine', 'A Thing Called Love', 'I Promise You', 'Papa Was A Good Man', 'Tear-Stained Letter', 'Mississippi Sand', 'Daddy', 'Arkansas-Lovin' Man', 'The Miracle Man'

America (1972) (Columbia): Opening Dialogue, 'Paul Revere', 'Begin Westward Movement', 'The Road To Kaintuck', 'To The Shining Mountains', 'The Battle Of New Orleans', 'Southwestward', 'Remember The Alamo', 'Opening Of The West', 'Lorena', 'Gettysburg Address', 'The West', 'Big Foot', 'Like A Young Colt', 'Mister Garfield', 'A Proud Land', 'The Big Battle', 'On Wheels And Wings', 'Come Take A Trip In My Airship', 'Reaching For The Stars', 'These Are My People'

Any Old Wind That Blows (1973) (Columbia): 'Any Old Wind That Blows', 'Kentucky Straight', 'The Loving Gift', 'The Good Earth', 'Best Friend', 'Oney', 'Ballad Of Annie Palmer', 'Too Little, Too Late', 'If I Had A Hammer', 'Country Trash', 'Welcome Back Jesus'

The Gospel Road (1973) (Columbia): 'Praise The Lord', Introduction, 'Gospel Road – Part One', 'Jesus – Early Years', 'Gospel Road – Part Two', 'John The Baptist', 'Baptism Of Jesus', 'Wilderness Temptation', 'Follow Me, Jesus', 'Gospel Road – Part Three', 'Jesus Announces His Divinity', 'Jesus', Opposition Is Established', 'Jesus' First Miracle', 'He Turned The Water Into Wine – Part One', 'State Of The Nation', 'I See Men As Trees Walking', 'Jesus Was A Carpenter – Part One', 'Choosing Of Twelve Disciples', 'Jesus' Teaching', 'Parable Of The Good Shepherd', 'Two Greatest Commandments', 'Greater Love Hath No Man', 'John The Baptist's Imprisonment And Death', 'Jesus Cleanses Temple', 'Jesus Upbraids Scribes And Pharisees', 'Jesus In The Temple', 'Come Unto Me', 'The Adulterous Woman', 'Help – Part One', 'Jesus And Nicodemus', 'Help – Part Two', 'Sermon On The Mount', 'Blessed Are', 'The Lord's Prayer – Amen Chorus', 'Introducing Mary Magdalene', 'Mary Magdalene Speaks', 'Follow Me', 'Magdalene Speaks Again', 'Crossing The Sea Of Galilee', 'He Turned The Water Into Wine – Part Two', 'He Turned The Water Into Wine – Part Three', 'Feeding The Multitude', 'He Turned The Water Into Wine – Part Four', 'More Jesus Teaching', 'Living Water And The Bread Of Life', 'Gospel Road – Part Four', 'Jesus And Children', 'Children', 'Four Months To Live', 'Help-Part Three', 'Help-Part Four', 'Raising Of Lazarus', 'Jesus' Second Coming', 'Jesus' Entry Into Jerusalem', 'Burden Of Freedom', 'Jesus Wept', 'Burden Of Freedom', 'Jesus Cleanses Temple Again', 'Feast Of The Passover', 'Lord, Is It I?', 'The Last Supper', 'John 14: 1–3', 'And Now He's Alone', 'Agony In Gethsemane', 'Jesus Before Ciaphas, Pilot And Herod', 'Burden Of Freedom', 'Crucifixion', 'Jesus' Last Words', 'Jesus' Death', 'Earthquake And Darkness', 'He Is Risen', 'Mary Magdalene Returns To Galilee',

'Jesus Appears To Disciples', 'The Great Commission', 'Ascension – Amen Chorus', 'Jesus Was A Carpenter – Part Two'

Johnny Cash And His Woman (1973) (Columbia): 'Color Of Love', 'Saturday Night In Hickman County', 'Allegheny', 'Life Has Its Little Ups And Downs', 'Matthew 24 (Is Knocking At The Door)', 'City Of New Orleans', 'Tony', 'The Pine Tree', 'We're For Love', 'Godshine'

Ragged Old Flag (1974) (Columbia): 'Ragged Old Flag', 'Don't Go Near The Water', 'All I Do Is Drive', 'Southern Comfort', 'King Of The Hill', 'Pie In The Sky', 'Lonesome To The Bone', 'While I've Got It On My Mind', 'Good Morning Friend', 'I'm A Worried Man', 'Please Don't Let Me Out', 'What On Earth Will You Do (For Heaven's Sake)'

The Junkie And The Juicehead Minus Me (1974) (Columbia): 'The Junkie And The Juicehead Minus Me', 'Don't Take Your Guns To Town', 'Broken Freedom Song', 'I Do Believe', 'Old Slewfoot', 'Keep On The Sunny Side', 'Father And Daughter (Father And Son)', 'Crystal Chandeliers And Burgundy', 'Friendly Gates', 'Billy And Rex And Oral And Bob', 'J-E-S-U-S', 'Lay Back With My Woman'

John R. Cash (1975) (Columbia): 'My Old Kentucky Home', 'Hard Times Comin'', 'The Lady Came From Baltimore', 'Lonesome To The Bone', 'The Night They Drove Old Dixie Down', 'Clean Your Own Tables', 'Jesus Was Our Saviour', 'Reason To Believe', 'Cocaine Carolina', 'Smokey Factory Blues'

Look At Them Beans (1975) (Columbia): 'Texas 1947', 'What Have You Got Planned Tonight Diana', 'Look At Them Beans', 'No Charge', 'I Hardly Ever Sing Beer Drinking Songs', 'Down The Road I Go', 'I've Never Met A Man Like You Before', 'All Around Cowboy', 'Gone', 'Down At Drippin' Springs'

One Piece At A Time (1976) (Columbia): 'Let There Be Country', 'One Piece At A Time', 'In A Young Girl's Mind', 'Mountain Lady', 'Michigan City Howdy-Do', 'Sold Out Of Flagpoles', 'Committed To Parkview', 'Daughter Of A Railroad Man', 'Love Has Lost Again', 'Go On Blues'

Last Gunfighter Ballad (1977) (Columbia): 'I Will Dance With You', 'Last Gunfighter Ballad', 'Far Side Banks Of Jordan', 'Ridin' On The Cottonbelt', 'Give It Away', 'You're So Close To Me', 'City Jail', 'Cindy, I Love You', 'Ballad Of Barbara', 'That Silver Haired Daddy Of Mine'

The Rambler (1977) (Columbia): 'Hit The Road And Go', Dialogue, 'If It Wasn't For The Wabash River', Dialogue, 'Lady', Dialogue, 'After The Ball', Dialogue, 'No Earthly Good', Dialogue, 'A Wednesday Car', Dialogue, 'My Cowboy's Last Ride', Dialogue, 'Calilou', Dialogue

I Would Like To See You Again (1978) (Columbia): 'I Would Like To See You Again', 'Lately', 'I Wish I Was Crazy Again', 'Who's Gene Autry?', 'Hurt So Bad', 'I Don't Think I Could Take You Back Again', 'Abner Brown', 'After Taxes', 'There Ain't No Good Chain Gang', 'That's The Way It Is', 'I'm Alright Now'

Silver (1979) (Columbia): 'The L&N Don't Stop Here Anymore', 'Lonesome To The Bone', 'Bull Rider', 'I'll Say It's True', 'Ghost Riders In The Sky', 'Cocaine Blues', 'Muddy Waters', 'West Canterbury Subdivision Blues', 'Lately I've Been Leanin' Towards To The Blues', 'I'm Gonna Sit On The Porch And Pick On My Old Guitar'

Rockabilly Blues (1980) (Columbia): 'Cold Lonesome Morning', 'Without Love', 'W-O-M-A-N', 'Cowboy Who Started The Fight', 'The Twentieth Century Is Almost Over', 'She's A Goer', 'It Ain't Nothing New Babe', 'One Way Rider'

The Baron (1981) (Columbia) 'The Baron', 'Mobile Bay', 'The Hard Way', 'A Ceiling, Four Walls And A Floor', 'Hey, Hey Train', 'The Reverend Mr Black-Lonesome Valley', 'The Blues Keep Getting Bluer', 'Chattanooga City Limits Sign', 'Thanks To You', 'Greatest Love Affair'

The Survivors (1982) (Columbia) (with Jerry Lee Lewis and Carl Perkins): 'Get Rhythm', 'I Forgot To Remember To Forget', 'Goin' Down The Road Feelin' Bad', 'That Silver Haired Daddy Of Mine', 'Matchbox', 'I'll Fly Away', 'Whole Lotta Shakin' Goin' On', 'Rockin' My Life Away', 'Blue Suede Shoes', 'Peace In The Valley', 'Will The Circle Be Unbroken?', 'I Saw The Light'

The Adventures Of Johnny Cash (1982) (Columbia): 'Georgia On A Fast Rain', 'John's', 'Fairweather Friends', 'Paradise', 'We Must Believe In Magic', 'Only Love', 'Good Old American Guest', 'I'll Cross Over Jordan', 'Sing A Song', 'Ain't Gonna Hobo No More'

Johnny 99 (1983) (Columbia): 'Highway Patrolman', 'That's The Truth', 'God Bless Robert E. Lee', 'New Cut Road', 'Johnny 99', 'Ballad Of The Ark', 'Joshua Gone Barbados', 'Girl From The Canyon', 'Brand New Dance', 'I'm Ragged But I'm Right'

Highwayman (1985) (Columbia) with The Highwaymen: 'Highwayman', 'The Last Cowboy Song', 'Jim, I Wore A Tie Today', 'Big River', 'Committed To Parkview', 'Desperadoes Waiting For A Train', 'Deportee', 'Welfare Line', 'Against The Wind', 'The Twentieth Century Is Almost Over'

Rainbow (1985) (Columbia): 'I'm Leaving Now', 'Here Comes That Rainbow Again', 'They're All The Same', 'Easy Street', 'Have You Ever Seen The Rain', 'You Beat All I Ever Saw', 'Unwed Fathers', 'Love Me Like You Used To', 'Casey's Last Ride', 'Borderline (A Musical Whodunnit)'

Heroes 1986 (Columbia) with Waylon Jennings: 'Folks Out On The Road', 'I'm Never Gonna Roam Again', 'American By Birth', 'Field Of Diamonds', 'Heroes', 'Even Cowgirls Get The Blues', 'Love Is The Way', 'The Ballad Of Forty Dollars', 'I'll Always Love You (In My Own Crazy Way)', 'One Too Many Mornings'

Class Of '55: Memphis Rock & Roll Homecoming (1986) (Columbia) with Roy Orbison, Jerry Lee Lewis, and Carl Perkins: 'Birth Of Rock And Roll', 'Sixteen Candles', 'Class Of '55', 'Waymore Blues', 'We Remember The King', 'Coming Home', 'Rock And Roll (Fais-Do-Do)', 'Keep My Motor Running', 'I Will Rock And Roll With You', 'Big Rain From Memphis'

Johnny Cash Is Coming To Town (1987) (Mercury): 'The Big Light', 'Ballad Of Barbara', 'I'd Rather Have You', 'Let Him Roll', 'The Night Hank Williams Came To Town', 'Sixteen Tons', 'Letters From Home', 'W. Lee O'Daniel (And The Light Crust Doughboys)', 'Heavy Metal (Don't Mean Rock And Roll To Me)', 'My Ship Will Sail'

Water From The Wells Of Home (1988) (Mercury): 'Ballad Of A Teenage Queen', 'As Long As I Live', 'Where Did We Go Right', 'Last Of The Drifters', 'Call Me The Breeze', 'That Old Wheel', 'Sweeter Than The Flowers', 'A Croft In Clachan (The Ballad Of Rob MacDunn)', 'New Moon Over Jamaica', 'Water From The Wells Of Home'

Highwayman II (1990) (Columbia) with The Highwaymen: 'Silver Stallion', 'Born And Raised In Black And White', 'Two Stories Wide', 'We're All In Your Corner Tonight', 'American Remains', 'Anthem '84', 'Angels Love Badmen', 'Songs That Make A Difference', 'Living Legends', 'Texas'

Boom Chicka Boom (1990) (Mercury): 'A Backstage Pass', 'Cat's In The Cradle', 'Farmer's Almanac', 'Don't Go Near The Water', 'Family Bible', 'Harley', 'I Love You, Love You', 'Hidden Shame', 'Monteagle Mountain', 'That's One You Owe Me'

The Mystery Of Life (1991) (Mercury): 'The Greatest Cowboy Of Them All', 'I'm An Easy Rider', 'The Mystery Of Life', 'Hey! Porter', 'Beans For Breakfast', 'Goin' By The Book', 'Wanted Man', 'I'll Go Somewhere And Sing My Songs Again', 'The Hobo Song', 'Angel And The Badman'

American Recordings (1994) (American Recordings): 'Delia's Gone', 'Let The Train Blow The Whistle', 'The Beast In Me', 'Drive On', 'Why Me Lord', 'Thirteen', 'Oh Bury Me Not', 'Bird On A Wire', 'Tennessee Stud', 'Down There By The Train', 'Redemption', 'Like A Soldier', 'The Man Who Couldn't Cry'

Up Through The Years (1994) (Bear Family): 'Cry! Cry! Cry!', 'Hey! Porter', 'Folsom Prison Blues', 'Luther Played The Boogie', 'So Doggone Lonesome', 'I Walk The Line', 'Get Rhythm', 'Train Of Love', 'There You Go', 'Goodbye Little

Darling Goodbye', 'I Love You Because', 'Straight A's In Love', 'Next In Line', 'Don't Make Me Go', 'Home Of The Blues', 'Give My Love To Rose', 'Rock Island Line', 'Wreck Of The Old '97', 'Ballad Of A Teenage Queen', 'Big River', 'Guess Things Happen That Way', 'Come In Stranger', 'You're The Nearest Thing To Heaven', 'Blue Train'

The Road Goes On Forever (1995) (Liberty) with The Highwaymen: 'The Devil's Right Hand', 'Live Forever', 'Everyone Gets Crazy', 'It Is What It Is', 'I Do Believe', 'The End Of Understanding', 'True Love Travels On A Gravel Road', 'Death And Hell', 'Waiting For A Long Time', 'Here Comes That Rainbow Again', 'The Road Goes On Forever'

Unchained (1996) (American Recordings): 'Rowboat', 'Sea Of Heartbreak', 'Rusty Cage', 'The One Rose', 'Country Boy', 'Memories Are Made Of This', 'Spiritual', 'Kneeling Drunkard's Plea', 'Southern Accents', 'Mean Eyed Cat', 'Meet Me In Heaven', 'I Never Picked Cotton', 'Unchained', 'I've Been Everywhere'

VH1 Storytellers (1998) (American Recordings) with Willie Nelson: 'Ghost Riders In The Sky', 'Worried Man', 'Family Bible', 'Don't Take Your Guns To Town', 'Funny How Time Slips Away', 'Flesh And Blood', 'Crazy', 'Unchained', 'Night Life', 'Drive On', 'Me And Paul', 'I Still Miss Someone', 'Always On My Mind', 'Folsom Prison Blues', 'On The Road Again'

American III: Solitary Man (2000) (American Recordings): 'I Won't Back Down', 'Solitary Man', 'Lucky Ole Sun', 'One', 'Nobody', 'I See A Darkness', 'The Mercy Seat', 'Would You Lay With Me?', 'Field Of Diamonds', 'Before My Time', 'Country Trash', 'Mary Of The Wild Moor', 'I'm Leavin' Now', 'Wayfaring Stranger'

American IV: The Man Comes Around (2002) (American Recordings): 'The Man Comes Around', 'Hurt', 'Give My Love To Rose', 'Bridge Over Troubled Water', 'I Hung My Head', 'First Time Ever I Saw Your Face', 'Personal Jesus', 'In My Life', 'Sam Hall', 'Danny Boy', 'Desperado', 'I'm So Lonesome I Could Cry', 'Tear Stained Letter', 'Streets Of Laredo', 'We'll Meet Again'

SOURCES

So much has been written about Johnny Cash since the mid-Fifties – in books, newspapers, magazines, journals, liner notes, and internet material – that it would be impossible to credit every source. However with the able and generously given assistance of the staff at the Country Music Foundation and the Nashville Public Library I was able to see a broad swathe of American and Canadian press clippings going right back to the early stages of Johnny Cash's career. Although the articles came from numerous publications (many of which are doubtless now defunct), the majority were contained in *The Nashville Banner* and *The Tennessean*. Among numerous articles in the British press, those in *The Guardian* and *The Daily Telegraph* – encompassing respective left- and right-wing views (like Cash himself) – struck me as containing the most acute observations. Magazines that were especially helpful included *Country Music* and *Country Music People*.

In addition I was fortunate to be given access to the private collections of some long-serving Johnny Cash fans in Britain, including rare tribute magazines and fan club documents that often contained features and comments which never entered the wider public domain. One collector provided a tape of an entire Johnny Cash concert from an early British tour that he obtained via a carefully concealed tape recorder.

The internet of course provides a forum for many of those with interests in Johnny Cash to publish a diverse range of material – some of which was useful, as were various record and CD liner notes.

Of the many books published about Johnny Cash (and various areas associated with his life and career), the following were consulted for additional information and/or inspiration:

A Boy Named Cash. The Johnny Cash Story. Albert Govoni. Lancer Books, 1970.
A Johnny Cash Chronicle. I've Been Everywhere. Peter Lewry. Helter Skelter. 2001.

A Satisfied Mind: The Country Music Life Of Porter Wagoner. Steve Eng. Rutledge Hill Press. 1992.

All The Gold In California. Larry Gatlin with Jeff Lenburg. Thomas Nelson Publishers. 1998.

America's Music: The Roots Of Country. Robert K Oermann. Turner Publishing, Inc. 1996.

Among My Klediments. June Carter Cash. Zonderban Publishing House. 1979.

Are You Ready For The Country. Peter Doggett. Penguin. 2000.

Catalyst: The Sun Records Story. Colin Escott and Martin Hawkins. Aquarius. 1975.

Classic Bob Dylan 1962 – 1969. My Back Pages. Andy Gill. Carlton.

Classic Country: Legends Of Country Music. Charles K Wolfe. Routledge. 2001.

Country: Living Legends And Dying Metaphors In America's Biggest Music. Nick Tosches. Secker & Warburg. 1985.

Country Music Culture: From Hard Times To Heaven. Curtis W Ellison. University Press of Mississippi. 1995.

Country Music USA: A Fifty Year History. Bill C Malone. The University of Texas Press. 1968.

Creating Country Music: Fabricating Authenticity. Richard A Peterson. University of Chicago Press. 1997.

Definitive Country: The Ultimate Encyclopedia Of Country Music And Its Performers. Barry McCloud. Perigee Books. 1995.

Down At The End Of Lonely Street: The Life And Death Of Elvis Presley. Peter Brown and Pat Broeske. Heinemann. 1997.

The Ultimate Elvis (Elvis Presley Day By Day). Patricia Jobe Pierce. Simon and Schuster. 1994.

Elvis: The Golden Anniversary Tribute. Richard Peters. Pop Universal/Souvenir Press. 1984

Finding Her Voice: The Illustrated History Of Women In Country Music. Mary A Bufwack and Robert K Oermann. Henry Holt. 1993.

Honky Tonk Angel: The Intimate Story Of Patsy Cline. Ellis Nassour. Virgin Books. 1994.

Good Rockin' Tonight. Colin Escott with Martin Hawkins. Virgin Books. 1992

Great Balls Of Fire: The True Story Of Jerry Lee Lewis. Myra Lewis with Murray Silver. Virgin. 1982.

Hank Williams: The Biography. Colin Escott with George Merritt and William MacEwen. Little Brown and Co. 1994.

Inside Country Music. Larry E Wacholtz. Billboard Publications, Inc. 1986.

In The Country Of Country: People And Places In American Music. Nicholas Dawidoff. Faber & Faber. 1997.

Johnny Cash. Frank Moriarty. Metro Books. 1997.

Johnny Cash (Pop Culture Legends). Sean Dolan. Chelsea House Publishers. *1995.*

Johnny Cash: The Autobiography. Johnny Cash with Patrick Carr. Harper-Paperbacks. 1997.

Johnny Cash: Winners Got Scars Too. Christopher S Wren. Abacus. 1974.

Living Proof. Hank Williams, Jr with Michael Bane. G P Putnam's Sons. 1979.

Lost Highway: Journeys And Arrivals Of American Musicians. Peter Guralnick. David R Godine. 1979.

Louisiana Hayride Years: Making Musical History In Country Music's Golden Age. Horace Logan with Bill Sloan. St Martin's Griffin. New York. 1998.

Man In White. Johnny Cash. Corona. 1986

Marty Robbins: Fast Cars And Country Music. Barbara J Pruett. The Scarecrow Press, Inc. London. 1990.

More Memories. Ralph Emery with Tom Carter. G P Putnam's Sons. 1993.

Music USA: America's Country And Western Tradition. Charles T Brown. Prentice – Hall. 1986.

Nashville: Music City USA. John Lomax III. Harry N Abrams, Inc. 1985.

Nashville Babylon. Randall Riese. Guild Publishing. 1989.

No Direction Home: The Life And Music Of Bob Dylan. Robert Shelton. Penguin. 1986.

Pat Boone: The Authorised Biography. Paul Davis. HarperCollins. 2001.

Readin' Country Music. The South Atlantic Quarterly. Winter 1995. Duke University Press.

Ring Of Fire: The Johnny Cash Reader. Michael Streissguth Editor. Da Capo Press. 2002.

Say It One Time For The Broken Hearted: The Country Side Of Southern Soul. Barney Hoskyns. Fontana. 1987.

Sing Your Heart Out, Country Boy. Dorothy Horstman. Country Music Foundation Press. 1996.

Stars Of Country Music. Edited by Bill C Malone and Judith McCulloh. University of Illinois Press. 1975.

Tennessee Music: Its People And Places. Peter Coats Zimmerman. Odyssey. 1998.

The Blackwell Guide To Recorded Country Music. Edited by Bob Allen. Blackwell Publishers. 1994.

The Country Music Story. Goldblatt and Shelton. The Bobbs-Merrill Company, Inc. 1966.

The Day The Music Died: The Last Tour Of Buddy Holly, "Big Bopper", And Ritchie Valens. Larry Lehmer. Schirmer Books. 1997.

The Grand Ole Opry History Of Country Music. Paul Kingsbury. Villard Books. 1995.

The Man In Black. Johnny Cash. Hodder & Stoughton 1975.

The New Johnny Cash. Charles Paul Conn. Hodder Christian Paperbacks. 1973.

The Sound Of Light: A History Of Gospel Music. Bowling Green State University Popular Press. 1990.

The Women Of Country Music: Singers And Sweethearts. Joan Dew. Dolphin Books. 1977.

Three Chords And The Truth: Hope, Heartbreak And Changing Fortunes In Nashville. Laurence Leamer. HarperCollins. 1997.

Waylon: An Autobiography. Waylon Jennings with Lenny Kaye. Warner Books. 1996.

Willie Nelson: Red Headed Stranger. Jim Brown. Quarry Music Books 2001.

Will You Miss Me When I'm Gone?: The Carter Family And Their Legacy In American Music. Mark Zwonitzer with Charles Hirshberg. Simon & Schuster. 2002.

ACKNOWLEDGEMENTS

I never did get to meet Johnny Cash. The first time I visited Nashville he had just suffered an allergic reaction to a throat spray, and was admitted to hospital as a precautionary measure. Unsurprisingly answering the questions I had was the last thing on his mind. On my second visit he was again in hospital with pneumonia and, again, an interview was out of the question.

However, I was fortunate to make the acquaintance of Johnny's brother Tommy, with whom I spent time in Nashville (with his delightful wife Marcy). Apart from the generous hospitality I was shown, Tommy took me to some key sites of relevance to his brother's story, such as the mansion in Hendersonville, The House Of Cash, the areas of land purchased and sold by Johnny and June over the years and the Hendersonville cemetery where many members of the Cash and Carter clan are buried. (Sadly, just as this book was being completed, June Carter Cash was also laid to rest there in May 2003.)

Tommy also introduced me to other members of the family including his sisters Joanne and Louise. Sadly, Louise too passed away in April 2003 making Johnny now the eldest survivor of the seven Cash siblings. When Tommy visited Scotland to headline a concert in Ayr, I was able to set up another show at Bein Inn, a thriving and imaginative music venue run by David Mundell near Glenfarg, a small town in Fife – part of the Cash ancestral lands around Strathmiglo. I acted as guide for Tommy and Marcy and we had a pleasant time driving around the countryside, with Tommy stopping every now and then to take photographs of signs such as Wester Cash and Cash Feus.

In the course of the time we spent together, as well as transatlantic communications, we talked a great deal about Johnny, professionally and personally and I am indebted to Tommy for the anecdotes and insights he so kindly gave me. Tommy also acted as an intermediary on occasion, getting answers to specific questions from Johnny himself. It's an honour to see his personal e-mails signed off as, "Your friend Tommy."

I did approach Rosanne Cash and John Carter Cash but they declined to be involved, though I was able to observe John Carter Cash at close quarters when I attended a show he played at the Bluebird Café in Nashville.

I was similarly unable to interview Marshall Grant and WS Holland who were with Johnny from his earliest days. Marshall Grant is, I understand, involved in another project about his former boss and did not reply to my inquiries.

WS Holland (alias Fluke) spoke to me on a number of occasions but though he told me to contact him when I got to Nashville with a view to us "hooking up", in the event, he chose not to give an interview. His position was paradoxical. On the one hand, he complained that books, magazines, articles and television programmes about Johnny "never told the real truth". Yet he declined the opportunity I gave him to put the record straight. It seems that he too is interested in writing his own version of the Cash story and as he is keen to point out, he "saw it all". Then again, Fluke has been talking in these terms for some time but has yet to put his plan into action.

Two men who have been closely involved with Johnny Cash in pivotal roles for many years, Jack Clement and Lou Robin, graciously consented to give interviews. Apart from obtaining much useful material, I was, as a cat lover, delighted to make the acquaintance of Jack's ginger tom Eugene, so full of character that despite his strong preference for dogs, Johnny Cash has been won over by Eugene's charms. Apart from providing me with anecdotes and opinions, I am grateful to George Hamilton IV for arranging a backstage pass to the Grand Ole Opry. It was my good fortune that the night I attended happened to coincide with the 4,000th Opry show.

On each of my Nashville visits I stayed with singer-songwriter Bob Cheevers to whom I am grateful to for being such a genial and informative host. On my second visit Bob gave me a lift to various parts of Nashville when, in the absence of my wife Judy and her excellent navigational skills, I didn't have the courage to hire a car and negotiate downtown Nashville and the interstate highways on my own. (Tommy Cash quite seriously offered to lend me his large white Cadillac, once owned by Connie Francis. I did not have the courage for that either!) I also immensely enjoyed a day in Memphis when Bob took Judy and I to visit Sun Studios and various areas of the city where Johnny Cash lived and worked prior to his success. Bob also introduced me to his friends and associates, some in the music business, all of whom had thoughts and opinions on Johnny Cash to share.

When placing press advertisements seeking material about Johnny Cash, I had little idea as to what response I would get. It was my good fortune that Murdoch Nicolson, Denis Bowerbank and John O'Neill are more than mere fans of Johnny Cash; they're devotees, fanatics and obsessives. The three have been collecting material relating to Johnny Cash for many years, much of which they freely made available to a complete stranger, thus providing me with many invaluable sources of information which would have been difficult or impossible to obtain elsewhere. I must single out Murdoch who, given his geographical proximity, was the recipient of my many e-mails requesting information, thoughts, video footage and tapes, to which he invariably responded promptly and effectively and for all of which I thank him.

I am also particularly grateful to Bill Black and Dick Barrie, two of Scotland's leading country music DJs. Bill lent me many books and magazines from his extensive collection and Dick entrusted me with a large number of albums which I have nervously looked after for the last nine months or so.

I also received assistance of great value from the following people to whom I am very grateful: David Allan, Sandra Black, Ian Boughton, Joe Brown, Tony Byworth, Ian Calford, Shawn Camp, Chris Charlesworth, Bill Chislett, Warren Davies, Ed Dixon, Peter Doggett, Narvel Felts, Jan Flederus, George Hamilton V, Dave Johnston, Sandy Kelly, Spencer Leigh, Peter Lewry (who runs a high quality Cash fanzine, *The Man In Black*, peter.lewry@ntworld.com), Sandy MacCalman, Robert Macmillan, Sue Marshall, Jo Miller, Ottilie Miller, Al Moir, Andy Neill, Christine Paice, Dave Roe, Rich Richardson, Neil Ross, David Sinclair, Simon Taylor, Robin West, Helen Wright, Frank Yonco.

Finally, my heartfelt thanks to Judy for giving me every kind of support it's possible for one human being to give to another.

INDEX

Queen Elizabeth II 367

Radio And Records (magazine) 349
Radiohead 340
Ragged Old Flag (album) 235, 236, 378
'Ragged Old Flag' 235, 293, 308, 309, 365, 368
Rainbow (album) 280, 379
Rambler, The (album) 249, 378
Ranch Party (TV show) 73
Raney, Wayne 23, 61
Reagan, Ronald 148, 164, 231, 235, 290, 293, 308
Rebel, The (TV show) 108, 119
Record Collector (magazine) 81
Red Cloud, Edger 173
Red Headed Stranger (album) 242
Red Hot And Blue (radio show) 45
Red Hot Chili Peppers 328, 347
Redford, Robert 200
Reed, Lou 326
Reeves, Jim 292
Reid, Don 128, 141
Reid, Harold 128, 142
'Remember The Alamo' 222
Return Of Roger Miller, The (album) 124
Revenge Of Coweta County (film) 270
Revolver (album) 144
Reynolds, Nick 367
Reznor, Trent 366
Rhodes, John David 181
Rich, Charlie 80, 265
Richards, Keith 249, 319, 363
Ride This Train (album) 91–93, 95, 319, 363, 374
Ridin' The Rails (film) 236, 237
Rigdon, Orvile 41
Riley, Billy Lee 71
Riley, Jeannie C 197, 211, 260
Ring Of Fire (album) 375
'Ring Of Fire' 117, 118, 129, 141, 143, 144, 166, 311, 324, 340, 349, 353, 356, 364
Ring Of Fire – The Best Of Johnny Cash (album) 118
Ritter, Tex 73, 92, 138, 142, 198, 210
Rivers, Carrie *see* Cash, Carrie
Rivers, John L (JC's grandfather) 7, 23, 37
Rivers, Ruth (JC's grandmother) 23
Road Goes On Forever, The (album) 341, 381
Roanoke Times (newspaper) 298
Robbins, Marty 69, 78, 95, 99, 190, 194, 211
Robbins, Tim 357
Robertson, Robbie 240
Robin, Lou 140, 192, 210, 219, 233, 253, 259–261, 278, 284, 289, 290, 309, 312,

313, 315, 321, 323, 328, 341, 342, 354, 368
Rock And Roll Hall Of Fame 319, 320, 347
'Rock And Roll Ruby' 113
'Rock Island Line' 58
Rockabilly Blues (album) 263, 264, 267, 379
Rockerfeller, Winthrop 170
Rock'n'Roll Circus (film) 172
'Rocket 88' 49
Rodgers, Carrie 109n
Rodgers, Jimmie 35, 41, 50, 73, 74, 109, 112, 115, 120, 141, 150, 187, 319, 334, 337, 348
Roe, Dave 326, 327, 333, 340, 341, 347, 348, 353, 364
Rogers, Kenny 211, 220, 262
Rolling Stone (magazine) 63, 102, 112, 179, 338, 339, 349, 361, 363, 367, 369
Rolling Stones, The 169, 172, 219, 233, 249
Rollins, John 232
Romanek, Mark 366
Ronstadt, Linda 211
Rooftop Singers, The 45n
Roosevelt, Eleanor 17, 167
Roosevelt, Franklin Delano 10, 11
Rosa, Stuart 222
Rouse, Ervin 129
Rouse, Gordon 129
'Route No. 1, Box 144' 195
Routh, Jack 296
Routh, John Jackson 296
Rowan and Martin's Laugh-In (TV show) 144, 187, 197
'Rowboat' 348
Rowland, Ross Jr. 245
Rubin, Rick 328, 329, 333, 334, 336, 337, 341, 347–349, 361, 362, 366, 368
'Rumba Boogie' 41
Run DMC 328
'Run Softly Blue River' 86
Runyon, Damon 101
'Rusty Cage' 348, 349

Saito, Takahiro 177
Sam & Dave 319
San Quentin 116, 120, 178–181, 189, 236
'San Quentin' 180
Sandburg, Carl 138
Saturday Night Live (TV show) 277
Schlitz, Don 249
Schneider, John 240
Scott, Sir Walter 25
Scruggs, Earl 153
Scruggs, Randy 367
Sebastian, John 154
'See Ruby Fall' 196